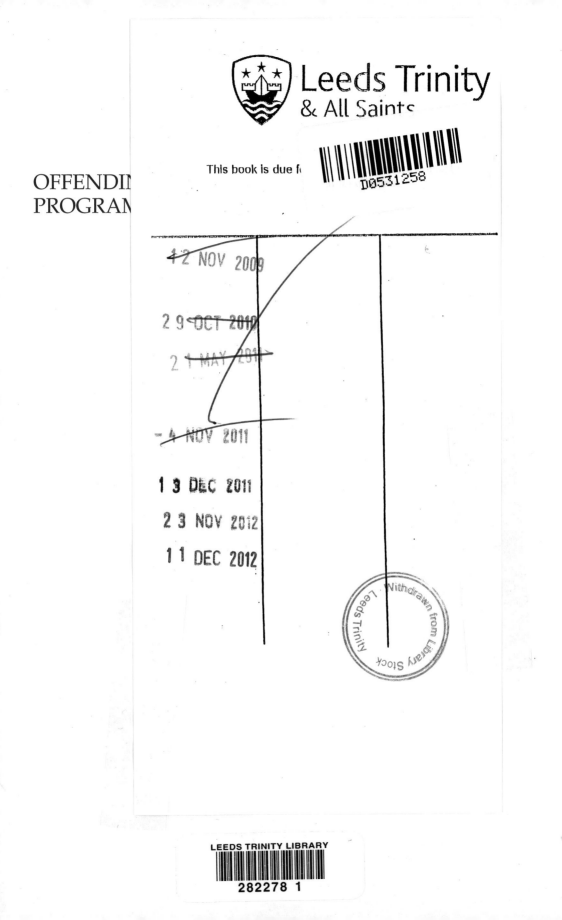

OFFENDI...
PROGRAM...

WILEY SERIES IN
FORENSIC CLINICAL PSYCHOLOGY

Edited by

Clive R. Hollin
Department of Health Sciences, University of Leicester, UK

and

Mary McMurran
School of Community Health Sciences, Division of Psychiatry,
University of Nottingham, UK

For other titles in this series please go to www.wiley.com/go/fcp

OFFENDING BEHAVIOUR PROGRAMMES
Development, Application, and Controversies

Edited by

Clive R. Hollin and Emma J. Palmer
University of Leicester, UK

John Wiley & Sons, Ltd

Copyright © 2006   John Wiley & Sons Ltd, The Atrium, Southern Gate, Chichester, West Sussex PO19 8SQ, England

Telephone   (+44) 1243 779777

Email (for orders and customer service enquiries): cs-books@wiley.co.uk
Visit our Home Page on www.wiley.com

Other Wiley Editorial Offices

John Wiley & Sons Inc., 111 River Street, Hoboken, NJ 07030, USA

Jossey-Bass, 989 Market Street, San Francisco, CA 94103-1741, USA

Wiley-VCH Verlag GmbH, Boschstr. 12, D-69469 Weinheim, Germany

John Wiley & Sons Australia Ltd, 42 McDougall Street, Milton, Queensland 4064, Australia

John Wiley & Sons (Asia) Pte Ltd, 2 Clementi Loop #02-01, Jin Xing Distripark, Singapore 129809

John Wiley & Sons Canada Ltd, 6045 Freemont Blvd, Mississauga, ONT, L5R 4J3

Wiley also publishes its books in a variety of electronic formats. Some content that appears in print may not be available in electronic books.

Library of Congress Cataloguing in Publication Data

Offending behaviour programmes : development, application, and controversies / edited by Clive R. Hollin and Emma J. Palmer.
      p.   cm. – (Wiley series in forensic clinical psychology)
      Includes index.
      ISBN-13: 978-0-470-02335-8 (cloth : alk. paper)
      ISBN-10: 0-470-02335-X (cloth : alk. paper)
      ISBN-13: 978-0-470-02336-5 (pbk. : alk. paper)
      ISBN-10: 0-470-02336-8 (pbk. : alk. paper)
      1. Criminals–Rehabilitation.   2. Criminals–Rehabilitation–Great Britain.   3. Criminals–Mental health services–Great Britain.   4. Prisoners–Mental health services–Great Britain.   5. Correctional psychology.   6. Group psychotherapy.   I. Hollin, Clive R.   II. Palmer, Emma J.   III. Series.
      HV9275.O355 2006
      365'.66–dc22   2006016674

British Library Cataloguing in Publication Data

A catalogue record for this book is available from the British Library

ISBN-13   978-0-470-02335-8 (ppc)   978-0-470-02336-5 (pbk)
ISBN-10   0-470-02335-X (ppc)   0-470-02336-8 (pbk)

Typeset in 10/12 pt Palatino by TechBooks, New Delhi, India
Printed and bound in Great Britain by Antony Rowe Ltd, Chippenham, Wiltshire
This book is printed on acid-free paper responsibly manufactured from sustainable forestry in which at least two trees are planted for each one used for paper production.

CH: For Kevin Howells, a proper academic.
EP: For Carl, my best friend.

CONTENTS

About the Editors   *page* viii

List of Contributors   ix

Series Editors' Preface   xi

Preface   xv

1 Offending behaviour programmes: history and development   1
  Clive R. Hollin and Emma J. Palmer

2 Offending behaviour programmes and contention:
  evidence-based practice, manuals, and programme evaluation   33
  Clive R. Hollin

3 General offending behaviour programmes: concept, theory,
  and practice   69
  James McGuire

4 Violent offender programmes: concept, theory, and practice   113
  Devon L. L. Polaschek

5 Sex offender programmes: concept, theory, and practice   155
  Ruth E. Mann and Yolanda M. Fernandez

6 Drug and alcohol programmes: concept, theory, and practice   179
  Mary McMurran

7 The implementation and maintenance of quality services in offender
  rehabilitation programmes   209
  Claire Goggin and Paul Gendreau

8 Offending behaviour programmes: controversies and resolutions   247
  Clive R. Hollin and Emma J. Palmer

Index   279

ABOUT THE EDITORS

Clive R. Hollin. Clive Hollin is Professor of Criminological Psychology at the University of Leicester where he is Head of the School of Psychology and a member of the Department of Health Sciences. Alongside his academic appointments he has worked as a prison psychologist, as Director of Rehabilitation in the Youth Treatment Service, and as a Consultant Forensic Psychologist at Rampton Hospital. His main research interest lies in the interface between psychology and criminology, particularly with reference to the management and treatment of offenders. He has published widely in the field of criminological psychology, including the best-selling text *Psychology and Crime: An Introduction to Criminological Psychology*, and the *Handbook of Offender Assessment and Treatment*. He is coeditor of the journal *Psychology, Crime, and Law*. Professor Hollin has worked as a consultant with several government departments and practice agencies, including the Prison and Probation Services, on the design, implementation, and evaluation of programmes to reduce offending. He is the 1998 recipient of the Senior Career Award for Distinguished Contribution to the Field of Criminological and Legal Psychology, presented by the Division of Criminological and Legal Psychology of The British Psychological Society.

Emma J. Palmer. Emma Palmer is Senior Lecturer in Forensic Psychology in the Department of Health Sciences at the University of Leicester. Her main research interests are the roles of parenting and social cognition in the development of juvenile delinquency, specifically moral reasoning; the design and evaluation of the effectiveness of interventions with offenders; assessment of risk and need; and bullying in prisons. She has published widely in these areas, including the text *Offending Behaviour: Moral Reasoning, Criminal Conduct, and the Rehabilitation of Offenders*. Dr Palmer has carried out research and consultancy work for a number of agencies, including the Prison and Probation Services and the Office of the Deputy Prime Minister examining offenders and their behaviour, and the design and evaluation of the effectiveness of interventions.

LIST OF CONTRIBUTORS

Yolanda M. Fernandez

Senior Psychologist, Department of Psychology, Millhaven Institution, PO Box 280, Bath, Ontario, K0H 1G0, Canada

Paul Gendreau

University Research Professor, Department of Psychology and Director, Centre for Criminal Justice Studies, University of New Brunswick, Saint John, New Brunswick, E2L 4L5, Canada

Claire Goggin

Instructor, Department of Criminology and Criminal Justice, St Thomas University, Fredericton, New Brunswick, E3B 5G3, Canada

Clive R. Hollin

Professor of Criminological Psychology, Henry Wellcome Building, School of Psychology, University of Leicester, Leicester, LE1 9HN, UK

Ruth E. Mann

Director, Sex Offender Treatment Programmes, HM Prison Service, Room 725, Abell House, John Islip Street, London, SW1P 4LH, UK

James McGuire

Professor of Forensic Clinical Psychology, Department of Clinical Psychology, University of Liverpool, The Whelan Building, Quadrangle, Brownlow Hill, Liverpool, L69 3GB, UK

Mary McMurran

Professor of Personality Disorder Research, Section of Forensic Mental Health, Division of Psychiatry, School of Community Health Sciences, University of Nottingham, Duncan Macmillan House, Porchester Road, Nottingham,

NG3 6AA, and Consultant Clinical and Forensic Psychologist, Llanarth Court Hospital, Raglan, NP5 2YD, UK

Emma J. Palmer

Senior Lecturer in Forensic Psychology, Clinical Division of Psychiatry, Department of Health Sciences, University of Leicester, Leicester General Hospital, Gwendolen Road, Leicester, LE5 4PW, UK

Devon L. L. Polaschek

Senior Lecturer in Criminal Justice Psychology, Department of Psychology, Victoria University of Wellington, PO Box 600, Wellington 6001, New Zealand

SERIES EDITORS' PREFACE

ABOUT THE SERIES

At the time of writing it is clear that we live in a period, certainly in the UK and other parts of Europe, if perhaps less so in areas of the world, when there is renewed enthusiasm for constructive approaches to working with offenders to prevent crime. What do we mean by this statement and what basis do we have for making it?

First, by "constructive approaches to working with offenders" we mean bringing the use of effective methods and techniques of behaviour change into work with offenders. Indeed, this view might pass as a definition of forensic clinical psychology. Thus, our focus is the application of theory and research in order to develop practice aimed at bringing about a change in the offender's functioning. The word *constructive* is important and can be set against approaches to behaviour change that seek to operate by destructive means. Such destructive approaches are typically based on the principles of deterrence and punishment, seeking to suppress the offender's actions through fear and intimidation. A constructive approach, on the other hand, seeks to bring about changes in an offender's functioning that will produce, say, enhanced possibilities of employment, greater levels of self-control, better family functioning, or increased awareness of the pain of victims.

A constructive approach faces the criticism of being a "soft" response to the damage caused by offenders, neither inflicting pain and punishment nor delivering retribution. This point raises a serious question for those involved in working with offenders. Should advocates of constructive approaches oppose retribution as a goal of the criminal justice system as a process that is incompatible with treatment and rehabilitation? Alternatively, should constructive work with offenders take place within a system given to retribution? We believe that this issue merits serious debate.

However, to return to our starting point, history shows that criminal justice systems are littered with many attempts at constructive work with offenders, not all of which have been successful. In raising the spectre of success, the second part of our opening sentence now merits attention: that is, "constructive approaches to working with offenders *to prevent crime*". In order to achieve the goal of preventing crime, interventions must focus on the right targets for behaviour change. In addressing this crucial point, Andrews & Bonta (1994, p. 176) have formulated the *need principle*:

> Many offenders, especially high-risk offenders, have a variety of needs. They
> need places to live and work and/or they need to stop taking drugs. Some
> have poor self-esteem, chronic headaches or cavities in their teeth. These are
> all "needs". The need principle draws our attention to the distinction between
> *criminogenic* and *non-criminogenic* needs. Criminogenic needs are a subset of an
> offender's risk level. They are dynamic attributes of an offender that, when
> changed, are associated with changes in the probability of recidivism. Non-
> criminogenic needs are also dynamic and changeable, but these changes are not
> necessarily associated with the probability of recidivism.

Thus, successful work with offenders can be judged in terms of bringing about
change in non-criminogenic need *or* in terms of bringing about change in criminogenic need. While the former is important and, indeed, may be a necessary
precursor to offence-focused work, it is changing criminogenic need that, we argue, should be the touchstone in working with offenders.

While, as noted above, the history of work with offenders is not replete with
success, the research base developed since the early 1990s, particularly the meta-
analyses (for example, Lösel, 1995), now strongly supports the position that effective work with offenders to prevent further offending is possible. The parameters
of such evidence-based practice have become well established and widely disseminated under the banner of "What Works?" (McGuire, 1995).

It is important to state that we are not advocating that there is only one approach
to preventing crime. Clearly there are many approaches, with different theoretical underpinnings, which can be applied. Nonetheless, a tangible momentum has
grown in the wake of the "What Works" movement as academics, practitioners,
and policy makers seek to capitalise on the possibilities that this research raises for
preventing crime. The task now facing many service agencies lies in turning the
research into effective practice.

Our aim in developing this series in forensic clinical psychology is to produce
texts that review research and draw on clinical expertise to advance effective work
with offenders. We are both committed to the ideal of evidence-based practice
and we will encourage contributors to the series to follow this approach. Thus, the
books published in the series will not be practice manuals or "cook books": they will
offer readers authoritative and critical information through which forensic clinical
practice can develop. We are both enthusiastic about the contribution to effective
practice that this series can make and look forward to continuing to develop it in
the years to come.

ABOUT THIS BOOK

There is now a vast body of research, commentary, and practice, stretching over
two decades, that constitutes the "What Works?" movement within offender treatment. Alongside this, there has also been a growth in questioning and criticism (for
example, Mair, 2004). As long as critics remain objective, rather than indulging in
extreme scepticism (Raynor, 2004), a dialectic is potentially energising. It is important to be reminded that it is premature and stultifying conceptually to drop the
question mark from the phrase "What Works?" The movement should be one of

science, not totalitarianism. We need to continue to ask, not just "what works?" but the infinitely more nuanced question, "what works with whom and under what conditions, and how do we know it?" Contributors to this text begin to address these complexities.

Within "What Works?" the desired outcomes have always been unequivocally to reduce antisocial behaviour and crime. Put simply, the aim is to reduce crime and crime is the outcome measure. Realising this seemingly simple aim is, however, anything but straightforward. There are difficulties with choosing specific crime outcomes (for instance, does any offence count as a failure or would a lesser offence mean a success?), difficulties with collecting valid outcome data (should we rely on sometimes inaccurate official data bases?), and difficulties in knowing what the specific effect of treatment has been amongst all the events that happen to offenders within the criminal justice system and beyond. It is imperative that we really know what works and do not base our treatments and service provision on spurious findings. This book contains expert analyses of fundamental and crucial research issues.

The pursuit of reduced recidivism through treatment has been seen by some to represent impersonal, mechanical, state-driven moral re-education, which, furthermore, does not really work (see, for example, Kemshall, 2004). This antipathetical stance fails to disentangle theoretical and implementation issues. Raynor (2004) acknowledges that the "What Works?" movement enjoys empirical support but that implementation problems in the UK, particularly the speed and magnitude of programme roll-out, have militated against good treatment integrity, hence compromising outcome. Implementation is a topic of paramount importance and is cogently addressed in this text.

"What Works?" meta-analyses have consistently shown that treatments work better in the community, and adherents of the movement have been vociferous in calling for less punishment and more help, more community orders and less use of prisons (Hollin, 2002; McGuire, 1995). Many forensic mental health professionals are working in prisons, which can be dehumanising, brutal, and damaging to prisoners. The sheer numbers of people sentenced to prison reduce opportunities for individualised approaches to treatment. Despite this, prison populations keep on rising. In many prisons, treatment programmes, along with other self-improvement services such as education and vocational training, are the human face of prison regimes. One question that urgently needs answers is: "what works and at what financial and social costs?"

In the community, services must be adequately resourced so that offenders who need treatment actually receive treatment, and that the treatment they receive is appropriate to their needs. Also, those who start treatment need to be supported towards programme completion. These matters are important because non-starters and non-completers appear more likely to be reconvicted than untreated offenders (Hollin et al., 2005; McMurran & Theodosi, in press).

Few, if any, treatments of any kind will work unless they are appropriate to the individual's needs, true to the supporting evidence, and undertaken with care and consideration. Suboptimal treatment implementation, whatever the reasons for it, and poor outcome evaluation, should not be tolerated, whether in health or in criminal justice services. This book is a welcome addition to Wiley's forensic clinical psychology series because of its potential to assist in the drive to improve quality in offender treatment.

REFERENCES

Andrews, D. A. & Bonte, J. (1994). *The psychology of criminal conduct*. Cincinnati, OH: Anderson.

Hollin, C. R. (2002). Does punishment motivate offenders to change? In M. McMurran (Ed.) *Motivating offenders to change: A guide to enhancing engagement in therapy* (pp. 235–249). Chichester: John Wiley & Sons.

Hollin, C. R., Palmer, E. J., McGuire, J., Hounsome, J., Hatcher, R. & Bilby, C. (2005). *An evaluation of pathfinder programmes in the Probation Service*. Unpublished report. London: Home Office.

Kemshall, K. (2004). Dangerous thinking: A critical history of correctional cognitive behaviouralism. In G. Mair (Ed.) *What matters in probation* (pp. 53–89). Cullompton: Willan Publishing.

Lösei, F. (1995). Increasing concensus in the evaluation of offender rehabilitation? *Psychology, Crime & Law, 2*, 19–39.

Mair, G. (Ed.) (2004). *What matters in probation*. Cullompton: Willan Publishing.

McGuire, J. (Ed.) (1995). *What works: Reducing reoffending*. Chichester: John Wiley & Sons..

McGuire, J. & Priestley, P. (1995). Reviewing "What Works": Past, present and future. In J. McGuire (Ed.) *What works: Reducing reoffending* (pp. 3–34). Chichester: John Wiley & Sons.

McMurran, M. & Theodosi, E. (in press). Is treatment non-completion associated with increased reconviction over no treatment? *Psychology, Crime & Law*.

Raynor, P. (2004). The Probation Service "Pathfinders": Finding the path and losing the way? *Criminal Justice, 4*, 309–325.

PREFACE

There is nothing new about rehabilitative efforts aimed at offenders. Since the turn of the twentieth century there have been concerted efforts to improve the lives of criminals so that they can live law-abiding lives. In order to achieve this goal a variety of approaches have been brought into play, ranging from welfare provision, training for employment, education, diversion from custody, and psychological and psychiatric treatment. All these approaches might claim a little success although it is difficult to point to any approach that might claim an unqualified, undisputed triumph. This is, of course, not an unexpected state of affairs: the complexity of human behaviour, within an equally complex social environment, makes it entirely unlikely that there will be a "magic bullet" that will rehabilitate all offenders with equal effectiveness.

In the latter part of the twentieth century there were two significant advances in the work with offenders within a treatment tradition. The first was the move away from treatment approaches based on models of psychopathology. The initial attempts at treatment of offenders were clearly based on direct transference of therapeutic techniques used in mainstream clinical practice. The transfer of clinical techniques to offender populations is clearly seen in the use of methods such as group therapy, counselling, and therapeutic communities. However, as the academic and research base has progressed within psychology so there has been a shift away from theories steeped in psychopathology, based on research with clinical samples, towards more mainstream psychological theories. In particular, there has been a significant influence from research and practice informed by behavioural theory and, in particular, Social Learning Theory (SLT).

Behavioural theories are intended to explain human behaviour, particularly behaviour within a social context. Thus, behavioural theory can be *applied* to give an account of criminal behaviour in the same way that it can be applied to other behaviours such as parenting, altruism, classroom behaviour, and so on. One of the hallmarks of SLT was that it brought the notion of cognition into the behavioural domain, giving rise to the term "cognitive-behavioural". A cognitive-behavioural analysis naturally gives rise to the development of cognitive-behavioural methods of bringing about changes in behaviour. Thus, cognitive-behavioural methods were applied, for example, within educational psychology and occupational psychology for a range of purposes such as improving pupil learning and improving managerial effectiveness.

The bringing together of research with offenders that looked at evidence within a cognitive-behavioural framework began to construct a new account of criminal behaviour. Criminal behaviour was not seen in terms of psychopathology but in terms of learned behaviour; in particular, behaviour that was learned within a social context. The way in which criminal behaviour was learned was no different to the way in which any other behaviour was learned and so was not "abnormal" or "deviant". Rather, criminal behaviour is a behaviour that in the main causes harm to other people and is not likely to lead to a particularly fruitful life for the apprehended offender. Thus, if new forms of behaviour can be learned that individual offenders can use to reduce their offending then there are clear advantages to such an approach. This approach, in which the emphasis is on learning new behaviours, is not "treatment" in the traditional sense of curing an ailment. Indeed, various terms have been coined, such as "psycho-educational", but these inevitably feel awkward and contrived and "treatment" remains in favour.

As cognitive-behavioural approaches to research and intervention gathered pace during the 1970s and 1980s an evidence base began to accumulate within this tradition, eventually giving rise to the second significant advance with regard to the development of offending behaviour programmes.

The publication of the meta-analyses of the effectiveness of intervention with offenders and the eventual synthesis of these studies coalesced around the notion of "What Works?". The practical basis of "What Works" is that, if treatment (in a cognitive-behavioural sense) is designed according to certain evidence-based principles, then there is a likelihood of reducing offending. In practice, this led in the late 1990s to concerted efforts to develop offending behaviour programmes according to "What Works" principles. Since the 1990s and into the twenty-first century a great deal of time and money has been directed at offending behaviour programmes.

Our aim in producing this book was to reflect on progress to date with the development, implementation, and evaluation of offending behaviour programmes. In particular, our thinking has been sharpened by our experience as researchers in a large-scale national evaluation of offending behaviour programmes in England and Wales. We wish to acknowledge the particular influence of other members of the research team – Charlotte Bilby, Ruth Hatcher and James McGuire – in all of those long meetings where we struggled with ideas, data, and the vicissitudes of Home Office micromanagement. Elaine Allen deciphered our editorial scribbles and transformed them into clean manuscripts. Finally, we are grateful to all our authors for the excellence of their work. We hope that our collective efforts will be seen as a genuine contribution to the field.

Clive Hollin
Emma Palmer

Chapter 1

OFFENDING BEHAVIOUR PROGRAMMES: HISTORY AND DEVELOPMENT

CLIVE R. HOLLIN AND EMMA J. PALMER
University of Leicester

INTRODUCTION

The history of crime tells us that the long-standing approach to crime reduction, across many cultures and civilisations, lay in the dispensation of punishment. The favoured punishments for crime took many forms, involving harsh penalties such as amputation, deportation, torture, and even death. It is arguable how effective such punitive strategies proved to be; certainly crime has never been eliminated from any society, but it might well be argued that those criminals who are executed commit very few crimes! It is only comparatively recently that changes in thinking within Western cultures came about that shifted legal systems away from immediate harsh sanctions to the notion that the punishment should fit the crime. The beginnings of classical theory, strongly influenced by Cesare Beccaria (b. 1738) and Jeremy Bentham (b. 1748), introduced to law the notion of utility. Following the principles of utility, the purpose of legal punishment is not to administer harsh punishment, but to deliver just enough punishment to deter the individual from further criminal actions and so prevent crime. Inherent in this approach, now enshrined in Western legal systems, is, first, that criminals act of their own free will in committing a crime, and second that criminals act in a rational manner when exercising free will. The principle of utility and its association with free will and rational choice does not always sit easily alongside psychological accounts of human action. Rather than free will, psychological theories may explain behaviour in terms of a complex interplay between biological, psychological, and social factors. The disparity between classical theory and some psychological theories produces a tension regarding the favoured means to reduce crime (Hollin, 2001a). While conservative classical theory favours punishment to deter the offender, the more liberal social and psychological theories prefer a response to crime that seeks to bring about a reduction in offending through some positive change. This change may be at a social level, as with the provision of welfare, or at an individual level as with attempts to rehabilitate the offender.

As McGuire (2002) suggests, these opposing strategies for reducing re-offending can be classified as *eliminative* or *constructional*. The rationale underpinning eliminative strategies is that linking criminal behaviour to aversive, punishing consequences can prevent it. Thus, within the criminal justice system this approach is seen in sanctions based on punishment and deterrence, such as fines, imprisonment, harsh prison regimes, and intensive supervision and surveillance. In contrast, constructional strategies seek to change criminal behaviour through providing offenders with socially acceptable alternatives to offending. This constructional approach may encompass education, skills training, employment skills training, anger management, and interventions designed to change attitudes and beliefs.

While it is debatable whether punishment motivates offenders to change (Hollin, 2002a), the issue of reducing re-offending has traditionally generated a great deal of discussion. The key questions are whether anything can be done to rehabilitate offenders effectively and, if so, which strategies are most effective in changing criminal behaviour and so preventing crime and reducing rates of re-offending. Moving to recent times, the debate has focused on the competing themes of "nothing works" against "what works".

"NOTHING WORKS"

The key paper in the "nothing works" stance is "What works? Questions and answers about prison reform" published in 1974 by Martinson. This paper, anticipating a fuller account of the literature (Lipton, Martinson & Wilks, 1975, p. 25) drew the conclusion that "With few and isolated exceptions, the rehabilitative efforts that have been reported so far have had no appreciable effect on recidivism." Other reviews published around that time had drawn similar negative conclusions about the effectiveness of rehabilitative efforts with offenders (for example, Robinson & Smith, 1971) but it was Martinson's paper that caught the attention of policy-makers.

The shift away from rehabilitation was felt during the 1980s, alongside a marked political move to the Right, with a view that the criminal justice system should administer "just deserts" to offenders. This return to an eliminative philosophy is seen in practice with the introduction of measures such as "short, sharp shock" prison regimes and boot camps. Despite some academic opposition citing effective interventions (for example, Gendreau & Ross, 1979) and Martinson's retraction of much of his earlier paper (Martinson, 1979), in practice there was a move away from rehabilitation and treatment towards more punitive measures. The later emergence of rational choice theory (Cornish & Clarke, 1986) prompted governments to invest in situational crime-prevention measures, such as CCTV, electronic tagging and alarms, leaving little room (or funding) for rehabilitation.

An important point highlighted by Martinson (1974) was that poor research methodologies may have been responsible for the negative, nothing works, findings

(Cooke & Philip, 2001). Indeed, Thornton (1987) criticised Martinson's approach to reviewing the evidence as too simplistic for such a complex issue. The problem inherent in narrative reviews lies in the selectivity and interpretation of the reviewer. The conclusions drawn from a narrative review of the literature are inevitably dependent upon the reviewer's own views and, as such, are inevitably open to charges of bias. In the 1980s, the emergence of the statistical technique of meta-analysis as a reliable means of distilling the consistent findings from large bodies of empirical literature became widely used in scientific disciplines. The main advantage of meta-analysis as compared to narrative review is that the process of meta-analysis is much more transparent in terms of the weight given to different studies, the systematic inclusion of key variables, and the process can be replicated. This is not to say that meta-analysis is perfect or without its critics (Hollin, 1999), but its widespread use across many academic disciplines has become an important means of distilling knowledge from large bodies of literature. The first meta-analytic studies of offender treatment appeared as the 1980s merged into the 1990s. The findings from these studies began to have an effect as they began to suggest what worked in reducing re-offending.

"WHAT WORKS?"

Meta-analysis is a statistical technique for reviewing the results of a large number of primary research studies, allowing overall trends in the accumulated data to emerge. Unlike traditional qualitative reviews of research, meta-analysis can control for variations and potential biases in the primary studies, and so produce a quantifiable treatment effect (Cohen, 1988; Glass, McGraw & Smith, 1981). In the offender treatment literature, for example, meta-analysts have developed coding systems that take into account study differences in areas such as offender group, offence type, follow-up period, criterion of outcome, and treatment setting (see Lipsey, 1992; Lipton, Pearson, Cleland & Yee, 2002a, 2002b; Redondo, Sánchez-Meca & Garrido, 2002). Complex coding systems can take account of differences between studies but the utility of meta-analysis can be compromised by the quality of the primary research studies, with problems potentially caused by a lack of or inadequate comparison groups, small sample sizes, and limited follow-up periods. Further, publication bias towards studies that show effects can lead meta-analytic reviews to produce biased results. These potential problems can be avoided as seen with the Correctional Drug Abuse Treatment Effective (CDATE) Study in the US (see Lipton et al., 2002a, 2002b), which consists of over 1 500 primary research studies of offender treatment, published and unpublished, conducted with adult and juvenile, drug abusing and non-drug abusing offenders from a large number of countries. However, this level of intensity of data gathering is neither quick nor cheap, requiring considerable time and funding.

As an outcome, meta-analyses produce effect sizes (ES), which provide a summary figure for the overall impact of an intervention. Following Rosenthal & Rubin (1982), ES can be interpreted as a binomial effect size display whereby it is the percentage difference between two groups – those receiving an intervention and those not receiving an intervention. Thus, a reconviction rate of 40 % in a treatment group as compared to 55 % in an untreated control group would produce an ES of 0.15. Across the offender treatment literature, the average ES of interventions with respect to recidivism has been reported as 10–12 % (Lösel, 1996, 1998). To place this in context, studies of the effect of common medicines have reported ES smaller than those for offender treatment: for example, Rosnow & Rosenthal (1988) reported an ES of 0.068 in a clinical trial of the effect of aspirin in reducing the risk of heart attacks, which is equivalent to a 6.8 % reduction in illness.

As of 2006 there have been 51 meta-analytic studies of offender treatment published since the first reported meta-analysis (Garrett, 1985). For a review see McGuire (2002). They incorporate hundreds of primary research studies (for example, Andrews et al., 1990; Antonowicz & Ross, 1994; Dowden & Andrews, 1999a, 1999b, 2000; Izzo & Ross, 1990; Lipsey, 1992; Pearson, Lipton & Cleland, 1997; Redondo, Sánchez-Meca & Garrido, 1999; Whitehead & Lab, 1989). The meta-analyses carried out by Andrews et al. (1990) and Lipsey (1992) are two of the most widely cited studies and can be used to illustrate this methodology.

Andrews et al. (1990) reported a meta-analytic review of 154 outcome effects from adult and juvenile offender treatment studies. Andrews et al. were concerned to determine whether interventions that applied principles of "human service" or *appropriate* correctional services would be more effective than those interventions that did not apply these principles. Appropriate correctional service was seen as consisting of three key principles: first, the *risk principle* whereby services are directed towards medium- to high-risk offenders; second, the *needs principle* in which interventions target offenders' criminogenic needs; third, *the responsivity principle* by which interventions are matched to offenders' learning styles. The findings of the meta-analysis supported the position that appropriate interventions, with a larger ES, were more effective than interventions classified as inappropriate. Lipsey's (1992) study is the largest published meta-analysis to date, consisting of 443 treatment studies involving juvenile and young offenders aged 12–21 years. Lipsey reported that taking re-offending as an outcome, constructional interventions that were multi-modal, behavioural, or skills-oriented in nature had a significant positive ES. However, *eliminative* deterrence-based interventions had a negative ES, with mixed results regarding the ES of employment-focused interventions.

Most meta-analyses have been carried out with male young offender populations but meta-analyses with other offender populations have been published, including women offenders (Dowden & Andrews, 1999a), sexual offenders (Alexander, 1999; Gallagher, Wilson, Hirschfield, Coggeshall & MacKenzie, 1999; Hall, 1995; Hanson et al. 2002; Polizzi, MacKenzie & Hickman, 1999), drink-drivers (Wells-Parker, Bangret-Downs, McMillen & Williams, 1995), violent offenders (Dowden & Andrews, 2000), and drug abusing offenders (Pearson & Lipton, 1999; Prendergast, Podus & Chang, 2000; Prendergast, Podus, Chang & Urada, 2002). The conclusions from these meta-analyses suggest that effective offender interventions are cognitive-behavioural in nature, take the form of structured programmes with specific aims and objectives, focus on offenders with a high risk of re-offending, have high levels of treatment integrity, are delivered by highly trained staff, have high levels of organisational support, and have in-built monitoring and evaluation procedures. The congruence in the outcome of the various meta-analyses has led to attempts to crystallise the findings into principles for effective practice in working with offenders to reduce re-offending.

Principles of Effective Practice

A number of syntheses of the meta-analyses are available (see, for example, Andrews, 1995, 2001; Gendreau, 1996; Hollin 1999; Lösel, 1995a, 1995b), which have informed the formulation of the principles of effective practice. Thus, as shown in Box 1.1, in defining "what works" in offender interventions, Andrews (1995, 2001) has derived the 18 "principles of human service" that underpin effective interventions.

Box 1.1   Principles of Effective Practice

1. Interventions with offenders should be based on a psychological theory of criminal behaviour.
2. This theory should have a personality and social learning theory focus to the risk factors for offending.
3. Strategies for intervention should be based on human service, rather than on principles of retribution, restorative justice, or deterrence.
4. Where possible interventions should take place in the community in natural settings (such as the family). However, when it is necessary to use custody, these facilities should be as community-oriented as possible.
5. Offenders' level of risk of reoffending should be assessed and used as the basis for allocation to services.
6. Offenders' dynamic criminogenic needs – those needs associated with their offending behaviour – should be assessed and used as targets for interventions.
7. Interventions should be multi-modal in nature in that they should target a range of criminogenic needs to reflect the fact that offending is associated with multiple risk factors.
8. Assessment of level of risk and criminogenic needs should be carried out using validated methods.
9. Interventions should have general responsivity, with services matched to offenders' learning styles, motivations, and abilities.
10. Interventions should have specific responsivity and be adapted to take account of the diversity of offenders (for example, in terms of age, gender, ethnicity/race, language) and their strengths and limitations.
11. Specific responsivity and offenders' strengths and weaknesses should be assessed in a routine manner, using specifically designed tools.
12. Organisational strategies should be in place to monitor the continuity of service, including provision for relapse prevention work.
13. Organisations should identify areas of practice in which staff may exercise their personal discretion in applying the principles of appropriate service. These areas should be made clear to all staff.

14. Organisations should develop a service-level policy and guidelines for the application of the principles of appropriate service and ensure that it is circulated to all staff.
15. Organisations should set up procedures to monitor the delivery and integrity of interventions, and for dealing with problems. These procedures should include issues such as staff selection, training, supervision, and recording of monitoring information on service delivery.
16. There should be a focus on the development of staff skills, including the abilities to develop relationships, motivate others, and structure programmes and sessions.
17. Managers should have the competencies expected of their staff, plus extensive knowledge and understanding of the principles underpinning interventions. They also need the ability to coordinate procedures associated with programme and site accreditation.
18. At an organisational level, programmatic intervention should be placed within a wider context, with attention paid to differences in local contexts and client groups so as to allow for adaptation of services as necessary.

Lists such as the one shown in Box 1.1 cannot provide an exhaustive set of principles that will absolutely guarantee success in reducing re-offending. However, it is also the case that the knowledge base on what works has significantly improved over the past decade. It is fair to say that we may have a reasonable degree of confidence that these principles provide strong guidance for the development and implementation of interventions, and so provide a basis from which to extend theory, research, and practice.

RESEARCH INTO PRACTICE

In the 1990s the use of manualised programmes to guide the delivery of an intervention was an established means of working in mainstream clinical psychology (Wilson, 1996), and in the specific field of offender treatment manualised programmes were beginning to appear (see Chapter 2 for a fuller discussion). The first offending behaviour programme to be widely used with offenders was Reasoning and Rehabilitation (R & R) developed in Canada in the late 1980s by Ross and Fabiano (Ross, Fabiano & Ewles, 1988; Ross, Fabiano & Ross, 1989). Taking this programme as a starting point, the introduction of offending behaviour programmes within the criminal justice system in England and Wales can be used to highlight many of the issues associated with programme development, implementation, and maintenance (see also Chapter 3 for a consideration of the R & R programme).

Reasoning and Rehabilitation (R & R)

Reasoning and Rehabilitation (R & R) was the first evidence-based, structured cognitive-behavioural programme intended to reduce re-offending. The programme is based on research concerned with offender's thinking styles and patterns which suggests associations between cognition and offending (Ross & Fabiano, 1985). The aim of R & R is to provide and promote alternative ways of thinking to enable the growth of thinking patterns and skills that are likely to promote prosocial behaviour. Thus, through the use of techniques such as role-playing, rehearsal, modelling, reinforcement, and cognitive exercises, R & R aims to promote reflective, rather than reactive, thinking. Specific targets for change include offenders' self-control, social problem-solving skills, social perspective-taking, critical reasoning, and attitudes and beliefs that support criminal behaviour, with an emphasis on practice to enhance learning and to show how these skills are relevant to everyday life (Goldstein, 1988).

Reasoning and Rehabilitation was designed to be delivered by a range of staff, including prison and probation officers, rather than just professional therapists. The tutors responsible for delivering the programme complete an intensive training process in order to gain the optimum level of skill for effective delivery. Reasoning and Rehabilitation places an emphasis on video monitoring of sessions and provision of formal feedback to staff to help ensure integrity of delivery. Since its inception, R & R has been used in a number of jurisdictions, in both institutional and community settings, including those in Canada, North America, England and Wales, Scotland, Spain, Germany, Scandinavia, Australia, and New Zealand. To date there have been several evaluations (for reviews see Robinson & Porporino, 2001; Tong & Farrington, 2006), which typically show positive results in terms of reconviction among male adults who complete the programme. However, less evidence of effectiveness is available with other offender populations.

The development of R & R in the mid-1980s dovetailed neatly with the emerging principles of effective practice derived from the meta-analyses during the 1990s. Thus, services working with offenders who were seeking to innovate and develop their practice turned to R & R as a readily available programme.

Straight Thinking on Probation (STOP)

In mid-1991, mid-Glamorgan Probation Service in Wales took the bold step of running an adaptation of the R & R programme (Knott, 1995; McGuire, 1995; Raynor & Vanstone, 1996). An evaluation of the programme reported that the actual and the predicted rates of reconviction were the same for the treatment and comparison groups at 12-months follow-up (Raynor & Vanstone, 1997). However, for those offenders who actually *completed* the programme there was a significantly lower reconviction rate than predicted, along with a significantly lower rate of custodial sentences upon reconviction. These positive results were not maintained at a 2-year follow-up.

Sex Offender Treatment Programme (SOTP)

In the early 1990s the English and Welsh Prison Service also pioneered development of treatment programmes based on cognitive-behavioural techniques (see also Chapter 5). The first programme to be developed was for sexual offenders, known as the *Sex Offender Treatment Programme (SOTP)* (Grubin & Thornton, 1994). From its beginning in the early 1990s, treatment for sex offenders in the English and Welsh Prison Service has developed today into a suite of programmes for sex offenders. The *Core SOTP* aims primarily to challenge the cognitions used by sex offenders to justify and excuse their crimes. The Core programme aims to help offenders develop new attitudes and so change their offending behaviour. A version of the Core programme for lower intellectually functioning offenders is available, termed the *SOTP Adapted programme*. The *Extended SOTP* offers a longer, more intensive further programme of work for high-risk and high-need sexual offenders who have completed the Core programme (Correctional Services Accreditation Panel, 2004).

More recently, an intervention for *low* risk sexual offenders, the *SOTP Rolling Programme*, has been introduced, which covers similar areas to the Core programme. Finally, the *Better Lives Booster SOTP Programme* has been developed for offenders who have successfully completed either the Core or the Extended SOTP programme. The Better Lives programme is designed to allow prisoners to concentrate on their individual treatment needs and to make plans for release. There are two versions of the Better Lives programme: a high intensity version for offenders who are close to their release date, and a low intensity version aimed at offenders who have completed an SOTP programme early in their sentence and require maintenance or refresher work during their time in custody. This programme has also been adapted for use with low intellectually functioning sexual offenders. Research evaluating the effectiveness of sexual offender programmes has shown mixed results (for a recent review, see Beech & Mann, 2002). Where positive results in terms of sexual reconviction have been found, these have typically been among medium-low and medium-high risk men who have been responsive to treatment (Beech, Erikson, Friendship & Ditchfield, 2001; Friendship, Mann & Beech, 2003b).

Community treatment programmes for sexual offenders also began to be implemented in England and Wales during the 1990s, with interventions typically providing about 50 hours of treatment (Barker & Morgan, 1993). By the mid-1990s Proctor & Flaxington (1996) reported a doubling in the number of probation areas offering sex offender programmes, and an increase in the average treatment duration to 81 hours. The first systematic evaluation of these programmes was carried out by Beckett, Beech, Fisher & Fordham (1994), using psychometric measures to assess psychological factors related to sexual offending. In this study, treatment success was greater among child molesters and low deviancy men and for longer programmes using highly skilled therapists.

A 2-year reconviction study of these men reported by Hedderman & Sugg (1996) showed a lower rate of sexual reconviction as compared to a comparison group, although there was no analysis of statistical significance. In 2001, Beech et al. reported a six-year follow-up of the 53 child molesters from the original Beckett et al. study. Although this study did not include a comparison group, only 10 % of those men who were classified as "benefiting from treatment" based on change on psychometric measures were reconvicted as compared to 23 % of those classified as "not having responded to treatment". Furthermore, rate of reconviction was also predicted by risk of reconviction using the Static-99 (Hanson & Thornton, 2000) and level of sexual deviancy.

Since the late 1990s three accredited programmes for sexual offenders have been developed and implemented within the Probation Service in England and Wales for use with both sexual offenders serving community sentences and those released on licence from prison. These programmes are the Community-Sex Offender Group Programme (C-SOGP) designed by West Midlands Probation Area and developed in collaboration with the Home Office; the Thames Valley-Sex Offender Group-work Programme (TV-SOGP) set up by the local health, police, and social services and developed with the Home Office; and the Northumbria-Sex Offender Group Programme (N-SOGP), developed by Northumbria Probation Area and staff from the Sexual Behaviour Unit, St Nicholas Hospital in Newcastle.

All three programmes target sexual re-offending among adult male offenders, with the TV-SOGP also including work to support the partners of perpetrators. The dosage of intervention received by offenders depends on assessed level of risk and deviance, ranging from 100 hours to 260 hours according to risk level and programme. A relapse prevention module is included in each programme, and forms the minimum requirement for each programme. Offenders who are released on licence from prison who have successfully completed the Prison SOTP may go directly to the relapse prevention modules, depending on initial assessment. More detailed descriptions of these three programmes are provided in Mandeville-Norden & Beech (2004).

To date, there have been few published evaluations of these three programmes, and those that do exist collected data prior to the programmes being accredited. Therefore, the programmes evaluated may differ from those currently being used. Allam (1998) reported a reconviction study of the pre-accredited West Midlands programme, comparing programme participants with a comparison group of sexual offenders who had received alternative community sentences. The follow-up period varied across the sample but was 2.5 years on average. Although no test of statistical significance was calculated, participants in the programme had lower rates of reconviction than the comparison group, a finding that held for child molesters (3.2 % versus 10.6 %), rapists (7.7 % versus 26.3 %), and exhibitionists (17.8 % versus 37.5 %).

Data were collected on participants in the TV-CSOG programme from 1995–1999, and re-offending examined using information from a Home Office database, a police database, and local probation files (Falshaw, Bates, Patel, Corbett & Friendship, 2003). After a mean follow-up period of 3.9 years (range 2.0–5.9 years), the two sources of official convictions suggested between 5 (3 %) and 15 (9 %) men had been reconvicted for a sexual offence. However, when information about any offence-related sexual behaviour (re-offending and reconviction) was examined from probation files, recidivism among the sample rose to 21 %.

Enhanced Thinking Skills (ETS)

Enhanced Thinking Skills is a general cognitive skills programme, developed by the English and Welsh Prison Service (Clark, 2000), which addresses similar targets to

R & R (see also Chapter 3). Initially used within the Prison Service, since 2000 it has been used in the National Probation Service in England and Wales. As with R & R, evaluations have shown ETS to be effective in institutional settings with adult male offenders who complete the programme (Blud, Travers, Nugent & Thornton, 2003; Cann, Falshaw, Nugent & Friendship, 2003; Falshaw, Friendship, Travers & Nugent, 2003; Friendship, Blud, Erikson & Travers, 2002; Friendship, Blud, Erikson, Travers & Thornton, 2003). Furthermore, the initial reconviction outcome data are positive for offenders who complete the programme in the community in England and Wales (Hollin et al., 2004). Once again, however, less evidence is available for other offender populations and settings.

Think First

The Think First programme is a third general cognitive skills programme developed in England and Wales (McGuire, 2000) and also initially used in the Prison Service and later in the Probation Service (see also Chapter 3). Think First is similar both to R & R and ETS in its content and aims, but differs in that it has a more explicit focus on offending behaviour and includes material requiring offenders to analyse specific offences they have committed. Think First includes pre-group sessions given to preparation, engagement and motivation work, and post-group sessions to work at relapse prevention strategies. A preliminary evaluation of Think First in the English and Welsh Probation Service (when it was called *Offence-Focused Problem Solving*) reported significant reductions in criminal attitudes and locus of control and significant increases in self-esteem after participating in the programme (McGuire & Hatcher, 2000). The evaluations conducted in the English and Welsh Probation Service have shown significant decreases in reconviction among offenders who complete the programme as compared to non-starters and non-completers (Hollin et al., 2004; Roberts, 2004).

DELIVERING AND MAINTAINING EFFECTIVE PRACTICE

As programmes gained a momentum during the 1990s it became apparent that two issues demanded attention if the principles of effective practice were to be translated into action. First, new and existing offending behaviour programmes would have to demonstrate that they embodied the principles that emerged from the meta-analyses. Second, if well-designed programmes are to be effective, then the quality of delivery is essential: high-quality delivery means that the programme sessions that are delivered in practice must be as close in content as possible to that intended by the programme developers. There are several publications that document a range of barriers – such as resource allocation, professional clashes, and management failure – to the successful implementation of programmes (Cullen & Seddon, 1981; Laws, 1974). As recognised by some practitioners and researchers, good programme management is the key to successful implementation of offending behaviour programmes (for example, Bernfeld, 2001; Hollin, Epps & Kendrick, 1995).

The problem of maintaining practitioner adherence to a set of methodological principles is common in clinical practice and has variously been called "treatment fidelity" (Moncher & Prinz, 1991) and "treatment integrity" (Quay, 1987). In the mainstream clinical literature the topic of treatment integrity continues to be seen as critically important with regard to its definition (Dobson & Singer, 2005), its implications for professional training (Flannery-Schroeder, 2005), and its interaction with outcome research (Perpletchikova & Kazdin, 2005). The importance of maintaining treatment integrity applies equally to offending behaviour programmes (Andrews & Dowden, 2005; Hollin, 1995). Indeed, exactly the same issue is apparent in other spheres of life: after a talk to a public audience (Hollin, 2002b), a comment was made from the floor that a recurrent problem in the insurance field is ensuring that those people selling policies actually do adhere to a set of legal and professional procedures.

The response to these two issues, ensuring high-quality programme development and managing treatment integrity in delivery, lies in the notion of *programme accreditation* and in systems of *programme audit*.

Programme Accreditation

As offending behaviour programmes were implemented in different countries, including England and Wales, Scotland, Canada, Scandinavia, Australia, and New Zealand, this led to the drawing up of formal procedures and guidelines for developing programmes. In the mid-1990s, with the adoption of SOTP and R & R, the English and Welsh Prison Service took on the pioneering task of developing accreditation criteria for the design of offending behaviour programmes. This initiative began, during a grey week in a hotel in East Grinstead, Sussex, with a small group of academics, consultants, and civil servants, under the stewardship of David Thornton, charged with the task of defining the gold standards by which offending behaviour programmes could be judged (Lipton, Thornton, McGuire, Porporino & Hollin, 2000). The product of the machinations of this group was a set of so-called accreditation criteria that aimed to set the standards by which programmes could be evaluated (Thornton, 1996). From 1996 onwards this same group, with several new members, met regularly over the next few years, refining the criteria (Thornton, 1998) and acting as a general accreditation panel (GAP) on behalf of HM Prison Service for a range of programmes. A similar but separate panel, the Sex Offender Treatment Accreditation Panel (SOTAP), composed of experts in the sex offender field, was instituted for SOTP. The work of these panels came to be seen as an important part of the drive within the Prison Service for high standards.

In 1999 the status of the panels changed significantly. The two panels, GAP and SOTAP, were amalgamated to form the Joint Accreditation Panel (JAP), with the additional remit that programmes delivered within the Probation Service also came under the new panel's sphere of activity. The formal status of JAP also changed as it became an advisory non-departmental public body with formal independence from the Home Office, and with an independent chair reporting directly to the Minister. In 2002 JAP was renamed the Correctional Services Accreditation Panel (CSAP). The formal duties of CSAP, as fell similarly to its predecessors, are to review the criteria for programme design and delivery, and where appropriate make recommendations for changes; to accredit programmes; to authorise audit procedures for programme delivery; to authorise the annual assessment of delivery quality; to conduct an annual review of developments in the evidence base and where appropriate provide advice from this review to inform the development of programme design; to provide advice on training; and to receive reports on the effectiveness of programmes and so advise on the implications of these reports (Prison Service Order 4360, 2004). In an exercise in reviewing the reviewers, the work of CSAP has been examined by a commissioned review team (Rex, Lieb, Bottoms & Wilson, 2003).

Accreditation Criteria

The gold standards for programme design, as originally formulated in the mid-1990s, have stood the test of time remarkably well. Currently, there are 10 accreditation criteria, which are similar to the original criteria, as shown in Box 1.2.

Box 1.2   Outline of CSAP Accreditation Criteria for Offending Behaviour Programmes

1. Programmes must have a clear model of change.
2. The selection of offenders must be justified.
3. Target a range of dynamic risk factors.
4. Programmes should use effective methods of change.
5. Programmes should be skills oriented.
6. Sequencing, intensity and duration of treatment should be justified.
7. Attention should be given to the engagement and motivation of offenders taking part in the programme.
8. Continuity of programmes and services within sentence planning.
9. Programmes should show how they will maintain integrity.
10. There should be procedures to allow the continued evaluation of a programme.

Model of Change

Programmes should have a clear theoretical model of change, fully articulated in a Theory Manual, which explains the principles by which the programme will achieve the intended outcome. This model will provide a coherent basis, supported by the theoretical and empirical literature, for the nominated targets and methods for change within the programme.

Selection of Offenders

Programmes will have clear criteria for the selection of offenders, with inclusion and exclusion criteria, as well as criteria for expelling offenders from the programme.

The procedures and assessments to be used for selection must also be fully detailed.

Target a Range of Dynamic Risk Factors

Dynamic risk factors are those aspects of an offender's functioning that are related to their offending and which can be changed. For example, a long history of offending is predictive of offending but cannot be changed: this would be a *static* risk factor. On the other hand, factors related to offending such as employment status and substance use can be changed and so are *dynamic* risk factors. Offending is often related to several risk factors, therefore programmes should target a justified range of dynamic risk factors. Further, procedures should be in place to measure any changes that occur in these factors over the course of the programme.

Effective Methods

The educational and behaviour change methods used to bring about change in offenders' dynamic risk factors, and hence their offending behaviour, should be supported by empirical evidence with the target population.

Skills Oriented Targets

While programmes might seek to bring about change in cognitive and affective aspects of an offender's functioning, they should encompass targets that are skills oriented. Therefore, programmes should aim to assist offenders develop those life and social skills that will help avoid offending and gain other rewards.

Sequencing, Intensity and Duration

Formally known as "dosage", this criterion is concerned with matching the level and intensity of the programme, in terms of number and frequency of sessions, with offenders' level of risk. Further, where offenders take part in more than one programme, the sequencing of programmes and components of treatment should be planned with regard to offenders' overall treatment needs.

Engagement and Motivation

From the point of selection to take part in a programme, attention should be paid to offenders' engagement and motivation. In this light, programme attendance and completion rates should be monitored, along with recording the reasons for non-attendance of sessions and non-completion of programmes.

Continuity of Programmes and Services

The provision of programmes should take place within a coherent sentence planning process. This point applies both within services and between services.

Maintaining Integrity

A programme must have strategies in place to monitor programme integrity in order to demonstrate that the sessions are being delivered as intended. These strategies should include procedures to provide staff with constructive feedback on their practice.

Ongoing Evaluation

There will be continued monitoring and evaluation of programmes with respect to their effectiveness. The evaluation should encompass both processes, as in change on the targeted dynamic risk factors, and outcome as with re-offending.

As discussed in Chapter 2, the emergence of programmes has seen a marked move towards the use of manuals. The CSAP requires all offending behaviour programmes seeking accreditation to be fully manualised, with no fewer than five manuals required. A *theory manual,* which details the theory and its supporting research evidence that underpins the programme's model of change. A *programme manual,* which details each programme session and links the targets for change to the model of change presented in the theory manual. An *assessment and evaluation manual* provides full details, including administration, scoring, and interpretation, for all the measures used for assessment and evaluation within the programme. A *management manual* detailing the procedures for staff selection, training, and appraisal; the criteria for the selection and assessment of offenders for the programme; the minimum operating conditions for the programme; procedures for monitoring and evaluating the programme; and the roles and responsibilities of staff relating to the programme. Finally, a *staff training manual* provides details of all training for those staff involved in the programme, including both management and delivery personnel, alongside details of the procedures for assuring the competence of staff and regular reviews of staff performance.

Thus, the accreditation criteria set high standards for the development, implementation, and maintenance of offending behaviour programmes. These standards give a clear platform for organisations seeking to develop programmes to meet the needs of their particular client group (Hollin, 2001b). Those organisations with similar programmes have developed parallel systems. For example, the Scottish Prison Service (SPS) has seven programme design accreditation standards, so that a programme must show the following: (1) that it has a clear rationale and outcomes are clearly stated; (2) that it uses effective methods of prisoner selection and support; (3) that it uses appropriate means of assessing prisoner progress; (4) that it ensures benefits for the prisoner both during and after delivery; (5) that there are criteria for selecting, training, and supporting delivery staff; (6) that the resources and conditions for implementation are identified; and (7) that there is a commitment to continuous quality improvement (Scottish Prison Service, 2003). The SPS Accreditation Panel works to these standards and each standard has a set of supporting criteria. For example, Standard 1 is that a programme has a clear rationale and outcomes are clearly stated and there are four supporting criteria to be met.

At the onset, the accreditation criteria were designed for use with "stand-alone programmes", such as R & R, where the programme is self-contained and delivered within a single setting such as a prison. As thinking has evolved, so programmes have been seen as a way of crossing institutional boundaries, linking work across a range of agencies. For example, the STOP programme developed by County Durham probation was designed to be delivered initially in prison then for the work to progress into the community, involving criminal justice agencies, state services such as health and education, and the voluntary sector (Hollin, 2002c). Other examples include resettlement programmes that are delivered through the prison door into the community (Lewis et al., 2003). The feature of such approaches is that they extend the notion of a programme to a means of working that seeks to work within and across the various systems responsible for public protection and the offender's welfare. This change in emphasis has been recognised with the development of a set of parallel accreditation criteria for *integrated systems* approaches to working with offenders. An integrated system is seen as a network of services to which offenders are referred based on their assessed level of risk and areas of need. An integrated system delivers a range of activities to offenders, such as accredited programmes, health services, accommodation services, and education, in a planned, managed, and coherent manner. However, as with stand-alone offending behaviour programmes, the main aim of an integrated system is to reduce offending. For comparison purposes, the nine CSAP accreditation criteria for integrated systems are as follows:

1. *Integrated models of change.* Systems should have explicit inter-related theoretical models of change, supported by the theoretical and empirical literature, that provide a clear basis for how the system will lead to changes in targeted areas and reduce offending.

2. *Assessment and allocation.* There should be clear criteria, including inclusion and exclusion criteria, for selection and allocation of offenders into systems and the various elements within the systems.

3. *Effective methods and services.* The methods and services used within systems to change offenders' risk factors or enhance protective factors to reduce offending should be supported by empirical evidence relevant to the target population.

4. *Skills and opportunities.* Systems should aim to provide offenders with life and social skills to help avoid offending and gain prosocial rewards.

5. *Sequencing, scale and intensity.* The allocation of offenders to services, in terms of scale, intensity, and sequencing of service delivery, should be matched to their level of risk.

6. *Engagement and motivation.* Systems should aim to engage and motivate offenders throughout their period of supervision.

7. *Planning and integration.* Systems should ensure that the different elements of intervention are integrated within a case management, supervision, or sentence plan.

8. *Monitoring to maintain effectiveness.* Systems should have quality assurance systems in place to monitor effectiveness, as well as procedures to deal with practice that departs from the plan.

9. *Ongoing evaluation.* Systems should be continually evaluated with respect to their effectiveness: effectiveness might include change in targeted dynamic risk factors, enhancement of protective factors, and levels of offending.

As is the case with stand-alone programmes, integrated systems are also required by CSAP to submit documentation when seeking accreditation. This documentation takes the form of a Core Manual with two main sections: the *theory and design* section and the *implementation and evaluation* section. The *theory and design* section will give the theoretical base and model of change for the integrated system, supported by the empirical literature relevant to the targeted population. This section should specify the targeted risk factors and how each element of the system will target these risk factors. The elements of the system should be detailed in terms of their aims, objectives, and content, and the association between these elements and the model of change should be shown using supportive evidence. This section of the manual should also discuss diversity issues, the interaction between elements of the system, and the model of overall case management.

The *implementation and evaluation* section describes each element of the system and its interaction with other elements to set the benchmark for delivery. The minimum operating requirements for delivering the system should be laid out, alongside exactly how the elements link together in practice. Staff roles and responsibilities should be detailed in this section, along with procedures for assurance of staff competencies, including training, assessment, and regular performance reviews. The procedures for selection of offenders should be outlined, including details of assessment tools and guidelines for their use and interpretation, alongside treatment integrity and audit procedures, and details of evaluation systems, including administration and interpretation information on tools used in these procedures.

Although separate criteria exist for stand-alone programmes and integrated systems, the parallels between the two are evident from an accreditation perspective. In both cases the aim is to set high standards with respect to quality of the design of offending behaviour programmes. While the drive for excellence in programme design was an obvious step towards effective practice, the eventual outcome of any programme ultimately depends on the quality of its delivery. In order to determine the quality of delivery it is necessary to have a means by which to conduct a programme audit.

Programme Audit

The concept of programme audit as a means of ensuring high levels of treatment integrity was a new idea in the Prison Service in England and Wales in the mid-1990s. The general assumption in many areas of practice is that practitioners have autonomy to do what they judge to be in the best interests of their clients. Within the context of manualised behaviour change programmes, the concept of treatment integrity challenges this assumption of practitioner autonomy. Hollin (1995) draws on the wider therapeutic literature to describe three threats to programme integrity. First, *programme drift* refers to the gradual shift over time in the practices and aims of a programme, perhaps as practitioners change and focus is lost. Second, *programme reversal* where there is active resistance and opposition to the programme methods and there are efforts to undermine the workings of the programme. Third, *programme non-compliance,* which refers to a situation where practitioners decide independently to re-work the programme, adding new sessions and dropping others, introducing new methods, and altering the targets for change. In all three cases, to a greater or lesser extent, the end result is the same: the programme's integrity is compromised and, following one of the key findings from the meta-analyses, its potential effectiveness curtailed.

A system of regular programme audit provides one means with which to try to detect active threats to integrity and so maintain high levels of practice. Hollin (1995) describes three sources of information that can be used to manage integrity. First, outside, independent observation of the conduct of programme sessions; second, client report of their experiences in participating in a programme; third, practitioner self-reports of their own practice. Of course, these three methods are not exclusive and, arguably, should all be used in order both to give a wide range of information and as a means by which to triangulate findings. As noted by Blud et al. (2003), the introduction of offending behaviour programmes into HM Prison Service was accompanied by a system of audit.

The Prison Service audit was conducted using an annual visit to each prison running offending behaviour programmes. Blud et al. note that the audit visit covered four areas. First, *institutional support* which is concerned with the operation and management of the programme within the prison. Second, *treatment support,* which covers issues such as the selection of staff to deliver the programme, the proper application of the selection criteria for prisoners who might enter a programme, and the supervision and support of staff delivering programmes. Third, *throughcare* refers to the continuity of work initiated in the programme across other services. Fourth, *quality of delivery* looks at aspects of programme delivery such as dropout and completion rates, and critically uses video monitoring of sessions to determine adherence to the programme manual.

The Scottish Prison Service (SPS) has seven standards to inform implementation accreditation (as opposed to design accreditation). These seven standards are: (1) that staff are appropriately managed and supported; (2) that staff are systematically selected; (3) that programmes are appropriately delivered; (4) that programmes are appropriately managed; (5) that suitable rooms and equipment are available; (6) that documentation is of a good standard; (7) that programmes are monitored and evaluated. In the SPS system, as with their programme design standards, each programme implementation standard has a set of supporting criteria that produces the evidence that the standard is being met. Further, alongside each criterion the sources for the evidence, which the audit team will approach, are made explicit. For example, Standard 1 of the Implementation Standards requires that staff are appropriately managed and supported. There are 13 criteria by which evidence is gathered for this criterion: for example, criteria 1.5 states "Programme facilitators are provided with initial and continued training and development"; the sources of evidence for this criterion are the programme manager in the prison and the SPS College records.

In a similar vein, *The Correctional Programme Assessment Inventory* (CPAI) (Gendreau, Goggin & Smith, 2002) provides a system for measuring programme quality (see also Chapter 7). As shown in Box 1.3, the 75-item CPAI gathers management information across six domains, proving a very full picture of the running

Box 1.3   Components in the CPAI (after Gendreau et al., 2002)

1. *Programme implementation.* The experience and qualifications of those who initiate a programme.
2. *Client pre-service assessment.* The assessment of offender risk and need in conjunction with the type of offender for whom the programme is intended.
3. *Programme characteristics.* The nature of the programme and the quality of the associated protocols and documentation.
4. *Staff characteristics.* The levels of staff experience and training in implementing and running programmes.
5. *Evaluation.* The type of quality assurance mechanisms in place, process evaluation, and outcome evaluation.
6. *Other.* The ethical guidelines and standards for the programme, and funding mechanisms to maintain the programme.

of a programme. Gendreau et al. (2002) report that the CPAI has been used widely in practice, with three large-scale programme reviews (involving a total of over 400 programmes) also conducted using the CPAI. Gendreau et al. use examples from these reviews, nested within the six domains that form the instrument, to give examples of how programme implementation and maintenance can go wrong in the real world.

The research evaluating multi-systemic therapy (MST) has consistently examined the role of treatment integrity (Brown et al., 1997; Henggeler, Melton, Brondino, Scherer & Hanley, 1997; Henggeler, Pickrel & Brondino, 1999). These studies have shown the value of therapists receiving high levels of management support through organisational policies, provision of appropriate resources, competitive salaries, and support for completing required documentation (for a summary, see Edwards, Schoenwald, Henggeler & Strother, 2001). A practical implication of this research has been the development of a site assessment checklist to assess organisations' ability to implement MST. This checklist assesses a wide range of issues, including broad topics such as an organisation's mission and service philosophy as well as specific issues like provision of computers, telephones, and fax machines for therapists (Edwards et al., 2001).

Similarly, Goldstein & Glick (2001) note four key management principles that underpin the successful implementation of Aggression Replacement Training (ART) (Goldstein, Glick & Gibbs, 1998). First, managers should respect the programme work and the staff who deliver it, and in turn practitioners should respect the work of managers. Second, there is a need for good communication among all staff involved in programme. Third, there should be a clear delineation of staff roles and responsibilities that provide clear lines of accountability. Fourth, shared ownership of the programme should be promoted through joint planning of the implementation and delivery of the programme.

In conclusion, by the end of the 1990s it was evident that the findings from the meta-analyses had been assimilated into mainstream thinking about offender rehabilitation. The basic work on programme accreditation and audit had been carried out, in the UK and elsewhere, and in the UK large-scales initiatives were being set up in both the Prison Service and the Probation Service. Indeed, an evaluation based on a sample of more than 4 000 offenders in the Canadian federal system (Robinson, 1995) illustrates the scale on which programme implementation could be contemplated. However, as discussed in Chapter 2, the shift from small, local projects to large, even national, initiatives brings its own problems.

2000 AND ONWARDS: WHAT'S HAPPENED?

Since the turn of the century there have been significant developments in three areas connected with offending behaviour programmes. First, the range of available programmes has increased markedly; second, there has been a growth in the number of published evaluations of programmes; third, following the large-scale, national implementation of programmes in the UK it is possible to gauge opinion regarding their reception into services.

Programme Development

Increasing the Range of Programmes

Programme development has become a widely appreciated skill and, as the most recent CSAP report shows, there is no shortage of well-developed, accredited programmes in the Prison and Probation Services of England and Wales (Correctional Services Accreditation Panel, 2004). Since its inception in 1999 JAP, later CSAP, has accredited 27 offending behaviour programmes and recognised or provisionally accredited four programmes, one integrated system, and a model for a prison therapeutic community. With the exception of the SOTP, the offending behaviour programmes developed during the early- and mid-1990s were *general* programmes in the sense that they did not discriminate between the types of offender or offence for which they were designed. (A *cognitive skills booster* programme, for use in the prison and probation services, for offenders who have completed one of the general offending behaviour programmes has been developed. Further, a one-to-one cognitive skills programme is available for use in the Probation Service for offenders for whom group work is not suitable (Priestley, 2000).)

Since 2000, however, a range of specialist programmes have been developed that target either specific offenders or specific offence types (Correctional Service Accreditation Panel, 2004). These accredited specialist programmes include three focused on violence and anger management. The *Cognitive Self-Change Programme* is an adaptation of a North American programme, and is accredited for use in the Prison Service. The Canadian programme *Controlling Anger and Learning to Manage It* (CALM) is a cognitive-behavioural programme used in both the prison and probation services. Finally, an adaptation of the US programme *Aggression Replacement Training* (ART) (McGuire & Clark, 2004) has been accredited for use in the Probation Service.

For domestic violence offenders there are two accredited programmes. The Prison Service uses an adapted version of the *Canadian Healthy Relationships Programme*, while the Probation Service delivers an *Integrated Domestic Abuse Programme* to male offenders, which is based on the Duluth model of working with domestic abusers and their victims (Pence & Paymar, 1993). A range of sex offender programmes suitable for use in the community are now accredited by CSAP, as detailed in the 2003–2004 CSAP Report: these three are the *Community-Sex Offender Group Programme*, the *Thames Valley-Sex Offender Group Programme*, and the *Northumbria-Sex Offender Group Programme*. A programme for psychopathic offenders, *Chromis*, has been developed for use in prisons and a pilot trial is underway in the Westgate Unit at HMP Frankland and the Peaks Unit at Rampton Hospital (HM Prison Service, 2005).

Various programmes for offenders who misuse substances have been developed within the Prison Service, with some programmes run in partnership with specialist drug agencies. These prison-based programmes include the *Substance Abuse Treatment Programme*, and the *Prisons Partnership 12-Step Programme*. There are four programmes of varying intensity, aimed at prisoners with different risk levels: *Prison-Addressing Substance-Related Offending* (P-ASRO), *FOCUS*, *Action on Drugs*, and *STOP*. Within the Probation Service there are two programmes for work with substance-misusing offenders, the programme *Addressing Substance-Related Offending* (ASRO); (McMurran & Priestley, 1999, 2004) is designed to be delivered in a group setting. A similar programme, *Priestley Reducing Individual Substance Misuse* (PRISM), is designed for delivery on a one-to-one basis. An accredited substance use programme with a different focus, used within the Probation Service, is the *Drink-Impaired Drivers* (DIDs) programme for drink-related driving offenders.

A therapeutic community (TC) operating within HMP Grendon has been accredited. This TC provides treatment for prisoners with specific emotional and psychological needs that are unlikely to be met through participation in shorter interventions. On average, prisoners stay in the therapeutic community for 18 months, with a recommended maximum of 3 years. Other accredited prison-based TCs address drug use and offending behaviour among prisoners with a substance-misuse problem, or offer cognitive-behavioural interventions within a therapeutic milieu.

Since 2000 one Integrated System, an *Enhanced Community Punishment* (ECP) programme, has been seen by the CSAP. This programme is for use with offenders serving a Community Punishment Order or the Community Punishment element of a Community Punishment and Rehabilitation Order in the Probation Service. The ECP Integrated System aims to reduce re-offending by maximising offenders' learning opportunities, both through high levels of contact with probation staff and via engagement in unpaid work in the community, for prosocial and anticriminal attitudes and behaviours.

The growth both in number of programmes and management sophistication in England and Wales can also be seen in several other jurisdictions. Of particular note are Canada and Scotland, which have a range of programmes and accompanying accreditation systems and criteria similar to those used in England and Wales.

Programme Design and Delivery

The effectiveness of a programme may be affected by the level at which an offender participates and engages in programme sessions. The responsivity principle, drawn from the meta-analyses, states that programme design and delivery style should be matched to offender characteristics in order to increase an offender's engagement with a programme (Andrews & Bonta, 2003; Andrews et al., 1990). Since 2000, increasing attention has been paid to making the responsivity principle operational. There are two issues to address in this respect. First, does the programme address the criminogenic needs of the target group? Second, is the programme content engaging and relevant to the target group?

As Ogloff (2002) notes, most offender treatment programmes are designed for white, adult, male offenders. It follows that it cannot be assumed that other offender groups, such as women, young offenders, and offenders from different ethnic and cultural groups, will present with the same criminogenic needs. It is entirely possible that at least some criminogenic needs will vary according to the personal, cultural, and social factors relevant to different offender groups. For treatment to be at its most effective, it should also be sensitive to these specific needs (Bonta, 1995). However, the process of establishing the exact nature of the criminogenic needs of different offender groups is a complex empirical task. Nonetheless, attempts have been made at designing programmes for specific offender groups. For example, the *Women's Acquisitive Crime* programme, designed by the Canadian company T3 Associates and run in the Probation Service, is intended for women offenders who have committed offences of an acquisitive nature (Lovbakke & Homes, 2004). This programme uses a motivational approach based on the Stages of Change model (Prochaska, Norcross & DiClemente, 1994). The principle of designing programmes for particular groups is further seen in programmes for young offenders (Ross & Hilborn, 2003), racially motivated offences (Hollin & Palmer, 2001), Black and Asian offenders (Powis & Walmsley, 2002; Stephens, Coombs & Debidin, 2004), and indigenous aboriginal offenders (Cull & Wehner, 1998).

With relevance to programme content, Andrews (2001) made the distinction between *internal* and *external* responsivity factors. Internal responsivity refers to the characteristics of offenders that may impact on their ability to participate in and benefit from treatment: this includes characteristics such as age, gender, ethnicity, intellectual functioning, levels of motivation, and other personality characteristics (Kennedy, 2000). Programme designers and practitioners can address these issues by ensuring that the content and pace of programmes are matched to these offender characteristics. In contrast, external responsivity refers to "organisational factors" such as characteristics of both the staff responsible for programme delivery and the physical setting in which a programme is offered.

Meta-analytic reviews have shown the importance of the responsivity principle in offender programmes (for example, Andrews et al., 1990; Lipsey, Chapman & Landenberger, 2001; Redondo et al., 2002). Further support for the role of responsivity can be found in meta-analyses with specific offender populations, including violent offenders (Dowden & Andrews, 2000), women offenders (Andrews & Dowden, 1999; Dowden & Andrews, 1999a), young offenders (Dowden & Andrews, 1999b), and sexual offenders (Gallagher et al., 1999; Polizzi et al., 1999).

Programme Evaluation

It might be thought at the outset that the case for offending behaviour programmes is proven, that the meta-analyses have shown that treatment "works". Indeed, the meta-analyses have highlighted an overall treatment effect nested within the literature, which offers support to this approach, but this effect is an aggregated statistical effect across different treatment modalities rather than a consistent effect of a single approach. A critical dimension in the development of "what works" offending behaviour programmes is the careful evaluation of the effects of individual programmes.

In practice, how to know whether or not an intervention is working is an issue faced in many fields (for example, Long & Hollin, 1998). With regard to evaluating offending behaviour programmes, Friendship, Falshaw & Beech (2003) present a comprehensive model that links the outcome of the programme with the climate of delivery and programme integrity.

Friendship et al. distinguish between short-term outcome, such as changes in the offenders' behavioural functioning, long-term outcome as in changes in offending, and the cost-effectiveness of the programme. Thus, assuming the programme is delivered with integrity, there are three dimensions to consider in evaluating programmes. First, do programmes impact on short-term *process* variables? Second, do programmes significantly effect the *outcome* targets? Third, are programmes *cost-effective* to deliver? Again, programmes within England and Wales can be used to highlight the issues in programme evaluation (for a more detailed consideration of these issues, see Chapter 2).

Evaluating Process

Offending behaviour programmes are designed to help the offender bring about change in some aspect of their functioning, such as anger control or employment skills, and through this change there is an increased likelihood of a reduction in criminal behaviour. One level of evaluation is therefore to see whether programmes are effective in modifying the targets they intend to change – the process by which the outcome of reduced offending is to be achieved. Blud et al. (2003) looked at the effects of taking part in two prison-based offending behaviour programmes, R & R and ETS, on pre- and post-programme scores on a range of measures of cognitive functioning. From an analysis of data gathered from over 2 500 prisoners, Blud et al. (2003, p. 74) noted that "The majority of measures in the assessment battery evinced modest change in the desired direction . . . indicating a particular impact of programmes on the targeted behaviour of short-cut, lazy problem-solving where little heed is paid to personal responsibility." This change was greater for women prisoners than for men, and for high- rather than low-need prisoners. Blud et al. were also able to report associations between process measures, programme management, and level of treatment integrity. These relationships were seen in the significant associations between efficient management of programme tutors within prisons and change on the assessment battery and rates of programme completion, and between video-monitoring scores of integrity and programme audit scores for institutional support for programmes and treatment management. As Blud et al. (2003, p. 78) conclude, "Better quality programme delivery was associated with better programme administration on all fronts." An important aspect of the Blud et al. study is the detailed analysis of process data, actually looking to see how the effects of a programme are mediated by offender characteristics and institutional performance.

Wilson, Attrill & Nugent (2003) investigated the effects of R & R and ETS on a range of process measures for three groups of offenders (including both men and women) serving prison sentences. The three groups were 2 537 non-acquisitive offenders who had no record of conviction for an acquisitive offence, 2 427 "medium acquisitive" offenders with between one and three convictions for acquisitive offences, and 3 339 offenders with more than four convictions for acquisitive offences. Following the offending behaviour programme, all three groups showed significant patterns of change, in the predicted direction, on a range of measures of cognitive functioning.

Evaluating Outcome

Beech et al. (2001) conducted a 6-year follow-up of 53 male sex offenders who had participated in community-based sex-offending programmes. They reported that the overall reconviction rate was 15 %: however, for those offenders who had responded to treatment the reconviction rate was 10 % compared to 23 % for men who had not responded to treatment. Friendship, Mann & Beech (2003a) compared the 2-year sexual offence reconviction rates for 647 men who had completed the prison-based Sex Offender Treatment Programme (SOTP) with those of a comparison group, composed of 1 910 men imprisoned for a sexual offence but who had not taken part in SOTP. The overall sexual offence reconviction rate was typically low for both the SOTP (2.6 %) and comparison groups (2.8 %), making it difficult to draw any firm conclusions about the effects of the programme. The issue of a low base rate in reconviction, as seen with sexual offending, is an issue that produces difficulties in programme evaluation (Friendship & Thornton, 2001). When Friendship et al. (2003a) compared the reconviction rates of the two groups for sexual *and* violent offences there was a trend to a significantly lower reconviction rate in the SOTP group.

The first large-scale evaluation of two prison-based general offending programmes, R & R and ETS, was reported by Caroline Friendship and her colleagues (Friendship et al., 2002; Friendship, Blud, Erikson, Travers & Thornton, 2003). The reconviction rate for the 667 offenders who took part in the programmes (including 66 offenders who did not complete their programme) was compared with a matched comparison group of 1 081 offenders who had not participated in a programme. The analysis looked at the reconviction rates according to assessed risk of reconviction: comparing the two groups, a significantly lower rate of reconviction, by up to 14 %, was found for medium-risk offenders in the programme group, with a similar tendency in the low- and high-risk comparisons. This difference between groups remained significant when logistic regression was used to control for factors such as age, previous convictions, and type of offence. These findings can be seen as consistent with the risk principle that emerged from the meta-analyses, such that programmes produce the least effect with low- and high-risk offenders.

A second evaluation of the prison-based R & R and ETS programmes has been reported by Louise Falshaw and her colleagues (Falshaw et al., 2003; Falshaw, Friendship, Travers & Nugent, 2004). This evaluation compared 649 male offenders who had participated in an offending behaviour programme (including the 10 % of offenders who failed to complete it) with 1 947 male offenders who had not taken part in a programme. There were no significant differences in the 2-year re-conviction rates of the two groups: the same finding was reported when the groups were divided, as in the Friendship study, according to risk of reconviction. When the analysis was recomputed excluding those offenders who had not completed their programme the same null finding remained.

Using the same methodology as in the Friendship and the Falshaw studies, Cann et al. (2003) compared the 1- and 2-year reconviction rates of 2 195 adult male offenders and 1 534 young offenders who had taken part in prison-based R & R and ETS programmes with matched comparison groups. As before, the group comparisons were made on the basis of assessed risk of reconviction. When all those who had started a programme were included, there was no significant difference in the 1- and 2-year reconviction rates for the programme starters and the comparison groups for either adult or young offenders. The dropout rate from the programmes was about 9 % for both adult and young offenders: when the dropouts were excluded from the analysis the 1-year reconviction rate for adult offenders was significantly lower than for the comparison group, with an overall reduction of 2.5 % and a reduction of 6.9 % for the high risk sub-group of offenders. A similar pattern was found for the young offenders, with an overall reduction of 4.1 % and 4.8 % for the high-risk sub-group. However, at 2-years reconviction these differences were lost and the reconviction rates for programme completers and the comparison group were no longer statistically different. Further analysis revealed that the 1-year programme effect for completers (adult and young offenders) was evident for ETS but not for R & R.

Evaluating Costs

There are many financial costs to running programmes, including staff training, equipment and premises, and staff time to run the project. Indeed, this point is true for any initiative intended to reduce crime and considerable expertise has accumulated in measuring the costs and benefits of preventing crime (Welsh, Farrington & Sherman, 2001). In order for programmes to be financially viable, which is not the same as socially valuable, they must deliver a saving. In this approach to evaluation the distinction is drawn between *cost-effectiveness* and *cost-benefit* analysis. As Dhiri, Goldblatt, Brand & Price (2001) explain, cost *effectiveness* is the cost of the input per unit of outcome: thus, cost-effectiveness might be expressed as the cost of a programme per reconviction prevented. A measure of cost-effectiveness such as reduced reconviction might, for example, be used to assess the relative merits of different types of programme, or the value of a programme in prison compared to just imprisonment. Dhiri et al. (2001) further explain that

> Cost-benefit analysis takes cost-effectiveness analysis a stage further by attaching monetary values to the outcomes of an intervention. Once both the costs of inputs and the values of outcomes (benefits) are expressed in monetary terms, a direct comparison can be made. (Dhiri et al., 2001, p. 188)

In practice both types of cost analysis are not easy to achieve. The process of costing a programme can be far from simple in terms of what to cost and gaining access to costs. For example, running a programme in a room in a prison will cost in terms of room space, heating, and lighting; how to aggregate these costs is a far from simple task. Further, what should be included if assessing the output costs for an intervention? A prevented crime will save costs within the criminal justice system for police, courts, prisons and probation; while there are broader savings to be had in terms of insurance costs, possible health costs, and victim suffering. Clearly, deciding what to cost and then calculating a figure are far from simple tasks (Cohen, 2001).

Welsh & Farrington (2001) present a review of research on the financial value of preventing crime. Setting three criteria for inclusion of an intervention in their review – a measure of personal crime, such that the victim was a person; an experimental or quasi-experimental research design; and availability of cost-benefit information – Welsh and Farrington were able to include 26 studies in their review. These studies spanned a wide range of crime prevention strategies ranging from improved street lighting to a scheme for supported work for offenders. Of these 26 studies, Welsh and Farrington identified seven that were grouped under the heading "correctional intervention". These seven studies had the common element of trying to change offender behaviour, although they used a variety of methods including counselling, diversion from custody, and services for substance abuse. While all the studies showed a positive cost-benefit ratio, none employed an intervention that would be recognisable as an offending behaviour programme. A full economic evaluation of the costs and benefits of an offending behaviour programme remains to be reported in the literature.

In summary, programme evaluation is absolutely central to the continued development and understanding of effective practice and, indeed, continues apace. The strength of any body of research lies in the diversity of its evidence: this diversity can be seen in recent publications that encompass empirical outcome studies (Van Voorhis, Spruance, Ritchey, Listwan & Seabrook, 2004), qualitative studies of programme delivery (Clarke, Simmonds & Wydall, 2004), and quantitative reviews (Wilson, Bouffard & Mackenzie, 2005).

CONCLUSIONS

In considering the development of offending behaviour programmes three fundamental points arise. First, the centrality of research in both the emergence of offending behaviour programmes and their continued evaluation. Second, the practical issues that arise in making research findings operational through policy. Third, relating to the first point, the political issues that arise in the interplay between evaluative research, experience from practice, and the reformulation of policy.

Looking at the first point, there are valid criticisms of the research base that informed the development of offending behaviour programmes. Similarly, there are limitations to the extant knowledge base and enduring criticisms of the methods used by researchers. The issues involved in clarifying the research relevant to offending behaviour programmes are considered in detail in Chapter 2. As explored throughout this book, there are a myriad of topics related to practice to consider, ranging from procedures for selection of offenders, practitioner skills, to service provision tailored for specific groups of offenders, such as women offenders, young offenders, and offenders from different ethnic groups. Finally, as the final chapter will discuss, there are significant issues in interpreting the evaluative research in order to reformulate policy to reinforce effective practice. Almost inevitably, there are areas of professional and political conflict, typically played out in acrimony and hostility, which sit alongside considerations of what makes for effective service provision and delivery.

REFERENCES

Alexander, M. A. (1999). Sexual offender treatment efficacy revisited. *Sexual Abuse: Journal of Research and Treatment, 11,* 101–116.

Allam, J. (1998). *Effective practice in work with sex offenders: A reconviction study comparing treated and untreated offenders.* West Midlands: West Midlands Probation Service.

Andrews, D. A. (1995). The psychology of criminal conduct and effective treatment. In J. McGuire (Ed.), *What works: Reducing reoffending – guidelines for research and practice* (pp. 35–62). Chichester: John Wiley & Sons.

Andrews, D. A. (2001). Principles of effective correctional programs. In L. L. Motiuk & R. C. Serin (Eds), *Compendium 2000 on effective correctional programming* (pp. 9–17). Ottawa: Correctional Service Canada.

Andrews, D. A. & Bonta, J. (2003). *The psychology of criminal conduct (3rd edition).* Cincinnati, OH: Anderson.

Andrews, D. A. & Dowden, C. (1999). A meta-analytic investigation into effective correctional intervention for female offenders. *Forum on Corrections Research, 11,* 18–21.

Andrews, D. A. & Dowden, C. (2005). Managing correctional treatment for reduced recidivism: A meta-analytic review of programme integrity. *Legal and Criminological Psychology, 10,* 173–187.

Andrews, D. A., Zinger, I., Hoge, R. D., Bonta, J., Gendreau, P. & Cullen, F. T. (1990). Does correctional treatment work? A clinically relevant and psychologically informed meta-analysis. *Criminology, 28,* 369–404.

Antonowicz, D. H. & Ross, R. R. (1994). Essential components of successful rehabilitation programs for offenders. *International Journal of Offender Therapy and Comparative Criminology, 38,* 97–104.

Barker, M. & Morgan, R. (1993). *Sex offenders: A framework for the evaluation of community-based treatment.* London: Home Office.

Beckett, R. C., Beech, A. R., Fisher, D. & Fordham, A. S. (1994). *Community-based treatment for sex offenders: An evaluation of seven treatment programmes.* London: Home Office.

Beech, A. R., Erikson, M., Friendship, C. & Ditchfield, J. (2001). *A six-year follow-up of men going through probation-based sex offender treatment programmes.* Home Office Research Findings No. 144. London: Home Office.

Beech, A. R. & Mann, R. E. (2002). Recent developments in the assessment and treatment of sexual offenders. In J. McGuire (Ed.), *Offender rehabilitation and treatment: Effective programmes and policies to reduce reoffending* (pp. 259–288). Chichester: John Wiley & Sons.

Bernfeld, G. A. (2001). The struggle for treatment integrity in a "dis-integrated" service delivery system. In G. A. Bernfeld, D. P. Farrington & A. W. Leschied (Eds), *Offender rehabilitation in practice: Implementing and evaluating effective programs* (pp. 168–188). Chichester: John Wiley & Sons.

Blud, L., Travers, R., Nugent, F. & Thornton, D. M. (2003). Accreditation of offending behaviour programmes in HM Prison Service: "What Works" in practice. *Legal and Criminological Psychology, 8,* 69–81.

Bonta, J. (1995). The responsivity principle and offender rehabilitation. *Forum on Corrections Research, 7,* 34–37.

Brown, T. L., Swenson, C. C., Cunningham, P. B., Henggeler, S. W., Schoenwald, S. K. & Rowland, M. D. (1997). Multisystemic treatment of violent and chronic juvenile offenders: Bridging the gap between research and practice. *Administration and Policy in Mental Health*, 25, 221–238.

Cann, J., Falshaw, L., Nugent, F. & Friendship, C. (2003). *Understanding what works: Accredited cognitive skills programmes for adult men and young offenders*. Home Office Research Findings No. 226. London: Home Office.

Clark, D. A. (2000). *Theory manual for Enhanced Thinking Skills*. Prepared for the Joint Prison Probation Accreditation Panel.

Clarke, A., Simmonds, R. & Wydall, S. (2004). *Delivering cognitive skills programmes in prison: A qualitative study*. Home Office Research Findings No. 242. London: Home Office.

Cohen, J. (1988). *Statistical power analysis for the behavioural sciences*, (2nd edition). New York: Academic Press.

Cohen, M. A. (2001). To treat or not to treat? A financial perspective. In C. R. Hollin (Ed.), *Handbook of offender assessment and treatment* (pp. 35–49). Chichester: John Wiley & Sons.

Cooke, D. J. & Philip, L. (2001). To treat or not to treat: An empirical perspective. In C. R. Hollin (Ed.), *Handbook of offender assessment and treatment* (pp. 17–34). Chichester: John Wiley & Sons.

Cornish, D. B. & Clarke, R. V. G. (Eds) (1986). *The reasoning criminal: Rational choice perspectives on crime*. New York: Springer-Verlag.

Correctional Services Accreditation Panel. (2004). *The Correctional Services Accreditation Panel report: 2003–2004*. London: Prison and Probation Services.

Cull, D. M. & Wehner, D. M. (1998). Australian Aborigines: Cultural factors pertaining to the assessment and treatment of Australian Aboriginal sexual offenders. In W. L. Marshall, Y. M. Fernandez, S. M. Hudson & T. Ward (Eds), *Sourcebook of treatment programs for sexual offenders* (pp. 431–444). New York: Plenum Press.

Cullen, J. E. & Seddon, J. W. (1981). The application of a behavioural regime to disturbed young offenders. *Personality and Individual Differences*, 2, 285–292.

Dhiri, S., Goldblatt, P., Brand, S. & Price, R. (2001). Evaluation of the United Kingdom's "Crime Reduction Programme": Analysis of costs and benefits. In B. C. Welsh, D. P. Farrington & L. W. Sherman, (Eds), *Costs and benefits of preventing crime* (pp. 179–201). Boulder, CO: Westview Press.

Dobson, K. S. & Singer, A. R. (2005). Definitional and practical issues in the assessment of treatment integrity. *Clinical Psychology, Science and Practice*, 12, 384–387.

Dowden, C. & Andrews, D. A. (1999a). What works for female offenders: A meta-analytic review. *Crime and Delinquency*, 45, 438–452.

Dowden, C. & Andrews, D. A. (1999b). What works in young offender treatment: A meta-analysis. *Forum on Corrections Research*, 11, 21–24.

Dowden, C. & Andrews, D. A. (2000). Effective correctional treatment and violent reoffending: A meta-analysis. *Canadian Journal of Criminology and Criminal Justice*, 42, 327–342.

Edwards, D. L., Schoenwald, S. K., Henggeler, S. W. & Strother, K. B. (2001). A multilevel perspective on the implementation of Multisystemic Therapy (MST): Attempting dissemination with fidelity. In G. A. Bernfield, D. P. Farrington & A. W. Leschied (Eds), *Offender rehabilitation in practice: Implementing and evaluating effective programs* (pp. 97–120). Chichester: John Wiley & Sons.

Falshaw, L., Bates, A., Patel, V., Corbett, C. & Friendship, C. (2003). Assessing reconviction, reoffending and recidivism in a sample of UK sexual offenders. *Legal and Criminological Psychology*, 8, 207–215.

Falshaw, L., Friendship, C., Travers, L. & Nugent, F. (2003). *Searching for what works: An evaluation of cognitive skills programmes*. Home Office Research Findings No. 206. London: Home Office.

Falshaw, L., Friendship, C., Travers, L. & Nugent, F. (2004). Searching for "what works": HM Prison Service accredited cognitive skills programmes. *British Journal of Forensic Practice*, 6, 3–13.

Flannery-Schroeder, E. (2005). Treatment integrity: Implications for treatment. *Clinical Psychology, Science and Practice*, 12, 388–390.

Friendship, C. & Beech, A. R. (2005). Reconviction of sexual offenders in England and Wales: An overview of research. *Journal of Sexual Aggression, 11*, 209–223.

Friendship, C., Blud, L., Erikson, M. & Travers, L. (2002). *An evaluation of cognitive behavioural treatment for prisoners.* Home Office Research Findings No. 161. London: Home Office.

Friendship, C., Blud, L., Erikson, M., Travers, L. & Thornton, D. M. (2003). Cognitive-behavioural treatment for imprisoned offenders: An evaluation of HM Prison Service's cognitive skills programmes. *Legal and Criminological Psychology, 8*, 103–114.

Friendship, C., Falshaw, L. & Beech, A. R. (2003a). Measuring the real impact of accredited behaviour programmes. *Legal and Criminological Psychology, 8*, 115–127.

Friendship, C., Mann, R. E. & Beech, A. R. (2003b). *The prison-based Sex Offender Treatment Programme – an evaluation.* Home Office Research Findings No. 205. London: Home Office.

Friendship, C., Mann, R. E. & Beech, A. R. (2003c). Evaluation of a national prison-based treatment programme for sexual offenders in England and Wales. *Journal of Interpersonal Violence, 18*, 744–759.

Friendship, C. & Thornton, D. (2001). Sexual reconviction for sexual offenders discharged from prisons in England and Wales: Implications for evaluating treatment. *British Journal of Criminology, 41*, 285–292.

Gallagher, C. A., Wilson, D. B., Hirschfield, P., Coggeshall, M. B. & MacKenzie, D. L. (1999). A quantitative review of the effects of sexual offender treatment on sexual reoffending. *Corrections Management Quarterly, 3*, 19–29.

Garrett, C. G. (1985). Effects of residential treatment on adjudicated delinquents: A meta-analysis. *Journal of Research in Crime and Delinquency, 22*, 287–308.

Gendreau, P. (1996). Offender rehabilitation: What we know and what needs to be done. *Criminal Justice and Behavior, 23*, 144–161.

Gendreau, P., Goggin, C. & Smith, P. (2002). Implementation guidelines for correctional programs in the "real world". In G. A. Bernfeld, D. P. Farrington & A. W. Leschied (Eds), *Offender rehabilitation in practice: Implementing and evaluating effective programs* (pp. 228–268). Chichester: John Wiley & Sons.

Gendreau, P. & Ross, R. R. (1979). Effective correctional treatment: Bibliotherapy for cynics. *Crime and Delinquency, 25*, 463–489.

Glass, G. V., McGraw, B. & Smith, M. L. (1981). *Meta-analysis in social research.* Beverly Hills, CA: Sage.

Goldstein, A. P. (1988). *The Prepare Curriculum.* Champaign, IL: Research Press.

Goldstein, A. P. & Glick, B. (2001). Aggression Replacement Training: Application and evaluation management. In G. A. Bernfeld, D. P. Farrington & A. W. Leschied (Eds), *Offender rehabilitation in practice: Implementing and evaluating effective programs* (pp. 122–148). Chichester: John Wiley & Sons.

Goldstein, A. P., Glick, B. & Gibbs, J. C. (1998). *Aggression Replacement Training (2nd edition).* Champaign, IL: Research Press.

Grubin D. & Thornton D. (1994). A national programme for the assessment and treatment of sex offenders in the English prison system. *Criminal Justice and Behavior, 21*, 55–71.

Hall, G. C. N. (1995). Sexual offender recidivism revisited: A meta-analysis of recent treatment studies. *Journal of Consulting and Clinical Psychology, 63*, 802–809.

Hanson, R. K. et al. (2002). First report of the Collaborative Outcome Data Project on the effectiveness of psychological treatment for sex offenders. *Sexual Abuse: A Journal of Research and Treatment, 14*, 169–194.

Hanson, R. K. & Thornton, D. M. (2000). Improving risk assessment for sex offenders: A comparison of three actuarial scales. *Law and Human Behavior, 29*, 119–136.

Hedderman, C. & Sugg, D. (1996). *Does treating sex offenders reduce re-offending?* Home Office Research Study No. 45. London: Home Office.

Henggeler, S. W., Melton, G. B., Brondino, M. J., Scherer, D. G. & Hanley, J. H. (1997). Multisystemic Therapy with violent and chronic juvenile offenders and their families: The role of treatment fidelity in successful dissemination. *Journal of Consulting and Clinical Psychology, 65*, 821–833.

Henggeler, S. W., Pickrel, S. G. & Brondino, M. J. (1999). Multisystemic treatment of substance-abusing and -dependent delinquents: Outcomes, treatment fidelity, and transportability. *Mental Health Services Review, 1*, 171–184.

HM Prison Service (2005). All-staff approach key to new psychopathy programme. *Prison Service News (Magazine)*. October. http://www.hmprisonservice.gov.uk/prisoninformation/prisonservicemagazine/index.asp?id=4300,18,3,18,0,0

Hollin, C. R. (1995). The meaning and implications of "programme integrity". In J. McGuire (Ed.), *What works: Reducing reoffending* (pp. 195–208). Chichester: John Wiley & Sons.

Hollin, C. R. (1999). Treatment programmes for offenders: Meta-analysis, "what works", and beyond. *International Journal of Law and Psychiatry*, 22, 361–372.

Hollin, C. R. (2001a). To treat or not to treat: An historical perspective. In C. R. Hollin (Ed.), *Handbook of offender assessment and treatment* (pp. 3–15). Chichester: John Wiley & Sons.

Hollin, C. R. (2001b). The role of the consultant in developing effective practice. In G. A. Bernfeld, D. P. Farrington & A. W. Leschied (Eds), *Offender rehabilitation in practice: Implementing and evaluating effective programs* (pp. 269–281). Chichester: John Wiley & Sons.

Hollin, C. R. (2002a). Does punishment motivate offenders to change? In M. McMurran (Ed.), *Motivating offenders to change: A guide to enhancing engagement in therapy* (pp. 235–249). Chichester: John Wiley & Sons.

Hollin, C. R. (2002b). *Understanding and working with the violent offender.* Presented in the Symposium Psychology at Leicester: Improving the quality of life. BA Festival of Science, University of Leicester, Leicester.

Hollin, C. R. (2002c). An overview of offender rehabilitation: Something old, something borrowed, something new. *Australian Psychologist*, 37, 159–164.

Hollin, C. R., Epps, K. J. & Kendrick, D. J. (1995). *Managing behavioural treatment: Policy and practice with delinquent adolescent.* London: Routledge.

Hollin, C. R., et al. (2004). *Pathfinder programmes in the Probation Service: A retrospective analysis.* Home Office Online Report 66/04.

Hollin, C. R. & Palmer, E. J. (2001). *Reducing reoffending by racially motivated offenders: A review of the evidence and survey of current practice in the Probation Service.* Grant Report for the Home Office, Research Development and Statistics Directorate.

Izzo, R. L. & Ross, R. R. (1990). Meta-analysis of rehabilitation programmes for juvenile delinquents. *Criminal Justice and Behavior*, 17, 134–142.

Kennedy, S. M. (2000). Treatment responsivity: Reducing recidivism by enhancing treatment effectiveness. *Forum on Corrections Research*, 12, 19–23.

Knott, C. (1995). The STOP programme: Reasoning and Rehabilitation in a British setting. In J. McGuire (Ed.), *What works: Reducing reoffending* (pp. 115–126). Chichester: John Wiley & Sons.

Laws, D. R. (1974). The failure of a token economy. *Federal Probation*, 38, 33–38.

Lewis, S., Vennard, J., Maguire, M., Raynor, P., Vanstone, M., Raybould, S. & Rix, A. (2003). *The resettlement of short-term prisoners: An evaluation of seven Pathfinders.* RDS Occasional Paper No. 83. London: Home Office.

Lipsey, M. W. (1992). Juvenile delinquency treatment: A meta-analytic inquiry into the variability of effects. In T. Cook, D. Cooper, H. Corday, H. Hartman, L. Hedges, R. Light, T. Louis & F. Mosteller (Eds), *Meta-analysis for explanation: A casebook* (pp. 83–127). New York, NY: Russell Sage Foundation.

Lipsey, M. W., Chapman, G. L. & Landenberger, N. A. (2001). Cognitive-behavioral programs for offenders. *Annals of the American Academy of Political and Social Sciences*, 578, 144–157.

Lipton, D. S., Martinson, R. & Wilks, J. (1975). *The effectiveness of correctional treatment: A survey of treatment evaluation studies.* New York: Praeger.

Lipton, D. S., Pearson, F. S., Cleland, C. M. & Yee, D. (2002a). The effects of therapeutic communities and milieu therapy on recidivism. In J. McGuire (Ed.), *Offender rehabilitation and treatment: Effective programmes and policies to reduce re-offending* (pp. 39–77). Chichester: John Wiley & Sons.

Lipton, D. S., Pearson, F. S., Cleland, C. M. & Yee, D. (2002b). The effectiveness of cognitive-behavioural treatment methods on recidivism. In J. McGuire (Ed.), *Offender rehabilitation and treatment: Effective programmes and policies to reduce re-offending* (pp. 79–112). Chichester: John Wiley & Sons.

Lipton, D. S., Thornton, D. M., McGuire, J., Porporino, F. J. & Hollin, C. R. (2000). Program accreditation and correctional treatment. *Substance Use and Misuse*, 35, 1705–1734.

Long, C. G. & Hollin, C. R. (1998). How do you know if your treatment of problem drinking is successful? *Clinical Psychology and Psychotherapy*, 5, 167–176.

Lösel, F. (1995a). The efficacy of correctional treatment: A review and syntheses of meta-evaluations. In J. McGuire (Ed.), *What works: Reducing reoffending – guidelines for research and practice* (pp. 79–111). Chichester: John Wiley & Sons.

Lösel, F. (1995b). Increasing consensus in the evaluation of offender rehabilitation? Lessons from recent research syntheses. *Psychology, Crime and Law*, 2, 19–39.

Lösel, F. (1996). Working with young offenders: The impact of the meta-analyses. In C. R. Hollin & K. Howells (Eds), *Clinical approaches to working with young offenders* (pp. 57–82). Chichester: John Wiley & Sons.

Lösel, F. (1998). Treatment and management of psychopaths. In D. J. Cooke, A. E. Forth & R. D. Hare (Eds), *Psychopathy: Theory, research and implications for society* (pp. 303–354). Dordrecht, The Netherlands: Kluwer Academic.

Lovbakke, J. & Homes, A. (2004). *Focus on female offenders: The Real Women Programme – Probation Service pilot*. Home Office Development and Practice Report 18. London: Home Office.

Mandeville-Norden, R. & Beech, A. R. (2004). Community-based treatment of sex offenders. *Journal of Sexual Aggression*, 10, 193–214.

Martinson, R. (1974). What works? Questions and answers about prison reform. *The Public Interest*, 35, 22–54.

Martinson, R. (1979). New findings, new views: A note of caution regarding sentencing reform. *Hofstra Law Review*, 7, 243–258.

McGuire, J. (1995). Reasoning and Rehabilitation programs in the UK. In R. R. Ross & B. Ross (Eds), *Thinking straight: The Reasoning and Rehabilitation program for delinquency prevention and offender rehabilitation* (pp. 261–282). Ottawa, Canada: Air Training and Publications.

McGuire, J. (2000). *Theory manual for Think First*. Prepared for the Joint Prison Probation Accreditation Panel.

McGuire, J. (2002). Integrating findings from research reviews. In J. McGuire (Ed.), *Offender rehabilitation and treatment: Effective programmes and policies to reduce re-offending* (pp. 3–38). Chichester: John Wiley & Sons.

McGuire, J. & Clark, D. (2004). A national dissemination program. In A. P. Goldstein, R, Nensén, B. Daleflod & M. Kalt (Eds), *New perspectives on Aggression Replacement Training: Practice, research, and application* (pp. 139–150). Chichester: John Wiley & Sons.

McGuire, J. & Hatcher, R. (2000). Offence-focused problem solving: Preliminary evaluation of a cognitive skills program. *Criminal Justice and Behavior*, 28, 564–587.

McMurran, M. & Priestley, P. (1999). *Addressing Substance-Related Offending (ASRO) and Programme for Reducing Individual Substance Misuse (PRISM). Section 1: Theory, evidence and evaluation*. Unpublished document, Home Office Pathfinder Unit.

McMurran, M. & Priestley, P. (2004). Addressing substance-related offending. In B. Reading & M. Weegmann (Eds), *Group psychotherapy and addiction* (pp. 194–210). London: Whurr Publishers.

Moncher, F. J. & Prinz, R. J. (1991). Treatment fidelity in outcome studies. *Clinical Psychology Review*, 11, 247–266.

Ogloff, J. R. P. (2002). Offender rehabilitation: From "nothing works" to what next? *Australian Psychologist*, 37, 245–252.

Pearson, F. S. & Lipton, D. S. (1999). A meta-analytic review of the effectiveness of corrections-based treatments for drug abuse. *The Prison Journal*, 79, 384–410.

Pearson, F. S., Lipton, D. S. & Cleland, C. M. (1997). *Rehabilitative programs in adult corrections: CDATE meta-analyses*. Paper presented at the Annual Meeting of the American Society of Criminology, San Diego, California, November.

Pence, E. & Paymar, M. (1993). *Education groups for men who batter: The Duluth model*. New York: Springer-Verlag.

Perpletchikova, F. & Kazdin, A. E. (2005). Treatment integrity and therapeutic change: Issues and research recommendations. *Clinical Psychology, Science and Practice*, 12, 365–383.

Polizzi, D. M., MacKenzie, D. L. & Hickman, L. J. (1999). What works in adult sex offender treatment? A review of prison- and non-prison-based treatment programs. *International Journal of Offender Therapy and Comparative Criminology*, 43, 357–374.

Powis, B. & Walmsley, R. K. (2002). *Programmes for black and Asian offenders on probation: Lessons for developing practice*. Home Office Research Study No. 250. London: Home Office.

Prendergast, M. L., Podus, D. & Chang, E. (2000). Program factors and treatment outcomes in drug dependence treatment: An examination using meta-analysis. *Substance Use and Misuse*, 35, 1931–1965.

Prendergast, M. L., Podus, D., Chang, E. & Urada, D. (2002). The effectiveness of drug abuse treatment: A meta-analysis of comparison group studies. *Drug and Alcohol Dependence*, 67, 53–72.

Priestley, P. (2000). *Theory manual for One-to-One programme*. Prepared for the Joint Prison Probation Accreditation Panel.

Prison Service Order 4360 (2004). London, UK: HM Prison Service. http://www.hmprisonservice.gov.uk/resourcecentre/psispsos/listpsos/

Prochaska, J. O., Norcross, J. C. & DiClemente, C. C. (1994). *Changing for good*. New York: William Morrow.

Proctor, E. & Flaxington, F. (1996). *Community based interventions with sex offenders organised by the Probation Service: A survey of current practice*. Report for ACOP Work with Sex Offenders Committee. England: Probation Service.

Quay, H. C. (1987). Institutional treatment. In H. C. Quay (Ed.), *Handbook of juvenile delinquency* (pp. 244–265). New York: John Wiley & Sons.

Raynor, P. & Vanstone, M. (1996). Reasoning and Rehabilitation in Britain: The results of the Straight Thinking on Probation (STOP) program. *International Journal of Offender Therapy and Comparative Criminology*, 40, 272–284.

Raynor, P. & Vanstone, M. (1997). *Straight Thinking on Probation (STOP): The mid-Glamorgan experiment*. Oxford: University of Oxford, Centre for Criminological Research, Probation Studies Unit No. 4.

Redondo, S., Sánchez-Meca, J. & Garrido, V. (1999). The influence of treatment programmes on the recidivism of juvenile and adult offenders: An European meta-analytic review. *Psychology, Crime and Law*, 5, 251–278.

Redondo, S., Sánchez-Meca, J. & Garrido, V. (2002). Crime treatment in Europe: A review of outcome studies. In J. McGuire (Ed.), *Offender rehabilitation and treatment: Effective programmes and policies to reduce re-offending* (pp. 113–141). Chichester: John Wiley & Sons.

Rex, S., Lieb, R., Bottoms, A. & Wilson, L. (2003). *Accrediting offender programmes: A process-based evaluation of the Joint Prison/Probation Services Accreditation Panel*. Home Office Research Study 273. London: Home Office.

Roberts, C. (2004). Offending behaviour programmes: Emerging evidence and implications for practice. In R. Burnett & C. Roberts (Eds), *What works in probation and youth justice: Developing evidence-based practice* (pp. 134–158). Cullompton: Willan Publishing.

Robinson, D. (1995). *The impact of cognitive skills training on post-release recidivism among Canadian federal offenders*. Report No. R-41, Research Branch, Correctional Services Canada, Ottawa, Canada.

Robinson, D. & Porporino, F. J. (2001). Programming in cognitive skills: The Reasoning and Rehabilitation programme. In C. R. Hollin (Ed.), *Handbook of offender assessment and treatment* (pp. 179–193). Chichester: John Wiley & Sons.

Robinson, J. & Smith, G. (1971). The effectiveness of correctional programs. *Crime and Delinquency*, 17, 67–80.

Rosenthal, R. & Rubin, D. B. (1982). A simple general purpose display of magnitude of experimental effect. *Journal of Educational Psychology*, 74, 166–169.

Rosnow, R. L. & Rosenthal, R. (1988). Focused tests of significance and effect size estimation in counseling psychology. *Journal of Counseling Psychology*, 35, 203–208.

Ross, R. R. & Fabiano, E. A. (1985). *Time to think: A cognitive model of delinquency prevention and offender rehabilitation*. Johnson City, TN: Institute of Social Sciences and Arts.

Ross, R. R., Fabiano, E. A. & Ewles, C. D. (1988). Reasoning and Rehabilitation. *International Journal of Offender Therapy and Comparative Criminology*, 32, 29–35.

Ross, R. R., Fabiano, E. A. & Ross, B. (1989). *Reasoning and Rehabilitation: A handbook for teaching cognitive skills*. Ottawa: The Cognitive Centre.

Ross, R. R. & Hilborn, J. (2003). *R & R 2: SHORT version for youth*. Ottawa: Cognitive Centre of Canada.

Scottish Prison Service. (2003). *Manual of standards and guidelines for the design accreditation of prisoner programmes and the implementation of programmes in establishments*. Edinburgh: Scottish Prison Service.

Stephens, K., Coombs, J. & Debidin, M. (2004). *Black and Asian offenders pathfinder: Implementation report*. Home Office Development and Practice Report 24. London: Home Office.

Thornton, D. M. (1987). Treatment effects on recidivism: A reappraisal of the "nothing works" doctrine. In B. J. McGurk, D. M. Thornton & M. Williams (Eds), *Applying psychology to imprisonment: Theory & practice* (pp. 181–189), London: HMSO.

Thornton, D. M. (1996). *Criteria for accrediting programmes 1996/1997*. London: Programme Development Section, HM Prison Service.

Thornton, D. M. (1998). *Criteria for accrediting programmes 1998/1999*. London: Programme Development Section, HM Prison Service.

Tong, L. S. J. & Farrington, D. P. (2006). How effective is the "Reasoning and Rehabilitation" programme in reducing re-offending? A meta-analysis of evaluations in four countries. *Psychology, Crime and Law, 12*, 3–24.

Van Voorhis, P., Spruance, L. M., Ritchey, P. N., Listwan, S. J. & Seabrook, R. (2004). The Georgia Cognitive Skills experiment: A replication of reasoning and rehabilitation. *Criminal Justice and Behavior, 31*, 282–305.

Wells-Parker, E., Bangret-Downs, R., McMillen, R. & Williams, M. (1995). Final results from a meta-analysis of remedial interventions with drink/drive offenders. *Addiction, 9*, 907–926.

Welsh, B. C. & Farrington, D. P. (2001). A review of research on the monetary value of preventing crime. In B. C. Welsh, D. P. Farrington & L. W. Sherman (Eds). (2001). *Costs and benefits of preventing crime* (pp. 87–122). Boulder, CO: Westview Press.

Welsh, B. C., Farrington, D. P. & Sherman, L. W. (Eds). (2001). *Costs and benefits of preventing crime*. Boulder, CO: Westview Press.

Whitehead, J. T. & Lab, S. P. (1989). A meta-analysis of juvenile correctional treatment. *Journal of Research in Crime and Delinquency, 26*, 276–295.

Wilson, D. B., Bouffard, L. A. & Mackenzie, D. L. (2005). A quantitative review of structured, group-orientated, cognitive-behavioural programs for offenders. *Criminal Justice and Behavior, 32*, 172–204.

Wilson, G. T. (1996). Manual-based treatments: The clinical application of research findings. *Behaviour, Research and Therapy, 34*, 294–314.

Wilson, S., Attrill, G. & Nugent, F. (2003). Effective interventions for acquisitive offenders: An investigation of cognitive skills programmes. *Legal and Criminological Psychology, 8*, 83–101.

Chapter 2

OFFENDING BEHAVIOUR PROGRAMMES AND CONTENTION: EVIDENCE-BASED PRACTICE, MANUALS, AND PROGRAMME EVALUATION

CLIVE R. HOLLIN
University of Leicester

The use of offending behaviour programmes within the criminal justice system raises several fundamental issues which have been a source of contention with respect to both the origins and development of practice and the evaluation of interventions. First, as is clear from the literature covered in Chapter 1, the development and implementation of offending behaviour programmes has been firmly rooted in the knowledge provided by the meta-analyses of the treatment effectiveness literature. Given this background, offending behaviour programmes are clearly an example of evidence-based practice within the criminal justice system. The strengths and weaknesses and advantages and disadvantages of an evidence-based approach to practice is widely debated in the parallel clinical literature. Many of the associated arguments played out in the clinical literature with respect to this particular area of contention are germane to the use of offending behaviour programmes in the criminal justice system.

Second, it is the case that a manual is often the vehicle for the delivery of offending behaviour programmes. Indeed, as discussed in Chapter 1, the Correctional Service Accreditation Panel requires programmes to be accompanied by no fewer than five different manuals. Again, there is nothing new about the use of manuals in mainstream clinical psychology and the attendant issues are much rehearsed in the attendant literature. There has been remarkably limited discussion of the overlap between the delivery of offending behaviour programmes via manuals and the contentious issues raised in the wider literature (Hollin, 2002a).

The third area of contention lies in evaluation of offending behaviour programmes. There are many arguments for and against rehabilitation of offenders and the desired outcome of this approach. However, the case has been stated, based on the meta-analyses, that with offending behaviour programmes the focus is fixed on reduced re-offending as the major outcome. The process of producing empirical evidence to show whether or not offending behaviour programmes can impact significantly on re-offending is a far from simple business. The decisions made by researchers with regard to the design of their outcome studies are of critical importance. The nature of the outcome evidence, highly dependent upon research design and methodology, will play a large part in considerations regarding the continued application and funding of offending behaviour programmes.

The purpose of this chapter is to explore these three broad areas of contention – evidence-based practice, behaviour change via manuals, and evaluation – in detail.

EVIDENCE-BASED PRACTICE

Those professions engaged in working constructively with people, including those in the health, educational, and criminal justice systems, must have some basis through which they conduct their practice. The basis on which a profession sets itself to practice is important as it sets the foundation from which to deliver services, to train newcomers to the profession, and to change and develop as a profession. The basis of professional practice, passed on through generations through training and supervision, therefore lies in a profession's accumulated body of knowledge.

It is appropriate at this point to comment on the use of terminology in the following sections. Within the medical and broader clinical literatures the terms "therapy", "treatment", and "patient" are in common usage. The use of these terms within the context of offending behaviour programmes could be seen as implying a medical model of offending, in which criminal behaviour is understood by recourse to a psychopathological position. It is not the intention here to use this approach and, in the context of offending behaviour programmes, terms such as therapy and patient are inappropriate. The difficulty arises in deciding which terms are appropriate to describe the process and interactions implicit within an offending behaviour programme. There are various possibilities, such as "psychoeducational", but inevitably these terms feel somewhat contrived. The term *"treatment"* is difficult as it can be used interchangeably with clinical terms, such as therapy, and hence has strong associations with psychopathology. On the other hand, "treatment" can be used in a broader sense to mean the application of a process, as for example, in the statistical treatment of data to produce empirical findings. It is in this wider sense of introducing a process to achieve a specified outcome that the term treatment is used here with regard to offending behaviour programmes. Thus, in the current context, treatment refers to a process by which to work with offenders in order to try to reduce re-offending.

What is the Basis of Professional Knowledge?

Faced with the issue of changing another person's behaviour, three distinct (but not exclusive) sources of knowledge can be drawn upon to inform professional practice. The first source of knowledge lies in a theoretical account of human behaviour that can be used to inform and guide a practitioner's understanding of the individual. It is this basic theoretical understanding of the individual, augmented over time by accumulated clinical experience, which is used to direct practice. Thus, knowledge progresses through the practitioner's gathering of direct experience with individual cases and through the pooling of professional wisdom. In this light, practice is close to an art, an expression of practitioners' theoretically informed, deep understanding of their clients and the issues they bring into treatment. As Seligman & Levant (1998) note, "Practitioners tend to be ideographic: they typically tailor their treatment on the basis of ongoing, often theory-driven assessments" (p. 211).

A second source of knowledge lies in the products of scientific enquiry, in an empirically tested and validated body of facts. This scientific approach depends on the accumulation of knowledge through the use of the best scientific methods to distinguish fact from whimsy, effective from ineffective methods of treatment. As Peterson (2004) notes, Paul Meehl is perhaps the best known proponent of scientific method as the preferred means to advance knowledge in clinical work (see, for example, Meehl, 1997). Finally, a third way lies in the notion of *scientist-practitioners*, professionals who use both empirical research and their own clinical experience to guide and inform their practice (Long & Hollin, 1997).

The professional debate engendered by these various positions is both long-standing and deeply felt. Peterson (2004) particularly cites Kimble's (1984) work as capturing the division between the "scientific" and "humanistic" orientations of groups of psychologists within the American Psychological Association. These two groups differed in theoretical orientation and in their values and beliefs regarding the optimum basis for the accumulation of knowledge. Indeed, Kimble suggests that the two groups represent different cultures within both psychology and professional practice. There is a substantial literature on these basic professional issues that crystallises around the notion of empirically validated treatments (Levant, 2004). The issues surrounding the use of evidence to inform healthcare treatment are of concern within both professions and the wider world. Within the confines of professional debate there are issues about how bodies of evidence are interpreted and applied to practice (Gonzales, Ringeisen & Chambers, 2002), particularly with regard to the development of new treatments (Clark, 2004). In the wider world the notion of evidence-based and empirically validated treatments has influenced which treatments will be offered within the public healthcare sector, which treatments will be supported by insurance policies, and what is taught to trainee professionals.

Without necessarily becoming immersed in philosophical debates about theories of knowledge that date from Locke to Rousseau (Russell, 1961), it might be expected that within professions the complexities of knowing about knowledge, the generation of knowledge, and the application of knowledge are generally understood. As Peterson (2004) comments, it is appreciated that "Science does not provide the only way of knowing. It offers descriptions of what the world is *like*, not exclusive explanations of what the world *is*" (p. 198). Nonetheless, it sometimes appears that the polar extremes of the debate are incompatible, with claims that science is the only way to provide knowledge opposed by those who advocate a stance of anti-science and anti-empiricism. However, these two extremes, the two cultures, do not have to be exclusive and in conflict: scientists may have humanistic concerns; humanists are not necessarily opposed to science. It can be argued that the application of scientific methods provides the most dependable method available for answering many, but not all, questions. Although even within a broad scientific position there are strong disagreements regarding the meaning ascribed to science and what it means to be science-based. Gorman (2005) offers strong views on the scientific merits of drug and violence prevention programmes, suggesting that preoccupation with research design has led to a loss of scientific focus. In turn, equally strong counter-arguments have been made in response (Botvin & Griffin, 2005; Hawkins & Catalano, 2005). It is a question of balance, so that it is entirely legitimate, when the occasion demands, to advance clinical knowledge through the use of "unscientific" observation, narrative, individual case study, and aggregated case studies across individuals (see Clark, 2004). However, this does not mean that scientific evidence can be dismissed or ignored; rather it means that it has to be understood, evaluated, and applied within the context that it is gathered.

Offending behaviour programmes provide an excellent example of the way in which empirical evidence can drive policy and so influence practice. Given the above epistemological points, a narrower concern lies in the way that researchers gather the empirical evidence presented to policy makers.

The Gathering of Evidence

Seligman & Levant (1998) make the distinction between two types of outcome study that provide the evidence on which evidence-based treatments are based. The first type of study is *efficacy research*, which

> Tests a laboratory distillation of therapy. The therapy typically is manualised; is delivered for a fixed number of sessions; uses volunteers with well-diagnosed, relatively uncomplicated disorders; and makes random assignment to different treatments, including (it is hoped) placebo treatments. (Seligman & Levant, 1998, p. 211)

Seligman and Levant continue to make the argument that efficacy research produces imperfect data because the very conditions that make good research are diametrically opposed to the real world of therapy. In clinical practice, therapy ebbs, flows and changes, rather than strictly following a linear route via a manual; those people seeking help can make choices, rather than being randomly assigned to a treatment; therapy is open-ended, not a fixed number of sessions; and people may bring multiple complex problems, rather than single, uncomplicated disorders.

Seligman and Levant refer to the second type of study as *effectiveness research* that

> Investigates the outcome of therapy as it is actually delivered in the field ... Therapy investigated by the effectiveness method is typically done without a manual; duration is yoked to patient progress; often patients have multiple interacting problems, including comorbidities and Axis II diagnoses, and they choose the particular modality and therapist they believe in; and therapists take on the whole gamut of severity. (Seligman & Levant, 1998, p. 211)

Thus, effectiveness research is characterised by high levels of realism because it considers therapy as it is practised in the field.

It is efficacy research that dominates the literature given that most research is conducted by researchers who, naturally, have an interest in setting the parameters using good research methodology. In contrast, effectiveness studies are more difficult to set up and tend to be longer and more expensive than efficacy studies. If both approaches produced the same outcomes then, of course, the differences would not be so important. However, a uniformity of outcome from the two types of study is not invariably the case. Seligman & Levant (1998) note the contrast between studies of psychotherapy in which laboratory efficacy studies show limited success but effectiveness studies carried out in the field are much more positive. The points raised by Seligman and Levant are particularly germane to treatment delivered via manuals and to the design of evaluative research.

PROGRAMMES AND MANUALS

Most offending behaviour programmes are manual-based in the sense that the practical aspects of the intervention – such as the sequencing of sessions, the aims and objectives of sessions, the content of sessions, and the methods of delivery of sessions – are written down in detail in order to form a programme manual. In some systems there are other types of manual, such as management and research manuals, but the main concern is generally with programme manuals. There is a body of work that has looked at the views of professionals on the use of manuals in general (Najavits, Weiss, Shaw & Dierberger, 2000), and what makes a good manual in particular (Duncan, Nicol & Ager, 2004; Kendall, Chu, Gifford, Hayes & Nauta, 1998). With regard to the qualities of offender treatment programme manuals, McCulloch and McMurran (in press) report the findings of a survey of experts in the field of offender treatment. The experts considered that it is important that a manual has a clear exposition of both theory and aims and objectives, contains detailed instructions together with advice on delivery, and is presented in plain language and a user-friendly format.

Following the dissemination of the findings from the meta-analyses the manualised programme approach has become dominant in the delivery of offender treatment, probably for several reasons. First, programmes offer a ready means by which to train non-specialist staff, such as prison officers, to deliver interventions. Second, a large number of trained staff means that programmes can be delivered, particularly via groups, to an even larger number of offenders. Third, the use of programmes in which practitioners are required to adhere closely to a manual makes checks on programme integrity a clear-cut undertaking. Fourth, all the previous reasons facilitate the evaluation of programmes.

Within offender treatment, the use of a programmatic, manual-based approach to the delivery of treatment raises its own technical and managerial issues (Bernfeld, Farrington & Leschied, 2001), but it also raises the larger issue of whether manual-based programmes are the optimum means to deliver effective interventions. Given that the use of manuals is not limited to interventions with offenders, the same question has been debated in the wider clinical literature. Wilson (1996) outlines five main criticisms of manual-based treatments:

> They are conceptually at odds with fundamental principles of cognitive-behavioral therapy; they preclude idiographic case formulation; they undermine therapists' clinical artistry; they apply primarily to research samples which differ from the patients practitioners treat; and they promote particular "schools" of psychological therapy. (Wilson, 1996, p. 295)

Hollin (2002a) noted the general criticisms detailed by Wilson and applied them specifically to the treatment of offenders.

Negation of Theoretical Principles

In cognitive-behavioural treatment the intervention is usually designed to meet the individual needs of the client. However, a great deal of work with offenders is group-based, with offenders selected for a programme on the generic basis of their offence rather than their individual needs. This procedure leads, for example, to sex offender treatment groups in which offenders who commit violent sexual assaults on women participate in treatment alongside those men who sexually offend against children. Given the likely differences between these two types of sexual offender (see, for example, Marshall, 2001; Ward, Hudson & Keenan, 2001), the same treatment for both appears, at best, an uncertain option for effective treatment to reduce sexual offending.

It is likely that selection for offending behaviour programmes primarily on the basis of offence is the most efficient and cost-effective means of selection. However, this is a clear example of negation of theoretical principles with respect to basing treatment on individual need. The conflict between financial costs and individualised treatment highlights a tension in moving to the large-scale delivery of offending behaviour programmes.

Individual Case Formulation

Clinical treatment focuses, in the main, on the individual, so that traditionally cognitive-behavioural treatment incorporates individual assessment and case formulation leading to an individually tailored treatment plan. As noted with the example of sex offenders, the use of programmes may separate fine-grained clinical assessment from the planning and process of treatment (Persons, 1991). Thus, for example, there is a multitude of potentially important factors to consider in explaining sexual offending (Ward, Polaschek & Beech, 2006), with various implications for treatment (Marshall, Fernandez, Marshall & Serran, 2006). Given this complexity it seems likely that individual assessments would yield different treatment targets for different sex offenders. In which case why have a sex offender treatment programme with fixed treatment targets for all sex offenders?

Clinical Artistry

As Wilson (1996) notes, clinical artistry can be seen as a personal quality acquired by clinicians from their training and clinical practice, and hence their unique individual knowledge, understanding, and professional experience.

Advocates of clinical artistry note the importance of clinicians' judgement and decision-making with regard to their individual clients, and the ability of clinicians to "self-correct" in refining continually their assessment as treatment unfolds. Seligman & Levant (1998) have clear views on this issue of an individual treatment focus: "The essence of manuals is systematically minimizing individual tailoring (i.e., reducing independent thinking by therapists and downplaying specific needs of individual patients)" (p. 211). Wilson (1997), responding to similar views expressed by Hickling & Blanchard (1997), debates the associated issues, including clinical judgement versus actuarial prediction and the relationship between clinical experience and treatment outcome.

Given this debate, there is an obvious issue with regard to the interaction between clinical artistry and programme delivery. In the main, offending behaviour programmes leave little scope for practitioners to exercise clinical judgement or decision-making with respect to the content of the intervention. If clinical artistry is an important component of effective interventions, then highly structured programmes will eliminate this important element of treatment. On the other hand, if clinical artistry is neither essential nor desirable its expression within a structured programme may well be detrimental to programme effectiveness. Indeed, the main threats to programme integrity (Hollin, 1995) lie in programme non-compliance, in which practitioners make *ad hoc* adjustments to the programme, and in programme reversal where practitioners work in ways that are contrary to the design of the programme. As programme integrity is a key "what works" principle (Andrews & Bonta, 2003), whether or not to allow clinical artistry in its fullest sense is a significant problem in the delivery of offending behaviour programmes.

Research Samples Versus Real Clients

Wilson (1996) suggests that the issue here is that the population samples in clinical research are carefully selected for research purposes and so are not representative of the more complex clinical populations found in practice. This selection effect may at times be apparent in clinical research, but if researchers describe the selection criteria for their study populations then any differences with mainstream clinical populations will be clear to see.

Schools of Therapy

The use of manuals is typically, but not always, associated with cognitive-behavioural treatment with the attendant possibility that by focusing on one specific approach other types of intervention may be ignored. Arguably, a focus on a single approach to treatment may prevent or delay the development of new, improved interventions. In the treatment of offenders, where there is a lack of outcome evidence comparing different approaches to intervention, any theoretical monopoly may hinder advancement of understanding of effective practice.

In summary, there are concerns regarding individualised treatment and case formulation, the applicability of the research on unrepresentative samples, and the dominance of a particular theoretical model. Thus, the conclusion is that manual-based treatment programmes – with offender as well as general clinical populations – may not be the most effective in bringing about change at the individual level. On the other hand, there are clear advantages to the use of offending behaviour programmes, incorporating the principle of effective practice (Andrews & Bonta, 2003), in terms of utilising a wide range of staff to deliver programmes on a large scale. Given the advances and investments that have been made over the past decade in the development and running of offender treatment programmes, how might the above criticisms be used to inform the design of the next generation of programmes?

The final chapter will return to these points, however attention now turns to the second of Seligman and Levant's concerns, the evaluation of treatment effectiveness.

EVALUATIVE RESEARCH

As offending behaviour programmes are designed to reduce offending it is important to ask the question of whether they do, indeed, produce the intended outcome. Of course, the same question can be asked of any intervention within the criminal justice system and, indeed, of the evaluation of interventions in general. In discussing programme evaluation in the context of domestic violence programmes, Gondolf (2004) makes the following comment, which applies equally to any offending behaviour programme:

> [Evaluation] is a difficult and complex task that complicates the interpretation of the evaluation results. As has been the case in other fields, such as alcohol, sex offence, and depression treatment, different program conceptions, outcome measures, research designs, and statistical analyses can produce contrary results . . . Program evaluations that specifically address these sorts of issues are likely to further their validity, and those that at least acknowledge them will help clarify interpretation of the results. (Gondolf, 2004, pp. 607–608)

In seeking to evaluate the effects of various different types of treatment within the criminal justice system researchers have used a range of research methodologies, both quantitative and qualitative. The task of evaluative researchers is to attempt to draw conclusions about a programme that are as generally applicable as possible, but which are necessarily made on the basis of a limited sampling of the programme. It is therefore important that researchers design evaluative studies to the highest possible standards in order to protect and enhance the validity of their conclusions.

Validity

Validity is an important consideration in the design of evaluation studies. Cook & Campbell (1979) make the distinction between four types of validity, which are discussed here with particular reference to offending behaviour programmes.

Construct Validity

Construct validity refers to the researchers' ability precisely to define and measure the constructs that define the programme. Threats to construct validity would include whether the programme was delivered as intended (treatment integrity) and the reliability and validity of the outcome measure used to measure the effects of the programme (for example, cognitive change, re-conviction).

External Validity

This aspect of validity refers to the degree to which the research findings can be generalised across factors such as setting and people, and how the effects are moderated by these factors. Thus, for example, can the effects of programmes in prisons be generalised to the community? If a programme is successful with male offenders, can it be assumed that it will be successful with female offenders?

Internal Validity

Internal validity refers to the critical issue of change: does an offending behaviour programme actually bring about any observed, measurable changes in offending? One way to try to increase internal validity is to compare a treated sample with an untreated control sample on the same outcome measure to determine what happens in the absence of the intervention. There are multiple threats to internal validity when evaluating offending behaviour programmes. For example, rather then being treatment-neutral, the comparison group may actually receive some form of treatment; there may be selection problems that potentially introduce an experimental bias, such that offenders in the treatment group systematically differing in some important way from those in the comparison group; or differences and changes in measurement might be introduced over the duration of the evaluation.

Statistical Conclusion Validity

Finally, statistical conclusion validity refers to the statistical aspects of the study such as significance testing and the use of statistics such as confidence intervals, effect sizes, and odds ratios. The obvious threats to statistical conclusion validity, in offending behaviour programmes as elsewhere, lie in the use of inappropriate statistical techniques and degree of statistical power within individual studies.

In any quantitative study all four types of validity are important and, in practice, they are not independent of each other or even necessarily sympathetic. Thus, an evaluative study may attempt to maximise its internal validity, say by strict sampling criteria, and by absolute, rigorous control over the conduct of the offending behaviour programme. However, these efforts to achieve high internal validity may be introduced at the expense of external validity. The procedures used to increase internal validity may create such artificial circumstances that the findings from the evaluation are meaningless in the real world where tight control over selection and treatment integrity are not feasible (the study has low external validity). In most evaluations there is a trade-off between internal and external validity in order to attempt to maximise internal validity while maintaining a reasonable level of external validity. Evaluators of offending behaviour programmes will strive for knowledge of construct validity by seeking to encompass measures of treatment integrity within the design of the study. In addition, there are vigorous debates around the preferred statistical approach to understanding the data that emerges from programme evaluations (Gendreau, 2002), and in the correspondence between what is significant statistically as opposed to clinically (Jacobson & Truax, 1991).

Scientific Methods Scale

In practice researchers have a range of methodologies and designs that can be used to conduct evaluative studies. Of course, not all these methodologies are of equal utility, and there have been various attempts to classify the strengths and merits of quantitative research methods. In the current criminological literature the Scientific Methods Scale, devised for the Maryland Report (Sherman et al., 1997), is perhaps the most widely disseminated (Farrington, Gottfredson, Sherman & Welsh, 2002) and applied (Wilson, Bouffard & Mackenzie, 2005)

Classification System

As shown in Box 2.1, the Scientific Methods Scale covers a wide range of research designs, ranging from the most basic correlational design at one extreme to a fully randomised control trial at the other. As Farrington et al. (2002) note, the Scientific

Box 2.1   The Scientific Methods Scale (After Sherman et al., 1997)

1. A simple correlation between a crime prevention programme and some measure of crime.
2. A temporal sequence between the crime prevention programme and the measure of crime clearly observed; or the use of a comparison group but without demonstrating comparability between the comparison and treatment groups.
3. A comparison between two or more groups, one participating in the programme, the other not.
4. A group comparison, with and without the programme, in which there is control of relevant factors or a non-equivalent comparison group with only minor differences from the treatment group.
5. Random assignment to groups with analysis of comparable units for programme and comparison groups.

Methods Scale has its focus on *internal* validity; it should not be taken as referring to the other three types of validity.

Of the five research designs shown in Box 2.1 it is the latter three that are generally taken as producing evidence that is at least of acceptable scientific quality. Following Wilson et al. (2005), Level 3 equates to a low-quality quasi-experimental design, with the drawback of threats to internal validity produced by uncontrolled differences between the treatment and comparison groups that may introduce a selection bias. Level 4 is a high-quality quasi-experimental design, in which the absence of randomisation to condition (treatment and comparison) is countered by either methodological or statistical control of group differences. Finally, Level 5 is an experimental design in the proper sense, with randomisation of allocation to condition: these particular types of studies are generally referred to as randomised control trials (RCTs).

Of the three stronger designs, across disciplines Level 5 is taken to be the gold standard for the treatment evaluation and, as Cure, Chua, Duggan & Adams (2005) state, "This applies equally to research into the criminal justice system" (p. 185). However, as Farrington et al. (2002) note, "While randomized experiments in principle have the highest interval validity, in practice they are uncommon in criminology and also often have implementation problems" (p. 17). In sympathy with the point made by Farrington et al., Gondolf (2004) states that in the real world of applied research, it may often be difficult even to "Conduct some of the most basic evaluation designs in a criminal justice setting" (p. 612). Given the importance of the design used in the evaluation of offending behaviour programmes, this topic warrants further discussion. Following the Scientific Methods Scale, the pivotal discussion hinges on the relative utility of quasi-experimental and experimental designs.

However, before looking as this issue of design, it is worth noting that the Scientific Methods Scale has been adapted by Home Office researchers to assess reconviction studies (Friendship, Street, Cann & Harper, 2005). The Home Office scale is shown in Box 2.2 and its relationship with the Scientific Methods Scale, as shown in Box 2.1, is evident.

Now, as Farrington et al. (2002) stress, the Scientific Methods Scale "Focuses only on internal validity" (p. 17) although, as they explain, adjustments to the scale can be made in light of other aspects of the design and running of a study. The Home Office adaptation of the SMS loses the original intent of the scale – the assessment

---

Box 2.2   The SMS as Adapted by the Home Office for Reconviction Studies (After Friendship et al., 2005)

1. Reconviction measured for intervention group only.
2. Comparison of actual and predicted reconviction for intervention group only.
3. A comparison of the reconviction rates from treatment and unmatched controls.
4. A comparison of the reconviction rates from treatment and controls matched on theoretically relevant factors.
5. A comparison of the reconviction rates from treatment and control groups with randomisation to group.

of the internal validity of a study – and instead purports to be an unqualified means by which to assess the *overall* quality of a study. In the absence of any scientific justification, or even reasoned argument, for the shift in what the adapted scale claims to measure, the veracity of the scale is doubtful at best. Nonetheless, Debidin & Lovbakke (2005) use the "re-conviction scale" in order to give ratings to a string of studies investigating the effects of offending behaviour programmes. On this dubious basis they discuss the findings from "higher quality" and "lower quality" as if the scale had proven utility. Chitty (2005) seriously compounds the error in stating that "To help fellow researchers and correctional stakeholders to understand the quality (and hence value) of the research evidence and following from the work first done by Sherman, this report has proposed a hierarchy of research standards for reconviction studies" (p. 80). Ironically, given the scientific validity of the "re-conviction scale", Chitty (2005) then condemns the extant research as "sub-optimal".

Quasi-experimental Designs

As commentators such as Farrington et al. (2002) and Gondolf (2004) have stated, for practical reasons quasi-experimental designs, rather than fully experimental designs, are most often chosen for programme evaluation. The main reason for this choice lies in the difficulties inherent in setting up a study with random allocation of offenders to conditions. When offenders are ordered by the court to attend a programme as part of their sentence, as say with Probation, then randomisation faces two difficulties. First, randomisation would require courts, or more specifically judges and magistrates, to give sentences that randomly assign offenders to programmes. Second, in the absence of randomisation through the court, organisations would need powers of "sentence-override" in order to allocate offenders randomly to non-treatment conditions. The complications inherent in either of these options would deter most researchers, particularly when an evaluation is constrained by time.

The next difficulty arises when attempting to randomise offenders to conditions within an organisation. For example, as discussed in Chapter 1, HM Prison Service runs offending behaviour programmes for sex offenders. In a randomised trial of the programme those sex offenders who agree to take part in a programme (a choice which introduces a selection effect in itself) would be randomly allocated to treatment and non-treatment conditions. In theory this is a straightforward procedure; in practice there are two issues that immediately spring to attention. First, there are problems around withholding treatment: if treatment is withheld and the offender leaves prison and commits further sexual offences, then the question is invariably asked whether these offences and the suffering of victims might have been prevented with treatment. Indeed, the question might rightly be asked whether the withholding of treatment flies in the face of the purpose of the Prison Service to assist offenders to lead good and useful lives. Second, allocation to a non-treatment condition may be detrimental to the individual prisoner, in that not participating in treatment, so not changing their level of risk, might change decisions about security classification, Parole Board decisions, and so on.

It is not difficult therefore to envisage legal challenges to any decision to withhold treatment.

Thus, there is a "Catch 22" in designing evaluation studies within the criminal justice system: randomised studies are said to be the gold standard and are encouraged by the research community; however, attempts to implement such studies are broadly discouraged by the constraints of the system. The practical answer is to find another approach, which is where quasi-experimental, or non-random, designs come into play. One of the main procedural points with the use of quasi-experimental designs lies in the assembling of a control (or comparison), non-treatment group that has not been referred to treatment. Inspection of the literature suggests that there are three main strategies used by researchers to gather control groups. The first strategy is to match control and experimental groups on key variables that may be related to outcome. For example, this approach to matching was used by Friendship, Blud, Erikson, Travers & Thornton (2003) in their evaluation of cognitive skills programmes for imprisoned offenders. Friendship et al. used an existing database of prisoners to form a matched comparison group for treated prisoners: thus, the treatment and comparison groups were matched on variables – including current offence, sentence length, age at discharge from prison, length of discharge, number of previous sentences, and probability of re-conviction score – which are consistently predictive of offending. However, despite the large number of prisoners (1 801) from which to draw a matched group, Friendship et al. found that "It was not possible to find an exact match for every treated offender on the matching variables" (p. 105). In order to overcome this problem, Friendship et al. matched by target range, rather than by an exact match, so that offenders were matched within 5-year age bands, by four bands of risk of re-conviction, and so on. While this strategy is acceptable, it has two main disadvantages: first, it blunts the exactness of the match between any pair of treated and untreated offenders; second, the sensitivity of measurement of important variables is diminished when continuous variables, such as age and risk of re-conviction score, are reduced to bands of scores.

A different approach is not to control by exact matching of cases but to introduce two strategies to attempt to control for potential differences between treatment and comparison groups. The first strategy is to attempt to form broadly similar treatment and comparison groups at the onset of the evaluation. Second, alongside this broad group equivalence aspect of the design, it is also possible to introduce statistical control of key variables using well-established statistical methods. For example, these design and control strategies were used by Hollin et al. (2004) in an evaluation of offending behaviour programmes conducted in the Probation Service in England and Wales. The comparison group was drawn from a database of offenders who had served a period on probation but had not participated in an offending behaviour programme. Inspection of the characteristics of the treatment and comparison groups showed that they were broadly similar on a range of variables, and they were also a reasonable match to the national profile of offenders serving probation orders. When comparing the outcome for the two groups with regard to re-conviction, Hollin et al. used multivariate statistics to control for a string of key variables that included age, risk of re-conviction score, and offence type. The main disadvantage with this approach is that, despite attempts to control procedurally statistically differences between groups, the absence of randomisation allows the probability of some systematic variation between groups. Any between-group difference in outcome might be a consequence of this initial variation rather than the treatment.

The types of research design used by Friendship et al. (2003) and by Hollin et al. (2004) are referred to by Wilson et al. (2005) as "high-quality quasi-experimental", which contrasts with "low-quality quasi-experimental" designs. In low-quality designs there are threats to the internal validity of the study by using, for example, non-equivalent treatment and comparison groups, or comparing programme completers with programme dropouts. As Babcock, Green & Robie (2004, p. 1031) comment, there is a risk that quasi-experimental designs, perhaps particularly low-quality quasi-experimental designs, have "The methodological problem of 'stacking the deck' in favour of treatment."

Thus, in the absence of randomisation, quasi-experimental designs provide an alternative that can be employed to evaluate offending behaviour programmes. The primary difficulty with quasi-experimental designs lies in satisfactorily matching treatment and controls. Indeed, even with a strong set of control variables the criticism remains that some key variables might not be controlled, either by matching or statistically, thereby introducing a bias into the findings. A particular problem lies in comparing programme completers with programme dropouts as a control group, on the basis that those who complete a programme and those who drop out may have different characteristics and this difference introduces a bias into the study. This point regarding dropouts is valid with respect to the internal validity of a study, however, as Gondolf (2004) suggests, it is entirely realistic to study naturally occurring treatment subgroups. Indeed, studying what happens in the real world of treatment delivery, in other words trying to achieve good external validity, may lead to greater understanding of programmes. The study of treatment subgroups will be discussed below, following a consideration of the use of randomised designs in the evaluation of offending behaviour programmes.

Randomised Experimental Designs

As Farrington & Welsh (2005) note, randomised experiments are relatively uncommon in criminology – particularly so outside the US. In the UK there is currently a drive towards randomised studies. As a Home Office researcher in a Home Office publication stated:

> There is a need to develop randomised control trials in the correctional services, so that our knowledge of what works is truly improved and the existing equivocal evidence is replaced with greater certainty and ultimately, greater confidence for the correctional services that they are delivering effective interventions with offenders. (Chitty, 2005, p. 80)

The theme of research design emerges elsewhere in the same government publication (written and edited by Home Office researchers Harper & Chitty, 2005): Elliott-Marshall, Ramsey & Stewart (2005) suggest that, although there is a substantial body of evidence to suggest that interventions can reduce re-offending, "There is limited evidence to demonstrate what impact these interventions have in practice. There is also evidence of research failure . . . the design of most studies looking at outcomes is significantly below the gold standard" (p. 68). The same orchestrated theme appears again in the same publication:

> Current evidence in the UK is predominately based on quasi-experimental or non-experimental evaluation studies, which makes it difficult to attribute the outcomes to the effects of the treatment or intervention . . . . Outcome studies therefore should be based on more effective research designs. (Debidin & Lovbakke, 2005, p. 51)

The language used in this Home Office publication is of interest on two fronts. First, there is reference to "the existing *equivocal* evidence", the "limited evidence", and that it is "difficult" to interpret any evidence from a quasi-experimental study. It might be concluded from these comments that, in truth, there is very little empirical evidence of any value to inform our understanding of "what works". Second, there is a repeated call for gold-standard research, so that there is a "need to develop randomised control trials" to address the "research failure" of studies that fall below the gold standard, and that "more effective research designs" are required. Thus, it might be inferred that any evidence other than from an RCT is not to be trusted, that the current research is failed research, and that the solution to all this lies in conducting new RCTs. Notwithstanding the irony that much of the evidence that informed the development of "what works" came from quasi-experimental studies, it is self-evident that RCTs would be a welcome addition to any body of knowledge. However, whether RCTs really offer the promised land of "greater certainty" and "greater confidence" than what is currently available is questionable.

This issue can be looked at in two ways. First, what type of evidence do RCTs produce? Second, is the evidence from randomised experimental studies significantly different from that produced by quasi-experimental studies?

What Evidence do RCTs Produce?

In their overview of clinical trials, Everitt & Wessely (2004) make the following observation:

> The simpler the intervention, the easier the trial. The RCT methodology was developed principally for drug interventions, in which both intervention and control can be easily controlled and described. Later, the methodology was adapted for psychological interventions, the principal differences included the impossibility of ensuring double blindness, and the difficulties in ensuring treatment fidelity. (Everitt & Wessely, 2004, p. 64)

However, as Everitt and Wessely further note, many psychological interventions, specifically including cognitive-behavioural treatments, can be classified as "complex interventions". Following Medical Research Council (MRC) guidelines, Everitt and Wessely suggest that the development and evaluation of complex interventions should pass through various stages as shown in Box 2.3.

Box 2.3   Stages in the Development and Assessment of Complex Interventions (After Everitt & Wessely, 2004)

1. *Theory.* The development of the theoretical basis of the intervention.
2. *Modelling.* The development of and understanding of the intervention and its effect using small-scale surveys, focus groups, and observational studies.
3. *Exploratory trial.* Preliminary evidence is gathered in support of the intervention.
4. *Definitive RCT.* A randomised study is conducted.
5. *Long-term implementation.* Can the intervention's effects be replicated over time and in different settings?

The proper conduct of an evaluation of a complex intervention, following MRC guidelines, is rarely seen in the offending behaviour programme literature. Indeed, it may sometimes appear that this evaluative procedure has been overlooked. For example, in attempting to justify the use of RCTs in criminal justice research, including offending behaviour programmes, the National Probation Service *What Works News* (December, 2004) contains a comment from a Home Office researcher that

> Some ethical concerns have been raised about RCTs because they involve denying a potentially beneficial intervention to offenders allocated to a control group. Importantly, an RCT would only be used where the effect of the intervention is not known, and the benefit needs to be established alongside evidence that it does not have harmful effects, before the intervention can justifiably be given to anyone.

If this statement is re-read thinking about the evaluation of a powerful drug it becomes rather startling! Would a drug be used in an RCT without a great deal of preparatory laboratory work, probably on animals, testing whether or not it produced the theoretically predicted effects or led to harm? The point is that with an RCT the intervention *is* given to people and there should be *a priori* justification for doing so. Such unqualified comments are misleading at best and, if they form the basis for the implementation of research, damaging at worst.

The process outlined in Box 2.3 appears relatively straightforward. However, following Hotopf (2002), Everitt & Wessely (2004) contrast the textbook design of an RCT in clinical practice with "what happens in the real world". For example, in an ideal design patients are randomly allocated to the treatment, in the real world allocation is by a complex process of explanation and negotiation; or, ideally patient and clinician are blind to the design, but in reality both are usually aware of the treatment. Gondolf (2004) also makes the comment that RCTs are extremely problematic to implement, as evidenced by experience in other fields such as public health and medicine. Indeed, rather than seeing a RCT as a singular, uniformly strong, design, it should be appreciated that the methodological quality of RCTs can vary considerably (Juni, Altman & Egger, 2001). The Jadad scale was devised to rate the quality of reporting of randomised trials (Jadad et al., 2001), and there are guides to spotting bias and methodological problems in RCTs (Lewis & Warlow, 2004).

Everitt and Wessely (2004), drawing on trials of healthcare interventions, make the distinction between *explanatory* trials and *pragmatic* trials. An explanatory trial measures the direct effect of the intervention: that is, under controlled conditions does the treatment have the intended effect on those for whom it was designed? A pragmatic trial measures what happens when the treatment is introduced into routine clinical practice. The explanatory trial is clearly a critical part of treatment evaluation: for example, a drug would not be introduced into routine clinical practice without a great deal of previous testing and investigation under controlled conditions.

Given these methodological and procedural points, the next consideration lies in the nature of the evidence produced by an RCT. The basis of an RCT is that those individuals put forward for treatment are randomly allocated to either a group that receives the specific treatment (the experimental group) and a group that receives no treatment, a placebo, or "treatment as usual" (the control group). Once allocated to a group the design unfolds over the period of the study and the outcome data are gathered. Notwithstanding the complexities of data presentation and statistical analysis (Everitt & Wessely, 2004), the outcome from an RCT is a comparison of the outcomes for those allocated to the experimental and control groups. The final experimental group will therefore contain all those individuals *allocated* to treatment, regardless of whether they actually receive the treatment or not.

As Everitt & Wessely (2004) note, there are various procedures that might be followed in making sense of the data produced by an RCT. One procedure is called *intention to treat* (ITT) analysis "In which analysis is based on original treatment assignment rather than the treatment actually received" (Everitt & Wessely, 2004, p. 90). Alternatively, *treatment received* (TR) analysis looks at what happens "According to the treatment ultimately received" (Everitt & Wessely, 2004, p. 90) by those individuals who satisfy the requirements of participation in the treatment. As Sherman (2003) comments, these alternatives are the point at which "Experimentalists often divide their own ranks" (p. 11). One school of thought, perhaps primarily from a research perspective, is that with an RCT an ITT analysis is the most pure form of analysis. Any attempt to form subgroups within the randomised conditions violates the randomisation of individuals to groups and hence damages the integrity of the design. Alternatively, it is not difficult to mount an argument from a more clinical perspective that little can be learned about the effectiveness of a treatment if significant numbers of the experimental group do not comply with the treatment regime. A poor outcome for those who do not participate in or dropout of treatment may well cancel out any positive outcomes for those who fully participate in the intervention. Indeed, the presumption that an ITT analysis, originally devised for biomedical trials, can be applied to psychotherapy research has been referred to as the "drug metaphor" (Shapiro et al., 1994). As in many other areas of research, ITT analysis is not a simple, uniform procedure. Hollis & Campbell (1999) conducted a survey of the use of ITT within RCTs published in medical journals. Noting that ITT is better applied to pragmatic trials, Hollis and Campbell concluded that their survey showed that "The intention to treat approach is often inadequately described and inadequately applied" (p. 674).

It may well be preferable to see these two styles of analysis, ITT and TR, as answering different questions. Sherman (2003) makes the point that:

> The ITT principle holds that an RCT can test the effects of trying to get someone to take a treatment and, thus, provides a valid inference about the effect of the attempt, as distinct from the actual treatment received. (Sherman, 2003, p. 12)

Similarly, Gondolf (2004, p. 610) comments that "The comparison of an experimental group versus control group, therefore, may tell less about treatment effectiveness and more about the procedures of referring to and retaining men in a certain program." On the other hand, a TR analysis provides an estimate, at the risk of some bias, of the actual effects of the treatment when delivered as intended. As Sherman suggests, an ITT analysis offers a test of a policy of offering something to a group; a TR analysis allows a test of a theory about what happens when that offer is taken up. Given the caveats with both styles of analysis, the obvious solution is to report both analyses, with attempts to correct for potential bias.

The problem of a balance between maximising experimental precision and reducing bias engages wider statistical issues. In discussing the need to move beyond ITT analyses, Goetghebeur & Loeys (2002) writing from a medical perspective comment that

> The more we seek to tailor possibly dynamic treatments to individual characteristics, encouraged by genetic discoveries, the more imperative it becomes to acknowledge treatment received as an important source of variation in treatment effect. (Goetghebeur & Loeys, 2002, p. 89)

They consider that modern statistical methods should add in a flexibility to incorporate the effects of exposure patterns on outcome. Where statisticians tread today, social scientists may follow tomorrow. The point made by Goetghebeur & Loeys (2002) regarding the analysis of randomised trials is part of a growing trend to question sole reliance on this design in clinical research.

Munro (2005, p. 381) makes the comment that "There is an increasing realisation that the issues that can be dealt with by the RCTs are limited." Munro is clear that RCTs provide important evidence but makes the point that as "There are important activities in clinical research that are neither randomized nor systematic" (p. 381), other research methodologies, such as observational studies, cannot be neglected. Stephenson and Imrie (1998) have made essentially similar points for the evaluation of behavioural interventions, arguing for pragmatic trials of complex interventions. Victoria, Habicht & Bryce (2004) suggest that in the search for evidence-based public health there are complexities in evaluative research that stem from differences in the dose of the intervention delivered to the target population, and differences in the dose-response relationship between intervention and impact. These difficulties, Victoria et al. suggest, mean that the evidence from RCTs must be accompanied by evidence from other designs and methods of evaluation. Gilbody & Whitty (2002) make essentially the same point with respect to the evidence base to inform the organisation and delivery of mental health services.

It appears that the trend in evaluative research is both to question the unqualified reliance on RCTs and to consider using a wide range of research designs to gain a full understanding of complex interventions.

Do RCTs Produce Findings that are Significantly Different from Quasi-experimental Studies?

Another way to consider the current state of knowledge is to ask whether RCTs produce different outcomes to quasi-experimental studies. As Heinsman & Shadish (1996) point out, it is possible to look empirically at the relationship between methodology and outcome. Heinsman & Shadish (1996) compared statistically the results of random and non-randomised experiments reported in four meta-analyses of different areas of psychological research. On the basis of their analysis they suggest that if "Randomized and nonrandomized experiments were equally well designed and executed, they would yield roughly the same effect size" (Heinsman & Shadish, 1996, p. 162). Of course, as already discussed, not all experiments, randomised or not, are conducted and reported with equal rigour. Heinsman and Shadish are able to point to two design features of quasi-experimental studies that increase the likelihood of their producing a reliable effect size. First, it is important to control the degree to which participants are able to self-select into and out of conditions, and it is also desirable to minimise attrition. Second, if there are substantial differences between groups at pre-test on the outcome variable this can produce, not surprisingly, large effects at post-test. Therefore group matching or other methods of control of key variables are to be advised. There are similar studies, perhaps most notably Lipsey & Wilson's (1993) examination of psychological, behavioural, and education treatment that reach conclusions in line with Heinsman & Shadish (1996).

Moving closer to offending behaviour programmes, Weisburd, Lum & Petrosino (2001) looked at the effect of research design across a range of outcome studies within the criminal justice system. The studies included in the analysis were selected from the Maryland Report (Sherman et al., 1997), which had been concerned with crime prevention in the seven broad areas of communities, corrections, families, labour markets, policing, and schools. Using the Scientific Methods Scale (Sherman et al., 1997), Weisburd et al. coded the studies and compared the outcomes according to experimental design. Notably, only 15% of the 308 studies included in the analysis had a fully randomised design. Following their analysis, Weisburd et al. concluded, unlike Heinsman and Shadish (1996), that "There is a moderate inverse relationship between the quality of a research design, defined in terms of internal validity, and the outcomes reported in a study" (Weisburd et al., 2001, p. 64). In other words, non-randomised studies consistently produce more positive effects than do randomised designs. Weisburd et al. are cautious in describing their research as a preliminary step but they do suggest that non-randomised designs may introduce a bias in favour of treatment. They suggest two possible explanations for this bias: first, practitioners "creaming" those cases they deem most suitable for intervention; second, self-selection for treatment by offenders who are motivated towards rehabilitation. In a balanced discussion, Weisburd et al. (2001, p. 66) make the further point that "Randomized studies may not allow investigators the freedom to carefully explore how treatments or programs influenced their intended subjects." In this light, it is likely that the Weisburd et al. analysis was based on randomised studies that reported ITT, rather then TR, designs.

An empirical approach to understanding the impact of experimental design and the eventual findings has been considered in several reviews of offending behaviour programmes. In one of the first large-scale meta-analyses of offender treatment studies, Lipsey (1992) coded methodological variables in the analysis. The major factor to emerge from this aspect of the analysis was influence of the pre-treatment equivalence of the treatment and control groups. Substantial differences between the two groups at the outset were strongly associated with greater differences after treatment. However, Lipsey makes the comment that

> More surprising was the finding that the nature of the subject assignment to groups (random versus nonrandom), often viewed as synonymous with design quality, had little relationship to effect size. What mattered far more was the presence or absence of specific areas of non-equivalence – for example sex differences – whether they occurred in a randomized design or not. (Lipsey, 1992, p. 120)

When control groups received some attention, typically described as "business as usual", there was a smaller effect size than when the control group received no treatment (although this pattern was not the case for offenders in contact with the probation service). Another methodological point that emerged from the meta-analysis was concerned with the effects of attrition. When attrition occurs, in either treatment or control groups, the effect size is lowered. Lipsey suggests that this may be due to either the loss of amenable young offenders from the treatment group, or the more delinquent young offenders dropping out of the control group. Finally, studies with larger samples tended to have smaller effect sizes. Lipsey suggests that this may be because smaller studies are carried out more carefully and have greater treatment integrity.

Lipsey, Chapman & Landenberger (2001) reported a systematic review, using meta-analytic techniques, of 14 studies giving outcomes from cognitive-behavioural interventions with offenders. The studies selected used either randomised allocation to condition (eight studies) or a non-random procedure (six studies) that did "not involve manifest differential selection" (Lipsey et al., 2001, p. 148). The six quasi-experimental studies did not involve groups formed by treatment procedures, such as completers versus dropouts, and the treatment and control groups had to be shown to be initially equivalent and matched on key variables, such as offence history. Comparison of the randomised and non-randomised studies showed that the non-randomised studies gave a marginally larger treatment effect but that there was no statistical difference in outcome between the two designs. Interestingly, Lipsey et al. (2001) divided studies into "demonstration" and "practical" studies. The former are studies that were set up and evaluated by researchers; the latter are programmes applied in routine correctional practice. The demonstration programmes were much more likely to have good outcomes, which bears some similarity with Lipsey's (1992) finding regarding sample size. It is unclear whether the advantage seen with demonstration projects is a function of tighter control over procedures (high treatment integrity), shorter follow-up periods in the demonstration projects, or the setting in which the intervention was conducted.

Babcock et al. (2004) reported a meta-analytic review of treatment for domestically violent men. The meta-analysis included quasi-experimental studies, most using a non-equivalent control group design, and experimental studies. Babcock et al. report that both types of design showed a significant treatment effect, with no difference in effect size according to type of design. A quantitative review of the offender treatment programmes reported by Wilson et al. (2005) compared findings from random allocation studies and high-quality studies that attempt statistical control for group differences. Wilson et al. reported that high-quality designs, as with random allocation and control using statistical methods, produce broadly similar findings.

In the field of sex offender treatment there is heightened debate about the use of random allocation in treatment outcome studies (Brown, 2005). Lösel & Schmucker (2005) conducted a meta-analysis of treatment effectiveness for sex offenders. Along with methodological characteristics such as sample size and length of follow-up, Lösel & Schmucker coded the studies for methodological quality using the Maryland Scientific Methods Scale. They reported that the findings from studies using randomised designs did not differ significantly from those using quasi-experimental designs. Lösel and Schmucker also reported that treatment completers showed better effects than controls, and that dropping out of treatment doubled the odds of further offending. However, studies using smaller samples reported larger treatment effects, but length of follow-up did not have a systematic relationship with treatment outcome. The relationship between sample size and strength of treatment effect is similar to that noted by Lipsey (1992) and Lipsey et al. (2001). Lösel and Schmucker then used hierarchical regression analysis to attempt to disentangle the actual effects of treatment from the influence of methodological variation across the studies. They reported that small sample size and the use of offenders who refused treatment as a control group were positively and significantly predictive of treatment outcome. The inclusion of dropouts in the composition of the treatment group was negatively and significantly predictive of outcome. Thus, as seen in other studies, the composition of the treatment and control group is critically important with respect to outcome. The point regarding poor outcome for treatment dropouts replicates an earlier finding reported by Hanson and Bussière (1998). In the Hanson and Bussière meta-analysis dropouts from sex offender treatment were at increased risk of both sexual and general offending. Hanson and Bussière suggest that the "dropout effect" may be due to high risk offenders being most likely to leave treatment, possibly because of low motivation to change.

Are RCTs Always the Gold Standard?

The meta-analyses have added to our understanding of the relationship between methodological issues and treatment outcome. It is plain that there is a strong body of opinion, not just in the field of criminal justice research, that RCTs do not invariably guarantee strong research (or good science). Slade & Priebe (2001) note that RCTs were imported from medicine into mental health service evaluation, contrasting the standard pharmacotherapy of the former with the psychological and social interventions characteristic of the latter. This contrast leads Slade & Priebe (2001, p. 287) to the view that "Regarding RCTs as the gold standard in mental health care research results in evidence-based recommendations that are skewed, both in the available evidence and the weight assigned to evidence." In the field of criminal justice research, Gondolf (2001) makes the observation that the process of randomisation can introduce bias as offenders who would otherwise have gone in different directions are pushed together for the sake of the experimental design. Gondolf also notes the dropout problem in that, with RCTs, dropouts continue to be part of the treatment condition. However, if offenders dropout of treatment there are liable to be sanctions, such as going to prison or changing treatment programmes. Indeed, as Gondolf (2001, p. 85) states, "The real world usually does not work the way an experiment does."

Farrington & Jolliffe (2002) examined the conditions that should be in place for an RCT outcome study of a therapeutic unit within a prison. They concluded that several measures would need to be put in place. These measures included prisoners being assessed in the eight prisons feeding into the programme; several hundred prisoners participating in the RCT; and shortening the length of the intervention. The logistical problems in implementing Farrington and Jolliffe's suggestions are obvious, while trying to ensure consistency in data collection of several hundred cases across eight prisons is an interesting proposition! If a RCT is not possible, Farrington & Jolliffe (2002, p. 4) recommended that "The treatment should be evaluated by using matched treated and control groups, by comparing before and after outcomes in each group, or by statistical adjustment (e.g., in a regression equation) for pre-existing differences between groups."

Hedderman (2004) makes the point that RCTs are difficult to implement and maintain in practice; similarly Gondolf (2004) observes that introducing an RCT can be disruptive to practice and may change the system that is being evaluated. There are other limitations to RCTs: Hedderman (2004, p. 187) states that "RCTs do not answer other important questions such as *why* an intervention works or *which parts* have the most effect" (p. 187). Hedderman further notes that well designed quasi-experimental studies, controlling static and dynamic factors, can reduce significantly the likelihood of selection effects introducing a bias into the design. Indeed, Gondolf states that, as more precise questions are asked about the variables associated with explaining treatment, such as dosage effects, so experimental studies shift towards quasi-experimental designs. As in much applied research the problem lies in balancing internal and external validity: as indicated by the Scientific Methods Scale, an RCT may provide high internal validity, but the cost may be low external validity, thereby reducing the generalisability of the outcome from the study.

Slade & Priebe (2001) offer a concise conclusion:

> Mental health research needs to span both the natural and social sciences. Evidence based on RCTs has an important place, but to adopt concepts from only one body of knowledge is to neglect the contribution that other, well-established methodologies can make . . . RCTs can give better evidence about some contentious research questions, but it is an illusion that the development of increasingly rigorous and sophisticated RCTs will ultimately provide a complete evidence base. (Slade & Priebe, 2001, p. 287)

The views expressed by Slade & Priebe (2001) are increasingly being recognised, even in fields such as medicine where RCTs are highly prized. For example, a series of papers in *The Annals of Internal Medicine* inclined to the view that systemic reviews should include high-quality studies, both randomised and non-randomised (Hartling et al., 2005; Norris & Atkins, 2005; Reed et al., 2005). Thus, rather than dismissing evidence from quasi-experimental studies, the constructive position was advocated of moving towards the development of guidelines for agreeing the characteristics of high quality studies (see Des Jarlais, Lyles & Crepaz, 2004). Indeed, moving beyond the experimental versus quasi-experimental debate, Gondolf (2001) considers "alternative designs" that have arisen from the view that neither experimental nor quasi-experimental designs are sufficiently realistic in that they fail to take account of the context in which the programme is delivered and how variations in the context might influence outcome. These alternative designs may encompass the application of complex statistical procedures, such as structural equation modelling, to qualitative studies using, say, techniques based on post-modern methodologies. An interesting variation within this theme is to look specifically at the relationship between an individual's responses to treatment, say in terms of change on a measure of risk or a psychometric scale, and then relate the level of clinical change with outcome.

An interesting approach, based on *responsiveness* to treatment, was used by Beech, Erikson, Friendship & Ditchfield (2001) in an evaluation of a sex-offender treatment programme. The approach adopted by Beech et al. is highly informative regarding the fine-grained impact of programmes but the comparison of responders and non-responders faces the same criticisms as other quasi-experimental designs. Finally, as Abracen & Looman (2004) remind us, it is important that evidence is seen in the context of informing theory, so that advances in theory can inform future research and practice.

In summary, it is clear that there are no easy solutions to the question of programme evaluation: there are a number of approaches, each with its own inherent strengths and weaknesses and its own advocates and critics. Regarding the specific focus on the use of RCTs in outcome studies, it is possible to discern a growing shift across several fields towards considering the evidence garnered using different experimental designs and approaches. This trend to a more considered, expansive view of research design contrasts with the narrow approach advocated in Chitty & Harper (2005). It is difficult to disagree with Raynor's (2004) appraisal of this apparent shift in official research policy: "Criminal justice research in Britain has suffered as a result of their [RCTs] rarity, but it would be unwise to put all our heuristic eggs in this one basket" (Raynor, 2004, p. 319). Similarly, it is disingenuous to dismiss the extant research as "suboptimal" and "equivocal": as evinced by several studies, the significance of research design in relation to outcome might well best be considered as an empirical matter. Finally, as stated by several commentators (for example, Gondolf, 2004; Hedderman, 2004; Raynor, 2004), RCTs say little about the many complex issues involved in the delivery of programmes and the processes of individual change during offenders' participation in programmes. In the quest for high levels of experimental control, it is important to be aware of the distinction between *efficacy* research and *effectiveness* research (Seligman & Levant, 1998). The former might produce high-quality data from a researcher's point of view, but the generalisability of these data in that they test what happens in the real world is questionable. A search for convergence in outcome from both approaches to research would surely offer the best approach.

Where Do We Stand?

Given the many issues nested within the question of research design, Hanson & Bussière's (1998) conclusions about sex offender treatment programmes perhaps offer a fair summary of the field in general. Hanson and Bussière note that the concerns regarding the conduct of research, as discussed above, have divided judgements regarding the effectiveness of treatment programmes. Nonetheless, the evidence does stack up in favour of a treatment effect, even if that effect cannot as yet be attributed with full confidence to the direct result of the intervention. Thus, Hanson and Bussière's comments regarding sex offender programmes can be taken as a neat summary of the current state of knowledge regarding offending behaviour programmes in general: "Even if we cannot be sure that treatment will be effective, there is reliable evidence that those offenders who attend and cooperate with treatment programs are less likely to offend than those who reject intervention" (Hanson & Bussière, 1998, p. 358). In other words, there is evidence for a *completion* effect, even if caution should be expressed about calling this a *treatment* effect.

One way to try to understand more about the effects of completion (and hence programmes) is to contrast completers with non-completers, who seem to fare worse than either completers or controls in terms of re-conviction. Again, this brings the question of research design into the equation. As would happen with an ITT analysis, should those offenders who dropout and fail to complete programmes simply be seen in terms of attrition from the treatment condition? Alternatively, from a TR perspective, would a better practical and theoretical understanding of programmes be developed from greater knowledge of non-completion?

The Non-completion Issue

As well as a "completion effect", several studies have reported a "non-completion effect", in that for an offender to start a programme but then to dropout and fail to complete may be disadvantageous with regard to recidivism (Cann, Falshaw, Nugent & Friendship, 2003; Hanson et al., 2002; Robinson, 1995). For example, in their prison-based study, Cann et al. (2003) reported that when they compared the re-conviction rates of all programme starters with a comparison group no treatment effect was found. However, when Cann et al. compared programme *completers* with the comparison group a significant treatment (or at least completion) effect was reported. Given that the total rate of non-completion in the Cann et al. study was just over 11 % of the sample, it is evident that even a small dropout rate can exert a major effect on the outcome of an evaluation.

An American study reported by Van Voorhis, Spruance, Ritchey, Listwan & Seabrook (2004) employed random assignment of parolees to experimental and control conditions. The parolees in the experimental condition took part in the R & R programme, with a 60 % rate of programme completion. Van Voorhis et al. conducted a direct comparison of the two experimental and control conditions, using several outcome measures, and failed to find a significant treatment effect. However, when the data were considered as being generated by *three* groups – completer, dropout, and comparison groups – then a significant treatment effect was evident for the completers in terms of both reduced re-offending and increased employment. Hollin et al. (2004) reported a similar pattern of results (without random allocation) with no indication of a treatment effect when comparing experimental and comparison groups, even with a high level of statistical control over variables such as age and risk. However, a significantly lower rate of re-conviction was found for programme completers compared to programme dropouts and to the non-treatment comparison group. Further, as a blunt test of integrity, Hollin et al. (2004) examined outcome for programme completers by "appropriateness", classified as "too low risk", "appropriate risk", and "too high risk", according to the stated risk criterion for programme allocation. The "appropriate" group had a significantly higher rate of re-conviction than the "too low" group, and a significantly lower rate of re-conviction than the "too high" group. Clearly, even within samples of offenders who complete programmes, there may be variations in outcome when the criteria for programme allocation are violated. McMurran & Theodosi (in press) conducted a meta-analysis of 16 outcome studies carried out with offenders in which the intervention involved cognitive-behavioural methods. They concluded that re-conviction rates are higher amongst non-completers than for those offenders who complete treatment.

Thus, the evidence points to higher rates of re-conviction in programme dropouts, reinforcing the point that non-completers should not be used as the sole comparison group in outcome studies. This particular finding then raises two further issues:

1. Are there discernable differences between completers and non-completers prior to allocation to programme and in their experience and reaction to the process of taking part in programmes?
2. Can the "completion effect" and the "non-completion effect", and hence the differences in re-conviction between completers and non-completers, be explained by any such differences?

Differences Between Completers and Non-completers

Wormith & Olver (2002) note the evidence suggesting that treatment non-completers are at an increased risk of recidivism, which should be a concern as "Offender noncompletion of treatment is endemic to all correctional intervention" (Wormith & Olver, 2002, p. 450). However, as they further note, there are few studies of the characteristics of those offenders who drop out of correctional treatment. Accordingly, Wormith and Olver examined treatment programme attrition among a Canadian federal correctional population, comparing the characteristics of programme completers and non-completers on a range of historical, demographic, and treatment process variables. In terms of background, the completers were more likely to have full-time employment prior to imprisonment and to have a higher degree of academic attainment; however, non-completers were at a higher risk of recidivism.

In testing for differences between completers and non-completers, Van Voorhis et al. (2004) used logistic regression to compare programme dropouts and completers.

They reported that dropouts were more likely to have a history of violence, to be younger, and to have dropped out of school; there was no significant difference between dropouts and completers on employment history, race, social class, substance use, or prior incarcerations. In agreement with Van Voorhis et al., Hollin et al. (2004) found that the dropouts in their study were significantly younger than the completers, had higher risk of reconviction scores, and more previous convictions. Thus, unlike Wormith & Olver (2002), both Van Voorhis et al. (2004) and Hollin et al. (2004) found that dropouts were significantly younger than completers.

In terms of treatment process, Wormith and Olver incorporated seven measures, including treatment motivation, relating to offenders' performance during treatment. Multiple regression of data from treatment process measures and risk revealed that rated improvement during treatment, attitude towards treatment, and risk level were the significant predictors of completion. Wormith and Olver make the observation that the predictors of dropout – risk, attitude, education, and employment – are familiar risk factors for offending (cf. Browne, Foreman & Middleton, 1998; Hanson & Bussière, 1998; Van Voorhis et al., 2004). While more fine-grained research is awaited – it might be expected that findings will vary across jurisdictions and by type of offender population (prison and community being an obvious example) – it appears that that there may be predictable differences between completers and dropouts.

Completion, Non-completion and Re-conviction

If there are predictable differences between completers and non-completers, are these differences related to the different rates of post-programme rates of re-conviction between the two groups? There are several options to consider in seeking an answer to this question.

The first option, predicated on the absence of randomised studies, sees any differences between completers and non-completers as immaterial in explaining the completion effect found in quasi-experimental studies. Rather, the completion effect is a preordained function of a non-randomised design: Debidin & Lovbakke (2005) state that reduced rates of recidivism in completers "May be interpreted as selection effects, that is, that the programme simply served to sort those who would do well anyway from those who would not, regardless of the treatment" (p. 47). This explanation therefore suggests that it is precisely those offenders who will not commit further offences, and of course not all offenders will re-offend, who elect to enter and complete treatment programmes. It follows logically from this proposition that, on the basis of the extant evidence, treatment and treatment completion is irrelevant in looking at outcomes. If this view is correct, it raises several interesting questions. Why do offenders who would "do well anyway" elect to partake in programmes? (Might the decision to take part in programmes be related to the differences between completers and non-completers?) If completers were "going to do well anyway", why is there is still a high rate of re-conviction amongst this group? Indeed, is it possible that for *all* those offenders who complete an offending behaviour programme and are not re-convicted, the programme content did not have *any* impact at all? At face value this seems unlikely: Clarke, Simmonds & Wydall (2004) have reported that programme completers who had left prison and had not been reconvicted said that they had used their "Improved thinking skills in their everyday lives since leaving prison" (p. 16).

Nonetheless, if it is possible to specify in advance the characteristics of non-reconvicting completers then, perhaps evoking the spirit of radical non-intervention (Schur, 1973), it would make sense to turn away these offenders from programmes.

The second option for accounting for the completion effect hinges on the concept of *motivation*. Debidin and Lovbakke (2005, p. 50) comment that "Completion rates are strongly linked to motivation", which presumably means motivation to change behaviour and stop offending. Thus, before they enter a programme those offenders who go on to complete the programme are strongly motivated to change their behaviour in order to stop offending. The supportive evidence for this commonsense view is, however, limited and sometimes contrary (Hanson & Bussière, 1998; Wormith & Olver, 2002).

The motivation option provides an interesting juxtaposition with the "would do well anyway" argument. Those offenders who are motivated to change complete their programme, but the eventual lower rates of reconviction among completers are not explicable as an effect of the programme. It follows that somehow motivation in and of itself must have a central place in explaining desistance from offending. Casey, Day & Howells (2005) have considered this assumption for one particular motivational model, the transtheoretical model (TTM) of change (Prochaska & DiClemente, 1984), with regard to offending behaviour programmes. Casey et al. concluded that "The application of the TTM to offenders and offending is that the stages of change construct is, by itself, unlikely to adequately explain the process by which offenders desist from offending" (Casey et al., 2005, p. 167). If motivation is important in understanding desistance from further offending, it seems highly likely that it will take an interactive role with regard to other factors in the offender's life.

The main problem with the unqualified use of the term "motivation" is the lack of precision in its meaning. As Drieschner, Lammers & Staak (2004) comment, there is interest in the broader clinical literature regarding the notion of treatment motivation, which "sharply contrasts with the almost chronic ambiguity of the concept" (p. 1116). This ambiguity has led to several attempts to refine the notion of motivation (see, for example, Viets, Walker & Miller, 2002), and to alternative conceptualisations of motivation such as "readiness for change" (for example, Howells & Day, 2003).

The notion of readiness for change may offer an explanation of the hypothesised selection effect regarding programme entry and completion. It may be that some offenders who enter programmes are ready to change, in the sense that they are ready to *try* to stop offending, and their completion of the programme and desistance from offending reflects both their readiness to change *and* the effects of the programme. Thus, the reported differences between completers and non-completers may actually be correlates of readiness to change. This view is in accord with the findings of Clarke et al. (2004) who reported that the desisting completers in their sample emphasised that readiness for change was critical in their completing and benefiting from a programme. However, accepting this view would mean accepting a treatment effect that negates the basis of the "would do well anyway" explanation.

Understanding more about readiness to change, programme completion, and desistance from offending should be a research priority.

The use of psychological terms such as motivation imply that the locus of change lies *within* the offender; as opposed to the *process* of individual change which is obviously particular to the offender (Day, Bryan, Davey & Casey, in press). An alternative to looking within the offender for explanations of programme completion is to follow programme theory and look at the *interaction* between the individual offender and the treatment environment. In other words, as Wormith & Olver (2002) suggest, to consider *responsivity*:

> To summarize this perspective, the means by which responsivity may affect outcome is by being sensitive to offender characteristics so that the design and delivery of services are more likely to engage the client, increase treatment completion, augment the acquisition of rehabilitative material, and reduce recidivism. (Wormith & Olver, 2002, p. 454)

In order to understand programme completion and non-completion from this perspective it is necessary to consider a range of environmental factors alongside the characteristics of the offender.

A number of studies have examined why, once having started a programme, offenders do not complete treatment. Wormith & Olver (2002) made the distinction between offenders who elected to withdraw from treatment and those expelled from treatment but found few differences between the two in terms of offender characteristics. McMurran & McCulloch (in press) interviewed prisoners who did not complete a programme (ETS) and, like Wormith & Olver (2002), found a range of reasons why offenders left a treatment programme: there were some administratively based early exits due to release from prison; some prisoners were expelled from the group; some prisoners left because of ill health; and some prisoners left of their own volition. Other non-completers said they did not like working in a group but would value one-to-one work. McMurran and McCulloch also looked at various aspects of motivation and found that the non-completers said that initially they were motivated to stop offending and to engage in the programme. However, once engaged in the programme some of the non-completers said that ETS was not relevant to their needs, which may be true if, say, substance use was their primary problem. It is also possible that some offenders drop out of treatment because, having started, they come to consider themselves as sufficiently motivated to change their behaviour and so decide that they do not need to complete the programme. If that were that the case, however, the outcome data regarding the high rates of reconviction for dropouts suggest that this is a mistaken judgement. A reconviction study of dropouts taking into account their reasons for dropping out of a programme would provide illumination.

In terms of the material, some non-completers said that ETS was too slow and patronising; others that it was too demanding. Another study of ETS, this time within a probation setting, reported that offenders with literacy problems were more likely to drop out of programmes than offenders without such problems (Briggs, Gray & Stephens, 2003). Clarke et al. (2004) comment that institutional factors, such as a long delay before starting the programme and the link between programme completion and parole, could impact on a prisoner's motivation to enter a programme. In these accounts there is a clear association between offender characteristics and organisational factors that is related to eventual programme completion or dropout.

Some studies have looked at the relative abilities of organisations to deliver programmes. In their study of the R & R programme with parolees in Georgia, Van Voorhis et al. (2004) noted an overall completion rate of 60 % across 23 programmes conducted in 16 parole districts. However, the completion rates varied considerably across parole districts, from a low of 42 % completion to a high of 80 %. Pelissier, Camp & Motivans (2003) used multivariate analysis of a range of individual- and treatment-level variables to build a model predicting treatment non-completion among prisoners participating in drug treatment. The Pelissier et al. study provides a model for studying the effects of individual and organisational factors on offending behaviour programmes.

Thus, there are a range of possibilities by which to account for the associations between completion, non-completion, and the outcomes of offending behaviour programmes. These explanations range from an artefact of research design, through motivation and readiness to change, to complex interactions between the individual offender, programme characteristics, and organisational functioning. A final possibility, which has received little attention in the offending behaviour literature, is that dropping out of a programme is in itself a harmful experience. Against a backdrop of the adverse factors predictive of non-completion, the dynamic experience of failure will be evaluated by the individual offender. The offender may, for example, take the view that he or she is hopeless, or beyond assistance, or that they have been let down by the system. Any of these or other interpretations of their non-completion may harden the offender's attitudes towards crime and their own criminal behaviour, increasing the likelihood of further offending.

In conclusion, evaluation of offending behaviour programmes is of central, critical importance for several reasons. In the history of criminological psychology there have been various attempts to use psychological theory to explain crime and to devise means of working with offenders to change their criminal behaviour (Crow, 2001; Hollin, 2002b). The advances that followed the publication of the meta-analyses, giving rise to the "what works" agenda, have led in some criminal justice systems to a large investment in offending behaviour programmes. Indeed, in the UK since the late 1990s, the development and application of offending behaviour programmes, based on psychological principles of behaviour change, has been evident on a scale never previously seen. This large-scale development presents psychology with both opportunities and threats. There are real opportunities to apply psychology in the public domain for the benefits of society: if offending behaviour programmes can be of benefit in reducing crime this is clearly of benefit to potential victims, to the offender and their families, and to the taxpayer in general. There are also opportunities to learn from the implementation and running of programmes: from research, for example, we can learn more about effective practice, we can develop theory, and we can refine research methodologies. For instance, the collection of papers edited by Ward & Eccleston (2004) demonstrates the multifaceted nature of such advances in knowledge. In effect, through maintaining the cycle of research into practice, it will prove possible to move treatment and rehabilitation within the criminal justice system to the next generation of interventions.

However, moving to threats, research within criminal justice settings will inevitably be shaped by political demands for quick outputs. Pawson (2002) makes exactly this point with regard to the political imperative for research findings:

> Evaluation research is tortured by time constraints. The policy cycle revolves quicker than the research cycle, with the results that "real time" evaluations often have little influence on policy making. (Pawson, 2002, p. 157)

As well as the pressures of time, there may be problems with the availability of data, conflicts regarding the optimum research design, and vested professional interests (Blumson, 2004; Hedderman, 2004). These pressures and constraints may, in turn, lead to compromises in research practice, the dissatisfaction of researchers with both the process of the research and the dissemination of their findings, and even conflict between independent researchers and the policy-makers that commissioned the research (Hope, 2004; Raynor, 2004). The need for researchers to manage the immediacy of these types of situation is counter-productive and it builds delay and uncertainty into the conduct of the research, exacerbating the demands of time. Thus, one threat to progress lies in grappling with short-term demands that may well hinder substantial progress that would contribute significantly to the larger picture. Another threat, which is perhaps even more of a concern, lies in the potential conflict (or even collusion) between political, administrative, and (allegedly) independent researchers when the evidence fails to support either policy or changes in policy (Hope, 2004).

It is clear that there is a great deal at stake with respect to evaluation: if research is flawed or narrow in design, compromised in execution, or seen not to be impartial then its value will be significantly diminished. It is absolutely essential that the research evaluating offending behaviour programmes is seen to be of high quality and conducted with integrity.

CONCLUSION

One of the fascinations of offending behaviour programmes is that they necessarily involve so many different areas. Among other issues, this chapter has variously touched on epistemology, debates in mainstream clinical practice, the niceties of experimental design and methodology in outcome research, and political and professional concerns in the application and use of knowledge. Obviously there are no easy, or even widely agreed, answers to the issues raised across such a broad spectrum. However, awareness of the range of issues discussed in this and the preceding chapter will hopefully set the following specialist chapters into context.

REFERENCES

Abracen, J. & Looman, J. (2004). Issues in the treatment of sexual offenders: Recent developments and directions for future research. *Aggression and Violent Behavior, 9*, 229–246.

Andrews, D. A. & Bonta, J. (2003). *The psychology of criminal conduct (3rd edition)*. Cincinnati, OH: Anderson Publishing.

Babcock, J. C., Green, C. E. & Robie, C. (2004). Does batters' treatment work? A meta-analytic review of domestic violence treatment. *Clinical Psychology Review, 23*, 1023–1053.

Beech, A. R., Erikson, M., Friendship, C. & Ditchfield, J. (2001). *A six-year follow-up of men going through probation-based sex offender treatment programmes*. Home Office Research Findings No. 144. London: Home Office.

Bernfeld, G. A., Farrington, D. P. & Leschied, A. W. (Eds). (2001). *Offender rehabilitation in practice: Implementing and evaluating effective programmes*. Chichester: John Wiley & Sons.

Blumson, M. (2004). First steps and beyond: The pathway to our knowledge of delivering programmes. *Vista, 8*, 171–176.

Botvin, G. J. & Griffin, K. W. (2005). Prevention science, drug abuse prevention, and Life Skills Training: Comments on the state of the science. *Journal of Experimental Criminology, 1*, 63–78.

Briggs, S., Gray, B. & Stephens, K. (2003). *Offender literacy and attrition from the Enhanced Thinking Skills programme*. National Probation Service, West Yorkshire.

Brown, S. (2005). *Treating sex offenders: An introduction to sex offender treatment programmes*. Cullompton: Willan Publishing.

Browne, K. D., Foreman, L. & Middleton, D. (1998). Predicting treatment dropout in sex offenders. *Child Abuse Review, 7*, 402–419.

Cann, J., Falshaw, L., Nugent, F. & Friendship, C. (2003). *Understanding what works: Accredited cognitive skills programmes for adult men and young offenders*. Home Office Research Findings No. 226. London: Home Office.

Casey, S., Day, A. & Howells, K. (2005). The application of the transtheoretical model to offender populations: Some critical issues. *Legal and Criminological Psychology, 10*, 151–171.

Chitty, C. (2005). The impact of corrections on re-offending: Conclusions and the way forward. In G. Harper & C. Chitty (Eds), *The impact of corrections on re-offending: A review of "what works"* (pp. 73–82). Home Office Research Study 291 (2nd edition). London: Home Office.

Clark, D. M. (2004). Developing new treatments: On the interplay between theories, experimental science and clinical innovation. *Behaviour Research and Therapy, 42*, 1089–1104.

Clarke, A., Simmonds, R. & Wydall, S. (2004). *Delivering cognitive skills programmes in prison: A qualitative study*. Home Office Online Report 27/04. London: Home Office.

Cook, T. D. & Campbell, D. T. (1979). *Quasi-experimentation: Design and analysis issues for field settings*. Boston, MA: Houghton Mifflin Company.

Crow, I. (2001). *The treatment and rehabilitation of offenders*. London: Sage Publications.

Cure, S., Chua, W. L., Duggan, L. & Adams, C. (2005). Randomised controlled trials relevant to aggressive and violent people, 1955–2000: A survey. *British Journal of Psychiatry, 186*, 185–189.

Day, A., Bryan, J., Davey, L. & Casey, S. (in press). The process of change in offender rehabilitation programmes. *Psychology, Crime, and Law.*

Debidin, M. & Lovbakke, J. (2005). Offending behaviour programmes in prison and probation. In G. Harper & C. Chitty (Eds), *The impact of corrections on re-offending: A review of "what works"* (pp. 31–55). Home Office Research Study 291 (2nd edition). London: Home Office.

Des Jarlais, D. C., Lyles, C. & Crepaz, N. (2004). Improving the quality of nonrandomized evaluations of behavioural and public health interventions: The TREND statement. *American Journal of Public Health, 94*, 361–366.

Drieschner, K. H., Lammers, S. M. M. & Staak, C. P. F. van der. (2004). Treatment motivation: An attempt for clarification of an ambiguous concept. *Clinical Psychology Review, 23*, 1115–1137.

Duncan, E. A. S., Nicol, M. M. & Ager, A. (2004). Factors that constitute a good cognitive behavioural treatment manual: A Delphi study. *Behavioural and Cognitive Psychotherapy, 32*, 99–213.

Elliott-Marshall, R., Ramsey, M. & Stewart, D. (2005). Alternative approaches to integrating offenders into the community. In G. Harper & C. Chitty (Eds), *The impact of corrections on re-offending: A review of "what works"* (pp. 57–74). Home Office Research Study 291 (2nd edition). London: Home Office.

Everitt, B. S. & Wessely, S. (2004). *Clinical trials in psychiatry.* Oxford: Oxford University Press.

Farrington, D. P., Gottfredson, D. C., Sherman, L. W. & Welsh, B. C. (2002). The Maryland Scientific Methods Scale. In L. W. Sherman, D. P. Farrington, B. C. Welsh & D. L. MacKenzie (Eds), *Evidence-based crime prevention,* (pp. 13–21). London: Routledge.

Farrington, D. P. & Jolliffe, D. (2002). *A feasibility study into using a randomised controlled trial to evaluate treatment pilots at HMP Whitemoor.* Home Office Online Report 14/02. London: Home Office.

Farrington, D. P. & Welsh, B. C. (2005). Randomized experiments in criminology: What have we learned in the last two decades? *Journal of Experimental Criminology, 1,* 9–38.

Friendship, C., Blud, L., Erikson, M., Travers, L. & Thornton, D. M. (2003). Cognitive-behavioural treatment for imprisoned offenders: An evaluation of HM Prison Service's cognitive skills programmes. *Legal and Criminological Psychology, 8,* 103–114.

Friendship, C., Street, R., Cann, J. & Harper, G. (2005). Introduction: The policy context and assessing the evidence. In G. Harper & C. Chitty (Eds),*The impact of corrections on re-offending: A review of "what works"* (pp. 1–16). Home Office Research Study 291 (2nd edition). London: Home Office.

Gendreau, P. (2002). We must do a better job of culminating knowledge. *Canadian Psychology, 43,* 205–210.

Gilbody, S. & Whitty, P. (2002). Improving the delivery and organisation of mental health services: Beyond the conventional randomised controlled trial. *British Journal of Psychiatry, 180,* 13–18.

Goetghebeur, E. & Loeys, T. (2002). Beyond intention to treat. *Epidemiologic Reviews, 24,* 85–90.

Gondolf, E. W. (2001). Limitations of experimental evaluation of batterer programs. *Trauma, Violence, and Abuse, 2,* 79–88.

Gondolf, E. W. (2004). Evaluating batterer counselling programs: A difficult task showing some effects and implications. *Aggression and Violent Behaviour, 9,* 605–631.

Gonzales, J. J., Ringeisen, H. L. & Chambers, D. A. (2002). The tangled and thorny path of science to practice: Tensions in interpreting and applying "evidence". *Clinical Psychology: Science and Practice, 9,* 204–209.

Gorman, D. (2005). Drug and violence prevention: Rediscovering the critical rational dimension of evaluation research. *Journal of Experimental Criminology, 1,* 39–62.

Hanson, R. K. & Bussière, M. T. (1998). Predicting relapse: A meta-analysis of sexual offender recidivism studies. *Journal of Consulting and Clinical Psychology, 66,* 348–362.

Hanson, R. K., et al. (2002). First report on the collaborative outcome data project on the effectiveness of psychological treatment for sex offenders. *Sexual Abuse: A Journal of Research and Treatment, 14,* 169–194.

Harper, G. & Chitty, C. (Eds). (2005).*The impact of corrections on re-offending: A review of "what works".* Home Office Research Study 291 (2nd edition). London: Home Office.

Hartling, L., McAlister, F. A., Rowe, B. H., Ezekowitz, J., Friesen, C. & Klassen, T. P. (2005). Challenges in systematic reviews of therapeutic devices and procedures. *Annals of Internal Medicine, 142,* 1100–1111.

Hawkins, J. D. & Catalano, R. F. (2005). Doing prevention research: A response to Dennis M. Gorman and a brief history of the quasi-experimental study nested within the Seattle Social Development Project. *Journal of Experimental Criminology, 1,* 79–86.

Hedderman, C. (2004). Testing times: How the policy and practice environment shaped the creation of "what works" evidence-base. *Vista, 8,* 182–188.

Heinsman, D. T. & Shadish, W. R. (1996). Assignment methods in experimentation: When do nonrandomized experiments approximate answers from randomized experiments? *Psychological Methods, 1,* 154–169.

Hickling, E. J. & Blanchard, E. B. (1997). The private practice psychologist and manual-based treatments: A case study in the treatment of post-traumatic stress disorder secondary to motor vehicle accidents. *Behaviour, Research, and Therapy, 35,* 191–203.

Hollin, C. R. (1995). The meaning and implications of "programme integrity". In J. McGuire (Ed.), *What works: Reducing reoffending* (pp. 195–208). Chichester: John Wiley & Sons.

Hollin, C. R. (2002a). An overview of offender rehabilitation: Something old, something borrowed, something new. *Australian Psychologist*, 37, 159–164.

Hollin, C. R. (2002b). Criminological psychology. In M. Maguire, R. Morgan & R. Reiner (Eds), *The Oxford handbook of criminology (3rd edition)* (pp. 144–174). Oxford: Oxford University Press.

Hollin, C. R. et al. (2004). *Pathfinder programmes in the Probation Service: A retrospective analysis.* Home Office Online Report 66/04. London: Home Office.

Hollis, S. & Campbell, F. (1999). What is meant by intention to treat analysis? Survey of published randomised control trials. *British Medical Journal*, 319, 670–674.

Hope, T. (2004). Pretend it works: Evidence and governance in the evaluation of the Reducing Burglary Initiative. *Criminal Justice*, 4, 287–308.

Hotopf, M. (2002). The pragmatic randomised control trial. *Advances in Psychiatric Treatment*, 8, 326–333.

Howells, K. & Day, A. (2003). Readiness for anger management: Clinical and theoretical issues. *Clinical Psychology Review*, 23, 319–337.

Jacobson, N. S. & Truax, P. (1991). Clinical significance: A statistical approach to defining meaningful change in psychotherapy research. *Journal of Consulting and Clinical Psychology*, 59, 12–19.

Jadad, A. R., et al. (2001). Assessing the quality of reports of randomized clinical trials: Is blinding necessary? *Controlled Clinical Trials*, 17, 1–12.

Juni, P., Altman, D. G. & Egger, M. (2001). Assessing the quality of controlled clinical trials. *British Medical Journal*, 323, 42–46.

Kendall, P. C., Chu, B., Gifford, A., Hayes, C. & Nauta, M. (1998). Breathing life into a manual: Flexibility and creativity with manual-based treatments. *Cognitive and Behavioral Practice*, 5, 177–198.

Kimble, G. A. (1984). Psychology's two cultures. *American Psychologist*, 39, 833–839.

Levant, R. F. (2004). The empirically validated treatments movement: A practitioner/educator perspective. *Clinical Psychology: Science and Practice*, 11, 219–226.

Lewis, S. C. & Warlow, C. P. (2004). How to spot bias and other potential problems in randomised controlled trials. *Journal of Neurology, Neurosurgery and Psychiatry*, 75, 181–187.

Lipsey, M. W. (1992). Juvenile delinquency treatment: A meta-analytic inquiry into the variability of effects. In T. D. Cook, H. Cooper, D. S. Cordray, H. Hartmann, L. V. Hedges, R. J. Light, T. A. Louis & F. Mosteller (Eds), *Meta-analysis for explanation: A casebook* (pp. 83–127). New York: Russell Sage Foundation.

Lipsey, M. W., Chapman, G. L. & Landenberger, N. A. (2001). Cognitive-behavioral programs for offenders. *Annals of The American Academy of Political and Social Science*, 578, 144–157.

Lipsey, M. W. & Wilson, D. B. (1993). The efficacy of psychological, educational, and behavioral treatment: Confirmation from meta-analysis. *American Psychologist*, 48, 1181–1209.

Long, C. G. & Hollin, C. R. (1997). The scientist-practitioner model in clinical psychology: A critique. *Clinical Psychology and Psychotherapy*, 4, 75–83.

Lösel, F. & Schmucker, M. (2005). The effectiveness of treatment for sexual offenders: A comprehensive meta-analysis. *Journal of Experimental Criminology*, 1, 117–146.

Marshall, W. L. (2001). Adult sexual offenders against women. In C. R. Hollin (Ed.), *Handbook of offender assessment and treatment* (pp. 333–348). Chichester: John Wiley & Sons.

Marshall, W. L., Fernandez, Y. M., Marshall, L. E. & Serran, G. A. (Eds). (2006). *Sexual offender treatment: Controversial issues.* Chichester: John Wiley & Sons.

McCulloch, A. & McMurran, M. (in press). The features of a good offender treatment programme manual: A Delphi survey of experts. *Psychology, Crime and Law.*

McMurran, M. & McCulloch, A. (in press). *Why don't offenders complete treatment? Prisoners' reasons for non-completion of a cognitive skills programme. Psychology, Crime, & Law.*

McMurran, M. & Theodosi, E. (in press). *Is offender treatment non-completion associated with increased reconviction over no treatment? Psychology, Crime, & Law.*

Meehl, P. E. (1997). Credentialed persons, credentialed knowledge. *Clinical Psychology: Science and Practice*, 4, 91–98.

Munro, A. J. (2005). The conventional wisdom and activities of the middle range. *British Journal of Radiology, 78*, 381–383.

Najavits, L. M., Weiss, R. D., Shaw, S. R. & Dierberger, A. E. (2000). Psychotherapists' views of treatment manuals. *Professional Psychology: Research and Practice, 31*, 404–408.

National Probation Service. (December, 2004). *What Works News*, Issue 19. London: Home Office.

Norris, S. L. & Atkins, D. (2005). Challenges in using nonrandomized studies in systematic reviews of treatment interventions. *Annals of Internal Medicine, 142*, 1112–1119.

Pawson, R. (2002). Evidence-based policy: In search of a method. *Evaluation, 8*, 157–181.

Pelissier, B., Camp, S. D. & Motivans, M. (2003). Staying in treatment: How much difference is there from prison to prison? *Psychology of Addictive Behaviors, 17*, 134–141.

Persons, J. B. (1991). Psychotherapy outcome studies do not accurately represent current models of psychotherapy: A proposed remedy. *American Psychologist, 46*, 99–106.

Peterson, D. R. (2004). Science, scientism, and professional responsibility. *Clinical Psychology: Science and Practice, 11*, 196–210.

Prochaska, J. O. & DiClemente, C. C. (1984). *The transtheoretical approach: Crossing traditional boundaries of therapy*. Homewood, IL: Dow Jones-Irwin.

Raynor, P. (2004). The Probation Service "Pathfinders": Finding the path and losing the way? *Criminal Justice, 4*, 309–325.

Reed, D. et al. (2005). Challenges in systematic reviews of educational intervention studies. *Annals of Internal Medicine, 142*, 1080–1089.

Robinson, D. (1995). *The impact of cognitive skills training on post-release recidivism among Canadian federal offenders*. Report R-41, Correctional Service of Canada, Ottawa, Canada.

Russell, B. (1961). *A history of western philosophy*. London: Allen & Unwin.

Schur, E. (1973). *Radical non-intervention: Rethinking the delinquency problem*. Englewood Cliffs, NJ: Prentice-Hall.

Seligman, M. E. P. & Levant, R. F. (1998). Managed care policies rely on inadequate science. *Professional Psychology: Research and Practice, 29*, 211–212.

Shapiro, D. A., Harper, H., Startup, M., Reynolds, S., Bird, D. & Suokas, A. (1994). The high water mark of the drug metaphor: A meta-analytic critique of process-outcome research. In R. L. Russell (Ed.), *Reassessing psychotherapy research* (pp. 1–35). New York: Guilford Press.

Sherman L. W. (2003). Misleading evidence and evidence-led policy: Making social science more experimental. *Annals of the American Academy of Political and Social Science, 589*, 6–19.

Sherman, L. W., Gottfredson, D. C., MacKenzie, D. L., Eck, J. E., Reuter, P. & Bushway, S. D. (1997). *Preventing crime: What works, what doesn't, what's promising*. Washington, DC: Department of Justice, National Institute of Justice.

Slade, M. & Priebe, S. (2001). Are randomised controlled trials the only gold that glitters? *British Journal of Psychiatry, 179*, 286–287.

Stephenson, J. & Imrie, J. (1998). Why do we need randomised controlled trials to assess behavioural interventions? *British Medical Journal, 316*, 611–613.

Van Voorhis, P., Spruance, L. M., Ritchey, P. N., Listwan, S. J. & Seabrook, R. (2004). The Georgia cognitive skills experiment: A replication of Reasoning and Rehabilitation. *Criminal Justice and Behavior, 31*, 282–305.

Victora, C. G., Habicht, J-P. & Bryce, J. (2004). Evidence-based public health: Moving beyond randomized trials. *American Journal of Public Health, 94*, 400–405.

Viets, V. L., Walker, D. D. & Miller, W. R. (2002). What is motivation to change? A scientific analysis. In M. McMurran (Ed.), *Motivating offenders to change: A guide to enhancing engagement in therapy* (pp. 15–30). Chichester: John Wiley & Sons.

Ward, T. & Eccleston, L. (2004). Offender rehabilitation. *Special Issue of Psychology, Crime and Law, 10(3)*, 221–345.

Ward, T., Hudson, S. M. & Keenan, T. R. (2001). The assessment and treatment of sexual offenders against children. In C. R. Hollin (Ed.), *Handbook of offender assessment and treatment* (pp. 349–361). Chichester: John Wiley & Sons.

Ward, T., Polaschek, D. L. L. & Beech, A. R. (2006). *Theories of sexual offending*. Chichester: John Wiley & Sons.

Weisburd, D., Lum, C. M. & Petrosino, A. (2001). Does research design affect study outcomes in criminal justice? *Annals of The American Academy of Political and Social Science, 578*, 50–70.

Wilson, D. B., Bouffard, L. A. & Mackenzie, D. L. (2005). A quantitative review of structured, group-orientated, cognitive-behavioural programs for offenders. *Criminal Justice and Behavior, 32*, 172–204.

Wilson, G. T. (1996). Manual-based treatments: The clinical application of research findings. *Behaviour, Research and Therapy, 34*, 295–314.

Wilson, G. T. (1997). Treatment manuals in clinical practice. *Behaviour, Research and Therapy, 35*, 205–210.

Wormith, J. S. & Olver, M. E. (2002). Offender treatment attrition and its relationship with risk, responsivity, and recidivism. *Criminal Justice and Behavior, 29*, 447–471.

Chapter 3

GENERAL OFFENDING BEHAVIOUR PROGRAMMES: CONCEPT, THEORY, AND PRACTICE

JAMES MCGUIRE

University of Liverpool

INTRODUCTION

In its speed and scale, the dissemination of structured offending behaviour programmes in criminal justice settings has been little short of remarkable. The present chapter focuses on part of that phenomenon, and has five inter-related objectives. The first is to describe the theoretical framework on which most offending behaviour programmes are based. The second is to survey the background evidence that provides a rationale for the use of programmatic methods. As other chapters of the book deal with specific structured activities applied to violent, sexual and drug-related offences, the present one will be devoted exclusively to what are known as "generic" or "general" offending behaviour programmes. The next objective, then, is to describe the three programmes of this type currently in most widespread use with adult offenders. The fourth objective is to collate the evidence that has emerged to date concerning the application of these programmes, and in particular whether or not such initiatives have satisfied one of the principal motivations for their use – the reduction of criminal recidivism. The chapter will close on the fifth and final objective, which is to discuss some unresolved issues surrounding various aspects of the programmes.

The extent of interest and the expansion of activity in this area are unprecedented but applying interventions in forms that can be described as programmatic is not in itself new. There are examples of this kind of work dating as far back as the 1940s; some were described in the first large-scale review of outcome studies of offender treatment published by Lipton, Martinson & Wilks (1975). In the ensuing decades there was a slowly but steadily increasing number of exploratory studies and experimental trials of structured forms of intervention. But the real era of

Offending Behaviour Programmes: Development, Application, and Controversies. Edited by C.R. Hollin and E.J. Palmer.
Copyright © 2006 John Wiley & Sons Ltd.

development in this sphere has probably been from *circa* 1990 onwards, with a virtually exponential growth occurring since that date.

The three programmes to be described in this chapter are as follows. The first is Reasoning and Rehabilitation (R & R). Developed in Canada by Ross & Fabiano (1985a), this programme has been used in both probation and prison settings in many countries. The original design has been slightly revised and R & R is now available in a number of different formats. The second programme is Enhanced Thinking Skills (ETS). Initially written "in house" as a shorter programme for use to complement R & R in the Prison Service in England and Wales, ETS has since been produced in a modified form for use in the Probation Service (Clark, 2000). The third is Think First (TF). The initial version of this programme was designed for use in probation services in England and Wales (McGuire, 1994) and subsequently revised, and also expanded into a longer version for use in prisons. Because these programmes share common theoretical and empirical roots and in several instances have been evaluated conjointly, in some sections of this chapter they will be discussed together, while in others they will be described separately.

As the title of this book implies, the deployment of these (and other) programmes has given rise to sizeable controversy (see Chapter 2). The word *programme* sounds sinister to some people as it conjures up images of a rigid and insensitive method of working. Indeed it appears to send shivers down the spines of some personnel working in criminal justice. The adoption of such practices has been disparaged as "Orwellian" and comparisons have been drawn with Cold War brainwashing techniques or *Clockwork Orange* scenarios. The reality is more mundane. Delivering programmes is plain hard work and requires considerable skill. It is also more humane and potentially liberating. When this work is done well, participants can make great personal gains, and staff can derive significant job satisfaction from their achievements.

RATIONALE FOR GENERAL OFFENDING BEHAVIOUR PROGRAMMES

Perhaps one of the defining aspects of a programme is the clarification of a proposed mechanism or *vehicle of change* that is thought to bring about the intended effects. What is the process that participating in any intervention will generate, which is expected to produce the outcomes that are the designer's and the delivering agency's ultimate goal? In the case of punishment of offenders it would presumably consist of personal distress resulting from loss of liberty, the general privations of prison life, or the physical hardships of a boot-camp regime. The urge to avoid a recurrence of these unpleasant events should ensure that the individual does not repeat the behaviour that brought them about. That, at least, is the essence of deterrence doctrine. Taking another example – for some types of therapeutic community, the change process would entail the experience of gradual re-socialisation and growth of personal insight as daily interactions with others shape new behaviours, feelings, or beliefs.

The three general offending behaviour programmes to be described here are all founded on the same conceptual basis, that of *cognitive social learning theory*. As originally formulated by Bandura (1977, 2001), this approach represents a synthesis of ideas from traditional behavioural learning theory with others from cognitive and developmental psychology. Studies carried out by Bandura and his colleagues showed that for an animal to learn it did not need to have direct experience of rewards and punishments as earlier stimulus-response theorists had proposed. It could learn indirectly, by observing outcomes of behaviour for other members of its species. Researchers hypothesised that such *observational learning* must rely on internal mechanisms, which could not be accounted for by direct conditioning alone. Bandura amassed a large quantity of evidence on the importance of learning from models in human development. Social learning theory posits both direct conditioning and observational learning from models as basic processes in development. Bandura identified three separate classes of models that were powerful in human learning: family members, particularly parents (or alternative caregivers); other immediate associates such as members of a peer group; and symbolic models, as encountered through the mass media.

From a behaviourist perspective there is an important distinction between the *eliminative* and the *constructional* approaches to bringing about behaviour change (Goldiamond, 1974). The former refers to the reduction of problematic behaviour by ensuring that its consequences are punishing for the individual. Deterrence and allied procedures in criminal justice rest on the concept of punishment, based on the assumption that, to avoid pain, patterns of behaviour that lead to it will diminish in frequency and even extinguish. By contrast, the constructional approach entails the reduction of undesirable behaviour (in this case, criminal activity) indirectly, through the promotion of alternatives, via application of positive reinforcement procedures and repertoire-building techniques. Individuals are given opportunities to learn new skills, notably ones that if used can enable them to solve problems they are faced with, and encouraged to apply them where possible. Thus, in cognitive and interpersonal skills training programmes of the types to be described below, the hypothesised mechanism of change is the acquisition of new capacities for analysing and solving problems, for interacting with others, or for the management of strong negative emotions. Nevertheless, ultimately, the choice as to whether to exercise such capacities remains with individuals themselves.

Social Learning and Differential Association

A number of criminological and psychological theorists have applied these theoretical approaches to the emergence of delinquency and to factors that maintain involvement in a criminal lifestyle (Nietzel, 1979). Fundamentally, criminal behaviour is considered to have its origins in socialisation, group interaction and interpersonal influence processes. Akers, Krohn, Lanza-Kaduce & Radosevich (1979) explicitly elaborated such a model, which they described as "A revision of differential association theory in terms of general behavioural reinforcement theory" (p. 637). These authors proposed that repeated criminal behaviour is learned through processes of imitation and differential reinforcement, by which individuals may arrive at evaluative definitions that are supportive of delinquent action. This process occurs in the context of social encounters, notably adolescent peer-groups.

Other theorists have attempted to devise more inclusive models by integrating concepts from social learning with other approaches in theoretical criminology. For example Elliott, Ageton & Cantor (1979) combined social learning theory with elements of strain theory and control theory. Individuals experience strain as a result of being unable to achieve success as defined by the culture to which they belong. In conditions of social disorganisation they will also be subject to relatively weak controls or attachments to conventional norms. Social learning processes then operate in such a way that the balance of their attachments shifts towards delinquent attitudes and activities, with criminal behaviour one result. The causal pathways within this and related models are not uni-directional, but are variously defined as bi-directional, reciprocal, or transactional. Thornberry (1987) delineated an interactional theory of delinquency that amalgamates similar explanatory concepts, but with a different balance of emphases. Catalano & Hawkins (1996) put forward an analogous perspective, synthesising yet another differential balance between social learning theory, control theory, and differential association theory in a developmental age-related model.

There is substantial empirical support for the role of social learning processes in the onset and maintenance of involvement in delinquency. Akers et al. (1979) initially tested their theory by conducting a self-report survey of involvement in substance abuse amongst a large sample of teenagers. They hypothesised that the relative proportions of influences within the groups to which individuals are exposed, conceptualised in learning-theory terms, instigates and sustains under-age alcohol consumption and illicit use of other drugs. Significant correlations were found between independent or predictor variables (measures of differential association and opportunities for social learning) and the dependent variables of interest (levels of substance misuse). The finding that there are close relationships between self-reported levels of offending and numbers of known delinquent peers or "criminal associates" has been reproduced in many studies (for example, Brownfield & Thompson, 1991; Matsueda & Anderson, 1998; Wright, Caspi, Moffitt & Silva, 2001). Thornberry (1996) has adduced a sizeable volume of evidence for the operation of bi-directional causal effects in social interaction processes. His model has also been extensively validated in the findings of the Rochester Youth Development Study, a longitudinal project on the development of delinquency (Thornberry, Lizotte, Krohn, Smith & Porter, 2003). Finally, a recent large-scale, meta-analytic review of a series of 140 studies (Sellers, Pratt, Winfree & Cullen, 2000, cited by Lilly, Cullen & Ball, 2002) has furnished substantial backing for social learning theory.

According to social learning and differential association theories, then, the interactive sequences inside familiar groups, and also within larger social networks, play a major role in leading individuals towards or away from offence behaviour. Interactions within groups both provide tangible examples of behaviour that individuals can adopt and simultaneously reinforce sets of attitudes supportive of or conducive to the commission of offences. Modelling and observational learning play a direct part in the establishment of patterns of delinquent behaviour; while symbolic learning and values-acquisition occur alongside them and further absorb individuals into the acceptance of or willingness to engage in offending. However, there is evidence that direct behavioural learning through modelling and imitation (as social learning theory would suggest) is a more potent factor in group influence than exposure to and assimilation of offence-supportive attitudes (as differential association theory would suggest). Warr & Stafford (1991) analysed data from respondents to the US National Youth Survey, concerning participation in three types of illicit behaviour: theft; cheating in exams; and using marijuana. The behaviour of friends was a stronger predictor of individuals' own actions than either their friends' or even their own expressed attitudes. In a very different context, working in a Bristol housing estate Light, Nee & Ingham (1993) interviewed young people and adults with histories of vehicle-taking. Their respondents named the influence of friends as the single most frequent motive for involvement in offending, and described having been taught basic driving skills by an older offender with more experience.

Cognition and Crime

To achieve a further increase in explanatory power, concepts from social learning theory and the empirical data generated by it can be combined with corresponding findings from studies of cognition and development. The result is arguably the most cohesive, intellectually rigorous and firmly grounded theoretical framework yet devised in its capacity to account for an extremely wide range of human action, including crime.

The accumulation and integration of evidence from numerous sources during the 1970s led to the emergence of what has retrospectively been entitled the "cognitive revolution", or cognitive-social-learning synthesis, in applied psychology. The impetus towards this departure came from a convergence of findings from numerous sources. They included the study of language and its role in self-regulation (Farber, 1963), research on family socialisation processes (see Patterson, 1982), explication of the links between cognitive events and emotional states (Novaco, 1975), and of the relationship between self-statements, emotions and behavioural change during therapy (Mahoney, 1974; Meichenbaum, 1977). This development was closely associated with the advent of the array of intervention methods collectively known as *cognitive-behavioural therapies*. Initially confined to the field of mental health – where these methods are now widely regarded as "treatments of choice" for a sizeable range of problems (Department of Health, 2001) – this approach has subsequently been extended to address problems in numerous other areas, including work in criminal justice (McGuire, 2000a).

With reference to criminal conduct, findings of this type were first formally integrated in the *cognitive model of offender rehabilitation* proposed by Ross & Fabiano (1985b). This was a variant of social learning theory with a particular focus on "cognitive skills". Developmental research showed that most ordinary, real-life problems arise in the interpersonal domain, and that solving them requires a particular set of skills or habits of thinking (Spivack, Platt & Shure, 1976). Using a series of specially designed psychometric tasks, Spivack & Levine (1963) had found highly significant differences in levels of these skills between young offenders in a residential reform school and general population samples. Subsequently Ross & McKay (1979) found initially favourable results through training young offenders in problem-solving and social skills.

Ross and Fabiano (1985b) reviewed allied literature and found evidence of several types of differences between persistent offenders and normative comparison groups on variables associated with cognitive functioning. These were related not to levels of intelligence as conventionally defined, but to performance on tasks that typified effective direction of thinking when faced with a problem. This type of performance was correlated with styles of management of self and of interpersonal encounters including stresses and conflicts. There was evidence that persistent offenders were more rigid in their thinking styles, more impulsive, less likely to delay action in order to contemplate alternative courses of action, and less likely to look ahead and anticipate the possible consequences of an action, including its potential impact on others. The available data at that stage were not wholly consistent and there are some notable gaps in the evidential case forwarded by Ross and Fabiano. Nevertheless, there seemed reasonable grounds for proposing that this approach was a valuable area in which to look for factors associated with frequent offending, which also held out the prospect of designing interventions through which the observed skill deficiencies could be remedied.

Skills of the kind discussed by Ross and Fabiano are usually acquired more-or-less automatically during development (Spivack et al., 1976). This transpires not through explicit instruction of the kind that happens in the classroom but through a far less formal, subtler, implicit social learning process that is embodied in everyday interactions. Thus, unless individuals are exposed to opportunities to observe and assimilate social problem-solving skills, they are unlikely to acquire them. Given certain socialisation experiences, they may even learn to act in ways that cause problems, such as speedily resorting to the use of force in an argument (Patterson, 1982). Ross and Fabiano suggested that individuals who lack or who habitually do not apply problem-solving skills are at risk of involvement in crime. For example they may resort to coercion as a means of resolving everyday difficulties with which they are faced. Their skill "deficits" are not in themselves direct causes of criminality. However, they may interact with other risk factors and with opportunities in the environment, so increasing the likelihood of criminal acts.

Progressively more evidence has accumulated illustrating the importance of cognition in the processes that lead someone to commit an offence. Alternatively, an offence may result from the absence of cognitive events that could inhibit such processes. The empirical basis for the hypothesised link between cognition and crime now derives not only from psychometric group comparisons, but from interview and self-report studies concerning a wide variety of offences including shop theft, vehicle taking, burglary, violence, armed robbery, and substance abuse (McGuire, 2004). Further supportive data come from research on cognitive distortions supportive of sexual abuse (Ward, Hudson & Keenan, 2001), and beliefs supportive of domestic violence (Russell, 2002). In circumstances where individuals experience loss of control, either through excitement, anger, fear, intoxication with alcohol or other substances, their capacities for clear or careful thinking diminish commensurately.

Social Problem-solving

Evidence from many sources indicates that there is an association between difficulties in solving problems, an upsurge of negative emotion, and accompanying risk of involvement in criminal activity. For example, amongst a large sample of young people followed in another longitudinal study, the Denver Youth Survey, there was a strong association between numbers of self-reported problems and seriousness of offending: "Amongst those facing only one problem, 7% are serious offenders, but among those facing four problems, 85% are serious offenders" (Huizinga, Weiher, Espiritu & Esbensen, 2003, p. 62). This pattern emerged for both males and females. The experience of personal difficulties across several areas of life is unfortunately sometimes accompanied by a lack of skills for addressing those problems and solving them in an effective way. Antonowicz & Ross (2005) and McGuire (2001, 2005a) have reviewed other research findings along similar lines.

Recurrent difficulties in solving problems can lead not only to negative emotions, but to personal crises that may be associated with committing a new offence. Zamble & Quinsey (1997) interviewed convicted adult offenders with an average of 25 previous convictions concerning factors that appeared to contribute to re-offending. The crimes for which they were re-arrested were often preceded by difficulties in coping and by poor self-management, characterised by an absence of a positive "problem-oriented" approach. For example, individuals ignored the problems they were experiencing, so allowing them to accumulate to intolerable levels, then adopted drastic solutions. In earlier research on how adult prisoners cope with problems, Zamble & Porporino (1988) found that less well adjusted prison inmates had more limited problem-solving skills. In a study exploring the factors associated with desistance from offending in a sample of adults on probation, Farrall (2002, p. 212) observed that "As the total number of 'problem' social circumstances facing the probationer increased, so desistance became less likely."

EVIDENCE BASE FOR PROGRAMME CONTENT

To establish a still firmer rationale for the use of cognitive/behavioural interventions in criminal justice, as Lilly et al. (2002) have pointed out, additional support for this perspective comes from two other sources. One is the series of findings obtained through large-scale reviews of predictive *risk factors* for criminal re-offending. The other is *outcome evidence* concerning the types of interventions that are most consistently associated with reductions in offender recidivism.

Risk Factors for Offending Behaviour

Many studies have now been published that investigated which demographic, criminological, family, social, and psychological variables yield the best predictions of subsequent involvement in criminal or other antisocial behaviour. Since self-report surveys and other studies show that a majority of citizens break the law at some point in their lives, such studies tend to focus on those sub-groups in which a pattern of offending has become repetitive or entrenched.

Research studies relevant to this point can be divided into two broad categories. Some of the factors of interest can be discerned from longitudinal research in which age cohorts are followed over an extended period of the lifespan (McGuire, 2004).

The majority of these can broadly be called *prospective* studies of predictive factors. Others involve examination of the relationships between factors "targeted" in intervention studies and the extent of reductions in recidivism subsequently observed. The latter could be called *retrospective* studies of predictive factors. The two types of studies complement each other and in both instances data from them can be integrated using meta-analytic techniques.

Several meta-analyses have been reported of risk factors for initial involvement and maintenance of delinquent behaviour amongst young people. Lipsey & Derzon (1998) synthesised findings from a number of longitudinal studies, attempting to locate those variables that would best predict serious or violent offending between the ages of 15 and 25 years. They combined data from 34 independent studies yielding a total of 155 effect sizes. Simourd & Andrews (1994) reviewed research, both published and unpublished, conducted in the 30 years prior to 1994. They located 60 studies, jointly producing a total of 464 correlation coefficients between a wide range of factors and involvement in delinquency. Cottle, Lee & Heilbrun (2001) reviewed 25 studies published between 1983 and 2000, comprising 22 independent samples. Hubbard & Pratt (2002) analysed predictors of delinquency amongst girls, surveying all relevant published studies, finding 97 effect size estimates from a combined sample of 5 981 offenders.

Amongst adults, the strongest predictors of offending have been investigated through an evolving series of meta-analyses by Gendreau, Little & Goggin (1996). Their database comprised a total of 131 studies published between 1970 and 1994, with an aggregate sample size of just under 700 000 participants, yielding a total of 1 141 correlations between predictor variables and recidivism. Gendreau and his colleagues surveyed 18 "predictor domains", encompassing demographic, family background, criminal history, and personal functioning variables.

The second category of reviews, employing a "retrospective" approach, has entailed testing the importance of separate predictor variables by comparing the relative impact of various types of intervention, focused on different aspects of individuals' functioning, on their rates of re-offending. With reference to young people, Dowden & Andrews (1999) reported the results of a series of meta-analyses on factors associated with re-offending. In relation to adult offenders, the largest review of this kind draws on an integrative evidence base of 372 studies of factors associated with offending. Andrews & Bonta (2003) have analysed these studies both in combination and in separate groupings defined by moderator variables such as gender, age, and ethnicity, and research variables including the specific ways in which crime was measured and the type of research design employed.

The net conclusion from these reviews is that the major factors with demonstrable links to risks of crime are the following. There is continuing support for the importance of "static" criminological variables such as a lengthy and varied history of anti-social behaviour; a family history of criminality; and experience of poor parental supervision and discipline. Persistent offending is also associated with low levels of personal, educational, vocational or financial achievement. However, certain key "dynamic" risk factors also emerge with a high degree of consistency, corroborated from both the "prospective" and "retrospective" approaches as described above. They include anti-social or pro-criminal attitudes, beliefs and cognitive-emotional states; association with pro-criminal peers, and a number of temperamental and personality factors including impulsivity, restless aggressive energy, egocentrism, and poor problem-solving and self-regulation skills. By contrast, in those studies where it has been assessed, socio-economic status, assumed in many criminological theories to be of major importance, consistently emerges as a fairly weak (low and non-significant) predictor.

Both Simourd & Andrews (1994) and Hubbard & Pratt (2002) found that the strongest predictors amongst females were similar to those for young males but some additional factors also emerged, including school relationships, history of physical or sexual victimisation, and family relationships. Recently Harper, Man, Taylor & Niven (2005) have also suggested that differential risk factors may operate for females and males respectively, at least to the extent that it should not be assumed that intervention programmes designed to address risk factors found amongst men will necessarily be appropriate for women offenders. Their proposal draws on unpublished Home Office data using the *Offender Assessment System* (OASys). These data showed that

> Female offenders had markedly higher levels of criminogenic need in the areas of relationships and emotional well-being, whereas male offenders had higher levels of need with regard to offending, alcohol misuse, thinking and behaviour and attitudes. (Harper et al., 2005, p. 26)

On this basis an action plan has been formulated to address how this information can be incorporated in programmes and other policy initiatives.

Risk Factors and "Cognitive Skills"

Studies along the foregoing lines have enabled researchers to identify and isolate some of the individual-level variables that contribute to risk of offending. A question that flows naturally from this is whether such factors are susceptible to change. Perhaps more important, could that change be planned and conducted by a process of formal training? Several studies carried out during the 1970s and early 1980s showed that a planned intervention is feasible and that individuals' levels of functioning in these areas can be self-consciously improved.

For example, some studies were focused on evaluation of single components of interpersonal problem-solving, such as the capacity to define problems or to generate alternative solutions. Successful training interventions to improve individuals' abilities in these areas were described (for example, Nezu & D'Zurilla, 1981; see McGuire, 2005a). Thus, when individuals were given explicit instructions and training on the process of defining and formulating problems, there were significant improvements in both the quantity and quality of solutions they generated and in the effectiveness of their decision-making.

Research showed that more complex aspects of social cognition and problem-solving were also amenable to training. Chandler (1973) examined the social-cognitive skill of perspective-taking in a group of persistent young offenders aged 11 to 13 years. Using specially designed role-playing and story-telling techniques, he found first that the young offender group was significantly more "egocentric" than a comparison group of non-offenders: that is, they appeared less able to adopt other people's perspectives. Forty-five youths were then randomly assigned to one of three conditions: the experimental group undertook a series of training sessions involving videotaped role-reversal exercises: the attention placebo group used video cameras to make tapes of other activities; while the no-treatment group had neither the intervention nor attention. On completing the sessions, the evaluation showed that the treated group improved significantly in their role-playing and perspective-taking abilities. In addition, an 18-month follow-up showed a significant reduction in the recidivism rate only amongst members of the experimental group.

As the cognitive procedures being described here are generally automatic, are helpful in achieving a goal and can be learned, they are analogous to those sequences known as "skills", which are more easily recognised in the motor domain – such as typing, knitting, swimming or riding a bicycle. The collection of capacities to generate ideas, adopt alternative perspectives, or formulate the steps necessary to solve a problem can also be conceptualised as skills. Thus "cognitive skills" programmes are so called because their objectives and the methods they employ are directed towards helping participants to acquire new routinised, goal-directed procedures for thinking about and solving their problems. They do so by acquiring and rehearsing procedures for analysing complex problems, practising skill components, re-assembling them, and then executing them in the realm of everyday functioning. In the learning environment, the preparatory work is done using specially devised materials and ready-made "worked examples"; participants then transfer what they have learnt to the "real world" of everyday lived experience. While that may sound initially abstract, the focus of such training is almost exclusively on the ordinary, familiar difficulties within the normal experience of many people, gradually moving forward to more challenging problems including ones generated by participants in cognitive skills groups.

The first systematic use of specially devised training to improve the skills of interpersonal problem solving was carried out with young children attending kindergarten and primary schools. Shure, Spivack & Jaeger (1972) trained a class of 4-year-old children from a deprived neighbourhood in the city of Philadelphia by means of a 50-session curriculum covering basic communication, self-awareness, and problem-solving skills. The latter included the ability to verbalise alternative possible solutions to problems, and to look forward so as to anticipate the consequences of an action. By comparison with attention-placebo and no-treatment control groups, the trained children showed greater improvement on problem-solving assessments and were more able to delay gratification following the sessions. There was also a close relationship between increased problem-solving skills and improved social behaviour. While not all of the findings were statistically significant, there were marked differences between the experimental and control groups on the majority of the indices used.

The first attempt to assemble and test a full "package" of training founded on these principles with offenders was described by Platt, Perry & Metzger (1980). These authors reported the results of the Wharton Tract Program, based in an open-door satellite unit designed to support offenders in transition from prison to the community. The participants were adult male offenders with lengthy histories of criminal behaviour and of heroin use. Platt and his colleagues combined two elements in a structured group intervention programme. The first element was a form of *guided group interaction*, a specified pattern of activity in which the group leader took an active role to emphasise the development of the group and to create a supportive atmosphere. Members were encouraged to think of themselves as agents of change for other group members. The second element was a focus on the learning of a series of communication and problem-solving skills. These skills included recognising problems, generating alternative ideas, consequential thinking, means-end thinking, decision-making and perspective-taking.

When followed up over a period of 2 years, group participants were reported by their parole officers to be significantly better adjusted than the comparison sample. They had a significantly lower re-arrest rate (49 % versus 66 %). Those who were re-convicted had a lower rate of re-commitment to institutions than comparison group members, implying their re-offences were of a less serious nature. Also, if they were re-arrested, this occurred after a longer average arrest-free period (238 versus 168 days) than for the control group members.

This type of approach, which typifies general offending behaviour programmes, reflects what has been called a *cognitive deficit* model, designed to impart skills that individuals have not acquired. The prime focus in other words is on the *structure* of cognition or how it operates. Taking the Reasoning and Rehabilitation programme as an example, its cardinal aim is to teach participants "how to think, not what to think" (Robinson & Porporino, 2001, p. 180). There are other approaches founded instead on a *cognitive distortions* model, focusing more on the *content* of cognition, overtly directed in other words at what an individual is thinking, his or her attitudes and beliefs. Such an approach forms part of some programmes designed to address sexual offending, domestic violence, and responsible driving.

There is clearly a great deal more to be learned about the factors that contribute to the occurrence and persistence of offending behaviour. Nevertheless the above integrative reviews advance our understanding to a sizeable extent, and the pattern that emerges from them is reasonably consistent. Obviously there are discrepancies within this body of research and there have been findings that are at odds with the model outlined here, which is not surprising given the complexity of the influences that are involved, and the wide assortment of studies. However, there are strong trends indicating that, excluding criminal history variables or "static risk factors" (which can scarcely be the target of preventive endeavours), there is a collection of variables that should be at the core of any concerted effort to reduce rates of re-offending amongst recidivist offenders. This list includes having a network of criminal associates; expressing antisocial attitudes; and a range of cognitive processes which also emerge in other research as being linked to the sequences of events that result in criminal acts. Moreover, studies have shown that at least some of these factors are susceptible to change through direct training.

These findings also provide further support for the explanatory power of a cognitive social learning model of the emergence and maintenance of criminality at the individual level. This is not an attempt by "psy-scientists" to "pathologise" offenders, as some criminologists would aver (Groombridge, 2001), since such processes are applicable across many other spheres of human activity. Nor is it a denial of the importance of environmental factors in giving rise to crime, whether with regard to multiple deprivation, opportunity structures, or other variables. All of these more-or-less certainly have some contributory role in the genesis of offending, and a comprehensive criminal justice policy would address all of them in some manner. Nevertheless, that is not an argument against also working with individuals themselves, which is the specific remit of criminal justice agencies such as prison and probation.

Overall, therefore, there are good grounds for concluding that there exists a clear and coherent rationale for the usage of intervention methods that can address some of the processes that lead to an ingrained pattern of criminal offending. Structured cognitive-behavioural programmes are explicitly designed for that purpose. However, there is an additional type of evidence relevant to their use, which comes from studies of the relative impact of different methods in reducing the re-offence rates of recidivist offenders.

Outcomes of Cognitive-behavioural Interventions

The meta-analytic evidence base for the claim that recidivism can be reduced by interventions focused at the individual or group level has been expanding gradually since the first review of this type was published in 1985 (Andrews, 2001; Hollin, 1999; McGuire, 2004). There are now no fewer than 52 relevant reviews employing statistical integration techniques (Hollin et al., 2005) (see also Chapter 1 and Chapter 7).

Most of the larger meta-analytic reviews that have subsumed a variety of intervention "modalities" have found cognitive-behavioural interventions to be reliably and consistently associated with larger effect sizes than those obtained for other methods. This emerges for example from the reviews by Andrews et al. (1990), Lipsey (1992, 1995), Lipsey & Wilson (1998), Pearson, Lipton & Cleland (1997), and Redondo, Sánchez-Meca & Garrido (2002). Some other approaches have also produced large effect sizes, although the evidence in support of them has been less consistent. Yet others, such as family-based interventions, have also generally yielded large positive effects but are designed for work with young offenders and would be impractical and probably unacceptable for use with adults.

Additional, smaller scale but specifically focused reviews have tested hypotheses directly relevant to cognitive social learning theory, examining the outcomes of specific forms of intervention associated with it. In a review of 17 studies, Mayer, Gensheimer, Davidson & Gottschalk (1986) found a mean correlation effect size of 0.33 which corresponds to respective recidivism rates for experimental and comparison samples of 33.5% versus 66.5%. Using a set of 46 studies, Izzo & Ross (1990) compared effect sizes for interventions that contained a focus on thinking or other "cognitive training" elements with those that lacked such ingredients. They found the mean effect size for the former to be 2.5 times greater than for the latter.

There are also several meta-analyses specifically designed to scrutinise the effectiveness of cognitive-behavioural (CB) interventions. One applied fairly liberal inclusion criteria and subsumed a total 68 studies with a wide range of evaluation designs (Lipton, Pearson, Cleland & Yee, 2002). The Lipton et al. (2002) review embraced both behavioural and cognitive-behavioural interventions, including some that were not in a "programmatic" format, and also reported on the effectiveness of cognitive-behavioural methods in relapse prevention in substance abuse treatment. The mean effect size across all studies was comparatively low (0.13) but it is statistically significant despite embracing findings from some poor-quality studies, raising the question of what would be found were attention limited to only those studies that employed better quality designs.

Another review, conducted within the framework of the Campbell Collaboration Crime and Justice Group, applied much stricter inclusion criteria, selecting only the highest quality evaluation designs (Lipsey, Chapman & Landenberger, 2001). It is widely acknowledged that randomised controlled trials and other designs with high internal validity offer certain advantages with respect to the inferential logic of hypothesis testing, and secure maximal control over extraneous variables. However, as discussed in Chapter 2, these standards are difficult to attain and often remain elusive in criminal justice settings. Random allocation is rarely feasible and experimental and comparison groups are usually non-equivalent. Lipsey and his colleagues confined their analysis to studies that met standards 4 and 5 of the *Maryland Scientific Methods Scale* (Farrington, Gottfredson, Sherman & Welsh, 2002b). Thus, only 14 studies were included, with either relatively strong randomised (8) or quasi-experimental (6) designs. The mean effect size across these studies was computed, yielding an odds ratio of 0.66; this represents a recidivism rate for programme participants that is approximately two-thirds of that for control samples. Larger effect sizes were found for "demonstration" than for "practical" programmes – that is, for interventions that had been set up as specially designed experiments, as opposed to others that were implemented within the "business as usual" of criminal justice services.

A third meta-analysis also focused only on carefully selected interventions that met specified criteria (Wilson, Bouffard & MacKenzie, 2005), although it was not limited only to randomised designs and incorporated studies published since the Lipsey et al. (2001) review. Results were collated from a set of 20 distinct studies yielding a total of 74 effect sizes. Of these studies, four (20%) employed random assignment. A further seven (35%) were classified as "high-quality quasi-experimental" designs in that attempts were made to control for group differences, and the remaining nine (45%) as "low-quality quasi-experimental" designs.

One of the interventions covered by this review was Moral Reconation Therapy (MRT), which by its title might sound as if it is based on a theoretical approach other than cognitive social learning. However, its model of change derives from Kohlberg's cognitive-developmental framework (see Palmer, 2003, for a detailed account of this field), and "The therapeutic elements are largely cognitive-behavioural" (Wilson et al., 2005, p. 180) in orientation. The six studies reviewed all produced significant positive results. There were seven evaluations of R & R, and seven studies of cognitive-behavioural interventions of various other types.

On the basis of their review Wilson and his colleagues concluded that "The evidence summarised in this article supports the claim that cognitive-behavioral treatment techniques are effective at reducing criminal behaviors among convicted offenders" (Wilson et al., 2005, p. 198). The mean effect size across the higher quality evaluation designs was 0.32. Furthermore, the evidence for the effectiveness of CB programmes was "Substantially stronger" than that obtained from a review of educational, vocational, and other work-oriented programmes for offenders (Wilson, Gallagher & MacKenzie, 2000).

Taking all the kinds of evidence reviewed so far into account, there is a sustainable rationale for embarking on the experimental use of programmes that draw on cognitive social learning theory and that apply interventions containing predominantly cognitive-behavioural components. Whether this can be done effectively on the scale with which it has been attempted in some jurisdictions is one of the controversies to which we will return later in this chapter.

PROGRAMME CONTENT AND APPLICATION ISSUES

In a number of countries, interest in the use of general offending behaviour programmes has developed apace in recent years, and several programmes have been accepted for widespread application in both prison and community settings. An elaborate procedure has been established for the independent validation or accreditation of programmes. In essence this is a form of quality control for both the admittance of the programmes into use and for monitoring the ensuing process of their delivery.

The development, operation and current status of accreditation criteria and associated processes have been discussed in Chapter 1 of the present volume. The three programmes under discussion here were among the first to be accredited for use in prisons in England and Wales, during the period 1996/7, by the then General Accreditation Panel (later the Joint Prison-Probation Accreditation Panel, then the Correctional Services Accreditation Panel). The same three programmes were, again at that early stage, amongst the first to be accredited for use in Probation Services, after procedures for the latter were established from 2000 onwards. All three programmes required some revisions before they were fully accepted by the various panels. Similar procedures for governing the inception of programmes have been devised in a number of other countries where these programmes are used.

The designated "target population" for the programmes consists of recidivist offenders – individuals who have been convicted on a number of previous occasions, usually for a variety of offences. In the typical case this will probably include both property crimes and offences against the person, though the former are likely to predominate. The programmes are tailored for those whose offence pattern suggests they might benefit from training in problem-solving, self-management, social skills, or who exhibit other risk factors of the types identified in the reviews cited above. In most agencies where the programmes are used, problems in these areas are assessed by means of a semi-structured interview administered at the referral stage. For the most part, individuals who have been convicted of sexual offences, domestic violence, drink-and-drive offences, or a marked pattern of substance-related offending, are referred to other more specialised programmes, some of which are described elsewhere in this book (see Chapters 4, 5 and 6).

Methods and Contents: Reasoning and Rehabilitation

As the first programme of its kind in the field, Reasoning and Rehabilitation (R & R) has in some respects set the standard against which others are measured. As mentioned at the outset of this chapter, people readily accept the use of a formal, structured sequence of activities delivered to groups in settings such as the school curriculum or in vocational training. But the idea that a similar principle can also be applied to engender behavioural or personal change amongst offenders has remained alien to many. From that perspective, assembling methods and materials that could be used in this way was a bold and innovative step.

Reasoning and Rehabilitation has been described as the product of a "40-year, multi-stage, field-theoretical research project that began in 1964" and so has undergone a number of developmental phases (Antonowicz, 2005, p. 164). Some of those phases, including initial pilot work, and the review of relevant literature, were touched upon earlier. The programme itself was first set out in manual form in the mid-1980s (Ross & Fabiano, 1985a). Some years later, in response to the requirements of accreditation processes, it was revised and supplemented with a specially written theory manual (Porporino & Fabiano, 2000). The materials are designed for use with groups of between 6 and 12 members. The original programme consisted of 35, later extended to 36 and then to 38 sessions each designed to last two hours, hence yielding 76 hours of "contact time". The pace at which sessions are delivered can vary according to the organisational needs within an agency, although a frequency of two to four sessions per week is recommended.

The total duration of R & R is low when set alongside the 240 hours required for completion of the Violence Prevention Program, developed by Correctional Service Canada (2002). Yet with the exception of treatment programmes for violent and sexual offenders which last considerably longer (see Chapters 4 and 5), R & R remains one of the most intensive programmes currently available. It entails a higher number of delivery/contact hours than the other general offending behaviour programmes to be considered here. Given this position, it is generally regarded as more suitable for offenders judged to be towards the higher end of the risk of reconviction spectrum. This view is reflected in the most recent data concerning its use in probation services in England and Wales (National Probation Directorate, 2004a) where almost 60 % of those attending have a predicted reconviction score above 71 % as assessed by the Offender Group Reconviction Scale (OGRS-2) (Copas & Marshall, 1998).

Also, in contrast to some other programmes that are grounded in a more flexible, less prescriptive manual format, within R & R the contents and mode of delivery of its component sessions are specified in considerable detail. This level of specification is quite different from programmes such as Violence Self-Risk Management developed in Vermont (Bush, 1995; Henning & Frueh, 1996). The sequence of activities that comprise each session is set out with clear instructions as to how each is to be run, and how connections are to be made between them. This high level of specification notwithstanding, it is repeatedly emphasised in training materials that delivering R & R is an extremely skilled process. It requires staff who are excellent communicators, who possess qualities such as warmth and openness alongside a capacity to set firm boundaries, who are skilled in working with groups and who can convey an enthusiasm and energy in their mode of interacting with them. Of course, they must also understand the theoretical basis of the programme and have a thorough working knowledge of its contents.

The programme materials are organised in a series of modules, each focused on specific target areas that are believed, on the basis of research evidence of the kinds reviewed earlier, to be dynamic risk factors for offender recidivism. However, there is a repeated emphasis on joining together the points that are addressed within individual sessions in order to consolidate learning, so maximising the possibility of its being executed in practice. The component areas are as follows.

Interpersonal Cognitive Problem-Solving Skills

Participants are taught a series of skills that will assist them in this domain, such as generating ideas, formulating means-end steps and anticipating consequences. They are taught how to analyse interpersonal problems and situations, how to understand and consider other people's values, behaviour and feelings, drawing on the seminal work of Spivack, Platt & Shure (1976).

Social Skills

Carrying out actions in the interpersonal domain requires behavioural skills and these, too, are a focus of the programme. There is a specified cycle of activity for the learning and practice of each skill, which involves defining the skill, demonstration, practice and feedback, following the format devised by Goldstein, Sprafkin & Gershaw (1976).

Self-Control

To address problems of impulsiveness and the risk of losing control, participants are taught to stop and think before they act; to give measured thought to plans for solving problems and to consider all the likely consequences before making any decision and acting on it.

Emotional Management

This material focuses on avoidance of excessive emotional arousal, as occurs in anger and other strong feeling states, drawing on the methods developed by Novaco (1975) and now widely used in anger management and allied therapeutic approaches.

Creative Thinking

This module focuses on methods designed to reduce conceptual rigidity, and to help participants acquire skills of alternative thinking. Exercises are used that illustrate how to access a larger number of ideas and to evaluate them, drawing particularly on the methods developed by Edward de Bono (1981).

Critical Reasoning

These sessions focus on logical reasoning, objective and critical thinking, helping individuals to apply rationality, to avoid distorted perspectives and to examine the issue of personal responsibility for action.

Values Enhancement

These sessions are designed to enable participants to move through moral-developmental stages from a more egocentric, self-serving approach to a consideration of the needs of others based on a series of moral reasoning exercises. The materials draw on Lawrence Kohlberg's model (Palmer, 2003) and on the use of specially created dilemmas to stimulate questioning and reflection.

Meta-cognition

These materials, forming components of many sessions, are designed to help participants become steadily more aware of their own thinking processes, comprehend the links between their own thoughts, feelings and behaviour and to appreciate the extent to which this can be consciously self-managed.

Several different types of training methods and learning experiences are incorporated in R & R sessions. There is some direct instruction, giving explanations of concepts and of the format of structured exercises, though the proportion of instruction is deliberately kept low. A high level of active participation is sought, using group brainstorming, worksheets, thinking games, role-plays, guided discussion and other techniques. There are specially prepared role-play vignettes ("skits"), set up so as to focus on the practice and application of designated skills. At different moments participants observe each other and may act as models or as providers of feedback. At numerous points individuals work in varying configurations within the parent group, including pairs or trios, or with the group sub-divided in half, or other syndicate arrangements. Throughout, there is an emphasis on the use by tutors of "Socratic questioning", in which they attempt to engender problem-solving skills in participants, by framing interactions in a style designed to activate particular sequences of thought.

An additional feature of the programme, reaching back to the much earlier work of Ross & McKay (1979) is the concept of "helper therapy". Group participants are encouraged to practise their skills outside the formal sessions and to observe themselves doing so. This practice especially includes interactions with others where there may be opportunities to assist them in solving problems as doing so is one method of achieving generalisation of learning beyond the training environment, in order to facilitate transfer of skills to real-life problem situations.

As the longest standing programme in the field and the one that is most widely known amongst both practitioners and researchers, R & R is also almost certainly the most broadly disseminated correctional treatment programme yet devised for adult offenders. It was piloted in Canadian federal prisons during 1988/9 and implemented on a national basis from 1990 onwards. Group facilitators or coaches were given an intensive 10-day training workshop as preparation for delivering the sessions. Initial studies showed that the programme was reaching an appropriate target population – prisoners assessed as being at a relatively high risk of re-offending and who manifested the cognitive skill deficits that are the programme's targets (Fabiano, Porporino & Robinson, 1990). Two edited volumes drew together relevant background research and initial outcome studies (Ross, Antonowicz & Dhaliwal, 1995; Ross & Ross, 1995). In 2003/4 R & R was scheduled for delivery in 26 prison establishments in England and Wales (Cann, Falshaw, Nugent & Friendship, 2003), and since 2000 it has also been implemented in probation services. Antonowicz (2005) reports that in the intervening period since its development it has been used in almost every state in the US, and in a total of 17 different countries, and he estimates that over 50 000 offenders have completed R & R.

Methods and Contents: Enhanced Thinking Skills

Enhanced Thinking Skills (ETS) is a 20-session programme directed towards a portion of the targets focused on by R & R (Clark, 2000). Sessions are designed to last between two and two-and-a-half hours. It was developed by psychology staff within the Prison Service in England and Wales as a parallel but shorter programme that could complement the use of R & R, designed for offenders at a lower risk of reconviction on the OGRS-2. The selection criteria specify ETS as being suitable for those whose scores fall in the OGRS-2 range 31 % to 74 %. In 2003/4 ETS was scheduled for delivery in 89 prison establishments in England and Wales, with a target of 5 568 completions (Cann et al., 2003).

Not surprisingly, given its shorter duration, ETS employs a somewhat more limited range of methods and materials than R & R. Its prime focus is on interpersonal problem-solving, social skills, and moral reasoning exercises. For most modules there are fewer sessions than in the corresponding component of R & R, though ETS contains a slightly greater amount of time dedicated to perspective-taking. However, the emphasis on making linkages between session objectives and outcomes, and of review of activities in order to inter-connect and reinforce different learning points is, if anything, strengthened in ETS. Programme training materials particularly highlight the use of "Socratic questioning" during sessions. Enhanced Thinking Skills materials have been particularly thoroughly analysed with reference to how tutor skills can be identified, trained and evaluated, and associated intake training and skills validation processes are very rigorous. Tutors are carefully selected and managed through a multi-stage process. The style of the ETS programme manual has also been followed in an accompanying accreditation manual, applicable to both ETS and R & R, which both acts as a further stage of training for previously trained tutors and as a vehicle for judging the maintenance of the required facilitator competences.

An element of "pro-social modelling" is also important in delivering any programme of this kind and this, too, receives particular emphasis in ETS. This means that, as far as possible, facilitators adopt and display a positive, constructive style of interaction between themselves and the participant group. In seeking to promote an active, problem-solving frame of mind there is a continuing need to discern socially acceptable solutions and to avoid appearing to endorse antisocial attitudes or criminogenic thinking.

Methods and Contents: Think First

There are two principal forms of the Think First (TF) programme. The more widely used is applied in probation and other community corrections settings, and in its current version it consists first of four pre-group sessions lasting approximately 1 hour each, three conducted on an individual basis and one as an introductory group meeting. These pre-group sessions are followed by 22 2-hour group sessions, and six individual 1-hour post-group sessions (total contact time thus being 54 hours). Some of the post-group sessions are designed to take place immediately after the group programme and to set the scene for continuing individual supervision by case managers. Other post-group sessions occur after a gap of approximately 3 months, as a form of relapse prevention. The design of the prison-based version is more straightforward, entailing group sessions only (30 sessions of 2 hours each).

Think First is a synthesis of two main elements (McGuire, 2000b). In common with R & R and ETS, the first is a cognitive-social-learning model of change, applying specific methods of problem-solving, self-management, and social skills training. The second is a focus on offending behaviour and an analysis of crime events. This focus is intended to enable individuals to address and plan behaviour change and maintenance of gains. The overall objective is to help individuals acquire, develop and apply a series of social problem-solving and allied skills that will enable them both to manage difficulties in their lives, and to avoid future re-offending.

The cognitive skills training elements within TF draw on the same background theory and evidence as those that influenced R & R and ETS and, not surprisingly, they are essentially similar in content. There are, however, some stylistic differences, and the structure of TF permits slightly greater scope for practitioners to make minor adaptations of content. This is allowed primarily to enhance the responsivity of the programme materials, in order to take account of variations in literacy levels amongst participants, and also client diversity with reference to gender, culture and ethnicity. These issues continue to be widely debated and we will return to them in the closing section of this chapter.

Nevertheless in common with R & R and ETS, Think First sessions are designed to impart a series of interpersonal problem-solving skills, adapting the sequence suggested by Spivack et al. (1976). They include, for example, the capacity, when faced with a personal difficulty, to do the following:

- Recognise that there is something wrong; to realise, and articulate to yourself, that you have encountered a problem (problem awareness).
- Identify the problem clearly by expressing it in words (problem identification).
- Collect information that will assist in solving the problem (information-gathering; distinguishing facts, opinions and guesses).
- Generate ideas for alternative courses of action that might be possible solutions to the problem (alternative thinking).

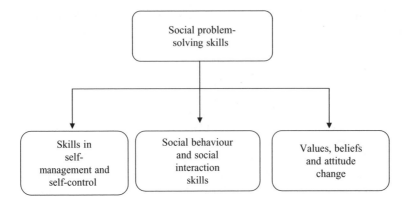

Figure 3.1   Conceptual structure of Think First.

- Formulate the steps that will be necessary to act on the solution (means-end thinking).
- Consider possible outcomes: anticipate the likely consequences of each course of action (consequential thinking).
- Make rational, well-informed choices between the available options (decision-making).

In addition, to become effective in problem-solving it is essential to control the impulse to act on the first idea that presents itself, and to manage the entire process without becoming overwhelmed (self-control training). Next, as most of the kinds of problems that beset individuals arise within the interpersonal domain, trying to solve them will entail applying behavioural interaction skills (social skills training). For the same reason, it will be necessary to understand and appreciate the perspectives of other people affected by the problem; with reference to criminal acts, this includes considering the impact of offences on victims (moral reasoning training, values and attitude change).

These areas are conceptually and methodologically inter-connected as depicted in Figure 3.1. Following the terminology of D'Zurilla, Nezu & Maydeu-Olivares (2004), when learning to solve problems and to promote effective functioning, it is helpful to distinguish two phases, of problem-solving and solution-implementation respectively. In this context, acquisition of problem-solving skill is seen as underpinning the changes that are then applied in practice in other segments of the work.

Probably the most distinctive feature of the TF programme however is that it is based on the guiding principle that an individual's offence itself should be a prime focus of interest in any work undertaken with him or her. The modification of a specific pattern of behaviour is more likely to be achieved if it is approached directly and attention is focused on it than if it is addressed only by indirect means. Group participants therefore analyse their own offences, and attempt to trace the factors that have contributed to their occurrence. Whilst this might seem a self-evidently useful thing to do, for many years criminal justice agencies almost steadfastly ignored the offence as a subject of discussion between offenders and correctional staff. Yet it is the occurrence of a criminal act that has provided the grounds for the individual's contact with the penal system.

Individuals participating in offending behaviour programmes cannot, however, be coerced into considering aspects of their offence behaviour in a confrontational or punitive manner. On the contrary, experience demonstrates that the overwhelming majority accept the rationale for doing so as a basis for change. But, once again, embarking on this process entails a high level of skill on the part of facilitators. It is possible to combine a firm and rigorous approach that motivates individuals to take responsibility for their actions, with a positive and empathic interactive style of the kind established as a prerequisite of effective personal counselling. As with R & R and ETS, the difficulty of working in this way has all too often been under-estimated. Think First was initially designed on the assumption that the tutors who would deliver the programme already possessed many of the required skills. A recent meta-analytic review has supplied clear evidence of the association between staff practices and the outcomes of offender intervention programmes (Dowden & Andrews, 2004).

The offence-focused component of the TF programme emerged from earlier research on preparing prisoners for return to the community. Following survey work on the self-reported problems of male prisoners, a form of pre-release training programme was designed and subsequently delivered by specially trained prison officers (Priestley et al., 1984). Follow-up suggested that the programme had been of considerable help to ex-prisoners in securing jobs, and managing a range of other difficulties including accommodation, family issues, money difficulties and alcohol abuse. Overall however, none of this had any observed impact on criminal re-offending. With one exception: where, at the request of prisoners, sessions had been devoted to aggression management, the subsequent records of those prisoners showed a significant reduction in violent re-offending (Priestley et al., 1984). This finding led to a literature review and series of proposals concerning direct work on offending behaviour (McGuire & Priestley, 1985). A fuller account of the development of Think First and of its composition and delivery is given by McGuire (2005b).

In both the prison and probation versions of TF, participants carry out a process of self-assessment of their problems using a specially designed problem checklist. One session is devoted to completing and scoring this checklist, yielding a problem profile, which group members then discuss collectively. This procedure in turn leads to a focus on offending behaviour as a problem. Participants select a single offence incident and analyse it in some detail using the "5-WH" format (What, Who, When, Where, Why); they then survey a series of such incidents to detect patterns across them. In essence, they engage in a functional analysis of their own crime histories, and then present the results of this analysis to the other members of the group. Later sessions use familiar cognitive-behavioural exercises such as A-B-C diaries, thinking reports, and tension thermometers (a variant of subjective units of distress) to examine different factors that may have contributed to criminal acts. Problem-solving and skills training methods are then applied to develop strategies for avoidance of further offending, and also to address other problems in individuals' lives.

Programme Delivery and Management

As outlined in Chapter 1, the process of accreditation that has been developed in England and Wales and applied to many programmes described in this book has two principal areas of focus. The first is on the nature of programmes themselves and whether they fulfil a series of criteria that will allow them to be used in a prison or probation setting. The second is on the process of implementation, the appropriateness of how it is done, the level of resources provided, the quality of delivery of the sessions and numerous other related matters (see also Chapter 7).

Understandably the precise management of programmes differs between prison and probation settings respectively although both have to achieve certain minimum standards. At any given prison site, there should be a Tripartite Programmes Team, consisting of a programme manager (usually one of the prison's assistant governors), a treatment manager (usually a forensic psychologist), and a through care manager (usually the senior probation officer allotted to the prison). There are set procedures that must be followed with regard to staff supervision, video-recording of sessions, recording of attendance and reasons for non-attendance, logging of tutor meetings, and filing of communications concerning participants.

Parallel arrangements are established within probation settings. Whereas for prisoners attendance at offending behaviour programmes is voluntary (although it may be strongly recommended as part of an individual sentence plan), in probation, attendance is part of a legal sanction. It is made an additional requirement of either a community rehabilitation order, or a community rehabilitation and punishment order, in accordance with the Powers of Criminal Courts (Sentencing) Act 2000. Failure to attend a programme may therefore mean that an individual could be returned to court; despite these structures, as we shall see later, there is considerable attrition due to non-attendance. Each offender is supervised by a case manager, who is responsible for coordinating all aspects of the order to which he or she has been made subject. Programme delivery is usually the responsibility of a specialist team located at a given programmes site, to which individuals are referred prior to appearing in court. As within prisons, numerous aspects of attendance, staff supervision, meetings and communications are documented and records kept for scrutiny through an annual programmes audit, details of which are presented in Chapter 1.

For all three programmes, both in prisons and the community, the frequency and timing of delivery of sessions has been varied to some extent to meet local institutional or service requirements. The most common modes of delivery to date have been frequencies of between two and four sessions per week. However slight variations on this are not uncommon. There is evidence from outcome research on Think First that the achievement of a minimum of eight hours of group sessions per week, is associated with superior results in terms of both attendance and reduced rates of reconviction (Ong, Al-Attar, Roberts & Harsent, 2003). This pattern may be because a higher intensity of effort builds a momentum in participation and individual change, but in the absence of further research this must remain speculative.

All three programmes under discussion here are highly structured with a prearranged sequence of themes, session objectives, and component exercises. As the preceding discussion indicates, however, some degree of flexibility is important in how issues are introduced; in the concrete, everyday examples used; and in specific facets of language or references to lifestyle that will reflect the composition of each new group. The greater the scope allowed for staff discretion within this procedure, the more challenging is the issue of maintaining treatment integrity. Outcome research shows that unless there is adherence to the conceptual model on which a programme is based, integrity may be compromised and outcome effects poorer as a result (Hollin, 1995; Lipsey, 1995).

For the programmes described here and others currently used in criminal justice in the United Kingdom, integrity is monitored by means of two principal mechanisms. First, tutors are allocated planning and debriefing time linked to delivery of sessions, and treatment managers supervise their work on a regular basis. For each programme there is a specified ratio of delivery sessions to supervision sessions, and records are maintained of all these activities. Other specific mechanisms are in place for each of the three programmes respectively. Second, sessions within prisons are videotaped and a random selection viewed by independent observers using specially devised rating scales. Ratings are made of tutors' treatment adherence, style of delivery, and group facilitation skills. Scores are converted into a composite index, the implementation quality ratio, part of a comprehensive audit process that yields annual "performance indicators" (see Chapter 1).

A specially designed cognitive skills "booster" programme has been developed to refresh and reinforce learning, designed for "graduates" of the three group-based general offending behaviour programmes and by 2004 had been implemented in 14 probation service areas (National Probation Directorate, 2004b). This programme lasts for a maximum of 12 sessions and is generally delivered at an interval of 3 to 6 months after completion of the main programmes.

OUTCOME EVIDENCE

The number of evaluative outcome studies of the three programmes just described has been steadily increasing over recent years (see also Chapters 1 and 7). Given the scale of its dispersal, R & R is the most frequently evaluated programme, to the extent that there have been enough outcome studies to support the conduct of meta-analyses focused on it alone. However, as the programmes have major conceptual similarities, and have also been used in varying permutations by some of the same criminal justice agencies, several evaluation studies have dealt with two or even all three of them in the same project. In what follows, studies that have focused on single programmes will be discussed first, before describing other evaluations that subsumed two or three of the programmes conjointly. In each case, research on how the programmes were perceived, and on short-term change usually assessed using psychometric methods, will be discussed first, before moving on to explore follow-up studies of criminal recidivism.

As judged by the initial reports of Fabiano et al. (1990) R & R, more familiarly known in Canadian prisons simply as the Cognitive Skills Training Program, was well received by prisoners who reported making important personal gains from it. Large majorities of respondents to survey questions concerning eight areas of personal functioning commented favourably on the benefits of participation, 97 % stating that they had used the skills they had learned, and describing the content as highly relevant to their lives. In a qualitative study in six prisons in England and Wales, Clarke, Simmonds & Wydall (2004) conducted 113 interviews with prisoners and staff concerning their experience of R & R or ETS. Again, most said they had benefited from joining the programmes, commented they would like to have done so earlier in their sentences, and prisoners held their tutors in high regard.

With regard to measured short-term change, Robinson, Grossman & Porporino (1991) reported encouraging outcomes from the delivery of R & R to Canadian federal prisoners. The measures used in this study included a semi-structured interview to assess cognitive skills; behavioural ratings completed by staff; a self-report measure of pro-criminal attitudes; and a self-report scale of impulsivity and empathy. Programme participants were compared with a pilot control sample with a similar risk profile. Examination of pre-to-post test scores showed that the treatment group made statistically significant changes on 18 out of the 20 measures used. While there were also some significant changes amongst the comparison sample, the treatment group changes were significantly larger on 14 out of the 18 measures.

Two more recent studies, both with very large sample sizes, have reported on short-term change in psychometric assessments of cognitive skills and other variables targeted within both R & R and ETS programmes (Blud & Travers, 2001; Blud, Travers, Nugent & Thornton, 2003). The former examined the "psychometric impact" of the two programmes on several key target areas assessed using the *Problem-Solving Inventory*, a multi-dimensional instrument specially devised by the Prison Service for this purpose (Clark, 2000), based on the Adolescent Problem Inventory (API) developed by Freedman et al. (1978). The API yields scores on assertive problem solving; suggesting alternatives, and generating solutions. Data were analysed for a sample of 1 910 prisoners who had completed R & R and for 6 636 who had completed ETS. Data were collected at three time-points: prior to each prisoner's commencement of the programme; immediately following completion; and at a short-term follow-up 2 months afterwards. There were "Statistically significant changes in the desired direction on all the key measures in the test battery" (Blud & Travers, 2001, p. 256). Expressed as effect sizes the observed changes varied between 0.22 and 0.43. There was evidence of reasonable level of maintenance of these gains at the follow-up. There was no clear differential impact of the two programmes across the sample as a whole but women offenders were found to make greater improvements in alternative-solution think following participation in R & R.

In another study, Wilson, Attrill & Nugent (2003) analysed a further set of data with the principal aim of testing whether there was a differential impact of these programmes on participants who had committed property offences only as compared with those who had committed offences against the person. Cognitive skills variables were analysed for a sample of 7 997 male and 306 female prisoners. Contrary to the findings obtained in Canadian prisons (see below), and the trend observed in meta-analyses that have addressed this question, the results of the pre- and post-intervention tests indicated that property offenders benefited just as much from cognitive skills training as did non-property offenders. However these are short-term, intermediate target results only and no data are available on whether the pattern emerges in post-release recidivism.

The earliest criminological outcome evaluations of R & R exemplified the extent of differences in scale that occur in this field. The first reported study by Ross, Fabiano & Ewles (1988) described the results of the Pickering experiment, a project based in Ontario province. Offenders placed on probation were randomly assigned to one of three groups. The first was standard probation contact or "business as usual", essentially amounting to a "no treatment" control. The second was a life skills programme that functioned as an "attention-placebo" condition; the third was R & R. Sample sizes were fairly small (23, 17, and 22 respectively) and the follow-up period only 9 months. The effect size was highly significant however, with recidivism rates for the three groups being 70 %, 48 % and 18 % respectively; corresponding rates of re-incarceration (a proxy measure indicative of the seriousness of new offences) were 30 %, 11 % and 0.

By contrast, another study reported by Robinson (1995) was a much larger scale evaluation for Correctional Services Canada, with a sizeable sample of federally sentenced prisoners (n=1 444). There was a striking reduction in recidivism of 36.4 % amongst those completing the programme as compared with controls (Robinson, 1995; Robinson & Porporino, 2001). Effects were however moderated by offence type: programme completers with records of violent, sexual and substance-related offending were less likely to be re-convicted than those with histories of property crimes.

Despite not being fully tested at that stage, as a result of its promising early findings usage of R & R became widely distributed in England and Wales from the early 1990s onwards, initially in probation settings (McGuire, 1995), and subsequently on a pilot basis in prisons (Williams, 1995). The STOP experiment in the Mid Glamorgan area of South Wales in the early 1990s was perhaps the initiation of "evidence-based probation" wherein research findings provided the grounds for a significant experiment in the content of offender supervision (Raynor, 2004a). Raynor & Vanstone (1996) reported encouraging outcome data at a 6-month follow-up but the observed effects disappeared at 12 and 24 months (for a fuller description of this pilot, see Chapter 1).

The subsequent delivery of both R & R and ETS on a mammoth scale in the Prison Service has been evaluated in four follow-up studies. The first (Friendship, Blud, Erikson & Travers, 2002; Friendship, Blud, Erikson, Travers & Thornton, 2003) reported recidivism outcomes for 667 adult males who participated in either R & R or ETS between 1992 and 1996. This study "adopted a retrospective quasi-experimental design – the relevant variables are controlled for after the treatment intervention" (Friendship et al. 2002, p. 3). Participants were compared with 1 801 non-participants matched on a number of relevant variables. Two years following release there was a 14 % reduction in reconviction among medium-low risk offenders, an 11 % reduction among medium-high risk offenders, and a 5 % reduction amongst high-risk offenders across the two programmes. The overall treatment effect was highly significant. The second study focused on a later cohort, those attending R & R or ETS between 1996 and 1998. Falshaw, Friendship, Travers & Nugent (2003) compared outcomes for 649 programme participants with a matched comparison group of 1 947 non-participants. Here however, 2-year re-conviction rates showed no significant differences between treatment and comparison samples. In the third study of a still later cohort who attended programmes in the period 1998–2000, Cann et al. (2003) extended the scope of the evaluation to include young and adult offenders. Two samples, respectively of 1 534 young and 2 195 adult prisoners were followed up for a period of 2 years after release. Outcomes were compared with those for equivalent-sized samples of non-participants. There was no significant difference between the two samples using an "intention-to-treat" design (see Chapter 2), however when programme dropouts were excluded, the 1-year reconviction rates were significantly lower for those who completed programmes than for the matched comparison groups. Amongst adult males, there was a 2.5 % difference in re-conviction for programme completers, and a 6.9 % reduction for the highest risk band. Amongst young offenders, there was an overall 4.1 % difference and a 4.8 % reduction for the high-risk band. These differences arose mainly from the impact of the ETS programme. However, none of the observed effects was maintained 2 years following release from prison. On the basis of such findings, some authors have been particularly critical of R & R (Wilkinson, 2005), drawing responses such as that of Wilson (2005), who maintained that programmatic intervention is so widespread as to have changed the recidivism rate on a substantial scale, which seems rather unrealistic.

In a subsequent study, Cann (2006) reported one-year and two-year follow-up findings for female offenders who attended prison-based cognitive skills programmes between 1996 and 2000. The number of participants here was much lower than amongst the male prison population, and no statistically significant differences in re-conviction rates were obtained. Several reasons were offered, including the low risk level of most participants, making it questionable whether they were suitable for the programmes. Also, "there is a lack of robust evidence that the deficits targeted by these programmes are criminogenic for female offenders" (2006, p. 5). The programmes were designed for male offenders and adapted only minimally for females. Thus the question of responsivity is raised, and there were also possible difficulties related to the limited scale of the implementation, with integrity being compromised by irregular programming of sessions.

The only study where ETS has been evaluated separately from R & R was reported by Farrington et al. (2002a) where the programme was one component of a multi-faceted treatment regime, making the effects of participation *per se* difficult to discern. This was a comparison between two intensive institutional regimes for young offenders, one primarily austere, disciplinarian and militaristic in orientation, the other physically demanding but also including basic skills training, ETS, vocational training, and a community placement. Evaluation showed that only the latter regime had an impact on subsequent offending, with experimental participants committing fewer offences than controls over a 2-year follow-up period. However, as mentioned, the contribution of ETS to this is not possible to disentangle from the global effect. The poorer showing of the former regime is consistent with meta-analytic findings on the effects of boot camps (MacKenzie, Wilson & Kider, 2001).

With respect to R & R, more encouraging findings have been obtained from studies in other countries including the US (Van Voorhis, Spruance, Ritchey, Listwan & Seabrook, 2004) and Sweden (Berman, 2004). Neither of these studies showed overall differences between assigned treatment and comparison samples but when analyses were conducted separating programme completers from those who dropped out, the former were found to have significantly lower rates of recidivism. The latter study also found that effects were moderated by risk level, with higher risk offenders and those with convictions for violence showing larger changes. This point was not noted in the Georgia study, though here positive effects of R & R participation were found in relation to subsequent patterns of employment.

Two recent reviews have summarised findings across a number of evaluations of R & R. Using a narrative approach Antonowicz (2005) surveyed 22 studies from a number of countries including Canada, four American states (California, Colorado, Georgia, and Texas), the UK, Spain, Sweden and Germany. This review included studies with adult and young offenders, prisoners, parolees and probationers. Four studies reported pre-to-post test data only, so applying a "ballot-box" method Antonowicz classified the remaining 18 according to whether the results were "positive" or "mixed" regarding recidivism outcomes, placing 11 in the former and 7 in the latter category.

Tackling a mostly overlapping set of studies Tong & Farrington (2006) have reported a meta-analysis integrating 16 recidivism follow-up evaluations carried out in four countries (Canada, the US, the UK and Sweden), and subsuming 26 separate comparisons. Expressed as an odds ratio, these authors found a mean effect size of 1.16 ($p < 0.0001$), alternatively represented as a 14 % decrease in recidivism for R & R participants across all studies: Tong and Farrington comment that "R & R programme participants were less likely to reoffend compared to controls in most evaluations" (Tong & Farrington, 2006, p. 17). Effects with regard to revocation of parole, technical violations or re-incarceration were not significant. Several other non-significant trends were noted: effect sizes were larger in community than institutional settings, for lower than higher risk offenders, and for offenders in the 30–39 age group than those in younger or older age strata. There was little information to shed light on this but where comparisons were feasible it appeared that the programme produced either nil or negative effects with offenders from ethnic minorities (in Canada and the US). Such a finding is at odds with meta-analytic evidence concerning programmes (Wilson, Lipsey & Soydan, 2003), although that review was conducted with reference to younger age groups. This caveat notwithstanding, Tong & Farrington's (2006) conclusion concerning the general impact of R & R was nevertheless favourable, and they make a number of valuable recommendations concerning future research.

In the meta-analysis reported by Wilson et al. (2005), cited earlier, on average R & R performed less well than either Moral Reconation Therapy (MRT) or the other assorted group of cognitive-behavioural interventions studied. Respective mean effect sizes from higher quality studies were: for MRT, 0.33; for the mixed bag of other cognitive-behavioural approaches, 0.49; and for R & R, 0.16. There was also more heterogeneity amongst the results for R & R than for the other approaches. It was thought possible that this might be due to the large-scale implementation of R & R in some settings and a consequent compromising of programme integrity. Although in an earlier review Allen, Mackenzie & Hickman (2001) found that evaluations of R & R were generally of a superior quality methodologically, they too drew a similar conclusion, that findings related to the programme were insufficiently consistent and even contradictory.

Evaluation: Think First

The direct forerunner of Think First, entitled *Problem-Solving Training and Offence Behaviour* (McGuire, 1994), was initially piloted in three probation service areas in England (Devon, Greater Manchester and Teesside). It was selected by the probation service as a Pathfinder programme when that policy initiative was announced in 1998, and thereafter extended to 31 of the 42 Probation Service areas. In the 3-year period from April 2001 to March 2004, a total of 11 624 offenders completed this programme. The programme is also used by the Scottish Prison Service, and in four Australian states (Victoria, New South Wales, South Australia, and Western Australia).

A few studies have provided data on the short-term impact of this programme, using repeated measures designs. McGuire & Hatcher (2001) reported pre-post psychometric data for 225 offenders who completed the programme in the three initial probation areas. This study was based on a fairly limited set of measures and there was no untreated comparison group. Significant changes in predicted directions were found for total scores and most sub-scales of a criminal attitudes scale, and on measures of impulsiveness, empathy and self-esteem. Ong et al. (2003) found a mixed, but predominantly positive set of results in a separate study of another sample from the three pilot areas. The authors used a series of measures of social problem solving, impulsiveness, locus of control, social reflection, criminal attitudes, perspective-taking and situational response assessments. Of 30 sub-scale scores obtained, 22 changed in the expected direction with 10 being statistically significant. The remaining eight changed in the opposite direction and one was statistically significant. Steele (2002a) has analysed a set of pre-to-post psychometric data from a sample of probationers who completed the programme in the Merseyside probation area during 2002. This was a small sample but all scores showed changes in predicted directions and several were statistically significant, most notably those on the *Social Problem-Solving Inventory* (revised) (D'Zurilla et al., 2004).

For the prison programme, McGuire (2005b) has reported on an analysis of pre-to-post scores for a sample of 405 prisoners who completed the prison version of the TF programme. The results show positive and highly significant changes on 12 out of the 15 measures, including scales for assessment of impulsivity, empathy, locus of control, socialisation, self-esteem, increased use of assertive responding, and decreased use of aggressive responding. Data are also available from a proportion of these prisoners who were available for further evaluation approximately 10 weeks after completion of the programme, showing that the gains were maintained. Unfortunately, no normative or control samples have been available with which to compare these data.

To date, only a few recidivism outcome studies have been reported for Think First. An initial unpublished evaluation of the pre-Pathfinder programme (Stewart-Ong, Harsent, Roberts, Burnett & Al-Attar, 2003, cited by Debidin & Lovbakke (2005) yielded disappointing results, in that the experimental group fared less well than a prison comparison sample. However, the groups were not equivalent and the latter had an anomalously low rate of re-offending. In another study, working at a local level, Steele (2002b) reported a 1-year follow-up of the programme in a single probation area. Those offenders who completed the programme had a significantly lower re-conviction rate than non-completers; their rate was also below that of the control group but the latter difference was not statistically significant. When attention was focused only on those offenders who properly met the programme's selection criteria, the reconviction rate for completers was substantially below that for controls (33 % as against 53 %).

More recently Roberts (2004) has reported a two-year follow-up evaluation of the programme in the three Pathfinder probation areas where it was originally piloted. Taking prior differences in risk level into account, there were significant differences in reconviction rates at six, 12, and 18 months follow-up, and a small but non-significant difference at 2 years (see also Stewart-Ong et al., 2004). The association between completion and reconviction rates was moderated by risk level. No effect of programme completion was evident for lower-risk offenders, but

> In relation to medium risk offenders (OGRS-2 scores of 41–75) and higher risk offenders (OGRS-2 scores of 76 plus) there were significant differences with lower rates for completers than non-completers and non-starters. (Roberts, 2004, p. 136)

However, the possibility remained that the observed differences were due to a self-selection effect, in that participants in the full programme were more motivated to avoid re-offending; an issue to be discussed again below.

Pathfinder Evaluation Project

In probation settings, two inter-related studies by a project team based at the universities of Leicester and Liverpool have shown significant effects on recidivism across all three of the general offending behaviour programmes being described here. This study also incorporated evaluation of an individualised general offending programme ((One-to-One) Priestley, 2000) and other "offence-specific" offending behaviour programmes focused on substance abuse, violence, domestic violence, and drink-driving. The latter programmes and their implementation are described in a separate "process evaluation" report (Hollin et al., 2002).

The outcome evaluation was carried out in two phases. In the first, the retrospective study (Hollin et al., 2004), the experimental group was composed of offenders sentenced to a Probation Order (now called a Community Rehabilitation Order) between January 2000 and December 2001, with a requirement to attend an offending behaviour programme. In the second, the prospective study (Hollin et al., 2005), the experimental group was composed of offenders sentenced during 2002 to a Community Rehabilitation Order or Community Punishment and Rehabilitation Order, with a requirement to attend one of seven Pathfinder programmes. After systematic data checking 16 Probation Service areas were included in the retrospective analysis and 15 in the prospective study.

This project constitutes the largest evaluation of community interventions for offenders conducted to date. The comparison group for the first study consisted of a random sample of 2 630 offenders given community sentences in seven probation service areas during 2001 without a requirement to attend an offending behaviour programme. Information concerning the comparison group was drawn from the Home Office's Probation Index database. For the second study that cohort was supplemented by data from two other areas bringing the comparison group sample size to 3 305 offenders. Reconviction data were collected over a period of between 12 and 18 months.

In the first study 2 141 offenders had been allocated to R & R, ETS or Think First, and in the second, 2 409. As the objective of this research was to evaluate the effects of the programmes, in both studies data for those who attended all programme sessions ("completers") and those who did not do so ("non-completers") were first of all analysed jointly, forming an "intent-to-treat" experimental group. The groups were then analysed separately, forming a three-group design (the initial remit of the study) alongside the comparison sample. In the second study, the non-completion group was further dismantled into those who failed to commence the programmes ("non-starters") and those who commenced but failed to complete ("drop-outs"). The completion rates for R & R, ETS and TF were respectively: in study one, 21.20 %, 28.93 % and 38.03 %; in study two, 17.91 %, 22.67 % and 33.52 %. In the second study, the respective non-starter rates were 54.73 %, 55.92 % and 43.25 %, and the drop-out rates for those who did start were 60.45 %, 48.56 % and 40.93 %.

With respect to recidivism a similar pattern of findings was obtained across all three programmes in both studies. Direct comparisons between the experimental group as a whole and the control sample showed a higher rate of recidivism amongst the former. However, the predicted reconviction scores for those allocated to programming (risk levels for future offending as measured by the OGRS-2) were significantly higher than for the controls in both cohorts. These prior differences between the samples were taken into account through the use of multivariate analysis (sequential logistic regression).

The results of the retrospective analysis showed that completing a general offending behaviour programme made participants 33.9 % less likely to be reconvicted (as compared to non-completers and the comparison group). Being a non-completer made an offender 57.2 % more likely to be reconvicted (as compared to completers and the comparison group).

Across all three programmes, completers showed the lowest reconviction rate, and non-completers the highest, with the comparison group between the two. This finding was statistically highly significant for the sample as a whole and for each programme separately. Data pertinent to this finding for the prospective phase of the research are displayed in Table 3.1. A similar pattern of findings emerged as in the earlier retrospective analysis.

In these studies it was not possible to take account of self-selection and motivation as a possible factor influencing the outcome. It is possible that those participants who complete programmes possess some feature, such as determination to succeed, that differentiates them from others and that this factor rather than programme participation accounts for their reduced offending (Chitty, 2005). It seems unlikely, however, that motivation alone can provide an explanation of the findings. Many individuals motivated to avoid offending nevertheless fail to do so in the absence of other factors; equally, adherence to treatment may be evidence that programmes helped them achieve their goals. Results from a number of studies that have found

Table 3.1 Percentage reconviction rates from a prospective evaluation of general offending behaviour programmes (Hollin et al., 2005)

Sub-group	Reasoning and Rehabilitation	Enhanced Thinking Skills	Think First
Completers	34.96	42.64	37.41
Non-starters	80.86	80.04	74.35
Non-completers	81.48	75.81	71.63
Comparison	63.66	63.66	63.66
Regression model	38.37	73.36	80.53
χ^2	$p < 0.001$	$p < 0.001$	$p < 0.001$

differential effects by risk-bands also argues against an explanation purely in terms of self-selection and motivation.

These conclusions are supported by some further analyses. First, it was noted that a proportion of those allocated to the programmes obtained OGRS-2 scores above or below the designated risk bands for referral. Detailed analysis showed that the most reliable effects on recidivism were obtained amongst those who fell within the bands thought appropriate for the programmes. Second, for a proportion of the sample, data were available concerning case managers' estimates of offenders' motivations to change. No association could be found, however, between these ratings and subsequent completion or recidivism outcomes. Third, completion rates for general offending behaviour programmes in the community have been gradually increasing (National Probation Directorate, 2004a). Taking Think First as an example, during the period 2001–2004 the national average completion rate (expressed as a fraction of commencements) rose by nearly 50 %, from 39.5 % to 58.5 % (McGuire, 2005b); that trend has continued in 2004/5. It is difficult to conjecture why such a rise should have occurred in the national pool of motivated offenders over a relatively short period. Programme completion is more likely to have been a function of agency and organisational change than of motivational change at the individual level. If personal motivation is an unlikely explanation for increasing completion rates, it seems equally unlikely as an explanation for differential recidivism outcomes.

FUTURE DIRECTIONS

In the UK, the inception and steady dissemination of offending behaviour programmes is just one aspect of a broader trend within prison, probation and youth justice services. This is one strand of the British government's Crime Reduction Programme, a major policy initiative which with regard to the probation service represents, as Raynor has portrayed it, "Recent history's most spectacular example of a wholesale conversion to evidence-based practice" (Raynor, 2004a, p. 161). Colloquially termed the "what works movement", this departure has given rise to considerable controversy, an issue that is considered in more detail in Chapter 2. It has been variously claimed that the evidence supporting it is thin and spurious

(Mair, 2004), that it represents a shift towards greater social control (Kemshall, 2002), even that it contains an intrinsic repressiveness (Boone, 2004). The equivocal nature of some of the findings emerging from recent evaluations has added to an underlying tone of scepticism (Merrington & Stanley, 2000, 2004, 2005). Apart from offending behaviour programmes, other elements within this policy framework include projects on prisoner resettlement (Lewis, Maguire, Raynor, Vanstone & Vennard, 2003), teaching basic skills (McMahon, Hall, Hayward, Hudson & Roberts, 2004), and community service (Rex, Gelsthorpe, Roberts & Jordan, 2004).

Space limitations preclude an in-depth examination of the full range of questions raised within this debate, but this final section will briefly review several of the most vital issues (for a fuller discussion, see McGuire, 2005c). (A number of these issues are also considered in Chapter 8 of this volume.) The principal problems identified with reference to offending behaviour programmes include their very unsatisfactory rates of commencement and completion. Others include their alleged failure to address diversity amongst offender populations in terms of gender, ethnicity, and other dimensions; and that they are likely to solidify patterns of social exclusion by making inadequate provision for those with literacy problems. More generally, the process of transferring "what works" research findings into practice has been castigated for neglect of implementation issues. To make matters worse, the latter has been compromised by the introduction of target-setting and enforcement procedures, and major organisational changes that were part of other policy agendas (Raynor, 2004b).

Attrition

As we saw earlier, attrition occurs in two phases: failure to commence programmes to which individuals have been sentenced, and drop-out during the programme itself. In the evaluations outlined above, R & R, ETS and Think First were found to show unacceptable rates of both non-commencement and of completion, particularly in the community.

Compliance with community sentences poses a perennial problem in the criminal justice system. Persistent offenders may be resistant to legal sanctions, many are beset with numerous problems and some have chaotic lifestyles. In such a context new initiatives may take some time to achieve their targets. When Day Training Centres were established in England and Wales in the 1970s, rates of attendance and completion were at first extremely poor. Indeed, in some locations it was only after the introduction of a structured programme (not at that time offence-focused) that absenteeism was meaningfully reduced (Priestley et al., 1984). As previously noted, there have now been progressive rises in completion rates for general offending behaviour programmes (National Probation Directorate, 2004a).

Such observed annual increases suggest that the initially low participation rates were not due solely to poor compliance or lack of motivation on the part of offenders. In a study of the factors associated with failure to commence programmes in the West Yorkshire Probation Area, Briggs & Turner (2003) discovered that attrition was often due to organisational factors. In some instances there was no group programme available at the required time; or offenders were subject to breach of probation proceedings for separate reasons. A miscellany of other influences included travel distances to programme sites, health problems, or missed communications. There were local variations within the probation area studied that were unlikely to be explicable in terms of factors within individual offenders. Another segment of attrition may be due to the system of centrally determined targets for the numbers of completions to be attained annually within probation areas, which may have led to inappropriate referrals and allocations, so increasing the likelihood of non-attendance. Other types of Pathfinder programmes, focused on "traditional" objectives of probation work such as securing employment, have shown similarly low rates of attendance (Haslewood-Pocsik, Merone & Roberts, 2004).

Westmarland, Hester, Reid, Coulson & Hughes (2002) investigated the factors associated with attrition amongst offenders allocated to Think First in the Northumbria probation area. They found a number of differences between those likely to complete or not complete the programme. The former tended to have longer criminal records: they had committed an average of 33 previous offences across a 13-year period. They identified stress as a current major problem; were less likely to have poor self-esteem identified as a problem; and more likely to accept responsibility for their offending. Feedback concerning the programme was predominantly very positive, and a sizeable majority of offenders (62%) considered that it would help them avoid re-offending. However, some offenders were deterred by being in a group and most felt very negatively about the prospect of completing psychometric assessments. In a small-scale interview study carried out in prisons, McMurran & McCulloch (2005) found that group working was also a source of dissatisfaction for prisoners who did not complete ETS. Other reasons for dropping out, in this prison sample, included a sense that although they were motivated to stop offending and to participate in treatment, ETS was less relevant to their needs, or the chance to attend came at the wrong time. Even in this sample, two-thirds considered that the programme was telling them things they needed to know. Hence, most of the 18 non-completers interviewed expressed negative feelings about leaving the programme and only two expressed positive feelings about doing so. Some found the programme insufficiently stimulating, others found it too exacting.

It appears likely that a proportion of programme attrition may be due to the literacy demands of offending behaviour programmes. For example with reference to ETS, Briggs, Gray & Stephens (2003) found that offenders with literacy problems were more likely to drop out than others without such problems. Structured programmes in general have been found to make demands in excess of the attainment levels of many of those required to attend (Davies, Lewis, Byatt, Purvis & Cole, 2004). This finding applied to skills in the area of speaking and listening as much as to written material. To take account of these difficulties a number of modifications have been made to the language used in the manuals, and further guidance given concerning adaptations of the material, through an internal mechanism of "change control" established within the National Probation Directorate.

Overall, however, the views of various critics of these approaches notwithstanding, there is no firm evidence from any studies that failures to attend structured programmes can be directly explained to any significant extent by widespread aversion amongst offenders to their objectives, methods or contents. Recent steady improvements in completion rates may be more a function of improvements in case management than any other single factor (Blumsom, 2004).

Implementation Problems

Raynor (2004b) has considered whether the disappointing results of the Pathfinder evaluations can be attributed to failures of theory (the programmes, or the model on which they were based are wrong), implementation (the way things were put into practice was wrong), or research (the design of the evaluations provided neither an adequate test of effectiveness, nor any means to understand effects that were found). Raynor dismisses the first possibility on the grounds that there is copious evidence from elsewhere – portions of it reviewed in the present chapter – on the effectiveness of the approach that underpins cognitive-behavioural programmes. The possibility nevertheless remains that, measured against the recommendations made by Lipsey (1995), all current offending behaviour programmes represent too weak a dose of intervention to achieve their desired effects.

Implementation problems seem a far more likely explanation of the pattern of findings obtained to date. Many observers agree that until recently this topic was a sorely neglected one (Gendreau, Goggin & Smith, 1999). Palmer (1996) sought to distinguish between *programmatic* and *non-programmatic* aspects of interventions. The former include all the categories and elements of programmes themselves. The latter include a range of factors that are widely considered to be prerequisites to success but are much more difficult to specify: they include staff characteristics; features of staff-client interactions; and aspects of the settings in which programmes are delivered. While not integral components of the definition of most programmes, these issues often play a critical part in determining outcomes (see Chapter 7). In recent years questions of implementation have begun to receive the attention they require, and have been analysed in greater depth and with increasing sophistication by several authors (such as Andrews, 2001; Bernfeld, Farrington & Leschied, 2001).

With reference to the specific difficulties that beleaguered the process of "rolling out" structured programmes, during the period of experimentation many other changes were occurring simultaneously. The administrative climate in which this work was done was a rapidly evolving one that created many uncertainties, and it would be surprising if that had not induced some unease amongst practitioners: indeed, it is widely acknowledged that it did. As described by other authors (Ellis & Winstone, 2002; Raynor, 2004b), the process of implementing Pathfinders spanned a period when the probation and prison services in England and Wales were undergoing considerable organisational change.

That context indicates another reason that has been offered for the inconsistent and sometimes disappointing outcomes. The pace and scale of dissemination of programmes may have resulted in a decline in treatment integrity, despite there being numerous mechanisms in place designed to preserve it. In the absence of clear supporting evidence it is not adequate to resort to the reflex excuse that poor results must be due to poor programme delivery. In the Falshaw et al. (2003) study, site audits were taken into account and showed no association with outcomes. Even so, during the study period programmes were being delivered at no fewer than 72 prisons. Another more potent factor may be motivation and enthusiasm, amongst both participants and practitioners, to engage with programmes.

As was discussed in Chapter 2, the third possibility is that the design of evaluations renders it difficult to draw clear conclusions regarding effectiveness (Hedderman, 2004). For example, the finding that programme non-completers usually fare worse than completers (with untreated comparison groups somewhere in between) is taken to imply that positive outcomes amongst the latter are primarily if not entirely a function of prior differences in motivational levels. In an analysis of findings relevant to this question, McMurran & Theodisi (2005) have reviewed results from 16 studies of cognitive behavioural and therapeutic community programmes and found that this pattern does not always emerge: recidivism rates for untreated comparison samples are sometimes higher than those for drop outs. Equally important, there can be a variety of reasons for dropping out, and although some of them are correlated with risk factors and may well be a function of motivation, there are also positive reasons for discontinuing a programme, alongside others that are a function of organisational rather than participant variables.

These considerations allow us to arrive at a more complex model and a more nuanced understanding of programme effects. Outcome results are a function of the programme ingredients in combination with individual motivation and readiness to change, as has been proposed in relation to anger management (Howells & Day, 2003). Hence it does not follow that those who succeed on completion of programmes would have "done well anyway" (Hollin, 2005). Change is difficult, and even in the face of considerable personal cost of repeated criminality, many well motivated offenders do not succeed in their attempts at it (Maruna, 2001). The most consistent interpretation of the range of evidence currently available is that general offending behaviour programmes are an important element in enabling a proportion of offenders to steer their lives away from repetitive involvement in criminality. As the programmes have become more firmly established, much continues to be learned that will enable that proportion to be increased and maximised.

The Future of Offending Behaviour Programmes

As these debates proceed, a variety of adaptations continue to be made in the programmes themselves. For R & R, the programme has been applied in a high security hospital (Donnelly & Scott, 1999), and there is an updated overview of the background literature (Ross & Hilborn, in press). Several variants of the materials are now available including a short version for adults (R & R2) (Ross & Hilborn, 2005), a version for young people, and another for work with families (Antonowicz, 2005). The Think First programme has also been employed in secure mental health services (Fleck, Thompson & Narroway, 2001). There is a shorter version for work with young offenders, and a new adaptation developed in Victoria, Australia, for working with offenders who have learning disabilities (Lambrick, Bergman & Persson, 2005).

The extent to which programmes continue to be used and become still more widely adopted may be crucially influenced by the outcomes of recent and ongoing research, an issue that is considered in Chapter 2. Criminal justice agencies in several countries are conducting experiments along similar lines to those in the UK, albeit mainly on a more modest scale. Ogloff & Davis (2004) have emphasised the potentially very high price to be paid if the current investment in rehabilitative activities does not yield visibly affirmative outcomes. It could well transpire that if results fall below expectations, the allegorical law-and-order pendulum will once more swing back to the punitive end of its trajectory – and stay there. The net effect of programme failure, real or apparent, might be that the viability of rehabilitation is not only doubted but rejected. This may be a rather cynical note on which to end, but unless they are instantly impressive and easily communicated, even positive results may be consigned to the historical obscurity of the unpublished project report. In the absence of eureka-style findings, the longevity and durability of programme usage may depend on a range of organisational and political factors, some of which are very difficult to foresee.

REFERENCES

Akers, R. L., Krohn, M. D., Lanza-Kaduce, L. & Radosevich, M. (1979). A social learning theory of deviant behavior. *American Sociological Review, 44*, 635–655.

Allen, L. C., MacKenzie, D. L. & Hickman, L. J. (2001). The effectiveness of cognitive-behavioral treatment for adult offenders: A methodological, quality-based review. *International Journal of Offender Therapy and Comparative Criminology, 45*, 498–514.

Andrews, D. A. (2001). Principles of effective correctional programs. In L. L. Motiuk & R. C. Serin (Eds), *Compendium 2000 on Effective Correctional Programming* (pp. 9–17). Ottawa: Correctional Service Canada.

Andrews, D. A. & Bonta, J. (2003). *The psychology of criminal conduct (3rd edition)*. Cincinnati, OH: Anderson Publishing.

Andrews, D. A., Zinger, I., Hoge, R. D., Bonta, J., Gendreau, P. & Cullen, F. T. (1990). Does correctional treatment work? A clinically relevant and psychologically informed meta-analysis. *Criminology, 28*, 369–404.

Antonowicz, D. H. (2005). The Reasoning and Rehabilitation Program: Outcome evaluations with offenders. In M. McMurran & J. McGuire (Eds), *Social problem solving and offending: Evidence, evaluation and evolution* (pp. 163–181). Chichester: John Wiley & Sons.

Antonowicz, D. H. & Ross, R. R. (2005). Social problem solving deficits in offenders. In M. McMurran & J. McGuire (Eds), *Social problem solving and offending: Evidence, evaluation and evolution* (pp. 91–102). Chichester: John Wiley & Sons.

Bandura, A. (1977). *Social learning theory*. New York: Prentice-Hall.

Bandura, A. (2001). Social cognitive theory: An agentic perspective. *Annual Review of Psychology, 52*, 1–26.

Berman, A. H. (2004). The Reasoning and Rehabilitation Program: Assessing short- and long-term outcomes among male Swedish prisoners. *Journal of Offender Rehabilitation, 40*, 85–103.

Bernfeld, G. A., Farrington, D. P. & Leschied, A. W. (Eds) (2001). *Offender rehabilitation in practice: Implementing and evaluating effective programs*. Chichester: John Wiley & Sons.

Blud, L. & Travers, R. (2001). Interpersonal problem-solving skills training: A comparison of R & R and ETS. *Criminal Behaviour and Mental Health, 11*, 251–261.

Blud, L., Travers, R., Nugent, F. & Thornton, D. (2003). Accreditation of offending behaviour programmes in HM Prison Service: "what works" in practice. *Legal and Criminological Psychology, 8*, 69–81.

Blumson, M. (2004). First steps and beyond: The pathway to our knowledge of delivering programmes. *Vista: Perspectives on Probation, 8*, 171–176.

Boone, M. (2004). *Does What Works lead to less repression? The justification of punishment according to What Works.* Paper delivered at the Societies of Criminology 1st Key Issues Conference, Paris.

Briggs, S., Gray, B. & Stephens, K. (2003). *Offender literacy and attrition from the Enhanced Thinking Skills programme.* National Probation Service, West Yorkshire.

Briggs, S. & Turner, R. (2003). *Barriers to starting programmes: Second phase report.* National Probation Service, West Yorkshire.

Brownfield, D. & Thompson, K. (1991). Attachment to peers and delinquent behaviour. *Canadian Journal of Criminology, 33*, 45–60.

Bush, J. (1995). Teaching self-risk-management to violent offenders. In J. McGuire (Ed.), *What Works: Reducing reoffending: Guidelines from research and practice* (pp. 139–154). Chichester: Wiley.

Cann, J. (2006). *Cognitive skills programmes: Impact on reducing reconviction among a sample of female prisoners.* Findings 276. London: Home Office Research, Development and Statistics Directorate.

Cann, J., Falshaw, L., Nugent, F. & Friendship, C. (2003). *Understanding what works: Accredited cognitive skills programmes for adult men and young offenders.* Home Office Research Findings No. 226. London: Home Office.

Catalano, R. F. & Hawkins, J. D. (1996). The social development model: A theory of antisocial behavior. In J. D. Hawkins (Ed.), *Delinquency and crime: Current theories* (pp. 149–197). Cambridge: Cambridge University Press.

Chandler, M. J. (1973). Egocentrism and anti-social behaviour: The assessment and training of social perspective-training skills. *Developmental Psychology, 9*, 326–332

Chitty, C. (2005). The impact of corrections on re-offending: Conclusions and the way forward. In G. Harper & C. Chitty (Eds), *The impact of corrections on re-offending: A review of "what works".* Home Office Research Study 291. 2nd edition. London: Home Office.

Clark, D. A. (2000). *Theory manual for Enhanced Thinking Skills.* Prepared for the Joint Prison-Probation Accreditation Panel. London: Home Office.

Clarke, A., Simmonds, R. & Wydall, S. (2004). *Delivering cognitive skills programmes in prison: A qualitative study.* Home Office Research Findings No. 242. London: Home Office.

Copas, J. & Marshall, P. (1998). The offender group reconviction scale: A statistical reconviction score for use by probation officers. *Applied Statistics, 47*, 159–171.

Correctional Service Canada (2002). *Violence Prevention Programs.* http://www.csc-scc.gc.ca/text/prgrm/correctional/vp_e.shtml

Cottle, C. C., Lee, R. J. & Heilbrun, K. (2001). The prediction of criminal recidivism in juveniles: A meta-analysis. *Criminal Justice and Behavior, 28*, 367–394.

Davies, K., Lewis, J., Byatt, J., Purvis, E. & Cole, B. (2004). *An evaluation of the literacy demands of general offending behaviour programmes.* Home Office Research Findings No. 233. London: Home Office.

Debidin, M. & Lovbakke, J. (2005). Offending behaviour programmes in prison and probation. In G. Harper and C. Chitty (Eds), *The impact of corrections on re-offending: A review of "what works".* Home Office Research Study 291. 2nd edition. London: Home Office.

de Bono, E. (1981). *CORT Thinking Program.* New York: Pergamon Press.

Department of Health (2001). *Treatment choice in psychological therapies and counselling: Evidence based clinical practice guideline.* http://www.doh.gov.uk/mentalhealth/treatmentguideline/index.htm

Donnelly, J. P. & Scott, M. F. (1999). Evaluation of an offending behaviour programme with a mentally disordered offender population. *British Journal of Forensic Practice, 1*, 25–32.

Dowden, C. & Andrews, D. A. (1999). What works in young offender treatment: A meta-analysis. *Forum on Corrections Research, 11*, 21–24.

Dowden, C. & Andrews, D. A. (2004). The importance of staff practice in delivering effective correctional treatment: A meta-analytic review of core correctional practice. *International Journal of Offender Therapy and Comparative Criminology, 48*, 203–214.

D'Zurilla, T. J., Nezu, A. M & Maydeu-Olivares, A. (2004). Social problem solving: Theory and assessment. In E. C. Chang, T. J. D'Zurilla & L. J. Sanna (Eds), *Social problem solving: Theory, research, and training* (pp. 11–27). Washington, DC: American Psychological Association.

Elliott, D. S., Ageton, S. S. & Cantor, R. J. (1979). An integrated theoretical perspective on delinquent behavior. *Journal of Research in Crime and Delinquency, 16*, 3–27.

Ellis, T. & Winstone, J. (2002). The policy impact of a survey of programme evaluations in England and Wales. In J. McGuire (Ed.), *Offender rehabilitation and treatment: Effective programmes and policies to reduce re-offending* (pp. 333–358). Chichester: John Wiley & Sons.

Fabiano, E. A., Porporino, F. J. & Robinson, D. (1990). *Rehabilitation through clearer thinking: A cognitive model of correctional intervention.* Report B-04. Ottawa: Correctional Service of Canada.

Falshaw, L., Friendship, C., Travers, R. & Nugent, F. (2003). *Searching for "What Works": An evaluation of cognitive skills programmes.* Home Office Research Findings No. 206. London: Home Office.

Farber, I. E. (1963). The things people say to themselves. *American Psychologist, 18*, 185–197.

Farrall, S. (2002). *Rethinking what works with offenders: Probation, social context and desistance from crime.* Cullompton: Willan Publishing.

Farrington, D. P. et al. (2002a). *Evaluation of two intensive regimes for young offenders.* Home Office Research Study No. 239. London: Home Office.

Farrington, D. P., Gottfredson, D. C., Sherman, L. W. & Welsh, B. C. (2002b). The Maryland Scientific Methods Scale. In L. W. Sherman, D. P. Farrington, B. C. Welsh & D. L. MacKenzie (Eds), *Evidence-based crime prevention* (pp. 13–21). London: Routledge.

Fleck, D., Thompson, C. L. & Narroway, L. (2001). Implementation of the Problem-Solving Skills Training Programme in a medium secure unit. *Criminal Behaviour and Mental Health, 11*, 262–272.

Freedman, B. J., Rosenthal, L., Donahoe, C. P., Schlundt, D. G. & McFall, R. M. (1978). A social-behavioral analysis of skill deficits in delinquent and non-delinquent adolescent boys. *Journal of Consulting and Clinical Psychology, 46*, 1448–1462.

Friendship, C., Blud, L. Erikson, M. & Travers, R. (2002). *An evaluation of cognitive behavioural treatment for prisoners.* Home Office Research Findings No. 161. London: Home Office.

Friendship, C., Blud, L. Erikson, M., Travers, R. & Thornton, D. (2003). Cognitive-behavioural treatment for imprisoned offenders: An evaluation of HM Prison Service's cognitive skills programmes. *Legal and Criminological Psychology, 8*, 103–114.

Gendreau, P., Goggin, C. & Smith, P. (1999). The forgotten issue in effective correctional treatment: Program implementation. *International Journal of Offender Therapy and Comparative Criminology, 43*, 180–187.

Gendreau, P., Little, T. & Goggin, C. (1996). A meta-analysis of predictors of adult recidivism: What works! *Criminology, 34*, 575–607.

Goldiamond, I. (1974). Toward a constructional approach to social problems: Ethical and constitutional issues raised by applied behavior analysis. *Behaviorism, 2*, 1–84.

Goldstein, A. P., Sprafkin, R. P. & Gershaw, N. J. (1976). *Skill training for community living.* New York: Pergamon Press.

Groombridge, N. (2001). Pathology. Entry in E. McLaughlin & J. Muncie (Eds), *The Sage dictionary of criminology.* London: Sage Publications.

Harper, G., Man, L-H., Taylor, S. & Niven, S. (2005). Factors associated with offending. In G. Harper & C. Chitty (Eds), *The impact of corrections on re-offending: A review of "what works".* Home Office Research Study No. 291. 2nd edition. London: Home Office.

Haslewood-Pocsik, I., Merone, L. & Roberts, C. (2004). *The evaluation of the Employment Pathfinder: Lessons from Phase I, and a survey for Phase II.* Home Office Online Report 22/04. London: Home Office.

Hedderman, C. (2004). Testing times: How the policy and practice environment shaped the creation of "what works" evidence base. *Vista: Perspectives on Probation, 8*, 182–188.

Henning, K. R. & Frueh, B. C. (1996). Cognitive-behavioral treatment of incarcerated offenders: An evaluation of the Vermont Department of Corrections' Cognitive Self-Change Program. *Criminal Justice and Behavior, 23*, 523–542.

HM Prison Service (1999). *Criteria for accrediting programmes 1998–99.* London: HM Prison Service, Offending Behaviour Programmes Unit.

Hollin, C. R. (1995). The meaning and implications of programme integrity. In J. McGuire (Ed.), *What works: reducing reoffending: Guidelines from research and practice* (pp. 195–208). Chichester: John Wiley & Sons.

Hollin, C. R. (1999). Treatment programmes for offenders: Meta-analysis, "what works", and beyond. *International Journal of Law and Psychiatry*, 22, 361–372.

Hollin, C. R. (2005). *Treatment completion: Impact on evaluation design and outcome.* Paper presented at the 15th European Conference on Psychology and Law, Vilnius, Lithuania.

Hollin, C. R. et al. (2004). *Pathfinder Programmes in the Probation Service: A retrospective analysis.* Online Report 66/04. London: Home Office.

Hollin, C. R., McGuire, J., Palmer, E. J., Bilby, C., Hatcher, R. & Holmes, A. (2002). *Introducing Pathfinder programmes into the Probation Service: An interim report.* Home Office Research Study No. 247. London: Home Office.

Hollin, C. R., Palmer, E. J., McGuire, J., Hounsome, J., Hatcher, R. & Bilby, C. (2005). *An evaluation of Pathfinder Programmes in the Probation Service.* Unpublished research report to the Home Office Research, Development and Statistics Directorate.

Howells, K. & Day, A. (2003). Readiness for anger management: Clinical and theoretical issues. *Clinical Psychology Review*, 23, 319–337.

Hubbard, D. J. & Pratt, T. C. (2002). A meta-analysis of the predictors of delinquency among girls. *Journal of Offender Rehabilitation*, 34, 1–13.

Huizinga, D., Weiher, A. W., Espiritu, E. & Esbensen, F. (2003). Delinquency and crime: Some highlights from the Denver Youth Survey. In T. P. Thornberry & M. D. Krohn (Eds), *Taking stock of delinquency: An overview of findings from contemporary longitudinal studies* (pp. 47–91). New York: Kluwer Academic/Plenum Publishers.

Izzo, R. L. & Ross, R. R. (1990). Meta-analysis of rehabilitation programmes for juvenile delinquents. *Criminal Justice and Behavior*, 17, 134–142.

Kemshall, H. (2002). Effective practice in probation: An example of "advanced liberal" responsibilisation? *The Howard Journal of Criminal Justice*, 41, 41–58.

Lambrick, F., Bergman, J. & Persson, P. (2005). *Cognitive-behavioural group program for people with cognitive impairment.* Statewide Forensic Services, Department of Human Services, Victoria.

Lewis, S., Maguire, M., Raynor, P., Vanstone, M. & Vennard, J. (2003). *The resettlement of short-term prisoners: an evaluation of seven Pathfinder programmes.* Home Office Research Findings No. 200. London: Home Office.

Light, R., Nee, C. & Ingham, H. (1993). *Car theft: The offender's perspective.* Home Office Research Study No. 130. London: HMSO.

Lilly, J. R., Cullen, F. T. & Ball, R. A. (2002) *Criminological theory: Context and consequences (3rd edition).* Thousand Oaks, CA: Sage Publications.

Lipsey, M. W. (1992). Juvenile delinquency treatment: A meta-analytic inquiry into the variability of effects. In T. Cook, D. Cooper, H. Corday, H. Hartman, L. Hedges, R. Light, T. Louis & F. Mosteller (Eds), *Meta-analysis for explanation: A casebook* (pp. 83–127). New York: Russell Sage Foundation.

Lipsey, M. W. (1995). What do we learn from 400 studies on the effectiveness of treatment with juvenile delinquents? In J. McGuire (Ed.), *What works: reducing re-offending: Guidelines from research and practice* (pp. 63–78). Chichester: John Wiley & Sons.

Lipsey, M. W., Chapman, G. L. & Landenberger, N. A. (2001). Cognitive-behavioral programs for offenders. *Annals of the American Academy of Political and Social Science*, 578, 144–157.

Lipsey, M. W. & Derzon, J. H. (1998). Predictors of violent or serious delinquency in adolescence and early adulthood: A synthesis of longitudinal research. In R. Loeber & D. P. Farrington (Eds), *Serious and violent juvenile offenders: Risk factors and successful interventions* (pp. 86–105). Thousand Oaks, CA: Sage Publications.

Lipsey, M. W. & Wilson, D. B. (1998). Effective intervention for serious juvenile offenders: A synthesis of research. In R. Loeber & D. P. Farrington (Eds), *Serious and violent juvenile offenders: Risk factors and successful interventions* (pp. 313–345). Thousand Oaks, CA: Sage Publications.

Lipton, D. S., Martinson, R. & Wilks, J. (1975). *The effectiveness of correctional treatment: A survey of treatment evaluation studies.* New York: Praeger.

Lipton, D. S., Pearson, F. S., Cleland, C. M. & Yee, D. (2002). The effectiveness of cognitive-behavioural treatment methods on recidivism. In J. McGuire (Ed.), *Offender rehabilitation and treatment: Effective programmes and policies to reduce re-offending* (pp. 79–112). Chichester: John Wiley & Sons.

MacKenzie, D. L., Wilson, D. B. & Kider, S. B. (2001). Effects of correctional boot camps on offending. *Annals of the American Academy of Political and Social Science, 578*, 126–143.

Mahoney, M. J. (1974). *Cognition and behavior modification.* Cambridge, MA: Ballinger.

Mair, G. (2004). The origins of what works in England and Wales: A house built on sand? In G. Mair (Ed.), *What matters in probation* (pp. 12–33). Cullompton: Willan Publishing.

Maruna, S. (2001). *Making good: How ex-convicts reform and rebuild their lives.* Washington, DC: American Psychological Association.

Matsueda, R. L. & Anderson, K. (1998). The dynamics of delinquent peers and delinquent behavior. *Criminology, 36*, 269–308.

Mayer, J. P., Gensheimer, L. K., Davidson, W. S. & Gottschalk, R. (1986). Social learning treatment within juvenile justice: A meta-analysis of impact in the natural environment. In S. A. Apter & A. P. Goldstein (Eds), *Youth Violence: Programs and prospects* (pp. 24–38). Elmsford, NJ: Pergamon Press.

McGuire, J. (1994). *Problem-Solving Training and Offence Behaviour.* Unpublished manual and support materials. Department of Clinical Psychology, University of Liverpool.

McGuire, J. (1995). Reasoning and Rehabilitation programmes in the UK. In R. R. Ross & B. Ross (Eds), *Thinking Straight: The Reasoning and Rehabilitation Program for Delinquency Prevention and Offender Rehabilitation.* Ottawa: AIR Training & Publications.

McGuire, J. (2000a). *Cognitive-Behavioural approaches: An introduction to theory and research.* London: Home Office.

McGuire, J. (2000b). *Think First: Programme manual.* London: National Probation Service.

McGuire, J. (2001). What is problem-solving? A review of theory, research and applications. *Criminal Behaviour and Mental Health, 11*, 210–235.

McGuire, J. (2004). *Understanding psychology and crime: Perspectives on theory and action.* Maidenhead: Open University Press/McGraw-Hill Education.

McGuire, J. (2005a). Social problem solving: Basic concepts, research, and applications. In M. McMurran & J. McGuire (Eds), *Social problem solving and offending: Evidence, evaluation and evolution* (pp. 3–29). Chichester: John Wiley & Sons.

McGuire, J. (2005b). The Think First programme. In M. McMurran & J. McGuire (Eds), *Social problem solving and offending: Evidence, evaluation and evolution* (pp. 183–206). Chichester: John Wiley & Sons.

McGuire, J. (2005c). Is research working? Revisiting the research and effective practice agenda. In J. Winstone & F. Pakes (Eds), *Community justice: Issues for probation and criminal justice* (pp. 257–282). Cullompton: Willan Publishing.

McGuire, J. & Hatcher, R. (2001). Offence-focused problem-solving: Preliminary evaluation of a cognitive skills program. *Criminal Justice and Behavior, 28*, 564–587.

McGuire, J. & Priestley, P. (1985). *Offending behaviour: Skills and stratagems for going straight.* London: Batsford.

McMahon, G., Hall, A., Hayward, G., Hudson, C. & Roberts, C. (2004). *Basic skills programmes in the probation service: An evaluation of the basic skills pathfinder.* Home Office Research Findings No. 203. London: Home Office.

McMurran, M. & McCulloch, A. (2005). *Why don't offenders complete treatment? Prisoners' reasons for non-completion of a cognitive skills programme.* Report to HM Prison Service.

McMurran, M. & Theodosi, E. (2005). *Is offender treatment non-completion associated with increased reconviction over no treatment?* Report to HM Prison Service.

Meichenbaum, D. (1977). *Cognitive-behavior modification: An integrative approach.* New York: Plenum Press.

Merrington, S. & Stanley, S. (2000). Doubts about the What Works initiative. *Probation Journal, 47*, 272–275.

Merrington, S. & Stanley, S. (2004). What works? Revisiting the evidence in England and Wales. *Probation Journal, 51*, 7–20.

Merrington, S. & Stanley, S. (2005). Some thoughts on recent research on pathfinder programmes in the Probation Service. *Probation Journal, 52*, 289–292.

National Probation Directorate (2004a). *Annual Report for Accredited Programmes 2003–2004.* London: Home Office.

National Probation Directorate (2004b). *Offending Behaviour Programmes: Cognitive Skills Booster and CALM Programmes.* Probation Circular 05/2005. London: Home Office.

Nezu, A. M. & D'Zurilla, T. J. (1981). Effects of problem definition and formulation on the generation of alternatives in the social problem-solving process. *Cognitive Therapy and Research, 5*, 265–271.

Nietzel, M. T. (1979). *Crime and its modification: A social learning perspective.* New York: Pergamon Press.

Novaco, R. W. (1975). *Anger control: Development and evaluation of an experimental treatment.* Lexington, KT: D. C. Heath.

Ogloff, J. R. P. & Davis, M. R. (2004). Advances in offender assessment and rehabilitation: Contributions of the risk-needs-responsivity approach. *Psychology, Crime and Law, 10*, 229–242.

Ong, G., Al-Attar, Z., Roberts, C. & Harsent, L. (2003). *Think First: An accredited community-based cognitive-behavioural programme in England and Wales. Findings from the prospective evaluation in three Probation Areas.* Oxford: Probation Studies Unit, Centre for Criminological Research, University of Oxford.

Palmer, E. J. (2003). *Offending behaviour: Moral reasoning, criminal conduct and the rehabilitation of offenders.* Cullompton: Willan Publishing.

Palmer, T. (1996). Programmatic and non-programmatic aspects of successful intervention. In A. T. Harland (Ed.), *Choosing correctional options that work: Defining the demand and evaluating the supply* (pp. 131–182). Thousand Oaks, CA: Sage Publications.

Patterson, G. R. (1982). *Coercive family process.* Eugene, OR: Castalia Publishing Company.

Pearson, F. S., Lipton, D. S. & Cleland, C. M. (1997). *Rehabilitative programs in adult corrections: CDATE meta-analyses.* Paper presented at the Annual Meeting of the American Society of Criminology, San Diego, November.

Platt, J. J., Perry, G. & Metzger, D. (1980). The evaluation of a heroin addiction treatment program within a correctional environment. In R. R. Ross & P. Gendreau (Eds), *Effective correctional treatment* (pp. 419–438). Toronto: Butterworths.

Porporino, F. J. & Fabiano, E. A. (2000). *Theory manual for Reasoning and Rehabilitation* (revised). Ottawa: T3 Associates.

Priestley, P. (2000). *Theory manual for One-to-One programme.* Prepared for the Joint Prison Probation Accreditation Panel.

Priestley, P., McGuire, J., Flegg, D., Barnitt, R., Welham, D. & Hemsley, V. (1984). *Social skills in prisons and the community: Problem-solving for offenders.* London: Routledge.

Raynor, P. (2004a). Seven ways to misunderstand evidence-based probation. In D. Smith (Ed.), *Social work and evidence-based practice* (pp. 161–178). London: Jessica Kingsley Publishers.

Raynor, P. (2004b). The Probation Service "Pathfinders": Finding the path and losing the way? *Criminal Justice, 4*, 309–325.

Raynor, P. & Vanstone, M. (1996). Reasoning and rehabilitation in Britain: The results of the Straight Thinking on Probation (STOP) programme. *International Journal of Offender Therapy and Comparative Criminology, 40*, 272–284.

Redondo, S., Sánchez-Meca, J. & Garrido, V. (2002). Crime treatment in Europe: A review of outcome studies. In J. McGuire (Ed.), *Offender rehabilitation and treatment: Effective programmes and policies to reduce re-offending* (pp. 113–141). Chichester: John Wiley & Sons.

Rex, S., Gelsthorpe, L., Roberts, C. & Jordan, P. (2004). *What's promising in community service: Implementation of seven Pathfinder projects.* Home Office Research Findings No. 231. London: Home Office.

Roberts, C. (2004). An early evaluation of a cognitive offending behaviour programme ("Think First") in probation areas. *Vista: Perspectives on Probation, 8*, 130–136.

Robinson, D. (1995). *The impact of cognitive skills training on post-release recidivism among Canadian federal offenders.* Report R-41. Ottawa: Correctional Service of Canada.

Robinson, D., Grossman, M. & Porporino, F. (1991). *Effectiveness of the Cognitive Skills Training Program: From Pilot to national implementation.* Report B-07. Ottawa: Correctional Service of Canada.

Robinson, D. & Porporino, F. J. (2001). Programming in cognitive skills: The reasoning and rehabilitation programme. In C. R. Hollin (Ed.), *Handbook of offender assessment and treatment* (pp. 179–193). Chichester: John Wiley & Sons.

Ross, R. R., Antonowicz, D. H. & Dhaliwal, G. K. (1995). *Going Straight: The Reasoning and Rehabilitation Program for delinquency prevention and offender rehabilitation.* Ottawa: AIR Training and Publications.

Ross, R. R. & Fabiano, E. A. (1985a). *Reasoning and Rehabilitation: Manual.* Ottawa: AIR Training & Associates.

Ross, R. R. & Fabiano, E. A. (1985b). *Time to think: A cognitive model of delinquency prevention and offender rehabilitation.* Johnson City, TN: Institute of Social Sciences and Arts, Inc.

Ross, R. R., Fabiano, E. A. & Ewles, C. D. (1988). Reasoning and Rehabilitation. *International Journal of Offender Therapy and Comparative Criminology, 32,* 29–36.

Ross, R. R. & Hilborn, J. (2005). *R&R2: Short Version for Adults.* Riga: Cognitive Centre of Estonia.

Ross, R. R. & Hilborn, J. (in press). *Time to think again: A prosocial competence model for the treatment of antisocial behaviour.* Ottawa: Cognitive Centre of Canada.

Ross, R. R. & McKay, H. B. (1979). *Self-mutilation.* Lexington, MA: D. C. Heath & Co.

Ross, R. R. & Ross, R. D. (Eds), (1995). *Thinking straight: The Reasoning and Rehabilitation Program for delinquency prevention and offender rehabilitation.* Ottawa: AIR Training and Publications.

Russell, M. N. (2002). Changing beliefs of spouse abusers. In J. McGuire (Ed.), *Offender rehabilitation and treatment: Effective programmes and policies to reduce re-offending* (pp. 243–258). Chichester: John Wiley & Sons.

Shure, M. B., Spivack, G. & Jaeger, M. (1972). Problem-solving thinking and adjustment among disadvantaged preschool children. *Child Development, 42,* 1791–1803.

Simourd, L. & Andrews, D. A. (1994). Correlates of delinquency: A look at gender differences. *Forum on Corrections Research, 6,* 26–31.

Spivack, G. & Levine, M. (1963). *Self-regulation in acting-out and normal adolescents.* Report No. M-4531. Washington, DC: National Institute of Health.

Spivack, G., Platt, J. J. & Shure, M. B. (1976). *The problem-solving approach to adjustment.* San Francisco, CA: Jossey-Bass.

Steele, R. (2002a). *Psychometric features of Think First participants pre and post programme.* Research and Information Section, National Probation Service, Merseyside.

Steele, R. (2002b). *Reconviction of offenders on Think First.* Research and Information Section, National Probation Service, Merseyside.

Stewart-Ong, G., Harsent, L., Roberts, C., Burnett, R. & Al-Attar, Z. (2003). *Think First prospective research study: Effectiveness and reducing attrition.* London: National Probation Service for England and Wales.

Thornberry, T. P. (1987). Toward an interactional theory of delinquency. *Criminology, 25,* 863–891.

Thornberry, T. P. (1996). Empirical support for interactional theory: A review of the literature. In J. D. Hawkins (Ed.), *Delinquency and Crime: Current theories* (pp. 198–235). Cambridge: Cambridge University Press.

Thornberry, T. P., Lizotte, A. J., Krohn, M. D., Smith, C. A. & Porter, P. (2003). Causes and consequences of delinquency: Findings from the Rochester Youth Development Study. In T. P. Thornberry & M. D. Krohn (Eds), *Taking stock of delinquency: An overview of findings from contemporary longitudinal studies* (pp. 11–46). New York: Kluwer Academic/Plenum Publishers.

Tong, L. S. J. & Farrington, D. P. (2006). How effective is the "Reasoning and Rehabilitation" programme in reducing re-offending? A meta-analysis of evaluations in three countries. *Psychology, Crime and Law, 12,* 3–24.

Van Voorhis, P., Spruance, L. M., Ritchey, P. N., Listwan, S. J. & Seabrook, R. (2004). The Georgia cognitive skills experiment: A replication of Reasoning and Rehabilitation. *Criminal Justice and Behavior, 31*, 282–305.

Ward, T., Hudson, S. M. & Keenan, T. R. (2001). The assessment and treatment of sexual offenders against children. In C. R. Hollin (Ed.), *Handbook of offender assessment and treatment* (pp. 349–361). Chichester: John Wiley & Sons.

Warr, M. & Stafford, M. (1991). The influence of delinquent peers: What they think or what they do? *Criminology, 29*, 851–866.

Westmarland, N., Hester, M., Reid, P., Coulson, S. & Hughes, J. (2002). *An investigation into the factors associated with attrition in the Northumbria Probation Think First Programme.* Sunderland: International Centre for the Study of Violence and Abuse, University of Sunderland.

Wilkinson, J. (2005). Evaluating evidence for the effectiveness of the Reasoning and Rehabilitation programme. *The Howard Journal of Criminal Justice, 44*, 70–85.

Williams, N. (1995). Cognitive skills groupwork. *Issues in Criminological and Legal Psychology, 23*, 22–30.

Wilson, D. B., Bouffard, L. A. & MacKenzie, D. L. (2005). A quantitative review of structured, group-oriented, cognitive-behavioral programs for offenders. *Criminal Justice and Behavior, 32*, 172–204.

Wilson, D. B., Gallagher, C. A. & MacKenzie, D. L. (2000). A meta-analysis of corrections-based education, vocation and work programs for adult offenders. *Journal of Research in Crime and Delinquency, 37*, 568–581.

Wilson, R. J. (2005). Are cognitive problem-solving skills programmes really not working? A response to "Evaluating evidence for the effectiveness of the Reasoning and Rehabilitation Programme". *The Howard Journal of Criminal Justice, 44*, 319–321.

Wilson, S., Attrill, G. & Nugent, F. (2003). Effective interventions for acquisitive offenders: An investigation of cognitive skills programmes. *Legal and Criminological Psychology, 8*, 83–101.

Wilson, S. J., Lipsey, M. W. & Soydan, H. (2003). Are mainstream programs for juvenile delinquency less effective with minority youth than majority youth? A meta-analysis of outcomes research. *Research on Social Work Practice, 13*, 3–26.

Wright, B. R. E., Caspi, A., Moffitt, T. E. & Silva, P. A. (2001). The effects of social ties on crime vary by criminal propensity: A life-course model of interdependence. *Criminology, 39*, 321–351.

Zamble, E. & Porporino, F. J. (1988). *Coping, behavior and adaptation in prison inmates.* New York: Springer.

Zamble, E. & Quinsey, V. L. (1997). *The criminal recidivism process.* Cambridge: Cambridge University Press.

Chapter 4

VIOLENT OFFENDER PROGRAMMES: CONCEPT, THEORY, AND PRACTICE

Devon L. L. Polaschek

Victoria University of Wellington, New Zealand

INTRODUCTION

Several distinct traditions have emerged in interventions for criminally violent behaviour. Programmes addressing partner-assault have – for the most part – developed quite separately from those for more generally violent offenders. Recently, strong interest has also developed regarding what to do with the highest risk people, especially those with severe forms of personality pathology such as psychopathy. This chapter reviews each of these areas in turn. Each section presents the programme rationale, evidence base, content and application, and outcome data. I conclude by noting the most pressing needs for further development, and consider areas in which these separate fields could inform each other. Research on women perpetrators, violence in gay and lesbian couples, and child abuse is largely omitted due to space constraints.

As the overwhelming majority of what is known concerns male perpetrators, the male pronoun will be used. The definition of violent behaviour central to this chapter mainly comprises *acts recognised as criminal forms of physical violence, whether or not they have been formally detected*. Even within this definition, however, the extent and severity of these acts varies widely.

PROGRAMMES FOR MEN WHO HAVE ASSAULTED THEIR PARTNERS

Family violence is a particularly dramatic example of changing cultural mores and laws. Undoubtedly there is more progress to be made, but legislative changes over the last century in the Western world give women and children better protection from regular beatings, injury and premature death at the hands of the male head

Offending Behaviour Programmes: Development, Application, and Controversies. Edited by C.R. Hollin and E.J. Palmer.
Copyright © 2006 John Wiley & Sons Ltd.

of the household than in much of "civilised" human history (Gelles, 1993). This section traces the most important trends over the last 30 years. The term *intimate partner violence* (IPV) will be used predominately to refer to physical assaults by men on their domestic partners.

Feminist activism since the 1970s has greatly increased the visibility of men's IPV, and driven the development of interventions to protect women and children. However, recent scientific research suggests that significant reforms of programme provision for IPV perpetrators will be justified in the years ahead. Developmental and epidemiological research indicates that politically determined standards create programmes that may not meet the criminogenic needs of some men, and even that the programme theory needs re-examination.

Before discussing IPV programmes one central controversy must be addressed: that of gender and violence (see Archer, 2000; Felson, 2002 for reviews). For years, heated debate has surrounded the issue of whether women or men are "the most violent" in intimate partnerships, with each side supported by incompatible research traditions. Briefly, a theoretical perspective that IPV occurs in a mutual combat context has its roots in the family conflict perspective of Straus and Gelles (for example Straus & Gelles, 1986), whose data derive primarily from national community surveys. An opposing feminist perspective supported primarily from shelter and criminal justice system data is that men's IPV is part of a wider pattern of patriarchal control and complete domination of their partners' lives (Johnson, 1995), that the violence they subject their partners to is severe – even life-threatening – and that women can do little or nothing to stop it or to escape.

The debate is relevant to this review for two reasons. First, underlying it are two different theoretical rationales that imply distinct intervention strategies, and second, it is likely that patterns of IPV – who does it, in response to what, how severe is it, and other contextual factors – vary quite widely. Johnson (1995) has argued that these two research traditions tap into two somewhat distinct phenomena: (a) *common couple violence* (CCV) involving acts of relatively minor violence by either partner arising from escalated conflict and more highly represented in Straus and colleagues' survey research; and (b) *patriarchal terrorism* (PT) captured by feminist researchers working with shelter women fleeing from rarer cases of severe harm occurring "in a context of economic subordination, threats, isolation, and other control tactics" (Johnson, 1995, p. 284).

Most current interventions assume that, in Johnson's terms, offenders are PTs. However, Johnson's distinction – while a useful rubric – probably oversimplifies IPV heterogeneity. For example, Ehrensaft, Moffitt & Caspi's (2004) most severe were suggestive of *mutual* non-defensive violence.

RATIONALES FOR INTIMATE PARTNER VIOLENCE PROGRAMMES

Levels of Theory

Theories of IPV vary in whether they propose a single cause or multiple factors to explain behaviour. Multi-factorial theories purport to explain the heterogeneity of why individuals behave in an abusive manner through differences in the interactions of factors whose relevance varies for individual offenders. Competent single-factor theories primarily unpack the structures and processes associated with a particular factor that is seen to operate aetiologically in concert with others (Ward, Polaschek & Beech, 2005). However, older, less adequate single-factor theories implausibly promote themselves as complete etiological explanations, yet often lack detail about how the factor operates to increase risk.

The second relevant distinction is between specific theories and their source theories. Theoretical traditions (for example, psychodynamic, family-systemic, cognitive-behavioural) are often used as a basis on which to categorise theories. Ward et al. (2005) call these *source theories:* they specify very broad discipline-level principles about how general psychological phenomena function, but do not tell us exactly which factors are causal. So, specific theories built on the same source theory can vary widely and may be more or less adequate. For example, a programme based on social learning theory (the source theory) will assume that violent behaviour is learned and new non-violent behaviour may also be learned. However, in the history of IPV programmes this programme could target anger as the main cause of this violence, or patriarchal attitudes. Each intervention will be broadly cognitive-behavioural but the specific content and objectives of each programme will vary significantly.

Multi-factorial Frameworks

Truly multi-factorial theories are not evident in the domain, but several authors have suggested multi-factorial frameworks.

Ecological Frameworks

Dutton (1985) and Edleson & Tolman (1992) separately have applied Bronfenbrenner's (1979) nested ecological theory of human development to male IPV, thus drawing attention to the importance of factors outside of the perpetrator, and suggesting a range of intervention points (Edleson & Tolman, 1992). Bronfenbrenner delineated three levels of social context. First, the microsystem is the structural unit in which the man commits his assaults: thus it represents his most proximate level of social interaction. In male IPV, the relevant microsystem is likely to be the immediate family, covering such matters as the events that precede his assault, and both partners' responses to it. The macrosystem is the most remote level: it refers to the cultural templates (for example, for gender, ethnicity, social class) that help to shape individuals' most general "road maps" of how relationships work (Edleson & Tolman, 1992). The exosystem operates between the immediate family and the macrosystem: according to Edleson and Tolman, it has only an indirect effect on a violent man because it represents links between microsystems that do not include the man (for example, between agencies responsible for stopping men's IPV). They define links between the man's microsystem and others in his immediate social world as the mesosystem (such as peers, extended family, social services).

Alongside these levels of social context, a final level – the chronosystem – is based on the developmental history of a partner-violent man:[1] Dutton (1985) referred to this as the ontogenetic level.

The ecological framework provides two distinct intervention rationales. First, it can be used to plan, implement and evaluate a comprehensive societal response to male IPV, such as the myriad of 1980s North American community intervention projects (Edleson & Tolman, 1992). The best known of these projects are the Duluth-type models. Clearly in these projects, men's intervention groups are a cog in a much larger machine that aims to gain control of as many of the relevant systemic responses as possible. Edleson and Tolman also outlined how an ecological approach can be implemented in the men's assessment and in-group rehabilitation. This application emphasises social contextual factors in assessment, although intervention differs little from comprehensive feminist/cognitive-behavioural programmes described in a later section. Post-treatment, a full implementation of the model would have IPV men engage in social activism of their own, designed to change their own social networks, and even the wider social institutions that supported their violent behaviour (Edleson & Tolman, 1992). Ecological practitioners thus see a focus on individual men's change as "myopic" at best (Edleson & Tolman, 1992, p. 75).

Multivariate Developmental Models

An alternative source of multivariate models comes from the growing psychological literature on the longitudinal development of IPV risk. Holtzworth-Munroe & Stuart (1994) provide an example that, if developed into a fully-fledged theory, promises to have considerable fertility and explanatory depth. Briefly, their model integrates previous theory from a range of sources, and proposes distinct mixes of distal (genetic and childhood) and proximal (adult) factors in the development of three types of male IPV perpetrators. The three postulated types are: (a) family-only (FO) offenders, men whose assaults are relatively less severe and frequent than others, and occur only towards family members; the perpetrators oppose violent behaviour, have positive attitudes to their partners (Holtzworth-Munroe & Meehan, 2004), and are generally free of serious personality pathology (Holtzworth-Munroe & Stuart, 1994); (b) dysphoric/borderline (DB) men who commit moderately or severely violent acts as well as sexual assaults, but still mainly toward partners, and are psychologically distressed with features of borderline personality disorder and substance abuse; and (c) generally violent and antisocial (GVA) men, who are essentially chronically criminal antisocial or psychopathic individuals who moderately to severely assault their partners, often also sexually assault them, and abuse substances (Holtzworth-Munroe & Meehan, 2004; Holtzworth-Munroe & Stuart, 1994).

Holtzworth-Munroe & Stuart (1994) propose as relevant to the development of and intervention with men's IPV: (a) temperament, childhood family factors and peer experiences (distal factors); and (b) attachment, impulsivity, social skills

---

[1] Edleson and Tolman's *chronosystem* also includes the history of the development of the social systems at each of the levels.

and attitudinal variables (the proximal factors). For example they theorise that, for FO men, genetic influences are not relevant and developmental influences are limited to low to moderate violent victimisation in childhood, and minor involvement with antisocial peers. FO men are capable of empathy but may show insecure attachment – particularly the preoccupied, over-dependent style of attachment – to their proximal partners, will be somewhat impulsive, and may have some social skills deficiencies confined to their intimate relationships.

By contrast, DB men may be genetically predisposed to impulsivity, interpersonal aggression, personality disorder, and psychological distress. Their early family experiences are likely to include abusive and rejecting parental behaviour, and they will have some antisocial peer contacts. Unlike FO men, their attitudes to women and violence will tend to foster IPV. They will have adequate relationship skills but some difficulties with non-domestic social skills.

The development of men in the third group, GVA batterers, is characterised by the presence of most of the hypothesised risk factors for IPV. Holzworth-Munroe & Meehan (2004) suggested that these men will be genetically vulnerable to aggressive, impulsive and antisocial behaviour, and that these vulnerabilities will be enhanced by an abusive home environment, antisocial peer associations, and the development of dismissive attachment, poor empathic and other social skills and attitudes that support violence, hostility towards women and so on. Naturally, these are also risk factors for their diverse antisocial and violent behaviours, of which IPV is simply a subset.

The main implications of these developmental models for intervention is in recognising heterogeneity of both violent behaviour and treatment needs. When used in assessment, better tailoring of a treatment response can be undertaken. For example, DB men are unlikely to thrive in current feminist programmes but may need attachment-related intervention (see later section).

Single-factor Theories

Having examined multi-factorial frameworks, we turn now to three single-factor theories that have taken prominence in intervention: these are feminist, social learning, and family systems theory.

Feminist Explanations

From a psychological perspective, feminist theories draw on both social structure and learning paradigms (Ward et al., 2005). There is no single feminist theory, but the central tenets of this approach are that Western societies are primarily patriarchal in structure, implicitly entitling men to control the lives of women and children from the family level to that of the major social institutions (Stewart, Hill & Cripps, 2001). Within the family, men use physical violence as one of several strategies (including economic and psychological coercion) to maintain the subordination of women partners. Thus, men's IPV is a consequence of the application of learned social norms in the context of a social structure that enshrines male dominance (Adams, 1989).

In the late 1970s feminist theories corrected a misguided trend toward locating the causes of abuse within the psychopathology of individual abusers (Dutton, 1995b; Gelles, 1993), instead inspiring a multi-level programme of social activism designed to meet the needs of battered women (Cunningham et al., 1998). Feminist ideology underlies more programmes for male IPV than any other current theory.

Feminist theories can be seen by psychologists as a form of social learning theory. However, their major weakness – aside from their reductionist single-factor nature – is that there is no mechanism for accounting for the individual diversity that a growing body of research supports. Research findings from testing the theories' central predictions have been contradictory. For example, Sugarman & Frankel (1996) examined 29 studies of the relationships between gender roles and scripts and violence attitudes, and found that IPV offenders did not consistently endorse patriarchal ideology. Dutton's (1995b) review identified other empirical findings that are contrary to feminist predictions, and Dutton (1994) provided an extensive critique of the theory. At its simplest, it suffers from the same fate as all single-factor theories; complex social problems cannot be explained adequately by simple, single-factor responses (Stewart et al., 2001). The highly political nature of feminist theories has also created resistance to scientific evaluation.

Feminist theories have underpinned community intervention projects that include educational groups for perpetrators. Misuse of power and control are a major theme of feminist analyses, and the main focus of these education groups. For example, Pence & Paymar (1993) describe their model as being based on the theoretical idea that violence is used to control others. However, there is no significant explanatory depth in current feminist ideas about power and control; these issues arise in every intimate relationship (Jacobson & Gottman, 1998). The relative importance of the apparent control aspect of IPV remains poorly understood and consequently the empirical literature is confusing and unsupportive.

Social Learning Theory

Social Learning Theory (SLT) is the source theory that provides the underpinning to all cognitive-behavioural interventions: thus, family violence is learned both by direct if intermittent experience of its rewards – particularly through operant conditioning – and by vicarious learning in observing the modelling of others. Social learning theory postulates that children learn IPV-related cognitions and behaviours that ultimately they perpetuate in their adult family lives. It predicts that male children learn IPV from direct exposure to paternal modelling of partner assault, as well as from media, social institutions, peers, and wider social contacts (Cardin, 1994). Having become established as a behaviour, Bandura (1973) would hypothesise – as for aggression in general – that in addition to external reinforcement, IPV is maintained through the internal neutralisation of cognitions that would otherwise discourage such acts through self-censure (for example, depersonalising the victim, blaming alcohol for one's own violence).

Several lines of research provide some support for the influence of early exposure to violence and violent models on later endorsement and use of violence. In general, intergenerational transmission studies suggest a complex and imperfect relationship between childhood exposure and adult behaviour: only some of those who are exposed to violence actually carry it out themselves (see, for example, Stith et al., 2000). Exposure appears mediated by other variables, such as poor conflict resolution skills (Choice, Lamke & Pitman, 1995), alcoholism, and positive attitudes to the use of violence (Stith & Farley, 1993), but most studies that have combined predictors still account for no more than one-third of the variance at best, suggesting that other factors are also important (Capaldi & Clark, 1998; Ehrensaft et al., 2004).

Although SLT has been empirically supported in IPV, the evidence also demonstrates the complexity of what may be learned and how it may interact with other variables to enhance or even protect against adult violent behaviour in relationships (Cunningham et al., 1998). On a positive note, there is clearly little support for the deterministic folk theory that "violence *inevitably* begets violence". Viewing behaviour as learned gives optimism about the possibility of therapeutic change through new learning. Social learning theory's implications for treatment are that (a) violent behaviour and its associated cognitions are likely to be entrenched by adulthood, (b) alternatives to violence can be learned as responses to antecedent stimuli, and (c) IPV men are likely to have a variety of skill deficits that will also need remediation (for example, communication, problem-solving).

Family Systems Theory

Family systemic theoretical approaches are diverse, but remain controversial when applied to the aetiology of IPV (Geffner, Barrett & Rossman, 1995). Family systems (including couple-based) approaches grew from the recognition that intervening with the social system in which an individual was embedded could engender more efficient and effective change (Lane & Russell, 1989). However, some systemic approaches view IPV as the result of a "boundary disturbance in the family system whereby victims and perpetrators are linked in a circular and reciprocal process": in other words the family system itself is seen to maintain violence through "the roles, relations, and feedback mechanisms that regulate and stabilise the system" (Cunningham et al., 1998, p. 501).

For quite obvious reasons, therapeutic approaches based on this assumption brought systemic couples therapy into disrepute with feminist advocates in the 1970s. Amongst other difficulties, these approaches ignored the stability of men's IPV behaviour across relationships, the self-defensive nature of much of their partners' violence, the lack of safety for women in making them partially responsible for change, and the failure to hold perpetrators responsible for their own criminal behaviour.

Empirical investigations *have* found differences in various interaction-related variables for IPV men and women in relationships (see, for example, Babcock, Waltz, Jacobson & Gottman, 1993; Cordova, Jacobson, Gottman, Rushe & Cox, 1993). However, such findings are usually cross-sectional: the direction of causality cannot be established. Couples interventions for IPV are making a comeback on empirical grounds: they are discussed fully later in the chapter.

Borderline Psychopathology

Consistent with typological research, Dutton (1995a) has argued that a milder form of Borderline Personality Disorder, named Borderline Personality Organisation (BPO) causes IPV in some men. According to Dutton, childhood experiences predispose men with BPO to (a) viewing women in black-and-white terms, (b) blaming partners for their cyclical emotional neediness, (c) hypervigilance regarding possible abandonment, and angry responses to perceived attachment threats, and (d) acute anxiety and feelings of emptiness as a result of perceiving that their angry (and violent) behaviour has led to rejection. Dutton has provided some empirical support for his BPO theory (see, for example, Dutton, Saunders, Starzomski & Bartholomew, 1994; Dutton & Starzomski, 1994). Although there is no question that the BPO/attachment anger theory does not account for more than a minority of offenders – perhaps one-quarter according to Holtzworth-Munroe and Meehan (2004) – recent independent research on offender types has found that BPO men do not respond well to other treatments, suggesting that Dutton's work may constitute an important theory regarding treatment (Dutton, Bodnarchuk, Kropp, Hart & Ogloff, 1997; Holtzworth-Munroe & Meehan, 2004), and implying that systematic development of intervention for this group is overdue.

Conclusions

Programme development may lead treatment-related theory as often as it follows it. Programmes integrating feminist and social learning traditions dominate IPV despite no integrated treatment theory. The value of systemic processes is gaining some recognition, but intervention for IPV men with serious borderline personality pathology needs attention.

EVIDENCE BASE FOR IPV PROGRAMME TARGETS

For the last decade or so, there has been a strong emphasis on increasing programme effectiveness by targeting dynamic risk factors for the relevant offending type (see, for example, Andrews & Bonta, 1998). For IPV programmes, recent meta-analyses and better longitudinal studies of potentially changeable risk factors for IPV permit inferences about likely treatment targets. In one meta-analysis of dynamic predictors, Stith, Smith, Penn, Ward & Tritt (2004b) found that employment, education, and jealousy showed small effect sizes, attitude measures (support for violence, and traditional sex role ideology), marital dissatisfaction, anger or hostility, career or life stress, alcohol use, and depression obtained moderate effect sizes, and a large effect size was found for illicit drugs. Earlier narrative reviews (Holtzworth-Munroe, Bates, Smutzler & Sandin, 1997; Schumacher, Feldbau-Kohn, Slep & Heyman, 2001) support these findings and implicate other factors too, such as problem-solving, communication and assertiveness skills; and psychopathology as with antisocial personality, borderline personality, impulsivity, depression, attachment style (for example, dependence, fear of abandonment, suspicion, high nurturance needs, jealousy), and need for power.

Longitudinal research suggests the importance of the construct of *negative emotionality*, which appears to overlap a number of factors identified above. Moffitt, Robins & Caspi (2001) demonstrated the importance of this factor in predicting serious IPV in men and women. Negative emotionality is a complex but psychometrically robust construct (John & Srivastava, 1999) that encompasses a tendency towards experiencing affective volatility, anxiety, anger and fear, callousness, suspicion and hostility towards others, an expectation that others are out to harm one, and the enjoyment and pursuit of revenge towards others. Management of these propensities would thus appear to be an essential treatment target.

Ehrensaft et al. (2004) found, in the same New Zealand birth cohort, that IPV men had childhood externalising problems and adolescent psychopathology such as conduct disorder and attention deficit disorder. By adulthood, they exhibited enduring "disinhibitory behavioural pathology" (p. 268), an entrenched habit of using coercion to resolve interpersonal differences (Magdol, Moffitt, Caspi & Silva, 1998). Capaldi, Dishion, Stoolmiller & Yoerger (2001) found evidence of deviancy training effects: mutual hostile talk amongst peers at age 17 to 18 years predicted male IPV 3 to 5 years later, independently of antisocial and delinquent behaviour.

Norlander & Eckhardt (2005) report a meta-analysis of the role of anger and hostility in IPV. Anger is a particularly interesting variable to examine because anger management – rather like couples-based interventions – has been prohibited for use with IPV in many US state guidelines, on which state funding is contingent (Healey, Smith & O'Sullivan, 1998).

Although it is not yet clear theoretically *how* anger is related to violence, Norlander & Eckhardt's (2005) meta-analysis of 33 studies found that anger and hostility scores could distinguish IPV men from non-violent and maritally distressed men, and could distinguish men committing moderate/severe acts from those whose acts were of low/moderate severity. Of course these are correlational designs, but when taken in conjunction with the developmental research suggesting that negative emotionality does precede IPV, they argue for reconsidering anger and hostility as programme targets. Norlander & Eckhardt (2005) point out that the relevance of alcohol abuse as a dynamic risk factor was also often overlooked in treatment until recently (O'Farrell, Murphy, Stephan, Fals-Stewart & Murphy, 2004).

There are numerous methodological difficulties with the research reviewed in this section. The most serious problems are those of heterogeneity of offenders, and reliance on cross-sectional designs and official convictions. Overall, many of the factors identified above are not new, although significant progress has recently emerged in establishing that two of the most common, alcohol and drug abuse, and anger/hostility, are likely to constitute dynamic risks for IPV. Despite its weaknesses, this research suggests that IPV men have a range of treatment needs and it follows that the content of programmes should be tailored to the client group, and that individual assessment should lead to allocation to programmes that match identified needs.

PROGRAMME CONTENT AND APPLICATION ISSUES FOR IPV PROGRAMMES

Although a number of theories and frameworks with treatment implications were reviewed earlier, there are just three types of mainstream programmes: profeminist, cognitive-behavioural, and couples approaches.

Pro-feminist Group Programmes

Since the mid-1970s, educational group programmes have dominated the thera-peutic landscape. They seek to teach men that their IPV is part of a cluster of strategies for controlling women partners, and that it does not occur impulsively, or unpredictably (Mederos, 1999). These programmes hold men entirely respon-sible for their behaviour, and seek information from others (partners, courts) to ascertain the accuracy of batterers' reports. The Duluth model is the best known of these types of programme. "Duluth-style" programmes have proliferated through North America, the UK, and other Western nations (Balzer, 1999; Bilby & Hatcher, 2004; Dobash, Dobash, Cavanagh & Lewis, 1996). In this model, male batterer in-terventions exist within a community-based systemic response to IPV, which also coordinates agencies and government operations (such as police, courts, victim services, corrections) so that they share a common philosophy about IPV, commu-nicate with each other, and use their institutionalised power to ensure that IPV is treated as a crime that results in consistent sanctions.

Duluth's men's education programmes are not considered to engender change in men on their own, but rather, are thought to act in concert with consistent mes-sages and sanctions from other parts of the system. Groups usually comprise five to 15 mainly court-mandated men, with two facilitators, and comprise around 26 weeks of once-a-week sessions. The groups are often referred to as "psycho-educational" (see Adams, 1989), primarily because a core part of their content is facilitator-led pro-feminist analyses of IPV men's behaviour. The *power and control* and the *equality* wheels are used to focus IPV men on identifying their own abusive behaviour at the broadest level, and developing acceptable alternatives.

Pro-feminist programmes vary in the extent to which they include other treatment components. Participants may also be offered brief coverage of more traditional cognitive-behavioural skills for relationship development and anger management; for example, cognitive restructuring, self-talk strategies, time out, relaxation techniques, and other methods of arousal reduction (Edleson & Tolman, 1992; Pence, 1989).

Cognitive-behavioural Interventions

The term *cognitive-behavioural* refers to the source theory that informs us that the programme is broadly based on operant and respondent conditioning principles, and on social learning theory. As Saunders (1989) noted

> There is no monolithic theory or integrated set of procedures that can be called "cognitive-behavioral". Rather the term covers a collection of principles and procedures that many practitioners have not attempted to link theoretically. (Saunders, 1989, p. 77)

In the mid-1980s, *cognitive-behavioural* IPV programmes – again, in keeping with interventions throughout the offender rehabilitation domain – targeted individual offenders' anger, and were not as cognisant of social and socio-cultural influences on offending. These programmes were accused of the promotion of "non-violent terrorism" in an influential paper by Gondolf & Russell (1986). They suggested that this naïve, essentially folk model of why men hit their partners (Tavris, 1989) *increased* the danger to women and children. However, no empirical data were provided to support this view, and the pro-feminist backlash against anger management has probably stifled important research (Norlander & Eckhardt, 2005). Traditional elements of anger management are still built into programmes as noted above (such as time out, cognitive restructuring, relaxation training). However, as at 2006, although cognitive-behavioural and pro-feminist programmes can still be distinguished, considerable convergence exists in the predominant approach of "gender-based cognitive-behavioral counselling" (Gondolf, 2004, p. 606). Saunders & Hamill (2003) note succinctly that such programmes integrate the following four elements:

1. Skills training [that] is based on social learning assumptions about the behavioral deficits and behavioral excesses of offenders. Modeling of positive behavior by group leaders and behavioral rehearsal by members are used in skill-building approaches to enhance relationship skills that replace destructive behaviors.
2. Cognitive approaches [that] assume that faulty patterns of thinking lead to negative emotions, which in turn lead to abusive behavior. Restructuring of these thoughts is likely to reduce anger and the fear and hurt that often underlies it. These approaches can also be used to help men become aware of the core belief systems they developed in childhood, including rigid beliefs about gender roles.
3. Sex role resocialization [that] helps men see the negative effects of constricted male roles and the benefits of gender equality. Male dominance is viewed as one of the effects of this rigid socialization.
4. Methods to build awareness of control tactics [that] are designed to help men take ownership of their intentions to control others. An emphasis is placed on expanding the definition of abuse to include isolation, demeaning language, control of finances, and other means of control. Awareness is also built about the impact of the abuse on and building empathy for victims. (Saunders & Hamill, 2003, pp. 2–3)

The development of batterer programme standards has had an important influence on programme development. Today, such standards operate in 43 US states (Batterers' Intervention Services Coalition Michigan, 2002), and adherence is often mandatory for programmes that receive state funding (Austin & Dankwort, 1997; Tolman, 2001). There are strengths to mandated accreditation criteria: promotion of high standards of practice, collaboration between stakeholders and accountability. However, these standards have generally developed without reference to scientific research (Babcock, Green & Robie, 2004), and are so prescriptive in their laudable desire to protect victims that they stifle innovation.

At their worst, batterer standards represent the current "enshrining of early blind spots into rigid standards of practice" (Mederos, 1999, p. 136). Mederos noted further that

The aversion to approaches that do not focus on accountability has crystallised into a fear that to focus on other issues with batterers means a wholesale abandonment of concern for safety of battered women and for holding offenders responsible for their conduct. (Mederos, 1999, p. 135)

Mederos argued that the goals of such programmes are too narrow; they fail to recognise that there is heterogeneity among offenders' programme needs (for example, alcohol and drug problems).

Couple Counselling Approaches

Conjoint approaches have struggled to gain acceptability in recent years, no matter how carefully they may be implemented (Trute, 1998). There are two main concerns with these approaches: (a) that in conjoint intervention the woman victim is held at least partly responsible for her own victimisation, and (b) that couples work exposes her to increased danger, particularly if the partner is a patriarchal terrorist type (O'Leary, Hayman & Neidig, 1999). Consequently, couple counselling approaches are viewed as an inappropriate initial intervention in most batterer programme standards (Austin & Dankwort, 1997). For state-funded programmes, standards commonly either prohibit such interventions at any point (Healey et al., 1998), or at least until the IPV man has completed a group men's intervention and then achieved 6 months to a year free of violence (Austin & Dankwort, 1997), the so-called "second phase" approach to couple therapy (Trute, 1998).

There are two possible applications of conjoint therapy: (a) when one partner is the main perpetrator and the other wants to support him in stopping violence and making changes (for example, improving marital satisfaction), and (b) when both partners are instigators of violence. A third possibility, based on violence instigated by the woman partner only, has not yet received significant attention. If both partners are violent, as community-based research suggests, intervening with just one is unlikely to be effective (Stith, Rosen, McCollum & Thomsen, 2004a). Indeed, New Zealand longitudinal cohort research found that mild aggression was the domain of woman partners alone, and that moderate to serious violence was perpetrated by both partners (Ehrensaft et al., 2004). Such findings suggest the need to keep an open mind when assessing individuals' relationship violence patterns and intervention needs. It is likely that one cause of programme dropout, a serious problem in IPV intervention, may be the lack of fit between the client(s) goals – particularly in improving the quality of their domestic relationship – and the programme's narrow focus on stopping male aggression (Brown, O'Leary & Feldbau, 1997), regardless of context.

Of course, a great deal of caution should be exercised in offering conjoint approaches to couples where the man has been identified as violent. Guidelines have been suggested to meet these concerns. First, at the point of referral, care must be taken to ascertain accurately each partner's subjective experience. Both partners need to be motivated to stop their own violent behaviour (if present), and to continue with and improve their relationship (Stith et al., 2004b). If there is evidence of intimidation or subjugation (Jacobson & Gottman, 1998) or one partner – usually the woman – shows any anxiety or fear about a joint intervention, or does not wish to continue their relationship, if couples refuse to remove weapons from their houses or to sign a non-violence contract (Stith et al. 2004b), then a couples approach is certainly contraindicated (Greene & Bogo, 2002). Such information should be elicited, at least in part, from individual interviews with each partner. Similarly, evidence that either partner has needed medical attention for injuries, or that the man has ongoing alcohol dependence or a significant DSM-IV Axis I disorder are common exclusion criteria (O'Leary et al., 1999; Trute, 1998). Once a couple has been cleared to begin conjoint intervention, protocols regarding confidentiality of individual partners' information and ongoing individual safety assessments are vital to responsible implementation of such programmes (for example, Stith et al., 2004b).

Conjoint treatment can be delivered to individual couples, or in group format. Aside from the likely greater efficiency for service providers, the group approach has the advantage of providing additional social support for couples, the opportunity to learn from other couples' experiences, for other group members to challenge and influence one partner, and to raise issues that cannot be broached successfully at home (Stith, Rosen & McCollum, 2002; Stith et al., 2004a). There are advantages for therapists too. Men may behave more respectfully and indulge less in verbal "woman-bashing" when women are present. It may also be easier to observe evidence of how the man controls his partner, and other significant relationship dynamics, and consequently to make more rapid gains in having him take responsibility for his behaviour, and in enhancing his partner's ability to keep herself safe (Bograd & Mederos, 1999).

Stith and colleagues (Stith et al., 2004a; Stith, McCollum, Rosen & Locke, 2002; Stith, Rosen et al., 2002) offer one such programme: the Domestic Violence Focused Couples Treatment (DVFCT). They describe this programme as an integrative approach that includes feminist tenets, several family therapy models, and solution-focused therapy. Each partner attends gender-specific groups for at least 6 weeks prior to commencing conjoint treatment. The conjoint treatment has been offered for individual couples, and in groups (see the next section on treatment outcome). The treatment is manualised and is 12 sessions long.

Another well-established approach is Physical Aggressive Couples' Treatment (PACT), developed originally by Neidig and colleagues (see Heyman & Neidig, 1997; Neidig & Friedman, 1984) in which six to eight bi-directionally violent couples and male and female co-therapists work through a curriculum of about 14 sessions. Couples first learn to take responsibility for their own violent behaviour, how to cease all forms of violence (psychological and physical), and how to identify angry cognitions and manage them better. In later sessions relationship wellbeing and skills become the focus: improving communication skills, increasing positive relationship experiences and activities, and increasing respect for their partner (Cunningham et al., 1998; O'Leary et al., 1999). Physical Aggressive Couples' Treatment has been adapted for use with individual couples, and as a "second phase" intervention.

Conjoint couple approaches are likely to be particularly useful with voluntary clients, who often enter treatment because of marital distress and may not even disclose that one or both parties is violent (O'Leary et al., 1999). In addition to the exclusionary criteria reviewed above, their use with court-mandated clients is likely to be constrained by the high proportion who are not currently in a relationship (O'Leary et al., 1999).

OUTCOME EVIDENCE FOR IPV PROGRAMMES

The current consensus is either that IPV intervention has no effect (for example Hilton & Harris, 2005) or that it has a very small effect on subsequent offending (for example Bowen & Gilchrist, 2004). The difference in interpretation is accounted for by dispute over acceptable methodological standards, and poor evaluation design (see Chapter 2 for a fuller discussion of these issues). Most outcome studies are simply single-group post-test only or pre- and post-test designs (Davis & Taylor, 1999), or have compared treatment completers' outcomes with a comparison group – usually dropouts – when a substantial proportion of participants has dropped out. Selection bias in these quasi-experimental designs makes findings uninterpretable. Just four studies have used matched control groups of untreated offenders instead of dropouts. However, all have substantial methodological flaws that should have biased findings towards positive programme effects. Yet they found little or no difference in favour of treatment (Davis & Taylor, 1999).

Theoretically, the gold standard for human intervention evaluation design is the "true experiment" (Babcock et al., 2004), where potential participants are randomly allocated to different levels of intervention, usually including a no-intervention condition. In practice, even with quite large samples random allocation can still result in pre-test group differences on important characteristics. A strength of the IPV evaluation literature is that there have been at least five studies where allocation to intervention conditions has been randomised: Davis, Taylor, and Maxwell (1998) (see also Jackson et al., 2003); Dunford, 2000; Feder & Forde (1999) (see also Jackson et al., 2003), Ford & Regoli (1993), and Palmer, Brown & Berrera (1992). None of these programmes found a significant effect for group treatment versus no treatment using partner reports. However, attrition from the treatment groups ranged from 29 % to 60 %, creating a likely sampling bias despite initial randomisation. In addition, in Feder and Forde's study, administrative criminal justice issues (such as judicial "overrides") may have compromised random allocation in the first place (Babcock et al., 2004).

Davis & Taylor (1999) calculated effect sizes for the five best designed studies available at the time: they used an effect size statistic that did not control for sample size, and simply averaged the resulting statistics to estimate overall treatment effects. Three were quasi-experimental designs with a matched control group (not dropouts), and the other two were randomised experimental designs. Outcome relied on police records and overall effect sizes for each type of study were small.

Babcock et al. (2004) published the only true meta-analysis of treatment outcome to date. It is based on 22 studies from an original pool of 70: 48 studies without a comparison group or outcome data in the form of police or victim reports were eliminated to leave the five experimental studies mentioned above and 17 quasi-experimental studies, most of which still used only dropouts as comparisons. Therefore these studies suffer from likely pre-treatment differences between completers and dropouts that are biased towards producing an apparent treatment effect even when there is not one. By contrast, since the experimental studies suffer from significant dropout rates but retain dropouts' data in the treatment group outcome analyses, they inflate the likelihood of finding that the programme is ineffective when it actually works (Barbaree, 1997) because they count among the treated men those who were exposed only to little or no treatment (Gondolf, 2004).

With these limitations in mind, Babcock et al.'s (2004) main findings were as follows: (a) the method of recidivism report (police vs partner) had no influence on effect size, (b) regardless of report type, the effect size for experimental designs was negligible and a small effect size was found for quasi-experimental designs, (c) evaluations of Duluth-type programmes produced a small effect size with police reports, (d) CBT-type programmes (n = 3)[2] had no significant effect on recidivism in quasi-experimental studies that used police reports, (e) in quasi-experiments that used partner reports, both Duluth interventions and CBT had small effect sizes, and (f) there was no significant difference overall in effect sizes for experimental versus quasi-experimental designs (see Babcock et al., 2004; Gondolf, 2001; for detailed reviews of these studies).

Thus the most optimistic conclusion that can be reached – based on a liberal interpretation of what constitutes acceptable methodological rigour – is that the best programmes may help a little. However, there are so many possibilities for both programme and evaluation development that pessimism about effectiveness must be premature.

Gondolf and colleagues have led the way in developing evaluation approaches that address some of the concerns with the current research base, many of which have not even been covered here (see Gondolf, 2004). Two of his solutions are (a) multi-site evaluation designs, and (b) propensity analysis. Gondolf and colleagues employed a naturalistic design to compare IPV programmes across four sites. Within each site completers were compared with men who dropped out earlier than 2 months into the programme (a quasi-experimental design) and all four were typical pro-feminist cognitive-behavioural programmes. However, there were numerous differences between programmes: some included referral to additional interventions for alcohol or psychological difficulties, some were pre- and others post-conviction, programme length varied from 3 to 9 months, and so on. This well-resourced evaluation was able to follow 840 men and their female partners for four years from intake, collecting progress data periodically, and producing a raft of publications.

In contrast to much of the previous research, Gondolf & Jones (2001) found a medium effect size across all of the sites, when completers and dropouts were compared: 36% of completers and 55% of dropouts re-assaulted their partners. Using logistic regression to control for pre-existing differences between the two groups reduced this difference by 1%. An alternative analysis based on a form of structural equation modelling also found a moderate effect size (Gondolf & Jones, 2001). No significant differences were found across programmes over 30 months of follow-up (Gondolf, 2000).

Jones, D'Agostino, Gondolf & Heckert (2004) reported on a propensity score analysis conducted with the same data. Perhaps the most methodologically sophisticated technique yet used in IPV evaluations, propensity score analysis enables the

---

[2] Babcock et al. (2004) distinguish cognitive-behavioural programmes from feminist and psychoeducational approaches in their analysis. As noted earlier, and as they note themselves, there are grounds for regarding this distinction as potentially spurious.

matching of drop-outs and completers on their risk of dropping out, and then compares matched participants' recidivism outcome. Essentially, the matching is done by first conducting a logistic regression using variables known to predict treatment attrition. The samples are then divided into quintiles by rank ordering each sample on the propensity score for each case. This method appears to be an effective response to the dilemma of overestimating versus underestimating effectiveness by leaving out or including dropouts in the treatment group. Having conducted this analysis, Jones et al. were able to examine the relative re-assault rates in each quintile. Interestingly, overall there was a 13 % difference in favour of treatment completers, in the proportion of men who committed re-assaults for the whole sample, and the difference was in this direction for four of the five quintiles (range 9 % to 29 %). The differences were greater for the lower quintiles (the treatment effect was bigger for those most at risk of dropping out; probably a demonstration of the risk principle at work). Overall, then, Gondolf and colleagues' multi-site evaluation suggests that intervention can be effective with court-ordered men, particularly those who are relatively free of psychopathology (Jones et al., 2004).

Eckhardt, Holtzworth-Munroe, Norlander, Sibley & Cahill (in press) note, there are many differences between programmes that may influence outcome, including the degree to which they are embedded in other sanctions (Gondolf, 1999), perpetrator characteristics, and programme-specific practice differences (for example, consequences for non-attendance, length, range of services). We are a long way yet from understanding which of these factors, and in what combinations, may determine effective versus ineffective outcomes with offenders with particular criminogenic characteristics. However, evaluation design itself seems to be as big a barrier at present to understanding what works.

FUTURE DIRECTIONS FOR IPV PROGRAMMES

In recent decades, IPV programmes have recognised (a) the importance of patriarchal socio-cultural variables in promoting IPV; (b) the dangerousness of patriarchal terrorists and the need to assist women and children in escaping from them; (c) the importance of programme standards that curb some of the therapeutic practices that are most hazardous to women and children, hold perpetrators responsible for their own violent behaviour, promote intervention fidelity and coordinated supporting and sanctioning responses between government agencies, at least where government funding is concerned, and (d) the need for programme evaluation. Although still weak, this evaluation literature looks admirable alongside the research on general violence programmes.

Pro-feminist models do not translate into a plausible treatment theory. The dominant feminist intervention theory for IPV men is by implication that educating them that their attitudes are wrong, and sanctioning them will produce the desired behavioural change: violence desistance. On the face of it this looks like an "insight"-based model. The insight therapies have not generally been found to be effective with any but the lowest risk offenders (Holtzworth-Munroe & Meehan, 2004). However, the dominance of a political ideology over science has curbed innovation in programme development (Wileman, 2000), in part because of a concern that the use of alternative models will jeopardise victim safety. Victim safety is achieved best by (a) retaining system practices of checking independently and safely with different family members about current family safety, (b) retaining policies, legislation and practices that allow victims to remove themselves from relationships with perpetrators, and (c) developing more effective perpetrator intervention programmes. Innovation, particularly in directions consistent with "what works" in the offender rehabilitation literature, will be important in increasing programme impact, particularly in light of the longitudinal research on the characteristics of IPV offenders (Ehrensaft et al., 2004). In particular, the more seriously psychopathological and more broadly criminal subtypes of IPV offenders (for example, GVA and DB; Holtzworth-Munroe & Stuart, 1994), are likely to have a broad range of criminogenic needs that are not targeted in existing FO-type programmes.

In tandem, more research is needed on IPV offenders' criminogenic needs, so that programme evaluation can also examine links between dynamic risk factors and recidivism outcomes (Bowen & Gilchrist, 2004). Very few studies have yet made these links (see Eckhardt et al., in press, for an exception). Subtype research paves the way for programmes that better fit distinct clusters of offender needs.

Risk assessment also should become more routine, although current tools for IPV risk assessment generally perform poorly (Dutton & Kropp, 2000). The offender rehabilitation literature (Andrews & Bonta, 1998) would suggest that higher risk cases should be exposed to more intensive interventions (more hours, more criminogenic needs). Most interventions currently available are at the low intensity end: suited to low-risk, low-needs offenders, and do not screen for offender risk or need. Holzworth-Munroe & Meehan (2004) suggest that only one study to date has looked – even indirectly – at matching programme and offender subtype, but hypothesise that current low-impact IPV interventions may work best with FO men, as may conjoint interventions. Dysphoric/borderline men may need depression-related treatment as an adjunct, and GVA men are particularly likely to need interventions developed for more extensively antisocial individuals (see next section).

Generally violent and antisocial and DB men are probably more likely to be the IPV perpetrators in prison populations. Interventions in these settings are rare (Stewart et al., 2001), despite the prevalence of serious IPV even among low-security non-violent prisoners (White, Gondolf, Robertson, Goodwin & Caraveo, 2002), but should also be considered more often as a potentially more effective way of beginning behavioural change amongst the subtypes most likely to drop out of community-based intervention.

Then there is the issue of women IPV offenders: some women – in addition to, or instead of their partners – perpetrate significant violence within their intimate relationships. Again, cross-sectional research is demonstrating that a small proportion of young women initiate acts of serious violence and currently usually receive no intervention (Moffitt et al., 2001). Their intervention needs require further investigation, as do those of women non-perpetrators who wish to be involved in intervention with their violent male partners.

There is a sizeable body of research on treatment non-completion. Client factors have been investigated quite extensively but programme factors should now be studied too (Rooney & Hanson, 2001). Motivation/treatment readiness, and process issues are important areas for future attention too. Recent studies suggest that many IPV men come into programmes poorly matched to the stage at which the programme is pitched (Eckhardt et al., in press), and that the ability to form a therapeutic alliance also predicts outcome (Taft, Murphy, King, Musser & DeDeyn, 2003; Taft, Murphy, Musser & Remington, 2004).

Finally, cultural identity and match may be an important responsivity issue that has received surprisingly little therapeutic or research attention. Although culturally specific group programmes exist in isolated pockets (see, for example, Balzer, 1999). Gondolf & Williams (2001) observe that these are only one component of a fully integrated cultural initiative, with the need to develop tailored case management and to build specialised links with the wider community to better support change in the relevant men.

PROGRAMMES FOR GENERALLY VIOLENT MEN

Who are generally violent (GV) men? A reasonably robust criminological observation is that about one-half of all crime is carried out by about 5 % of the population (Farrington, Ohlin & Wilson, 1986): a group of predominantly male offenders who start their antisocial behaviour in childhood, and whose careers are characterised both by much more frequent and more violent offending than other offenders (Henry, Caspi, Moffitt & Silva, 1996). Examining the criminal histories of men imprisoned for serious violent offences reveals that they start offending early and continue their diverse criminal interests well into adulthood (Polaschek, Collie & Walkey, 2004). In short, not only are generally violent men violent toward a range of other people, they are generally criminal. Specialist violent offenders are very rare, raising the question "should rehabilitative programmes target the broad criminality of violent offenders, or just their violent offending"? We will return to this issue of programme focus later.

Rationale for General Violence Programmes

As with IPV, research reports on juvenile and adult violence programmes often devote little space to outlining the programme rationale. Ideally such rationales contain links to a relevant multi-factorial aetiological theory (Ward & Marshall, 2004). Fundamentally, aetiological theories need to be adapted to inform treatment. Programme designers need to decide which aetiological factors are relevant (distinguishing precipitating from maintaining factors), and which are capable of change (which factors are dynamic). Development of GV programmes does not yet appear to have reached this point (Howells & Day, 2002; Polaschek & Reynolds, 2001; Serin & Preston, 2001b), so this section simply outlines such a theory and notes how existing programme rationales could be fitted into it.

A number of developmental models of juvenile delinquency impose order on the numerous correlates of juvenile crime by laying out which variables come into play during each developmental period (for example, Pepler & Slaby, 1994). Moffitt (1993) made an influential theoretical distinction between *life-course persistent* offenders and *adolescence-limited* offenders, outlining two essentially separate theoretical accounts of how individuals participate in crime over their life-span. Her work accounts best for why most young delinquents do not persist with offending into adulthood. However, her *life-course persistent* (LCP) theory is described here because it is argued that it has unrecognised potential to offer a richer theoretical framework both for adolescent and adult violent offending intervention.

Moffitt (1993) proposed that the developmental trajectory for LCP offending begins with children who, prior to or soon after birth, are exposed to one or more influences (for example, maternal drug abuse, delivery complications, poor post-natal nutrition, inheritance from parents) that cause them to begin to develop particular neuropsychological characteristics, including early impairments in both verbal (for example, problem-solving, reading and writing, memory) and executive performance (ability to attend, and to self-regulate impulses). These difficult-to-raise children would elicit negative and inadvertently reinforcing responses from the best-equipped parents. However, their actual parents are likely to be genetically similar, thus creating an environment that enhances rather than suppresses their children's dispositional tendencies. In time their schools and neighbourhoods are also likely to respond to them in ways that, rather than correcting their difficulties, develop these difficulties into disordered conduct, which gradually builds itself into an entrenched antisocial personality style.

Moffitt (1993) then outlined processes that serve to consolidate this style. Risk factors continue to have a *direct* influence as the child ages (for example, irritability, leading to repetitive employment dismissal in adulthood, and economic hardship) and an *indirect*, but cumulative influence (for example, school failure, leading to poorer employment opportunities and economic hardship). According to Moffitt (1993, p. 683) "chains of cumulative and contemporary continuity" weave their way through the early years of LCP individuals, locking them into an increasingly focused repertoire of antisocial behaviours, and gradually crowding out opportunities to observe, learn, and practice pro-social behavioural skills and to take part successfully in non-criminal society.

Rationales for Juvenile Violence Programmes

Three types of juvenile offender programmes are described in this chapter. First, Goldstein and Glick's Aggression Replacement Training (ART) (Goldstein & Glick, 1987; Goldstein, Glick & Gibbs, 1998) is based on what the authors refer to as a *behavioural deficit* perspective. It assumes that youths acquire aggressive behaviours by social learning processes, and at the same time they fail to learn pro-social behavioural skills. Teaching them these skills, helping them to control anger, and motivating them to use these skills with moral reasoning training, and in some instances, intervening with the whole peer group to alter peer influences, all align with aspects of LCP theory. EQUIP – the second type of programme – encompasses ART in teaching multiple skills, but in addition it explicitly harnesses the peer group to motivate youths to learn by developing a positive helping-each-other culture that aims to undermine the detrimental effects of antisocial associates (Gibbs, Potter & Goldstein, 1995).

Programmes for youth implemented in the community also afford opportunities to intervene not only with the young person, but with the social influences around him. The third programme, multi-systemic therapy (MST) is one programme that with youth at imminent risk of institutionalisation, makes a comprehensive effort to address risk factors across multiple domains (individual, family, peer, school, and community) (Curtis, Ronan & Borduin, 2004), in the natural settings in which they arise. Thus, MST interventions are said to be targeted to an individual formulation of a particular youth's dynamic risks, drawing broadly on factors that developmental theories have identified as relevant for seriously antisocial youth (Henggeler & Sheidow, 2003). Caregivers and youths are then taught strategies to manage youth behaviour at home, with peers, and at school or work. Therapists help parents gain control over the consequences of their adolescent's pro-social and antisocial behaviour. To do this therapists may assist caregivers in improving their own competence through reducing substance abuse or family stress (Henggeler & Sheidow, 2003). The "programme theory" as such is listed as a set of treatment principles, such as "therapeutic contacts emphasise the positive and use systemic strengths as levers for change" and "intervention effectiveness is evaluated continuously from multiple perspectives with providers assuming accountability for overcoming barriers to successful outcomes" (Edwards, Schoenwald, Henggeler & Strother, 2001, p. 100). The appropriate selection of micro-level interventions previously established as effective with problematic youth behaviour (for example, pragmatic family systems interventions), delivered according to MST's general principles, is theorised to result in a reduction in the targeted antisocial behaviour. In order to ensure that the principles are adhered to and that the micro-level interventions are well chosen and implemented, rigorous therapeutic fidelity processes are put in place (Edwards et al., 2001).

Rationales for Programmes with Adults

Developmental theories like Moffitt's (1993) LCP theory appear to provide a fruitful aetiological account for violent adults as well as adolescents. Recent New Zealand research found tentative retrospective support for this claim: Wilson (2004) found that two-thirds of a sample of high-risk adult male prisoners could be classified as LCP using Moffitt's criteria. These men were estimated to have at least a 70 % chance of returning to prison for serious sexual or violent offending in the next five years. They were 27 years old on average, with a mean of six previous violent convictions each and seven imprisonment sentences (Wilson, 2004).

Outside of the realms of sexual violence (see Chapter 5) and IPV, there are very few specialist programmes for seriously violent men. Recently we reviewed programmes for serious adult violent offenders (Polaschek & Collie, 2004) and despite using liberal methodological criteria, we found just nine evaluations. These studies generally provided a little detail on content, and a paucity of information about the theoretical framework on which the treatment was based. Two approaches were identifiable: shorter programmes (less than 150 hours) focused primarily on a single theoretical factor, anger management; while more intensive programmes (greater than 300 hours) were multi-factorial, usually targeting antisocial cognition, anger management, skills training, and relapse prevention.

When a wider examination is undertaken of psychological rehabilitation approaches with violent offenders (including programmes without published evaluations), these same trends emerge (for example, Serin, 1994), although programmes use different labels for components that address common factors. For example, many anger management programmes, though oriented to increasing the regulation of angry affect, target attitudes and teach skills. The research supporting the status of these targets as criminogenic needs, and actual programme content are discussed in subsequent sections. The remainder of this section outlines the theoretical rationales for targeting these factors.

Anger Management

The rationale for using anger management interventions assumes that violent offenders' violence is caused or mediated by a tendency to experience anger more frequently and to express anger more often, and more violently than others. In other words, advocates of anger management for violent offenders see violent behaviour as a behavioural consequence of becoming angry (violent acts are "angry behaviours" – Howells, 2004, p. 190). Anger management for violent offenders (for example, Howells, Watt, Hall & Baldwin, 1997), is most often a version of Novaco's innovative (1975) adaptation of Meichenbaum's (1975) work, which has more often been implemented with non-correctional populations. Meichenbaum developed stress inoculation training (SIT) into a successful cognitive treatment for anxiety problems. The SIT approach to anger assumes anger is a type of affective stress reaction (Novaco, 1975, 1979). Anger arousal usually arises from an aversive event (usually social), which is then subject to two interrelated cognitive processes: appraisals of the meaning of the event, and expectations about such events and how one should respond to them. Appraisals and expectations interact to generate anger, which has both cognitive (labelling) and physiological (arousal) elements. Anger and cognitive processes both contribute to a behavioural reaction of antagonism or avoidance (Novaco, 1979). Edmondson & Conger (1996) suggested that the main goal of the SIT approach to anger management is to modify the cognitive aspects of the cycle: especially the appraisal of provocation (Novaco, 1979). Thus, aggression is seen to result ultimately from a maladaptive emotional response to a stressful event, and in this sense, anger management is a clinical rather than criminological approach to offender rehabilitation.

Edmondson & Conger (1996) have questioned the theoretical assumptions of SIT as an anger treatment on three grounds. Briefly, first they noted that there are important differences between anger and anxiety. Second, they suggested that gaining better control of arousal may not lead to more adaptive (non-violent) behaviour because the person may not have the requisite skills, or they may, but fail to use them (for example, because they anticipate negative consequences from others for doing so). The third challenge was on the grounds that automatic emotional processing is important in anger arousal, but SIT assumes conscious, controlled cognitive processing.

How substantial is the role of anger among the causes of violence in violent offenders? Howells (2004, p. 189) states "We might therefore label anger as a *contributing factor*, one that may affect the probability of violence, typically when it co-occurs with a number of other conditions." It can then be inferred that all of these "conditions" should be included in the theoretical rationale for violence interventions.

Multi-factorial Programmes

Current multi-factorial programmes rely on targeting a smorgasboard of criminogenic needs found in violent offenders, many of which are skills deficits similar to those addressed in the ART programme with young offenders. The lack of theory and the diversity of needs in serious violent offenders limits both current programme development and programme effectiveness (Serin, 1995). Serin and colleagues have put forward the best accounts to date of a scientifically based programme approach for violent offender rehabilitation, although they still fall short of theory status. Serin & Kuriychuk (1994) proposed that two factors, social cognitive deficits and poor self-regulation (impulsivity), interact synergistically to create the risk of violent behaviour in repetitively violent offenders. Serin & Brown (1996) elaborated this model into an information-processing approach to treating violent offenders and developed a new programme for "persistently violent offenders" based on this framework. The main differences between this approach and traditional anger management are that they explicitly add modules on treatment engagement issues, aggressive beliefs, impulse control, and moral reasoning.

EVIDENCE BASE FOR GENERAL VIOLENCE PROGRAMME TARGETS

Just one meta-analysis informs this domain: Dowden & Andrews (2000) found that targeting negative affect/anger, antisocial attitudes, and relapse prevention produced significant correlations with the size of the recidivism reduction in treated compared to untreated offenders, in programmes that measured violent recidivism as their outcome. However, this study included both sexual and domestic violence programmes; few of the studies included were for GV offenders. Multifactorial programmes generally address hostility and anger, impulsivity or lack of self-regulation, substance abuse, social information processing deficits, antisocial attitudes, and alcohol and drug problems (for example, Serin & Preston, 2001b). What evidence is there that each of these is a criminogenic need?

Attitudinal Factors

Generally criminal attitudes predict both violent and non-violent behaviour in violent offenders (for example, Gendreau, Goggin & Law, 1997). Slaby & Guerra (1988) demonstrated that attitudes to violence can also differentiate violent and non-violent youth. Polaschek et al. (2004) found small to moderate correlations with an actuarial estimate of risk of serious reconviction for both a general criminal attitudes measure and two scales of violent attitudes. Relatedly, violent individuals show biases in cognitive processing that suggest the overuse of highly developed hostile schemata, especially under conditions of uncertainty (Copello & Tata, 1990; Serin, 1991).

Impulsivity

Impulsivity can be conceptualised in three distinct but overlapping ways (White et al., 1994). First, it can be considered a cognitive processing deficit (Serin & Kuriychuk, 1994), the opposite of mental control, and related to executive functioning (White et al., 1994). A second way of viewing impulsivity is behaviourally, as a kind of disinhibition. The key concept here is the sensitivity of individuals to reward and punishment cues, and to changes in these contingencies: how quickly do they modify their behaviour? The third method of examining impulsivity is as an enduring personal characteristic. Again, in this tradition impulsivity is operationalised as distractibility, rule-breaking behaviour, unstable interpersonal relationships, a highly active behavioural style, and an inability to tolerate delays in gratification (White et al., 1994).

A number of studies have found impulsivity to be a prominent characteristic in violent men. The personality approach has been the most common: here impulsivity subscale scores from personality-scale measures are found to be higher in violent than in non-violent offenders (Nussbaum et al., 2002) or impulsivity subscales have also been found to predict violent and general offending (Craig, Browne, Beech & Stringer, 2004), and violent misconduct in prison (Wang & Diamond, 1999). A few studies have used other more task-oriented approaches (see, for example, White et al., 1994), particularly in studies of psychopathy (see Howland, Kosson, Patterson & Newman, 1993), which is relevant because impulsivity is part of the diagnostic criteria. Task measurement of impulsivity in violent offenders needs much more attention (Serin, 2004).

Affective Dyscontrol

There is some dispute about the empirical status of anger difficulties as a criminogenic need. Selby (1984) found that Novaco Anger Inventory scores were higher in violent than non-violent offenders. Cornell, Peterson & Richards (1999) found that scores on two self-report anger scales – the Novaco Anger Scale (NAS) (Novaco, 1994) and Spielberger's (1988) State-Trait Anger Expression Inventory (STAXI) – prospectively predicted institutional verbal and physical aggression but were not correlated with violence history. Mills & Kroner (2003) found the same two measures to be uncorrelated or weakly correlated to prior assaults, misconducts and reconviction. Loza & Loza-Fanous (1999a, 1999b) using several measures of anger and several risk measures found some significant differences between anger scale scores and level of risk, but few by comparison to the number of analyses undertaken, and on differences for violence history. They concluded that anger was not yet established as a worthwhile treatment target for violent offenders. However, Zamble & Quinsey's (1997) often-cited study found that re-offenders reported over five times the level of dysphoric affect of non-offenders in the 2 days prior to recidivating. So affective coping skills could be an important contributor to post-release success whether or not an offender shows up as "abnormal" on some form of dispositional self-report scale.

Other Needs

A number of other lifestyle-related variables also appear to be important criminogenic needs for violent offenders. Serin (1995) reported on a criminogenic needs assessment that covers seven broad areas, and that compares high risk/violent offenders with other offenders. The details about the exact nature of each need are not included but the high risk violent offenders' results show considerably higher need – and contrastingly, a marked absence of strengths in the same areas – for all seven needs domains: employment, marital/family relations, associations, substance abuse, community functioning, personal/emotional skills, and criminal attitudes. Research with both the Level of Supervision Inventory–Revised (LSI-R) with violent prisoners (see, for example, Hollin & Palmer, 2003), and the Violence Risk Scale (Wong & Gordon, 2000) find that needs such as marital/family relations, use of leisure time, use of alcohol and drugs, education/employment, companions, relationship quality, community support and history of compliance with supervision are important for violent offenders.

PROGRAMME CONTENT AND APPLICATION ISSUES FOR GENERAL VIOLENCE PROGRAMMES

Juvenile Violence Programmes

Aggression Replacement Training (ART)

Goldstein, Glick and colleagues developed the best-known multi-modal programme for aggressive and antisocial youth, described in several publications (for example, Goldstein & Glick, 1987, 1994; Goldstein et al., 1998; Goldstein, Nensén, Daleflod & Kalt, 2004; Reddy & Goldstein, 2001). There are three major components. First, groups of chronically aggressive adolescents undergo *structured learning training* (SLT): using expert modelling, role-playing and feedback on their own performance, they are taught how to carry out up to 50 skills for dealing with emotions, stress, goal-setting, planning and problem-solving, finishing with transfer training: generalising skills to home settings. The second component *anger control training* (ACT) is broadly similar to the adult anger management interventions described later in this section (Goldstein & Glick, 1994). The third component – moral education – was added to give violent young people more of an incentive to use their new pro-social skills, and is based on Kohlberg's (1969) research on enhancing adolescents' moral reasoning abilities by engaging in discussion of moral dilemmas in groups.

The full ART curriculum has been delivered in many formats, including groups for family members, and groups comprised of intact New York youth gang cohorts (Goldstein & Glick, 1994). The most common administration format is over 10 weeks with three sessions a week, one from each component. SLT and anger management sessions take less than an hour; moral education sessions may be twice as long. Programme delivery can be conducted by school teachers, counsellors, and caregivers for violent youths, with appropriate selection, training, and oversight for new programme leaders (Reddy & Goldstein, 2001). Groups can be closed or open, and are usually six to eight in size for the first two components (Goldstein & Glick 1987, 1994). Two group leaders are desirable for simultaneous modelling of skills teaching content, and managing aggressive and disruptive group behaviour (Reddy & Goldstein, 2001).

EQUIP

A newer approach, the EQUIP programme (Gibbs et al., 1995), integrates a peer-helping group format with cognitive-developmental and social information processing skills adapted from Goldstein's ART and Prepare (Goldstein, 1988) curricula, and Yochelson & Samenow's (1977) work. Seven to nine youths meet daily for 1 to one-and-a-half hours. The first treatment goal is to develop a prosocial group culture to motivate change. Once this is achieved, the teaching of the EQUIP curriculum commences (Gibbs, Potter, Barriga & Liau, 1996).

Multisystemic Therapy (MST)

The goal of MST is to deliver high-quality, personalised interventions to youth and family, at times and places of their choosing (Henggeler, Melton, Brondino, Scherer & Hanley, 1997) so that no two MST interventions are identical.

Therapists are grouped into teams of three to four Masters-level trained staff, with a caseload of between four and six families each (Henggeler & Sheidow, 2003). They deliver sessions mostly in homes or at school and a team member is available at any time. Treatment averages 40 to 60 hours over 3 to 6 months (Curtis et al., 2004). Targets of behaviour change often include youths' school or work performance, and peer associations (Henggeler & Sheidow, 2003). According to Edwards et al. (2001) the actual methods of intervention are an eclectic mix of "Evidence-based assessment and intervention strategies . . . (e.g., behavior therapy, cognitive behavior therapy, pragmatic family therapies)" (p. 111), and both the young person and caregivers may be taught strategies for behaviour change.

Programmes for Adults

Adult programmes have mainly been delivered in institutions, with all of their attendant challenges to therapeutic integrity and change (see Chapter 7). These programmes vary widely and three examples will be given below. For a prison programme to succeed, effectively addressing institutional challenges to programme implementation and management is as important as sound programme content. Serin & Preston (2001a) discuss the importance of appropriate site selection, staff selection and training, and programme marketing to referrers and offenders. They and others have noted the likely costs to therapy effectiveness of conflict between system factions in which the therapy is embedded (Gaes, 2001; Quinsey, Harris, Rice & Cormier, 1998).

Anger Management

A number of manualised programmes exist, most commonly based on Novaco's approach (Novaco, 1997). For example, in the 1980s the New Zealand Department of Justice developed the Video Anger Management Programme (VAMP) from Novaco's SIT approach. This 10-session programme teaches participants definitions of anger and violence, how to recognise their own anger, and to identify its developmental antecedents. Other elements include time out and relaxation training, recognising anger-inducing thinking, coping self-talk for provoking events, assertiveness, conflict resolution, and relationship skills (Howells et al., 2001).

The most important application issue with such stand-alone programmes concerns participant selection. Howells has noted that stress-inoculation-based anger management is not the treatment of choice: (a) when the violence arises from over-controlled rather than under-controlled anger, (b) when the violence has "a more instrumental and sadistic quality" (p. 172), such as in psychopaths, and (c) when violent behaviour occurs in the service of either immediate or both immediate *and* long-term goals (Howells, 1989). The violence of serious violent offenders commonly shares characteristics with both (b) and (c) above. Furthermore the programmes are typically of low-intensity. Together these factors suggest that stand-alone anger management will rarely be the treatment of choice for these men.

Multi-modal Programmes

Multi-modal programmes are generally more intensive. For example, the Correctional Service of Canada's Persistently Violent Offender treatment programme, comprises about 240 hours of mainly group sessions over 16 weeks (Serin, Preston & Murphy, 2001). The main referral criterion is a documented history of at least three separate violent acts. The programme has three distinct components. First is a motivational intervention that socialises offenders into programme requirements and group processes, and develops expectations of change. Second, participants develop a comprehensive socio-cognitive model of their risk factors for violence. Third, they are taught skills that are to serve as pro-social alternatives to violence, including managing affective arousal, cognitive restructuring, problem-solving, assertiveness, conflict resolution, altering lifestyle risk factors, and increasing self-control. Finally, individual violence relapse prevention plans are developed (see also Bettman, 2000).

Another high intensity and multimodal programme is the Rimutaka Violence Prevention Unit programme (Polaschek, Wilson, Townsend & Daly, 2005). Over 28 weeks, closed groups of 10 prisoners attend 12 hours of group treatment per week. Initial screening criteria are a current violent offence or significant history of violence, moderate to high actuarial risk of serious offending, and absence of factors that prevent adequate programme participation (such as major DSM-IV

Axis I mental disorder, major neurological impairment, very poor English language comprehension and expression). After a four-week assessment period, treatment commences with (a) identifying and presenting an offence chain; (b) restructuring offence-supportive thinking; (c) negative affect management; (d) victim empathy; (e) moral reasoning; (f) problem-solving; (g) communication and relationship skills; and (h) relapse prevention planning. The programme is highly structured with a range of practical, active learning methods used in delivery. There is an emphasis on participant contribution to sessions, and on modelling and rehearsing new skills in sessions, and then practising them out in the unit. The majority of participants in the VPU are Maori but, unlike Montgomery House, the programme is not specifically designed for Maori.

The final example is the Montgomery House Violence Prevention Programme (VPP) in Hamilton, New Zealand (Berry, 2003). It is unusual in two respects. First, it is an urban residential programme that takes both parolees and community-sentenced participants. Second, the programme creates a culturally supportive programme for Maori offenders, although non-Maori attend as well. The VPP opened in 1987 and currently takes closed groups of 12 men into 380 hours of programming. The VPP is based on a social learning model, implemented within a therapeutic community process that includes traditional Maori practices and protocols. Education and skills training are applied to a broad range of targets. Modules include anger control, communication, relationship and parenting skills, social problem-solving, alcohol, drug and health education, Tikanga and Te Reo Maori (Maori cultural and language instruction), budgeting, physical fitness training, and outdoor education (see Berry, 1999; Polaschek & Dixon, 2001).

OUTCOME EVIDENCE FOR GENERAL VIOLENCE PROGRAMMES

Interventions with Juveniles

Aggression Replacement Training

At least a dozen evaluations of ART have been reported (Goldstein et al., 1998). However, most have not measured aggressive behaviour per se, and used samples of predominantly non-violent youth. In the Annsville Youth Center study, Goldstein, Glick, Reiner, Zimmerman & Coultrey (1986) compared three groups of predominantly non-violent youths: a 10-week ART group (n = 24), a motivated untreated group (n = 24), and an unmotivated untreated group (n = 12). The evaluation examined whether ART participants learned the 10 pro-social skills they were taught, could perform them in new situations that were either similar or quite different to the original setting, whether the staff reported a reduction in behavioural incidents for participants, and whether they rated participants as more self-controlled or less impulsive than the other two groups. Compared to controls, the ART group was significantly improved on four of the 10 skills and on all other indices at 11 weeks. All controls were then ART-treated over weeks 11 to 20. A sample of post-release ART and non-ART trained youth also were compared on blind ratings by parole officers. Youths who had ART were reported to be performing better than controls at home, with peers, legally and overall, but not at school or work.

Coleman, Pfeiffer, and Oakland (1992) described improvement in just three skills with behaviourally disordered children and adolescents. There were no differences on moral development or out-of-treatment behaviour. Nugent (1999) implemented a condensed version of ART in a runaway shelter, and found women showed a marked reduction in antisocial behaviour. Goldstein et al. (1986) replicated exactly the Annsville study at the MacCormick Youth Center, a maximum-security institution for male youths aged between 13 and 21 years, incarcerated for serious sexual and violent offences. The ART group improved on the same four skills and on socio-moral reasoning. They significantly increased their use of pro-social skills and were less impulsive compared to both types of controls. However, the number and seriousness of behavioural incidents did not differ between groups, perhaps because of the very restrictive, controlled custody environment.

The Gang Intervention Project attempted to modify violent criminal youths' behaviour by intervening with an entire gang cohort. Goldstein & Glick (1994) reported significant improvements in all skill categories for ART-group members compared to pre-test and to controls, but no change in anger control scores, and improvement in only one area of community functioning – employment (Goldstein & Glick, 1994). Over 8 months of follow-up, 52 % of untreated and 13 % of ART youths were rearrested.

EQUIP

Few outcome studies of EQUIP are available. Leeman, Gibbs & Fuller (1993) randomly assigned incarcerated juveniles either to EQUIP or to one of two control groups. EQUIP youths showed significant reductions in self-reported and staff-reported misconduct. At 12 months post-release, 15 % of treated and 41 % of control youth had recidivated, but there are no specific figures for violent recidivism (see Gibbs et al., 1996). In New Zealand, EQUIP was implemented in the late 1990s in specialist units for young male offenders (YOUs) within the adult prison system. A preliminary evaluation compared 29 YOU men with 69 youths who had been imprisoned in the 2 years before the implementation of YOUs, and then released for at least 6 months at the time of data collection. Participants were not matched on risk indices other than age (mean = 17.7 to 17.9 years) and ethnicity (predominantly Maori). At follow-up most offenders in both groups had re-offended: there were no differences between groups, nor were there significant differences in subsequent re-imprisonment rates. However, 45 % of EQUIP youths were violently re-convicted compared to 25 % of non-EQUIP youths (Wilson, 2002). In a subsequent evaluation of another YOU in which the EQUIP programme may have been able to be implemented more rigorously,[3] and which also implemented a token economy regime, 44 EQUIP men were compared with 144 age-matched men who resided in the same prison prior to the development of YOUs. Follow-up ranged from 12 months to 2 years. Wilson (2003) found no differences in the proportion of

---

[3] More psychology staff time and more stable programme staffing were features of this evaluation environment.

offenders who acquired subsequent violent or general re-convictions, but significantly fewer YOU (EQUIP-treated) offenders were subsequently re-imprisoned, probably because untreated men who were re-convicted were more likely to receive multiple non-violent convictions that returned them to prison.

Multisystemic Therapy (MST)

Three randomised trials suggest that MST is very effective with chronic and violent youth (Borduin et al., 1995; Henggeler et al., 1997; Henggeler, Melton & Smith, 1992; Henggeler, Melton, Smith, Schoenwald & Hanley, 1993). For example, Borduin et al. (1995) randomly allocated 176 juvenile offenders to MST or individual therapy, finding a difference of 45 % in the number of youths who were rearrested at 4-year follow-up. Henggeler & Sheidow (2003) report that over all of these studies, which averaged 60 hours of service provision over three to 6 months, major improvements have been found in rates of arrest (25 % to 70 % reduction) and out-of-home placement (47 % to 64 % reduction). Multisystemic therapy has also improved other outcomes such as family functioning, adolescent mental health, and school attendance (Curtis et al., 2004), and the effects of treatment have persisted through more than a decade of follow-up. Schaeffer & Borduin (2005) followed Borduin et al.'s (1995) youths for 10 to 16 years after intervention, reporting that 50 % of MST adults, and 81 % of the routine-intervention controls had recidivated. Rates of violent re-arrest were 14 % for MST and 30 % for individual therapy. Control adults had more than twice as many overall and violent convictions. Overall, MST results appear to be impressive. The next step is to evaluate whether MST findings generalise to independent researchers and across sites outside of the US.

Interventions with Adults

Polaschek & Collie (2004) found four outcome studies that reported violent re-conviction, included an untreated control group and treated generally violent men in mainstream correctional settings. The Canadian Regional Health Centre (Pacific) Intensive Programme for Violent Offenders (IPVO) was a multiple-target programme that took 12 to 16 violent offenders into closed groups for up to 8 months, although the total treatment hours were not reported. The programme was described as both "cognitive behavioural and psychosocial dynamic" (Motiuk, Smiley & Blanchette, 1996, p. 10). Offenders were taught to identify components of their offence cycles and underwent addiction, communication, cognitive, relationships, anger management, and empathy modules. The 2-year follow-up data show no effect on either violent or general reconviction.

New Zealand's Montgomery House Violence Prevention Programme (VPP) has evaluations from two different programme periods. Dixon & Behrnes (1996) found that, over 5 years of follow-up, VPP completers showed medium and large reductions in general and violent reconviction respectively. Berry (1999, 2003) matched participants with untreated controls and over an average 17 months, Berry found a small decrease in violent reconviction for completers, and a significant increase for non-completers, compared to their matched controls. He also found an *increase* in non-violent re-offending as a function of treatment; he has attributed this to increased opportunity to offend, presumably among those who avoided incarceration by reducing their violent offending.

Polaschek et al. (2005) reported results for just 22 treated offenders from the first two years of operation at the Rimutaka Violence Prevention Unit programme, also in New Zealand, and a matched untreated group (from Berry, 1999, 2003). Data for treatment non-completers were not available for analysis. The VPU had a large effect on violent recidivism and a small reduction in non-violent offending and re-imprisonment. The problem with this design clearly is that the apparent treatment effect may be a function of selective retention of lower risk offenders, where risk has not been captured in the matching procedure.

None of these studies link changes in criminogenic needs to recidivism outcome: a necessary step if the treatment model itself is to receive any direct examination, and useful in studies where it is not clear why no effects were found. However, some programmes have measured change on relevant needs. Berry (1999) found improvements in attitudes towards women, self-esteem, wellbeing, and all of the subscales of the STAXI, but did not collect these data from the control group. Polaschek and Dixon (2001) reported increases in wellbeing and anger control from pre-programme to post-programme in both treated non-re-offenders and re-offenders. However, re-offenders scored higher throughout the programme until the follow-up, when their scores dropped. Bakker & Wilson (n.d.) found almost no changes on a large number of psychometrics administered to the VPU treatment group, and Motiuk et al. (1996) presented no scores or statistics but stated that the treated group showed improvement on most of the measures of anger or hostility, impulsivity, depression, and interpersonal problems. The control group also showed improved pre-post scores, but the magnitude of change was smaller; recall that this study showed no differences in recidivism between the treatment and control groups.

Anger Management

Novaco (1997) reviewed the few studies of anger management for mainstream (non-psychiatric) offenders: none appears to have examined subsequent violent or general offending as an outcome variable. Dowden, Blanchette & Serin (1999) evaluated the Anger and Other Emotions Management Programme (AOEMP) in a study that features large sample sizes, a 3-year follow-up period, and analyses by offender risk level. At first glance this is the only convincing demonstration that anger management can reduce violent recidivism in high-risk mainstream offenders with a history of violence: indeed this is the conclusion we reached previously (Polaschek & Collie, 2004). We noted too that such success was surprising given that AOEMP is a relatively low-intensity intervention of 25 two-hour sessions. Dowden et al. (1999) reported large effects for non-violent and violent recidivism: for the latter, just 9 % of high-risk treated men recidivated violently compared to 24 % of untreated men over an average of 513 days' follow-up (Dowden et al., 1999). No effect was found with low-risk offenders. The programme approach included rational-emotive therapy, Meichenbaum's Self-Instructional Training, and relapse prevention.

However, in a subsequent report, Dowden & Serin (2001) compared completers and controls with data for 76 dropouts, and found that over 3 years, the rates of recidivism were 5%, 17% and 40% respectively. They also found no difference between completers and controls on another outcome measure, number of post-programme violent institutional incidents. Overall, this is an interesting and methodologically sophisticated study. The attrition rate and the fact that non-completers recidivated violently at a rate eight times that of completers seriously threatens the view that this is an empirical demonstration of anger management programme effectiveness.

A number of anger-management interventions have monitored anger indices, but have often failed to demonstrate the expected changes on these measures as a function of intervention (Howells, 2004). Dowden et al. (1999) found increases in anger management skills, insight into anger problems, and anger self-competence were linked to survival in the AOEMP. However, trait and state anger changes, and impulsivity were not. Howells et al. (2001, 2005) conducted a large study of anger management with offenders, using a sample of several hundred male offenders including programme attendees and wait-list controls. Overall, the treated group changes were small and clinically non-significant. The largest intervention change was in "anger knowledge" suggesting some psycho-education had taken place. They concluded that there was a "need for caution in applying anger management indiscriminately with violent prisoners", and that "the impact of such programs is modest" (Howells et al., 2001, p. 106).

Most recently, Howells and colleagues have been concerned with increasing readiness for anger management, in recognition that offender responsivity barriers, or a lack of match between offender needs and programme stages are one of the significant causes of programme ineffectiveness (Howells & Day, 2003). Increased understanding of treatment readiness is thus likely to be very valuable in increasing the effectiveness of interventions. However, that offenders are not ready for anger management does not mean it will become an effective intervention when they are. Major sources of "lack of readiness" in serious violent offenders may themselves be criminogenic needs (for example, antisocial goals and values, attitudes that support the use of violence against others, social support from peers for violence, psychopathy and narcissism). A more theoretically elegant solution to this problem would be to offer a multi-modal programme that reinforced for offenders that the violence is multiply determined and targeted directly the factors that make violence ego-syntonic for such men.

PSYCHOPATHY

The investigation of the roles of psychopathy in crime and rehabilitation has been hampered both by variation in how the concept is defined, and inconsistent operationalisation (Lösel, 1998). In this section, psychopathy will be defined as it is in the Hare scales (Hare, 2003). Psychopathy is a construct important to violence treatment programmes because it statistically predicts both violence and treatment responsivity. Psychopathy also is important because of a recent enthusiasm for suggesting that psychopaths are virtually untreatable (Gacono, Nieberding, Owen,

Rubel & Bodholdt, 2001). This view seems to have been fuelled largely by the Oak Ridge therapeutic community studies (for example, Rice, Harris & Cormier, 1992), which demonstrated *increased* risk of recidivism in psychopaths who were treated compared to untreated controls. Actually, Salekin (2002) and D'Silva, Duggan & McCarthy (2004) have recently noted how little scientific research exists to answer the question of how treatment affects psychopaths.

Psychopathy and Violence: Common Aetiology?

The aetiology of psychopathy remains poorly understood. Salekin (2002) has suggested that there may be multiple aetiological routes, involving different proportions of contribution from temperamental and environmental factors. Some or all may overlap with aetiology for serious and chronic adult violence particularly if, as Lösel (1998) has suggested, serious violent offenders substantially overlap life-course persistent offenders (Moffitt, 1993).

A variety of studies have found small to moderate correlations between PCL-R scores and violent offending (see Hare, 2003 for a review). Hart (1998) noted that there are at least three possible mechanisms that may link the two concepts functionally. With regard to cognition, psychopaths show high rates of hostile attribution bias, perceptions that violence is rewarding, and attentional deficits (for example, the failure to attend to information that suggests that violence will not help them achieve their own long-term goals). In addition, the affective aspect shows that deficient feelings of empathy, guilt and fear fail to inhibit violent impulses out of concern either for one's own safety, or the wellbeing of others. Finally, in the behavioural domain, psychopaths tend to act before they think. This behavioural impulsiveness is likely both to increase the risk of violent acts directly, and also indirectly by facilitating proximal risk factors such as alcohol consumption (Hart, 1998).

Psychopathy and Responsivity

Characteristics of psychopathy affect treatment processes linked with programme effectiveness. Hallmarks of psychopathy interfere with the development of a therapeutic alliance (Taft et al., 2004), and may also disrupt or distort group cohesion, although there is little empirical evidence on this latter issue. Psychopaths' glibness and lying cause therapists to feel that the offender is "playing games". The inability of psychopaths to feel concern or distress about their behaviour, and their "here and now" focus hinder self-reflection and personal responsibility. Without these features, offenders often participate only to create an impression that will take them through some obstacle in the management system (for example, obtaining lower security, parole). Psychopaths' hostile schemas (Seager, 2005) and utilitarian relationship orientation predispose them to avoid any form of affective attachment to the therapist too. Together such features make developing an affective bond – the most important aspect of a therapeutic alliance (Jones & Pulos, 1993) – difficult for therapists.

Implications for Violent Offender Treatment Programmes

Recommendations and observations about treating psychopaths' violence and treating serious violent offenders overlap significantly. Violent psychopaths' needs have been found to be similar, though at a higher level than those of non-psychopathic violent offenders (Simourd & Hoge, 2000). Many of the characteristics of treatment recommended by experts (such as Wallace & Newman, 2004; Wong & Hare, 2005) contain elements of "best practice" for working with all serious, high risk offenders (for example, highly structured, intensive skills-based cognitive behavioural programmes, high levels of staff training and support, careful monitoring to maintain treatment integrity).

Therefore while the research literature on treatment outcome and process with psychopaths remains small, it is probably preferable to think of psychopathy in dimensional rather than taxonic terms when treating violent offenders, particularly with the more severely high-risk violent offenders. That is to say, the most optimistic approach is to treat psychopathic offenders as amongst the most difficult clients in violence programmes but to recognise that their characteristics and needs are also found in other serious violent offenders, albeit not necessarily as strongly (Simourd & Hoge, 2000).

FUTURE DIRECTIONS FOR GENERAL VIOLENCE PROGRAMMES

In this underdeveloped corner of offender rehabilitation, there are several pressing developmental needs. First, there is a need for more research on serious violent offenders in general. There are still few studies for example that have investigated their criminogenic needs and responsivity characteristics (for example, learning difficulties, ability to form a therapeutic alliance). Second, there is important work to be done on an adequate treatment theory for violent offending. Treatment theory is essential to programme design and evaluation because it helps determine the direction of development in programme content and implementation issues. Furthermore, it helps evaluators focus on what to measure in order to determine whether a particular programme is producing positive change, and to pinpoint why it is not, if it appears ineffective.

One important issue for treatment theory to address is the relationship between violence-related and non-violent crime-related criminogenic needs, and which programmes should target to be most effective. It is likely that the causes of violent and non-violent offending overlap but can also be separated somewhat. Support for this contention comes from longitudinal research. Henry et al. (1996), using a large cohort of New Zealand boys tracked from birth found that while it was true that those with violent convictions also had more non-violent convictions at age 18 years, a cluster of variables present early in life could uniquely predict their violent convictions. This variable was labelled *lack of control.* Caspi, Henry, McGee, Moffitt & Silva (1995, p. 59) described it as encapsulating an "inability to modulate impulsive expression, impersistence in problem solving, as well as sensitivity to stress and challenge that is expressed in affectively charged negative reactions." Scores on this variable as early as 5 years, were predictive of later behaviour (Henry et al., 1996). Third, although programmes for generally violent offenders are probably increasing, research into their effectiveness is still scarce and consequently there is little evidence to encourage correctional administrators to embark on projects to run such programmes. Much greater resources are needed to design and evaluate such programmes. In jurisdictions where there is some financial commitment to rehabilitation as well as incarceration, recognition that the target offenders are enormously overrepresented in crime may motivate the dedication of such resources.

REFERENCES

Adams, D. (1989). Feminist-based interventions for battering men. In P. L. Caesar & L. K. Hamberger (Eds), *Treating men who batter: Theory, practice, and programs* (pp. 3–23). New York: Springer.

Andrews, D. A. & Bonta, J. (1998). *The psychology of criminal conduct* (2nd edition). Cincinnati, OH: Anderson Publishing Co.

Archer, J. (2000). Sex differences in aggression between heterosexual partners: A meta-analytic review. *Psychological Bulletin, 126,* 651–680.

Austin, J. & Dankwort, J. (1997). *A review of standards for batterer intervention programs.* Retrieved 1 April 2005 from http://www.vaw.umn.edu/documents/vawnet/standard/standard.html

Babcock, J. C., Green, C. E. & Robie, C. (2004). Does batterers' treatment work? A meta-analytic review of domestic violence treatment. *Clinical Psychology Review, 23,* 1023–1053.

Babcock, J. C., Waltz, J., Jacobson, N. S. & Gottman, J. M. (1993). Power and violence: The relation between communication patterns, power discrepancies, and domestic violence. *Journal of Consulting and Clinical Psychology, 61,* 40–50.

Bakker, L. & Wilson, N. (n.d.). *Violence Prevention Unit: Psychological tests of change and recidivism evaluation.* Wellington, New Zealand: Department of Corrections Psychological Service unpublished report.

Balzer, R. (1999). Hamilton Abuse Intervention Project: The Aotearoa experience. In M. F. Shepard & E. L. Pence (Eds), *Co-ordinating community responses to domestic violence: Lessons from Duluth and beyond* (pp. 239–254). Thousand Oaks, CA: Sage.

Bandura, A. (1973). *Aggression: A social learning analysis.* Englewood Cliffs, NJ: Prentice-Hall.

Barbaree, H. (1997). Evaluating treatment efficacy with sexual offenders: The insensitivity of recidivism studies to treatment effect. *Sexual Abuse: A Journal of Research and Treatment, 9,* 111–128.

Batterers' Intervention Services Coalition Michigan (2002). Retrieved 1 April 2005 from http://www.biscmi.org/other_resources/state_standards.html

Berry, S. (1999). *The Montgomery House violence prevention programme: An evaluation.* Wellington, New Zealand: Department of Corrections Psychological Service.

Berry, S. (2003). Stopping violent offending in New Zealand: Is treatment an option? *New Zealand Journal of Psychology, 32,* 92–100.

Bettman, M. (2000). *Violence prevention program accreditation case file.* Ottawa, Ontario: Correctional Service of Canada.

Bilby, C. & Hatcher, R. (2004). *Early stages in the development of the Integrated Domestic Abuse Programme (IDAP): Implementing the Duluth Domestic Violence pathfinder.* Home Office Online Report 29/04. London: Home Office Research Development and Statistics Directorate. Retrieved 1 April 2005 from http://www.crimereduction.gov.uk/domesticviolence43.htm

Bograd, M. & Mederos, F. (1999). Battering and couples therapy: Universal screening and selection of treatment modality. *Journal of Marital and Family Therapy, 25(3),* 291–312.

Borduin, C. M. et al. (1995). Multisystemic treatment of serious juvenile offenders: Long-term prevention of criminality and violence. *Journal of Consulting and Clinical Psychology, 63*, 569–578.

Bowen, E. & Gilchrist, E. (2004). Comprehensive evaluation: A holistic approach to evaluating domestic violence offender programmes. *International Journal of Offender Therapy and Comparative Criminology, 48*, 215–234.

Bronfenbrenner, U. (1979). *The ecology of human development.* Cambridge, MA: Harvard University Press.

Brown, P. D., O'Leary, K. D. & Feldbau, S. R. (1997). Dropout in a treatment program for self-referring wife abusing men. *Journal of Family Violence, 12(4)*, 365–386.

Capaldi, D. M. & Clark, S. (1998). Prospective family predictors of aggression toward female partners for at-risk young men. *Developmental Psychology, 34*, 1175–1188.

Capaldi, D. M., Dishion, T. J., Stoolmiller, M. & Yoerger, K. (2001). Aggression toward female partners by at-risk young men: The contribution of male adolescent friendships. *Developmental Psychology, 37*, 61–73.

Cardin, A. (1994). Wife abuse and the wife abuser: Review and recommendations. *The Counseling Psychologist, 22*, 539–582.

Caspi, A., Henry, B., McGee, R., Moffitt, T. & Silva, P. (1995). Temperamental origins of child and adolescent behavior problems: From age 3 to age 15. *Child Development, 66*, 486–498.

Choice, P., Lamke, L. K. & Pittman, J. F. (1995). Conflict resolution strategies and marital distress as mediating factors in the link between witnessing interparental violence and wife battering. *Violence and Victims, 10*, 107–119.

Coleman, M., Pfeiffer, S. & Oakland, T. (1992). Aggression replacement training with behaviorally disordered offenders. *Behavioral Disorders, 18*, 54–66.

Copello, A. G. & Tata, P. R. (1990). Violent behaviour and interpretive bias: An experimental study of the resolution of ambiguity in violent offenders. *British Journal of Clinical Psychology, 29*, 417–428.

Cordova, J. Y., Jacobson, N. S., Gottman, J. M., Rushe, R. & Cox, G. (1993). Negative reciprocity and communication in couples with a violent husband. *Journal of Abnormal Psychology, 102*, 559–564.

Cornell, D. G., Peterson, C. S. & Richards, H. (1999). Anger as a predictor of aggression among incarcerated adolescents. *Journal of Consulting and Clinical Psychology, 67*, 108–115.

Craig, L. A., Browne, K. D., Beech, A. & Stringer, I. (2004). Personality characteristics associated with reconviction in sexual and violent offenders. *Journal of Forensic Psychiatry and Psychology, 15*, 532–551.

Cunningham, A., Jaffe, P. G., Baker, L., Dick, T., Malla, S., Mazaheri, N., et al. (1998). *Theory-derived explanations of male violence against female partners: Literature update and related implications for treatment and evaluation.* London: London Family Court Clinic.

Curtis, N. M., Ronan, K. R. & Borduin, C. M. (2004). Multisystemic treatment: A meta-analysis of outcome studies. *Journal of Family Psychology, 18*, 411–419.

Davis R. C. & Taylor B. G. (1999). Does batterer treatment reduce violence? A synthesis of the literature. *Women & Criminal Justice, 10(2)*, 69–93.

Davis, R. C., Taylor, B. G. & Maxwell, C. D. (1998). Does batterer treatment reduce violence? A randomized experiment in Brooklyn. *Justice Quarterly, 18*, 171–201.

Dixon, B. G. & Behrnes, S. (1996). *Violence prevention project reconviction study: Overview of study and findings.* New Zealand Department of Corrections Psychological Service unpublished report.

Dobash, R., Dobash, R., Cavanagh, K. & Lewis, R. (1996). *Research evaluation of programmes for violent men.* Edinburgh: The Scottish Office Central Research Unit.

Dowden, C. & Andrews, D. A. (2000). Effective correctional treatment and violent reoffending: A meta analysis. *Canadian Journal of Criminology, 42*, 449–467.

Dowden, C., Blanchette, K. & Serin, R. (1999). *Anger management programming for federal male inmates: An effective intervention.* Research report r-82. Ottawa, ON: Correctional Service of Canada.

Dowden, C. & Serin, R. (2001). *Anger management programming for offenders: The impact of program performance measures.* Research report r-106. Ottawa, ON: Correctional Service of Canada.

D'Silva, K., Duggan, C. & McCarthy, L. (2004). Does treatment really make psychopaths worse? A review of the evidence. *Journal of Personality Disorders, 18*, 163–177.

Dunford, F. W. (2000). The San Diego experiment: An assessment of interventions of men who assault their wives. *Journal of Consulting and Clinical Psychology, 68*, 468–476.

Dutton, D. G. (1985). An ecologically nested theory of male violence towards intimates. *International Journal of Women's Studies, 8*, 404–413.

Dutton, D. G. (1994). Patriarchy and wife assault: The ecological fallacy. *Violence and Victims, 9*, 167–182.

Dutton, D. G. (1995a). *The domestic assault of women: Psychological and criminal justice perspectives.* Vancouver, Canada: UBC Press.

Dutton, D. G. (1995b). Male abusiveness in intimate relationships. *Clinical Psychology Review, 15*, 567–581.

Dutton, D. G., Bodnarchuk, M., Kropp, R., Hart, S. D. & Ogloff, J. R. P. (1997). Wife assault treatment and criminal recidivism: An 11-year follow-up. *International Journal of Offender Therapy and Comparative Criminology, 41*, 9–23.

Dutton, D. G. & Kropp, P. R. (2000). A review of domestic violence risk instruments. *Trauma, Violence & Abuse, 1(2)*, 171–181.

Dutton, D. G., Saunders, K., Starzomski, A. & Bartholomew, K. (1994). Intimacy anger and insecure attachment as precursors of abuse in intimate relationships. *Journal of Applied Social Psychology, 24*, 1367–1386.

Dutton, D. G. & Starzomski, A. (1994). Psychological differences between court-referred and self-referred wife assaulters. *Criminal Justice and Behavior, 21*, 203–222.

Eckhardt, C., Holtzworth-Munroe, A., Norlander, B., Sibley, A. & Cahill, M. (in press). Readiness to change, partner violence subtypes, and treatment outcomes among men in treatment for partner assault. *Violence & Victims.*

Edleson, J. L. & Tolman, R. M. (1992). *Intervention for men who batter: An ecological approach.* Newbury Park, CA: Sage.

Edmondson, C. B. & Conger, J. C. (1996). A review of treatment efficacy for individuals with anger problems: Conceptual, assessment, and methodological issues. *Clinical Psychology Review, 16*, 251–275.

Edwards, D. L., Schoenwald, K., Henggeler, S. W. & Strother, K. B. (2001). A multilevel perspective on the implementation of multi-systemic therapy: Attempting dissemination with fidelity. In G. A. Bernfeld, D. P. Farrington & A. W. Leschied (Eds), *Offender rehabilitation in practice* (pp. 97–119). Chichester: John Wiley & Sons.

Ehrensaft, M. K., Moffitt, T. E. & Caspi, A. (2004). Clinically abusive relationships in an unselected birth cohort: Men's and women's participation and developmental antecedents. *Journal of Abnormal Psychology, 113*, 258–271.

Farrington, D. P., Ohlin, L. & Wilson, J. Q. (1986). *Understanding and controlling crime.* New York: Springer-Verlag.

Feder, L. & Forde, D. (1999). *A test of the efficacy of court-mandated counseling for convicted misdemeanor domestic violence offenders: Results from the Broward experiment.* Paper presented at the International Family Violence Research Conference, Durham, NH.

Felson, R. B. (2002). *Violence and gender re-examined.* Washington DC: American Psychological Association.

Ford, D. A. & Regoli, J. J. (1993). The criminal prosecution of wife batterers: Process, problems, and effects. In N. Z. Hilton (Ed.), *Legal responses to wife assault* (pp. 127–164). Newbury Park, CA: Sage.

Gacono, C. B., Nieberding, R. J., Owen, A., Rubel, J. & Bodholdt, R. (2001). Treating conduct disorder, antisocial, and psychopathic personalities. In J. B. Ashford, B. D. Sales & W. H. Reid (Eds), *Treating adult and juvenile offenders with special needs* (pp. 99–121). Washington DC: APA.

Gaes, G. (2001). Programme evaluation: Guidelines for asking the right questions. In L. L. Motiuk & R. C. Serin (Eds), *Compendium 2000 on Effective Correctional Programming.* Ottawa, Ontario: Ministry of Supply and Services.

Geffner, R., Barrett, J. J. & Rossman, B. B. R. (1995). Domestic violence and sexual abuse: Multiple systems perspectives. In R. H. Mikesell, D.-D. Lusterman & S. H. McDaniel

(Eds), *Integrating family therapy: Handbook of family psychology and systems theory* (pp. 501–517). Washington, DC: APA.

Gelles, R. J. (1993). Family violence. In R. L. Hampton, T. P. Gullotta, G. K. Adams, E. H. Potter & R. P. Weissberg (Eds), *Family violence: Prevention and treatment* (pp. 1–24). Newbury Park, CA: Sage.

Gendreau, P., Goggin, C. E. & Law, M. A. (1997). Predicting prison misconducts. *Criminal Justice and Behavior, 24*, 414–431.

Gibbs, J. C., Potter, G. B., Barriga, A. Q. & Liau, A. K. (1996). Developing the helping skills and prosocial motivation of aggressive adolescents in peer group programs. *Aggression and Violent Behavior, 1*, 283–305.

Gibbs, J. C., Potter, G. & Goldstein, A. P. (1995). *The EQUIP program: Teaching youth to think and act responsibly through a peer-helping approach.* Champaign, IL: Research Press.

Goldstein, A. P. (1988). *The Prepare curriculum: Teaching prosocial competencies.* Champaign, IL: Research Press.

Goldstein, A. P. & Glick, B. (1987). *Aggression Replacement Training: A comprehensive intervention for aggressive youth.* Champaign, IL: Research Press.

Goldstein, A. P. & Glick, B. (1994). Aggression Replacement Training: Curriculum and evaluation. *Simulation and Gaming, 25*, 9–26.

Goldstein, A. P., Glick, B. & Gibbs, J. C. (1998). *Aggression Replacement Training: A comprehensive intervention for aggressive youth (revised edition).* Champaign, IL: Research Press.

Goldstein, A. P., Glick, B., Reiner, S., Zimmerman, D. & Coultry, T. (1986). *Aggression Replacement Training.* Champaign, IL: Research Press.

Goldstein, A. P., Nensén, R., Daleflod, B. & Kalt, M. (2004). *New perspectives on Aggression Replacement Training: Practice, research, and application.* Chichester: John Wiley & Sons.

Gondolf, E. W. (1999). A comparison of four batterer intervention systems: Do court referral, program length, and services matter? *Journal of Interpersonal Violence, 14*, 41–61.

Gondolf, E. W. (2000). A 30-month follow-up of court-referred batterers in four cities. *International Journal of Offender Therapy and Comparative Criminology, 44*, 111–128.

Gondolf, E. W. (2001). Limitations of experimental evaluation of batterer programs. *Trauma, Violence & Abuse, 2(1)*, 79–88.

Gondolf, E. W. (2004). Evaluating batterer counseling programs: A difficult task showing some effects and implications. *Aggression and Violent Behavior, 9*, 605–631.

Gondolf, E. W. & Jones, A. S. (2001). The program effect of batterer programs in three cities. *Violence & Victims, 16*, 693–704.

Gondolf, E. W. & Russell, D. (1986). The case against anger control treatment programs for batterers. *Response to the Victimization of Women & Children. 9(3)*, 2–5.

Gondolf, E. W. & Williams, O. J. (2001). Culturally focused batterer counseling for African American men. *Trauma, Violence & Abuse, 2*, 283–295.

Greene, K. & Bogo, M. (2002). The different faces of intimate violence: Implications for assessment and treatment. *Journal of Marital and Family Therapy, 28(4)*, 455–466.

Hare, R. D. (2003). *Hare Psychopathy Checklist-Revised (PCL-R) (2nd edition).* North Tonawanda, NY: Multi-Health Systems.

Hart, S. D. (1998). Psychopathy and risk for violence. In D. J. Cooke, A. E. Forth, J. Newman & R. D. Hare (Eds), *Psychopathy: Theory research and implications for society* (pp. 355–373). Netherlands: Kluwer Academic Publishers.

Healey, K., Smith, C. & O'Sullivan, C. (1998). *Batterer intervention: Program approaches and criminal justice strategies.* Washington, DC: National Institute of Justice.

Henggeler, S. W., Melton, G. B., Brondino, M. J., Scherer, D. G. & Hanley, J. H. (1997). Multisystemic therapy with violent and chronic juvenile offenders and their families: The role of treatment fidelity in successful dissemination. *Journal of Consulting and Clinical Psychology, 65*, 821–833.

Henggeler, S. W., Melton, G. B. & Smith, L. A. (1992). Family preservation using multisystemic therapy: An effective alternative to incarcerating serious juvenile offenders. *Journal of Consulting and Clinical Psychology, 60*, 953–961.

Henggeler, S. W., Melton, G. B., Smith, L. A., Schoenwald, S. K. & Hanley, J. H. (1993). Family preservation using multisystemic treatment: Long-term follow-up to a clinical trial with serious juvenile offenders. *Journal of Child and Family Studies, 2,* 283–293.

Henggeler, S. W. & Sheidow, A. J. (2003). Conduct disorder and delinquency. *Journal of Marital and Family Therapy, 29,* 505–522.

Henry, B., Caspi, A., Moffitt, T. E. & Silva, P. A. (1996). Temperamental and familial predictors of violent and nonviolent criminal convictions: Age 3 to age 18. *Developmental Psychology, 32,* 614–623.

Heyman, R. E. & Neidig, P. H. (1997). Physical aggression couples treatment. In W. K. Halford & H. J. Markman (Eds), *Clinical handbook of marriage and couples intervention* (pp. 589–617). New York: John Wiley & Sons.

Hilton, N. Z. & Harris, G. T. (2005). Predicting wife assault: A critical review and implications for policy and practice. *Trauma, Violence & Abuse, 6,* 3–23.

Hollin, C. R. & Palmer, E. J. (2003). Level of Service Inventory – Revised profiles of violent and nonviolent prisoners. *Journal of Interpersonal Violence, 18,* 1075–1086.

Holtzworth-Munroe, A., Bates, L., Smutzler, N. & Sandin, E. (1997). A brief review of the research on husband violence. Part I: Maritally violent versus nonviolent men. *Aggression & Violent Behavior, 2,* 65–99.

Holtzworth-Munroe, A. & Meehan, J. C. (2004). Typologies of men who are maritally violent: Scientific and clinical implications. *Journal of Interpersonal Violence, 19,* 1369–1389.

Holtzworth-Munroe, A. & Stuart, G. L. (1994). Typologies of male batterers: Three subtypes and the differences among them. *Psychological Bulletin, 116,* 476–497.

Howells, K. (1989). Anger-management methods in relation to the prevention of violent behavior. In J. Archer & K. Browne (Eds), *Human aggression: Naturalistic approaches* (pp. 153–181). London: Routledge.

Howells, K. (1998). Cognitive behavioural interventions for anger, aggression and violence. In N. Tarrier, A. Wells & G. Haddock (Eds), *Treating complex cases: The cognitive behavioural therapy approach* (pp. 295–318). Chichester: John Wiley & Sons.

Howells, K. (2004). Anger and its link to violent offending. *Psychiatry, Psychology and Law, 11,* 189–196.

Howells, K. & Day, A. (2002). Grasping the nettle: Treating and rehabilitating the violent offender. *Australian Psychologist, 37,* 222–228.

Howells, K. & Day, A. (2003). Readiness for anger management: Clinical and theoretical issues. *Clinical Psychology Review, 23,* 319–337.

Howells, K. et al. (2001). *An evaluation of anger management programs with violent offenders in two Australian states.* Adelaide, Australia: University of South Australia Forensic and Applied Psychology Research Group.

Howells, K. et al. (2005). Brief anger management programs with offenders: Outcomes and predictors of change. *Journal of Forensic Psychiatry and Psychology, 16,* 296–311.

Howells, K., Watt, B., Hall, G. & Baldwin, S. (1997). Developing programmes for violent offenders. *Legal and Criminological Psychology, 2,* 117–128.

Howland, E. W., Kosson, D. S., Patterson, C. M. & Newman, J. P. (1993). Altering a dominant response: Performance of psychopaths and low-socialization college students on a cued reaction time task. *Journal of Abnormal Psychology, 102,* 379–387.

Jackson, S., Feder, L., Forde, D. R., Davis, R. C., Maxwell, C. D. & Taylor, B. G. (2003). *Batterer intervention programs where do we go from here?* Washington DC: NIJ.

Jacobson, N. & Gottman, J. (1998). *When men batter women: New insights into ending abusive relationships.* New York: Simon and Schuster.

John, O. P. & Srivastava, S. (1999). The big five trait taxonomy: History, measurement, and theoretical perspectives. In L. A. Pervin & O. P. John (Eds), *Handbook of personality (2nd edition)* (pp. 102–138). New York: Guilford.

Johnson, M. P. (1995). Patriarchal terrorism and common couple violence: Two forms of violence against women. *Journal of Marriage and the Family, 57,* 283–294.

Jones, A. S., D'Agostino, R. B., Gondolf, E. W. & Heckert, A. (2004). Assessing the effect of batterer program completion on reassault using propensity scores. *Journal of Interpersonal Violence, 19,* 1002–1020.

Jones, E. E. & Pulos, S. M. (1993). Comparing the process in psychodynamic and cognitive-behavioral therapies. *Journal of Consulting and Clinical Psychology, 61*, 306–316.

Kohlberg, L. (1969). Stage and sequence: The cognitive-developmental approach to socialization. In D. A. Goslin (Ed.), *Handbook of socialization theory and research* (pp. 347–480). Chicago, IL: Rand McNally.

Lane, G. & Russell, T. (1989). Second-order systemic work with violent couples. In P. L. Caesar & L. K. Hamberger (Eds), *Treating men who batter: Theory, practice, and programs* (pp. 134–162). New York: Springer.

Leeman, L. W., Gibbs, J. C. & Fuller, D. (1993). Evaluation of a multicomponent group treatment program for juvenile delinquents. *Aggressive Behavior, 19*, 281–292.

Lösel, F. (1998). Treatment and management of psychopaths. In D. J. Cooke, A. E. Forth, J. Newman & R. D. Hare (Eds), *Psychopathy: Theory, research and implications for society* (pp. 303–354). Netherlands: Kluwer Academic Publishers.

Loza, W. & Loza-Fanous, A. (1999a). Anger and prediction of violent and nonviolent offenders' recidivism. *Journal of Interpersonal Violence, 14*, 1014–1029.

Loza, W. & Loza-Fanous, A. (1999b). The fallacy of reducing rape and violent recidivism by treating anger. *International Journal of Offender Therapy and Comparative Criminology, 43*, 492–502.

Magdol, L., Moffitt, T. E., Caspi, A. & Silva, P. A. (1998). Developmental antecedents of partner abuse: A prospective-longitudinal study. *Journal of Abnormal Psychology, 107*, 375–389.

Mederos, F. (1999). Batterer intervention programs: The past, and future prospects. In M. F. Shepard & E. L. Pence (Eds), *Co-ordinating community responses to domestic violence: Lessons from Duluth and beyond* (pp. 127–150). Thousand Oaks, CA: Sage.

Meichenbaum, D. H. (1975). *Stress inoculation training.* New York: Pergamon.

Mills, J. F. & Kroner, D. G. (2003). Anger as a predictor of institutional misconduct and recidivism in a sample of violent offenders. *Journal of Interpersonal Violence, 18*, 282–294.

Moffitt, T. E. (1993). Adolescence-limited and life-course-persistent antisocial behavior: A developmental taxonomy. *Psychological Review, 100*, 674–701.

Moffitt, T. E., Robins, R. W. & Caspi, A. (2001). A couples analysis of partner abuse with implications for abuse-prevention policy. *Criminology and Public Policy, 1*, 5–36.

Motiuk, L., Smiley, C. & Blanchette, K. (1996). Intensive programming for violent offenders: A comparative investigation. *Forum on Corrections Research, 8*, 10–12.

Neidig, P. H. & Friedman, D. (1984). *Spouse abuse: A treatment program for couples.* Champaign, IL; Research Press.

Norlander, B. & Eckhardt, C. (2005). Anger, hostility, and male perpetrators of intimate partner violence: A meta-analytic view. *Clinical Psychology Review, 25*, 119–152.

Novaco, R. W. (1975). *Anger control: The development and evaluation of an experimental treatment.* Lexington, MA: Lexington Books.

Novaco, R. W. (1979). The cognitive regulation of anger and stress. In P. C. Kendall & S. D. Hollon (Eds), *Cognitive behavioral interventions: Theory, research and procedures* (pp. 241–285). New York: Academic Press.

Novaco, R. W. (1994). Anger as a risk factor for violence. In J. Monahan & H. J. Steadman (Eds), *Violence and mental disorder: Developments in risk assessment* (pp. 21–59). Chicago, IL: University of Chicago Press.

Novaco, R. W. (1997). Remediating anger and aggression with violent offenders. *Legal and Criminological Psychology, 2*, 77–88.

Nugent, W. R. (1999). The effects of aggression replacement training on male and female antisocial behavior in a runaway shelter. *Research on Social Work Practice, 9*, 466–482.

Nussbaum, D., Collins, M., Cutter, J., Zimmerman, W., Farguson, B. & Jacques, I. (2002). Crime type and specific personality indicia": Cloninger's TCI impulsivity, empathy, and attachment subscales in non-violent, violent and sexual offenders. *American Journal of Forensic Psychology, 20*, 23–56.

O'Farrell, T. J., Murphy, C. M., Stephan, S. H., Fals-Stewart, W. & Murphy, M. (2004). Partner violence before and after couples-based alcoholism treatment for male alcoholic patients: The role of treatment involvement and abstinence. *Journal of Consulting and Clinical Psychology, 72*, 202–217.

O'Leary, K. D., Heyman, R. E. & Neidig, P. H. (1999). Treatment of wife abuse: A comparison of gender-specific and conjoint approaches. *Behavior Therapy, 30*, 475–505.

Palmer, S. E., Brown, R. A. & Berrera, M. E. (1992). Group treatment program for abusive husbands: Long term evaluation. *American Journal of Orthopsychiatry, 62*, 276–283.

Pence, E. (1989). Batterer programs: Shifting from community collusion to community confrontation. In P. L. Caesar & L. K. Hamberger (Eds), *Treating men who batter: Theory, practice, and programs* (pp. 24–50). New York: Springer.

Pence, E. & Paymar, M. (1993). *Education groups for men who batter: The Duluth model.* New York: Springer.

Pepler, D. J. & Slaby, R. G. (1994). Theoretical and developmental perspectives on youth and violence. In L. D. Eron, J. H. Gentry & P. Schlegel (Eds), *Reason to hope: A psychosocial perspective on violence and youth* (pp. 27–58). Washington DC: APA.

Polaschek, D. L. L. & Collie, R. M. (2004). Rehabilitating serious violent adult offenders: An empirical and theoretical stocktake. *Psychology, Crime and Law, 10*, 321–334.

Polaschek, D. L. L., Collie, R. M. & Walkey, F. H. (2004). Criminal attitudes to violence: Development and preliminary validation of a scale for male prisoners. *Aggressive Behavior, 30*, 484–503.

Polaschek, D. L. L. & Dixon, B. G. (2001). The violence prevention project: The development and evaluation of a treatment programme for violent offenders. *Psychology, Crime, and Law, 7*, 1–23.

Polaschek, D. L. L. & Reynolds, N. (2001). Violent offenders: Assessment and treatment. In C. R. Hollin (Ed.), *Handbook of offender assessment and treatment* (pp. 415–431). Chichester, UK: Wiley.

Polaschek, D. L. L., Wilson, N. J., Townsend, M. & Daly, L. (2005). Cognitive-behavioral rehabilitation for high-risk violent offenders: An outcome evaluation of the violence prevention unit. *Journal of Interpersonal Violence, 20*, 1611–1627.

Quinsey, V. L., Harris, G. T., Rice, M. E. & Cormier, C. A. (1998). *Violent offenders: Appraising and managing risk.* Washington DC: American Psychological Association.

Reddy, L. A. & Goldstein, A. P. (2001). Aggression replacement training: A multimodal intervention for aggressive adolescents. *Residential Treatment for Children & Youth, 18*, 47–62.

Rice, M. E., Harris, G. T. & Cormier, C. A. (1992). An evaluation of a maximum security therapeutic community for psychopaths and other mentally disordered offenders. *Law and Human Behavior, 16*, 399–412.

Rooney, J. & Hanson, R. K. (2001). Predicting attrition from treatment programs for abusive men. *Journal of Family Violence, 16(2)*, 131–149.

Salekin, R. T. (2002). Psychopathy and therapeutic pessimism: Clinical lore or clinical reality? *Clinical Psychology Review, 22*, 79–112.

Saunders, D. G. (1989). Cognitive and behavioral interventions with men who batter: Application and outcome. In P. L. Caesar & L. K. Hamberger (Eds), *Treating men who batter: Theory, practice, and programs* (pp. 77–99). New York: Springer.

Saunders, D. G. & Hamill, R. M. (2003). *Violence against women: Synthesis of research on offender interventions* (No. NCJ 201222). Washington DC: National Institute of Justice.

Schaeffer, C. M. & Borduin, C. M. (2005). Long-term follow-up to a randomized clinical trial of Multisystemic Therapy with serious and violent juvenile offenders. *Journal of Consulting and Clinical Psychology, 73*, 445–453.

Schumacher, J. A., Feldbau-Kohn, S., Slep, A. M. & Heyman, R. E. (2001). Risk factors for male-to-female partner physical abuse. *Aggression and Violent Behavior, 6*, 281–352.

Seager, J. A. (2005). Violent men: The importance of impulsivity and cognitive schema. *Criminal Justice and Behavior, 32*, 26–49.

Selby, M. J. (1984). Assessment of violence potential using measures of anger, hostility, and social desirability. *Journal of Personality Assessment, 48*, 531–544.

Serin, R. C. (1991). Psychopathy and violence in criminals. *Journal of Interpersonal Violence, 6*, 423–431.

Serin, R. C. (1994). *Treating violent offenders: A review of current practices.* Report No. R-38. Ottawa: Correctional Research and Development, Correctional Services of Canada.

Serin, R. C. (1995). *Persistently violent (non-sexual) offenders: A program proposal.* Report No. R-42. Ottawa: Correctional Services of Canada.

Serin, R. C. (2004). Understanding violent offenders. In D. H. Fishbein (Ed.), *The science, treatment and prevention of antisocial behaviours. Volume 2: Evidence-based practice* (pp. 12–13). Kingston, NJ: Civic Research Institute.

Serin, R. C. & Brown, S. (1996). Strategies for enhancing the treatment of violent offenders. *Forum on Corrections Research, 8(3),* 45–48.

Serin, R. C. & Kuriychuk, M. (1994). Social and cognitive processing deficits in violent offenders: Implications for treatment. *International Journal of Law and Psychiatry, 17,* 431–441.

Serin, R. C. & Preston, D. L. (2001a). Designing, implementing and managing treatment programs for violent offenders. In G. A. Bernfeld, D. P. Farrington & A. W. Leschied (Eds), *Offender rehabilitation in practice* (pp. 205–221). Chichester: John Wiley & Sons.

Serin, R. C. & Preston, D. L. (2001b). Managing and treating violent offenders. In J. B. Ashford, B. D. Sales & W. H. Reid (Eds), *Treating adult and juvenile offenders with special needs* (pp. 249–271). Washington, DC: APA.

Serin, R. C., Preston, D. L. & Murphy, S. (2001). Programming for persistently violent offenders.*International Community Corrections Association Journal,* 19–23.

Simourd, D. J. & Hoge, R. D. (2000). Criminal psychopathy: A risk-and-need perspective. *Criminal Justice & Behavior, 27,* 256–272.

Slaby, R. G. & Guerra, N. G. (1988). Cognitive mediators of aggression in adolescent offenders: 1. Assessment. *Developmental Psychology, 24,* 580–588.

Spielberger, C. D. (1988). *State-Trait Anger Expression Inventory: Research edition professional manual.* Odessa, FL: Psychological Assessment Resources Inc.

Stewart, L., Hill, J. & Cripps, J. (2001). Treatment of family violence in correctional settings. In L. L. Motiuk & R. C. Serin (Eds), *Compendium 2000 on effective correctional programming.* Ottawa, Ontario: Ministry of Supply and Services.

Stith, S. M. & Farley, S. C. (1993). A predictive model of male spousal violence. *Journal of Family Violence, 8,* 183–201.

Stith, S. M., McCollum, E. E., Rosen, K. H. & Locke, L. D. (2002). Multiple couple group treatment for domestic violence. In F. Kaslow (Ed.), *Comprehensive textbook of psychotherapy* (Vol. 4.) (pp. 499–520). New York: Wiley.

Stith, S. M., Rosen, K. H. & McCollum, E. E. (2002). Developing a manualized couples treatment for domestic violence: Overcoming challenges. *Journal of Marital and Family Therapy, 28(1),* 21–25.

Stith, S. M., Rosen, K. H., McCollum, E. E. & Thomsen, C. J. (2004a). Treating intimate partner violence within intact couple relationships: Outcomes of multi-couple versus individual couple therapy. *Journal of Marital and Family Therapy, 30,* 305–318.

Stith, S. M., Rosen, K. H., Middleton, K. A., Busch, A. L., Lundeberg, K. & Carlton, R. P. (2000). The intergenerational transmission of spouse abuse: A meta-analysis. *Journal of Marriage & the Family. 6,* 640–654.

Stith, S. M., Smith, D. B., Penn, C. E., Ward, D. B. & Tritt, D. (2004b). Intimate partner physical abuse perpetration and victimization risk factors: A meta-analytic review. *Aggression and Violent Behavior, 10,* 65–98.

Straus, M. A. & Gelles, R. J. (1986). Societal change and change in family violence from 1975 to 1985 as revealed by two national surveys. *Journal of Marriage and the Family, 48,* 465–479.

Sugarman, D. B. & Frankel, S. L. (1996). Patriarchal ideology and wife-assault: A meta-analytic review. *Journal of Family Violence, 11,* 13–40.

Taft, C. T., Murphy, C. M., King, D. W., Musser, P. H. & DeDeyn, J. M. (2003). Process and treatment adherence factors in group cognitive-behavioural therapy for partner violent men. *Journal of Consulting and Clinical Psychology, 71,* 812–820.

Taft, C. T., Murphy, C. M., Musser, P. H. & Remington, N. A. (2004). Personality, interpersonal, and motivational predictors of the working alliance in group cognitive-behavioral therapy for partner violent men. *Journal of Consulting and Clinical Psychology, 72(2),* 349–354.

Tavris, C. (1989). *Anger: The misunderstood emotion.* New York: Simon & Schuster.

Tolman, R. M. (2001). An ecological analysis of batterer intervention program standards. *Journal of Aggression, Maltreatment and Trauma, 5*, 221–233.

Trute, B. (1998). Going beyond gender-specific treatments in wife battering: Pro-feminist couple and family therapy. *Aggression and Violent Behavior, 3*, 1–15.

Wallace, J. E. & Newman, J. P. (2004). A theory-based treatment model for psychopathy. *Cognitive and Behavioral Practice, 11*, 178–189.

Wang, E. W. & Diamond, P. M. (1999). Empirically identifying factors related to violence risk in corrections. *Behavioral Sciences and the Law, 17*, 377–389.

Ward, T. & Marshall, W. L. (2004). Good lives, aetiology and the rehabilitation of sex offenders: A bridging theory. *Journal of Sexual Aggression, 10*, 153–169.

Ward, T., Polaschek, D. L. L. & Beech, A. B. (2005). *Theories of sexual offending*. Chichester: John Wiley & Sons.

White. J. L., Moffitt, T. E., Caspi, A., Bartusch, J., Needles, D. J. & Stouthamer-Loeber, M. (1994). Measuring impulsivity and examining its relationship to delinquency. *Journal of Abnormal Psychology, 103*, 192–205.

White, R. J., Gondolf, E. W., Robertson, D. U., Goodwin, B. J. & Caraveo, L. E. (2002). Extent and characteristics of woman batterers among federal inmates. *International Journal of Offender Therapy and Comparative Criminology, 46*, 412–426.

Wileman, R. (2000). "Innovation should not be treason": Domestic violence interventions. *Australian and New Zealand Journal of Family Therapy, 21(1)*, 16–21.

Wilson, N. J. (2002). *Recidivism study Hawkes Bay Young Offenders Unit (YOU)*. New Zealand Department of Corrections Psychological Service: Unpublished internal memo, 1 November 2002.

Wilson, N. J. (2003). *Recidivism study of Waikeria Bay of Plenty Regional Prison Youth Offenders*. New Zealand Department of Corrections Psychological Service: Unpublished internal memo, 31 October 2003.

Wilson, N. J. (2004). *New Zealand high-risk offenders: Who are they and what are the issues in their management and treatment?* Wellington, New Zealand: Department of Corrections. Unpublished report, July.

Wong, S. & Gordon, A. (2000). *Violence risk scale*. Unpublished report for review purposes only.

Wong, S. & Hare, R. D. (2005). *Guidelines for a psychopathy treatment program*. Toronto, Canada: Multi-Health Systems.

Yochelson, S. & Samenow, S. (1977). *The criminal personality, volume 2: The change process*. New York: Jason Aronsen.

Zamble, E. & Quinsey, V. L. (1997). *The criminal recidivism process*. Cambridge, UK: CUP.

Chapter 5

SEX OFFENDER PROGRAMMES: CONCEPT, THEORY, AND PRACTICE

RUTH E. MANN* AND YOLANDA M. FERNANDEZ[†]

*HM Prison Service, England & Wales
[†]Correctional Service of Canada

INTRODUCTION

The danger of a gulf between psychological science and clinical practice is as relevant to sexual offender therapy as it is to the treatment of other disorders. The public may demand definitive answers: which parent should get custody? Is the rapist cured? Is the accusation accurate/true? Often, frustratingly, science offers only probabilities and likelihoods. Moreover, pure clinicians may claim that research captures only a glimpse of the real person or note that therapy was helping people long before science came along (Lilienfeld, Lynn & Lohr, 2003). However, therapies based on scientifically unvalidated claims rather than empirically supported findings may be at best ineffective and at worst harmful.

The treatment of sexual offenders provides a good example of a domain that has attempted to close the "scientist-practitioner gap". As with most scientifically validated therapies, sexual offender therapy has changed and improved with new research and information. Although many strategies for treating sexual offenders have been based on established paradigms from other validated therapies, researchers have striven to demonstrate similar validity for sexual offender populations. While early approaches to sex offender therapy relied heavily on anecdotal and case study examples, current research papers on sexual offenders are typically studies published in peer-reviewed journals, providing the opportunity for corrective feedback. The following chapter will describe the empirical bases for sexual offender treatment as it exists today. It is our belief that as research in this area continues, therapy for sexual offenders will continue to expand, evolve, and improve.

Offending Behaviour Programmes: Development, Application, and Controversies. Edited by C.R. Hollin and E.J. Palmer.
Copyright © 2006 John Wiley & Sons Ltd.

RATIONALE FOR SEX OFFENDER PROGRAMMES

Early approaches to treating sexual offenders were often psychoanalytic in nature. The focus was on helping the offender identify and resolve early life conflicts or traumas that were assumed to have triggered the offending behaviour. Sexual disorders, including sexual offending, were conceptualised as fixations at various stages of psychosexual development and were addressed through psychodynamic techniques such as free association and dream analysis. The evaluations of this approach to treatment have reported inadequate results (Crawford, 1981).

Although the development of behavioural approaches to treating sexual offenders marked an improvement, in terms of being more empirically based than psychoanalytic treatment, these approaches were also significantly limited in scope. Behaviourists viewed inappropriate sexual urges as "learned" through early sexual experiences that created associations with the deviant stimuli and were then maintained through masturbation and fantasy (McGuire, Carlisle & Young, 1965). Early articles on behavioural treatments were limited to case reports, with the majority using some form of aversion therapy (Marshall, Anderson & Fernandez, 1999). Aversive techniques made use of classical conditioning and punishment paradigms in which aversive events (for example, electric shock, a nausea-inducing substance) are paired with images of the behaviour to be eliminated. Socially condoned negative views of those who engage in inappropriate sexual behaviours most likely contributed to the general acceptance of aversive techniques for the treatment of sexual deviance (Marshall et al., 1999). As the area of sexual offender treatment has evolved most treatment programmes have become considerably more comprehensive, incorporating cognitive-behavioural and social learning approaches in addition to behavioural strategies. In fact, the Safer Society Press survey (2000) of sexual offender treatment programmes stated that the most commonly reported treatment approach for sexual offenders is cognitive-behavioural and delivered in a group format (86% of programmes for adult males and 89% of programmes for adolescents). Gene Abel and colleagues have been credited as the early leaders in the expansion of knowledge and treatment targets in sexual offender treatment (Abel, 1976; Abel, Barlow, Blanchard & Guild, 1977; Abel, Becker & Skinner, 1983; Abel, Blanchard & Becker, 1978; Abel, Osborn, Anthony & Gardos, 1992). Others soon followed this lead and programmes quickly became more comprehensive (Knopp, 1984; Marshall & Williams, 1975; Perkins, 1977). Interestingly, despite the widespread acceptance of the cognitive-behavioural model for treating sexual offenders, very little has been done until recently to provide robust empirical evaluations of treatment (as will be discussed later in this chapter). Nonetheless, cognitive-behavioural methods are now widely accepted as the most effective approach to the treatment of sexual offenders and are recommended by the Association for the Treatment of Sexual Abusers' (ATSA's) "Ethical Standards and Principles for the Management of Sexual Abusers" (Association for the Treatment of Sexual Abusers, 2001); a set of standards based on the research and agreement of identified specialists in the field of sexual offender treatment.

As noted, the Safer Society Press (2000) reported that the majority of sexual offender treatment programmes are cognitive-behavioural and delivered in a group format. There is, unfortunately, little research on the issue of group versus individual therapy in sexual offender treatment and it remains a contentious issue. Those who favour individual therapy describe numerous advantages to this approach such as increased confidentiality (noting that it is difficult to guarantee confidentiality in a group setting); greater opportunities to explore individual issues relating to an offender's offence cycle; and flexibility of session and overall treatment length (Abracen & Looman, 2004; Maletzky, 1993, 1998; Williams, 1995.) Advocates of individual therapy further suggest that individual sessions provide greater opportunity to address issues such as client reticence, anxiety, low functioning, disruptive behaviour, and difficult or embarrassing topics (Abracen & Looman, 2004). Maletzky (1999) proposed that groups can take on a tyrannical atmosphere when group members are allowed to make decisions on major issues, such as the continued participation of one group member.

Critics of individual treatment typically cite issues of cost and time as the biggest disadvantage with this approach. There is little doubt that one-on-one treatment is more time consuming, labour intensive and expensive than offering treatment in a group setting, and in this era of fiscal restraint among most organisations that is not an issue that can be dismissed lightly. However, many other advantages to group therapy have also been described by various authors. Jennings & Sawyer (2003) pointed out that according to theories of group process a group offers unique opportunities to its members that simply are not available in a one-on-one setting. They note that the basis of group therapy is that it gains its therapeutic potency from the interactions and relationships that emerge during the group process (Rutan & Stone, 1993; Yalom, 1995). Marshall and Barbaree (1990) indicated there is value in facilitating insight among group members and the presence of other participants provide opportunities for acquiring new perspectives that would not otherwise be available. Serran, Fernandez, Marshall & Mann's (2003) discussion of process issues in sexual offender therapy suggested that effective therapists may use group settings to their advantage to practise skills, promote reinforcement of individual gains, promote mutual encouragement and support, and create a positive therapeutic atmosphere. While proponents of individual therapy have commented that group treatment is more difficult to tailor to individual needs (Maletzky, 1999), Serran et al. proposed that more effective therapists may incorporate enough flexibility into their treatment programme appropriately to address individual issues within the group setting.

As noted earlier, commentators have looked at the issue of individual versus group treatment of sexual offenders, and even those who have been proponents of the individual approach (Maletzky, 1993, 1998) have questioned their previous conclusions in more recent papers, criticising the earlier research as retrospective, uncontrolled and geographically limited (Maletzky, 1999). Marshall & Williams (2000) contended that offering group therapy participants the option of one-on-one sessions may discourage offenders from discussing critical issues in group sessions. They concluded that there is no evidence that individual therapy is conducive to changes in sexual offenders and suggest that all treatment should be done in a group format. In contrast, Di Fazio, Abracen & Looman (2001) reported that participants specifically selected for individual therapy from those referred to their programme because of cognitive deficits and acute psychiatric symptoms, demonstrated post-treatment recidivism rates that were similar to the sexual offenders who participated in the full treatment programme. The authors concluded that high risk/high needs sexual offenders who also suffer from cognitive deficits, social skills deficits, and psychiatric problems may be better suited for, and benefit equally well from, individual therapy programmes. They noted that the requirements of a full treatment programme might be unrealistic for sexual offenders burdened with additional problems and that treatment material may be pared down and simplified during individual sessions. Of course, an alternative is to provide specialised programmes for sexual offenders who are lower functioning or suffer from psychiatric problems and many centres, such as HM Prison Service in England and Wales, have done just that.

EVIDENCE BASE FOR PROGRAMME TARGETS

What areas should sexual offender treatment target in order to be most likely to reduce recidivism? The Risk-Needs model of change for offender rehabilitation (Andrews & Bonta, 2003) suggests that treatment targets should be defined by dynamic criminogenic factors – those variables amenable to change that have been empirically linked to recidivism risk. This is essentially an atheoretical approach: a treatment programme can be created that targets multiple variables but for which a unifying underlying theory of sexual offending is not essential.

The types of criminogenic factors that have been most robustly established as predictive of sexual recidivism are static factors, which by definition are not amenable to treatment (Hanson & Bussière, 1998). Dynamic risk factors, which are potentially changeable, should therefore form a programme's targets, but these have been less conclusively established. However, recent meta-analyses (for example Hanson & Bussière, 1998; Hanson & Morton-Bourgon, 2004), large-scale follow-up projects (for example, Hanson & Harris, 2000) and psychometric classification studies (for example, Beech, Friendship, Erikson & Hanson, 2002) have produced reasonably consistent findings to inform treatment programme design. Current thinking has identified four domains of psychological risk factors for sexual offenders (Craissati & Beech, 2003; Hanson, 2000; Thornton, 2002): sexual arousal factors; attitudes tolerant of sexual assault; interpersonal deficits; and self-regulation deficits. Hanson (2000) also included a fifth domain concerned with negative social environment, but this could perhaps be viewed as involving situational rather than individual risk factors, in which case the problems might be more effectively targeted by a risk management strategy rather than a treatment programme.

It should be noted that not all sexual offenders will display deficits in all domains. Treatment planning should encompass comprehensive assessment and any programme, including manualised group programmes (see Chapter 2), should be flexible enough to accommodate offenders with different risk factors working within the same programme.

In suggesting suitable treatment targets, we will consider each of the four proposed risk domains in turn.

Sexual Arousal Factors

There is evidence that many child molesters prefer the idea of sexual relations with children to the idea of sexual intercourse with adults, and such a deviant preference has been clearly linked to recidivism risk (Hanson & Bussière, 1998; Hanson & Morton-Bourgon, 2004). This preference is likely to be especially true for offenders with young, male victims (Seto & Lalumière, 2001). There is less evidence for the notion that rapists of adult women show a preference for coercive sexual activity, although this is probably the case with the most dangerous, repetitive, rape offenders. Furthermore, many sexual offenders are found to be sexually pre-occupied, placing abnormally high emphasis on the need to have sexual relations frequently (Beech, 1997; Firestone et al., 1998; Hanson & Harris, 2000; Hanson & Morton-Bourgon, 2004).

Suitable targets for treatment within this domain, therefore, include the reduction of deviant sexual arousal and fantasy, increasing pleasure and arousal to ideas of consenting sex with other adults, and reduction of the level of importance placed on frequent sexual activity.

Attitudes Tolerant of Sexual Assault

Attitudes supporting sexual assault, such as child abuse supportive beliefs or rape myths have been extensively researched with respect to their relationship to recidivism risk. Many individual studies have found that child abuse supportive beliefs are held more strongly by child molesters than non-molesters (for example, Bumby, 1995) although the relevance of rape supportive beliefs for rapists is less well established (for example, Blumenthal, Gudjonsson & Burns, 1999). Moreover, the most recent meta-analytic study of dynamic risk factors for sexual offending did not find a strong predictive effect for offence-supportive attitudes (Hanson & Morton-Bourgon, 2004). Other types of dysfunctional thinking styles that have been identified in sexual offenders include sexual entitlement (Hanson, Gizzarelli & Scott, 1994), negative views of women and their sexuality (Malamuth & Brown, 1994; Marshall & Hambley, 1996) and general aggressive thinking (Thornton, 2002).

It is therefore recommended that treatment programmes address the way in which offenders view women and children, including processing errors they make in interpreting women's and children's behaviour, their beliefs about the lack of harm caused by sexual offending, and the way in which they see their rights towards these women and children in terms of sexual activity.

Interpersonal Deficits

Sexual offenders are known to exhibit a wide range of interpersonal deficits, which have been empirically related to sexual offending (Marshall et al., 1999). Sexual offenders tend to have negative expectancies of both themselves and others, suffering from low self-esteem (Thornton, Beech & Marshall, 2004), external locus of control, personal distress, and under-assertiveness (Fisher, Beech & Browne, 1993), emotional loneliness (Garlick, Marshall & Thornton, 1996), and paranoid hostility towards others (Firestone et al., 1998; Hanson & Bussière, 1998; Mann, 2005). Perhaps not surprisingly, given these symptoms, sex offenders often eschew intimate relationships with other adults and may feel that intimacy with children offers more safety (Fisher et al., 1993; Hanson & Morton-Bourgon, 2004). Therefore, appropriate targets for treatment within this domain include poor adult relationship skills, intimacy and attachment problems, over-sexualisation of relationships, failure to relate to others in emotionally supportive and intimate ways, difficulties with self-disclosure, and conflict resolution. Sexual offender programmes should aim to raise self-esteem, increase perceptions of personal autonomy, improve assertiveness and intimacy skills, and challenge paranoid and vengeful schemas about other people.

Self-regulation Deficits

Poor self-regulation is a key issue for criminality in general, and has also been found to be relevant to sexual assaulters (see, for example, Polascheck, Hudson, Ward & Siegert, 2001; Prentky & Knight, 1986; Prentky et al., 1991). Self-regulation problems can be divided into three aspects, following Thornton (2002): lifestyle impulsiveness (such as that associated with psychopathy), poor problem-solving, and lack of emotional regulation. Treatment programmes therefore should aim to reduce impulsivity, teach the skills necessary to think through problems and evaluate solutions logically ("detached coping"; Roger, 1995) as opposed to avoiding problems or reacting emotionally to them, and teach strategies for managing problematic emotions such as anger.

PROGRAMME CONTENT AND APPLICATION ISSUES

Most sexual offenders are treated in correctional or forensic settings, given that they rarely come to the attention of treatment providers unless they have been officially identified (typically through legal contacts). Andrews and colleagues (Andrews & Bonta, 2003; Andrews et al., 1990) have outlined the components of an effective correctional treatment programme for a general forensic population based on meta-analyses of the treatment literature, such as the need to target higher risk offenders, the advantages of behavioural over non-behavioural approaches, and the importance of anti-criminal modelling and reinforcement. Appropriate treatment targets include dynamic criminogenic needs, which are malleable to intervention. Andrews & Bonta (2003) argue that the above principles are also relevant to "unique" populations including female offenders, juvenile offenders, mentally disordered offenders, violent offenders, and sexual offenders, although they do note that factors such as inappropriate sexual arousal may be distinctive to sexual offenders.

As described above, programme targets in sexual offender treatment include sexual arousal factors, attitudes tolerant of sexual assault, interpersonal deficits, and self-regulation deficits. Each of these targets may be addressed in a variety of ways but while programmes vary to some degree from site to site there appears to be a general consensus as to the typical components that make up the content of sexual offender treatment programmes.

Sexual Arousal Factors

Attempts to modify sexual interests or preferences in the treatment of sexual offenders have typically utilised behavioural procedures. All of the procedures that have been developed or adopted for this use explicitly rest on behavioural principles; typically operant or Pavlovian conditioning processes. Aversive therapies of various kinds (electric, olfactory, or covert) were derived from research investigating methods of eliminating avoidance or escape behaviours in infrahuman animals (Laws & Marshall, 2003). Covert sensitisation, which involves the association between stimuli that match the typical sequence of behaviours that precede offending and relevant consequences, as well as masturbatory procedures designed to eliminate attraction to deviant acts (satiation) and enhance attraction to pro-social sex (masturbatory reconditioning), have been proposed as alternative, less punitive methods for reducing deviant arousal (Fernandez, Shingler & Marshall, 2006). However, various authors have expressed doubt that such procedures generate conditioned aversion to sexually inappropriate stimuli (Marshall & Eccles, 1993) and point out that there is no evidence that assessed reductions of deviant arousal in the treatment setting generalise to the client's real world.

Organic treatments have also been used for controlling deviant sexual arousal in some sexual offenders. Such treatments may include hormonal medications such as antiandrogen medication, surgical castration, or stereotaxic neurosurgery. These treatments effect changes in the body's neuroendrocrine systems by reducing the level of serum testosterone in the body, resulting in the reduction of sexual arousal (Bradford, 1985) or by reducing overt behaviours by surgically introducing lesions in the brain (Bradford, 1985). The limited research on castration, primarily conducted in Europe, does not specify the population of offenders sufficiently enough to evaluate the effect castration has had on reducing deviant sexual behaviours in groups of sexual offenders (Marshall, Jones, Ward, Johnston & Barbaree, 1991). While studies of antiandrogen medications have demonstrated success in suppressing overall sexual behaviours (Bradford, 1985, 1988, 1990; Fedoroff & Fedoroff, 1992; Kravitz et al., 1995; Marshall, 1993) they appear to be more appropriate for those sexual offenders for whom sexual motivation plays a significant role and not as a generalised treatment (Bradford, 1997). Additionally, difficulties associated with organic treatments of deviant sexual arousal include problems with patient compliance, side effects, and ethical issues related to performing irreversible procedures such as castration or stereotaxic surgery on patients.

There has been a move among sexual offender treatment programmes to include training in appropriate ways to meet sexual and relevant needs in prosocial ways (for example, enhancing attractiveness to adult consenting partners, self-confidence boosting, relationship skills training). Unfortunately, there has been a serious neglect of research attention on the evaluation of the effectiveness of these procedures with sexual offenders. Further research is needed to generate evaluations of the effectiveness of the procedures used to target deviant interests.

Attitudes Tolerant of Sexual Assault

Denial, minimisation, and/or rationalisation of offending is a dynamic factor that has long been considered important to sexual offending (Barbaree & Cortoni, 1993; Marshall, 1994; Scully & Marolla, 1984). In fact, reduction of denial and minimisations of offending behaviour tend to be the focus early in treatment as it is believed that overcoming denial and minimisation is necessary for a comprehensive and truthful offence analysis to take place (Maletzky, 1993). Group participation and process is essential at this point as other offenders within a group typically provide more credible challenges than the therapists to inappropriate thoughts and beliefs (Marshall et al., 1999). Therapists explain and encourage cognitive restructuring to encourage anti-offending thoughts and beliefs. Initially participants are challenged by the therapists and other group members but are eventually taught the skill of self-challenging.

Many treatment programmes also include a victim empathy component designed to challenge offender's justifications of their offending, expand self-challenging by improving the offender's understanding of the victim's experience, and create dissonance between pro-offending attitudes and the offender's self-concept by identifying short- and long-term effects of the offence on themselves, the victim, and others (Marshall et al., 1999). Since the mid-1990s, research on empathy in sexual offenders has supported focusing on victim specific empathy issues rather than working to increase generalised empathy in treatment participants (Fernandez, 2002). Methods used for such a purpose may include viewing or reading material relating to the experiences of sexual assault victims, writing letters of apology (not sent) to victims (Webster, 2002), and role-playing their victim in imaginary scenarios where offence-related consequences may be experienced (Daniels, Mann & Marshall, 2002; Webster, Bowers, Mann & Marshall, 2005). Empathy deficits have not been seen to predict recidivism risk (Hanson & Morton-Bourgon, 2004) but empathy work in treatment can be conceptualised as an approach which should impact upon offence-supportive attitudes such as justification for sexual offending; and this purpose is legitimate within the risk-need model of rehabilitation. Certainly, offenders themselves believe that empathy work is a crucially effective component of treatment (Wakeling, Webster & Mann, 2005).

Interpersonal Deficits

Early treatment programmes for sexual offenders traditionally focused on social skills such as dating skills (Marshall & McKnight, 1975) but more recently, targets have become more sophisticated (and less heterosexist) by focusing on intimacy skills such as expression of emotions and affection, and conflict resolution. In addition, some programmes have made a claim for the importance of attachment theory and have adopted approaches that encourage offenders to identify their predominant style within intimate attachments (Bartholomew, 1993). The three insecure attachment styles (preoccupied, fearful and dismissive) are defined in terms of self- and other-esteem and, consequently, treatment targets are easily identified once the attachment style is recognised. For example, preoccupied individuals would focus on developing self-esteem, fearful individuals would need to improve both self and other-esteem, and so forth.

The skills required for a successful intimate relationship are best rehearsed in roleplay (obviously necessitating a group treatment environment) and, if the offender's circumstances permit, also practised in real-life situations, with consequences being discussed in therapy sessions. For individuals with very severe intimacy skill deficits, the therapist would need to model (demonstrate) enactment of key skills before roleplay rehearsal would be an effective intervention.

Self-regulation Deficits

Treatment methods that have been found to be most beneficial with criminal offenders, including sexual offenders, involve modelling, graduated practice, behavioural rehearsal, reinforcement, and training in both problem-solving and moral reasoning (Andrews & Bonta, 2003). General self-regulation skills can improve through learning the skill of exploring costs and benefits of one's behaviour. Goal setting is designed to encourage clients to think before they act, consider the consequences, and evaluate long-term benefits for themselves.

The main focus of sexual offender treatment programmes is to assist offenders in preventing a relapse of their sexually inappropriate behaviour by improving their ability to regulate and manage themselves. Individuals are taught to anticipate and cope with the problem of relapse (Marques & Nelson, 1992). During treatment participants are directed to identify "risk factors" or cognitive and behavioural precursors relevant to their sexually aggressive behaviour. These factors, which are believed to increase their risk of re-offending, include internal elements such as depression, anger, intimacy issues, and substance abuse, as well as external aspects such as access to potential victims (Marshall et al., 1999) or interpersonal conflict (Proulx, McKibben & Lusignan, 1996). Treatment participants are then aided in developing self-management techniques aimed at dealing with the identified problematic patterns of thoughts and behaviours. Management techniques include both internal (for example, thought stopping, anger-management strategies, social skills, assertiveness training, problem solving, and intimacy skills) and external (for example, parole supervision) strategies. Deviant sexual responses to relieve emotional distress are another feature of the self-management of sexual offenders who have been found to over use sexual behaviours as a way of coping with various problems (Cortoni & Marshall, 2001). Problem-focused coping strategies are presented in treatment in an attempt to reduce reliance on sex as a coping strategy.

For sexual offenders who are habitually impulsive and poor at problem solving, we emphasise that cognitive skills training is an important adjunct to offence-focused treatment.

Programme Application

The heterogeneity of sexual offenders may create some difficulties in the application of treatment. There have been some attempts to address the issue of client variability by creating subsets of offender groups classified by offence type, DSM-IV diagnosis, or various classification systems (see, for example, Gebhard, Gagnon, Pomeroy & Christenson, 1965; Groth, 1979; Knight & Prentky, 1990; Seghorn & Cohen, 1980). However, Marshall et al. (1999) suggest that these attempts at classification offer little value and may, in fact, offer a disadvantage. Marshall and his colleagues comment that groups of "mixed" sexual offenders provide opportunities for insight, varying perspectives, as well as sharing of common experience.

The effectiveness of treatment ultimately lies in the hands of the therapists delivering treatment. The general clinical literature on therapist characteristics has clearly identified both therapist characteristics and techniques that predict beneficial changes in treatment and those that are related to negative treatment outcome. Historically treatment programmes directed toward problems that have typically been considered distasteful (for example, addictions or sexual deviance) have disregarded this research in favour of a confrontational approach to treatment (Fernandez & Serran, 2002; Kear-Colwell & Pollack, 1997; Miller & Rollnick, 1991). This negative stance is characterised by an aggressive and often denigrating challenging approach; hostile and/or angry interactions between therapist and client; an excessive emphasis in therapy on negative issues; lack of interest, optimism or belief in clients and their capacity to change; an absence of a collaborative approach to treatment; disregard of the influence of the therapist's interpersonal characteristics on treatment outcome; and goals that are avoidance based rather than directed toward aiding clients to develop a happy and fulfilling lifestyle (Marshall et al., 2003). Fortunately, there has been a recent move in the area of sexual offender treatment toward adopting a more positive, supportive approach. Marshall and colleagues have outlined the style and characteristics validated in the general therapeutic literature and in the limited number of studies completed with therapists delivering treatment to sexual offenders (Fernandez & Serran, 2002; Marshall et al., 2002; Marshall et al., 2003; Serran et al., 2003). Therapist characteristics and behaviours that enhance treatment effectiveness include empathy, genuineness, warmth, respect, support, asking open-ended questions, directiveness, flexibility, rewarding, encouraging participation, hope, confidence, and being emotionally responsive. Marshall and colleagues recommend a motivational style that requires challenging the clients but in a firm but supportive manner. Such an approach has been shown to be effective with substance abusers (Miller & Rollnick, 1991) and with various types of offenders. Encouragingly, other researchers have also begun to examine this neglected area in the sexual offender research literature (Beech & Fordham, 1997: Beech & Hamilton-Giachritsis, 2005; Drapeau, 2005; Garland & Dougher, 1991).

Little research has been conducted on the effectiveness of therapist combinations. Of the few studies on this topic it appears that more positive gains are associated with co-therapist teams who present as consistent, as opposed to inconsistent, to the group (Piper, Doan, Edwards & Jones, 1979). Interestingly, dissimilarity between the therapists (gender, age, race, or personality) was also associated with somewhat better outcome. Although no studies to date have examined the influence of therapist gender in sexual offender therapy, many programmes attempt to have male and female co-therapists, based on the assumption that having opposite gendered co-therapists provides opportunities for modelling appropriate and respectful male-female interactions.

OUTCOME EVIDENCE FOR SEX OFFENDER PROGRAMMES

The efficacy of sexual offender treatment remains an ardently debated issue. The problems of all offender rehabilitation outcome research apply (see Chapter 2), namely, difficulty in establishing a suitable control group, the problem of low base rates of sexual offending, and the understandable reluctance of policy-makers to support random allocation designs. Bearing these limitations in mind, we will briefly review some important single and meta-analytic studies of sexual offender treatment efficacy. Next we will summarise some of the current thinking about how evaluation research should be approached. We will also briefly consider the value of cost-benefit studies, and comparisons with treatment for other disorders.

Studies of Sexual Offender Treatment Efficacy

It is generally accepted that the only outcome for sex offender treatment that would satisfy the public, funding bodies, and governments is a reduction in sexual re-offending. Clinical change studies, while interesting and potentially valuable, are therefore insufficient unless they can be directly related to decreases in rates of recidivism. Hence, we will focus on studies which have evaluated treatment programmes in terms of their effect on re-offending (usually, but not always, defined in terms of reconviction). We will not enter here into a lengthy critique of published evaluation studies.

From the last decade, there have been four major meta-analytic or synthesised review studies of sexual offender treatment efficacy (although all have been subject to critique). First, Hall (1995) conducted a meta-analysis of 12 treatment studies. He found an overall "small but robust" treatment effect, equating to eight fewer sexual re-offenders per 100 treated. This was an overall finding – some programmes performed better than this, some worse. The more effective programmes were those that took either a cognitive-behavioural approach or a hormonal approach (prescribed medication). However, it was further established that a significant advantage of cognitive-behavioural programmes over hormonal programmes was their lower attrition rate: one-third of participants dropped out from cognitive-behavioural programmes compared to one-half of those in hormonal programmes. Hall's meta-analysis also established that programmes including rapists as well as child molesters performed as well as child-molester only programmes, and that community programmes seemed to do better than programmes sited in institutions.

A second, larger study combined 79 treatment outcome studies, although did not use a true meta-analytic design (Alexander, 1999). This study indicated that cognitive-behavioural and relapse prevention programmes performed the best overall in terms of reducing recidivism. The overall success rate for such programmes was to reduce reconviction by 10% points, from 17% to 7%. In other words, these programmes led to 10 fewer offenders for each 100 offenders treated. This study also suggested that treatment could reduce rates of reconviction in a variety of sex offender sub-populations, such as juveniles, incest perpetrators, child molesters, exhibitionists, and rapists. For each group, the effect of treatment was to reduce the recidivism rate to less than 10 %, even in groups where the untreated recidivism rate was as high as 25 %. In contrast to Hall's (1995) study, Alexander (1999) found that institution-based programmes performed slightly better than community programmes.

Third, Gallagher, Wilson, Hirschfield, Coggeshall, and MacKenzie (1999) conducted a "quantitative synthesis" of 25 sex offender treatment outcome studies, including but not limited to the studies covered by Hall's earlier meta-analysis. All bar one of the studies analysed related to treatment delivered in North America and more than half the treatments evaluated were cognitive behavioural. Overall, a statistically significant effect for treatment was observed, "Comparable to average effects found in other meta-analyses of psychological, behavioural and educational interventions" (Gallagher et al., 1999, p. 22). The strongest effects were found for behavioural, cognitive-behavioural (including relapse prevention), and chemical-medical treatments. The authors cautioned about drawing conclusions on the value of castration from the single study reviewed, where castration was found to be highly effective in reducing recidivism, because of the lack of replication of this finding and an uncertainty about pre-treatment differences between groups. Although augmented behavioural treatments (behavioural treatments with social skills and sex education training) and psychosocial treatments fared less well in terms of effectiveness, again design issues in the studies of these programmes prevented final conclusions being drawn about the ineffectiveness of these approaches.

Fourth, a high-profile collaborative study was published by a group of researchers operating on behalf of the Association for the Treatment of Sexual Abusers (ATSA) (Hanson et al., 2002). This review summarised data from 43 studies, combining over 9 000 sexual offenders. When "old-fashioned" programmes were removed from the analysis, and only the more modern cognitive-behavioural/relapse prevention and systemic programmes were examined, the impact of treatment was reasonably good. Such programmes brought about a reduction in recidivism of just over 7 % points: the re-offence rate was reduced from 17.4 % to 9.9 %. There was also a strong impact on general (non-sexual) recidivism, reducing this from 51 % to 32 %. The authors of this study concluded that modern sexual offender treatment is effective, although not spectacularly so.

However, some footnotes to the Hanson et al. (2002) study should be included. First, their review included just three studies that had employed a random allocation design: which is the most stringent methodology for evaluating treatment (for a fuller discussion of this issue, see Chapter 2). Only one of these three studies showed any treatment effect (Borduin, Henggeler, Blaske & Stein, 1990). Second, the performance of "non-current" or "old-fashioned" programmes in many cases actually was to increase recidivism. The variation in effect sizes from programme to programme means that the overall conclusion about the value of treatment masked considerable heterogeneity within the individual programmes.

It should be noted at this point that Thornton's (2005) critique of the design of virtually all sex offender treatment efficacy studies concluded that Hall's (1995) study and Alexander's (1999) study contained too many flawed studies, particularly studies comparing completers to non-completers rather than untreated controls, to be of much value. Thornton is kinder to the Hanson et al. (2002) study, concluding that their results could be regarded as "suggestive if not conclusive".

Kenworthy, Adams, Bilby, Brooks-Gordon & Fenton (2004) evaluated only randomised controlled trials involving the treatment of convicted or cautioned adult sexual offenders (including men with convictions for violence where a sexual element was present). Treatments included behavioural, cognitive-behavioural, psychodynamic, and psychoanalytic approaches. Results and recommendations were limited, but it appeared that cognitive-behavioural treatment reduced re-offending at 1-year follow-up, but psychodynamic group therapy was associated with increased re-arrest rates over a 10-year follow-up.

Whilst meta-analytic studies are generally considered most informative, given their large sample sizes, there are some single-sample studies that are worthy of note here because of particular innovations in design or because of particularly important lessons arising about the aspects of treatment that seem most crucial.

The Sex Offender Treatment Evaluation Project (SOTEP), which was one of the three random allocation designs considered by Hanson et al. (2002), was a large-scale, random allocation, evaluation of cognitive-behavioural treatment based on the relapse prevention model. The SOTEP, which ran for 10 years in Atascadero State Hospital, California, involved a highly structured group programme of cognitive, behavioural and skill-training activities (Marques, Nelson, Alarcon & Day, 2000) with additional speciality groups covering topics such as anger management, sex education, and social skills training. Further treatment, such as behaviour therapy to alter deviant sexual arousal, was offered according to need. After about 5 years at risk, there was a difference in recidivism rates between the treated and control groups of about 3 %, but this trend was not significant (Marques et al., 2000). However, the extensive data carefully collected by the SOTEP evaluation team has allowed for some important conclusions to be drawn about elements of effective treatment for sexual offenders. These are set out in Marques et al. (2000) and include the following points. First, sexual offenders with thought disorder symptoms did not seem to respond well to cognitive-behavioural treatment. Second, skills for coping with high-risk situations may not be sufficient as a programme aim; motivation and commitment to change are also vital issues to target. Third, avoidance by offenders of difficult personal issues (such as resolving own victimisation experiences) should be strongly challenged: "An attitude of 'I'll deal with that when I get out' was common among treatment failures" (Marques et al., 2000, p. 327). Fourth, management of negative emotional states should be given more weight in a programme's design. Fifth, coping skills practice should take priority over recognition of risky situations. Sixth, it was noted that all the treatment failures showed a marked lack of victim empathy. This analysis of what can be learned from the SOTEP is extremely important and these findings are, in our view, often overlooked.

Borduin et al. (1990) evaluated multi-systemic therapy for adolescent sexual offenders by comparing it with an individual counselling condition, using a random allocation design. The multi-systemic therapy (MST) was offered according to a theoretical model that holds that adolescent sexual offenders are embedded in a range of systems including their families, their peers, and their school (Henggeler, 1989). The sample size for this study was very small: only 10 adolescents completed treatment across both conditions. However, the findings indicated a considerable impact of treatment, with a much lower re-arrest rate for the MST group, and continuation of deviant behaviour in the individual therapy group. This study is included here because it indicates that treatment of adolescents can be effective as long the adolescent's context is taken fully into account. The MST approach seems to be worthy of larger-scale replication and evaluation for these younger offenders.

Friendship, Mann & Beech (2003) reported an evaluation of the multi-site prison sex offender programme operating in England and Wales (SOTP) (Mann & Thornton, 2000). The usual limitations of non-random allocation design were true of this study (see Chapter 2 for a fuller discussion of this issue). However, a feature of this study worthy of note is that the effectiveness of treatment was analysed by static risk level. The study found that a 160-hour, offence-focused, cognitive-behavioural programme (incorporating but not limited to relapse prevention work) was highly effective for medium risk offenders as assessed by the Static-99 (Hanson & Thornton, 2000). The impact on low risk offenders was not statistically significant but this was most probably due to the low base rate of offending for this group. There was no impact of treatment on recidivism for high-risk offenders. Friendship et al. concluded that high-risk men are likely to have entrenched levels of deviance and therefore require a higher dose of treatment and perhaps a broader range of treatment targets. Subsequently, the Prison Service has introduced extended treatment for high-risk men, although to date no reconviction data are available to assess its impact.

Cost-benefit Evaluations

Cost-benefit evaluations (Welsh & Farrington, 2001) attempt to determine whether the effect of the programme is sufficient to justify the money spent on delivering the programme. In their simplest form, cost-benefit analyses estimate the cost of programme delivery in monetary terms, and weigh this against the estimated value of the estimated effects of the programme. Obviously, it is going to be hard to produce an estimate of costs and benefits in monetary terms for sexual offender treatment, because emotional and psychological impact cannot be measured in precise financial terms. Estimates of criminal justice system costs for processing a reconviction can be made, but it must be emphasised that a cost-benefit analysis based solely on such data may not portray the full picture of an effective programme's value.

We are aware of only two published evaluations of the financial benefit of sexual offender treatment. Prentky & Burgess (1990) addressed the cost-effectiveness of treatment provided at the Massachusetts Treatment Center (MTC). In this study, 129 child molesters released from the MTC between 1960 and 1989 were followed up for an extended 20-year period. Thirty-two men re-offended within the first 5 years (a 25% failure rate) and, in total, 39 men had re-offended after 20 years. As offenders were not assigned to MTC by randomised allocation there was no obvious comparison group available so the authors relied on untreated recidivism rates from a study by Marshall and Barbaree (1988). Thus, a 40% recidivism for untreated sex offenders was adopted for comparative purposes. The estimated costs of the treatment included the following: costs of incarceration for 7 years (a figure thought to be reasonable for a repeat rape offence against a child); the total budget for rehabilitation divided by the number of treatment participants; and the total budget for custodial supervision divided by the total number of treatment participants. In total, this equated to $118 146 per man for treatment and $158 635 for incarceration. The costs of a re-offence were calculated by summing costs of apprehension and pre-trial investigation of the offender, trial costs, costs of incarceration and parole supervision. Victim-related expenses were calculated to include costs of social services, hospital and other medical expenses, witness services, and treatment for trauma. The analysis concluded that, "For every 1 000 child molesters released from prison, the cost to society over a 5 year period would be nearly $68 million greater for offenders who received no treatment prior to release" (Prentky & Burgess, 1990, p. 113).

The limitations of this study are obvious: all costs are only estimates and thus the final figures are likely to be inaccurate, and the use of untreated offender recidivism rates from another jurisdiction may be an inappropriate choice. However, even if these limitations had led to the benefits being over-estimated and the costs under-estimated, it is still likely that treatment would represent excellent value for money.

Marshall (1992) applied the costs estimated by Prentky and Burgess (1990) to his own programme, which had achieved a reduction in recidivism from 35% to less than 10% (Marshall & Eccles, 1991). He took into account the estimation that when previously convicted sexual offenders re-offend, they do so against more than one victim. He concluded that for every 100 sexual offenders treated, at least 50 offences were prevented, at a saving (after programme costs were deducted) in excess of $4 million (Canadian).

A subsequent cost-benefit analysis of sex offender treatment was conducted by Donato & Shanahan (1999). This study attempted to calculate both tangible costs (for example, costs of government services, costs of offender incarceration) and intangible costs of child sex abuse in order to estimate as fully as possible the benefits of reducing recidivism. Unsurprisingly, the authors concluded that it was extremely difficult to arrive at accurate estimates of costs, and so they produced a range of estimates of costs and benefits according to different levels of treatment effectiveness. The cost of treatment was estimated, from an average of four treatment programmes in Australia and New Zealand, at $10 000 (Australian) per prisoner. For an 8% reduction in recidivism rates, and assuming one re-offence per recidivist, the minimum estimated benefit of treating 100 offenders was $258 000 and the maximum estimated benefit was $1.85 billion. The authors concluded that

> The magnitude of the problems of child sexual abuse generally, and offences by recidivists in particular, is such that its costs are substantial and the associated benefits to be achieved from appropriate treatment programs high. (Donato & Shanahan, 1999, p. 6)

Comparison of Sex Offender Treatment with Treatments for Other Disorders

Another innovative approach to qualifying the value of sex offender treatment has been to compare its effectiveness with other recognised treatments for mental and physical health problems. Marshall & McGuire (2003) examined the magnitude of the effect size of sex offender treatment (and offender treatment more generally) and found that, in all cases, effect sizes were equal to or greater than treatments for other groups. The effect size for current sex offender treatments, drawn from the Hanson et al. (2002) study described above, was calculated at 0.28. This figure compared extremely favourably, for example, with an effect size of 0.03 for chemotherapy for breast cancer, and 0.15 for bypass surgery, and was slightly better than the effect size of AZT for AIDS (0.23).

Recommended Future Evaluation Approaches

Hanson (2000) identified four types of research design for sexual offender out-come research: completers versus dropouts (non-completers), successful versus unsuccessful completers, incidental comparison groups, and random assignment (see Chapter 2 for a consideration of these). Thornton (2005) has sternly reviewed these different approaches to evaluation design. He concluded that non-completers are a "non-overlapping and biased" comparison group and designs based on this approach are unsafe. Incidental comparison groups are also potentially un-safe because they will include refusers and offenders who would have been non-completers had they begun treatment; both types of offender would not have been found in a treatment completer group. Thornton concluded that, short of random allocation, which is held to be the superior design, the most favourable groups for comparison are sexual offenders from facilities or areas which did not provide treatment (just about acceptable) and (more acceptably) sexual offenders assigned to different forms of treatment. Even with these designs, treatment and compar-ison groups should be compared on as wide a range of pre-treatment factors as possible, and statistical adjustments should be made to observed recidivism rates in response to identified differences (see Chapter 2).

Ways of managing the low base rate problem are discussed by Falshaw, Bates, Patel, Corbett & Friendship (2003), and by Friendship & Thornton (2001). Further-more, Friendship et al. (2003) found that combining sexual and violence recidivism rates increases the base rate of offending to a level where significant differences between groups are possible, without compromising on standards of outcome that are important to policymakers and the general public. Finally, we recommend that more programme evaluators adopt a cost-benefit methodology in assessing the impact of sexual offender treatment. Even though the impact of current treatments may not always appear remarkable, a cost-benefit approach is likely to show that treatment is highly cost-effective.

Sex Offender Treatment Effectiveness: Conclusions

The four major meta-analytic studies of sexual offender treatment efficacy all indi-cate that a cognitive-behavioural or relapse prevention programme for sexual of-fenders can reduce levels of sexual re-conviction, often to less than 10 %. This seems to be a justifiable conclusion even when the programmes treat mixed offender types, and whether they are sited in an institution or in the community. However, the impact of treatment is not astounding. There is also a suggestion that some types of treatment make sexual offenders worse. Current treatments, using cognitive-behavioural methods and incorporating the relapse prevention approach, which target evidence-based dynamic criminogenic risk factors, are very likely to be cost-effective and there are indications that they are at least as effective as many well-accepted treatment procedures for physical health problems.

FUTURE DIRECTIONS FOR SEX OFFENDER PROGRAMMES

Thus far in this chapter we have confined ourselves to discussing the more straight-forward aspects of treatment for sexual offenders, such as commonly accepted treatment targets and methods. We have not touched on the less-defined areas of treatment where research (and in some cases, theory) is urgently needed. For instance, there are unresolved debates on issues such as the treatability of psychopaths (for example, Barbaree, Seto & Langton, 2001; Looman, Abracen, Serin & Marquis, 2005; Seto & Barbaree, 1999; Wong, 2004); and responsivity issues for sexual offenders with other personality disorders (for example, Buschman & Van Beek, 2003). As discussed in this chapter, meta-analytic overviews of treatment outcome provide a reasonably consistent picture of treatment effectiveness but there remains a need for work to try and define more clearly the essential elements of the more effective treatment programmes. Studies such as those reported by Mann, Webster, Schofield & Marshall (2004) and Webster et al. (2005) provide examples of how alternative treatment procedures (in these cases, alternative approaches to relapse prevention and empathy development respectively) can be compared in terms of their effectiveness. In particular, treatments aimed at reducing deviant sexual arousal and increasing appropriate arousal need to be evaluated. Early studies evaluating behavioural procedures were generally limited to case study designs, and many "modern" programmes contain little if any work designed specifically to address sexual deviance. Partly this limitation may be due to the difficulties in assessing change against this target, with another ardent debate to be had about the relative merits of phallometric assessment, polygraph, and some of the newer assessment technologies such as viewing time measures (Laws & Gress, 2004).

While interventions based on the relapse prevention model remain popular and are indicated to be reasonably effective, the analysis of Marques et al. (2000) would also indicate some limitations to the approach, especially if it is rigidly conceptualised. We suggest that relapse prevention can be a useful organising framework for summarising issues addressed in treatment in a succinct and memorable way for the offenders concerned. However, relapse prevention itself does not allow for the more intensive work that may need to take place with higher risk higher need offenders, such as those with extensive dysfunctional thinking patterns. In such cases, the cognitive therapy model would suggest that schema-focused cognitive therapy may be warranted (Mann & Beech, 2003; Mann & Shingler, 2006), but so far this approach has not been formally validated for sexual offender treatment.

As we have noted above, research has only recently begun to focus on the process aspects of sexual offender treatment, such as therapist characteristics.

Debates about the benefits of group vs individual therapy are conducted on the basis of clinical experience rather than empirical evidence, and yet many organisations have policies that mean that only one or other approach is available.

To conclude, in this chapter we have summarised some of the generally agreed criminogenic needs of sexual offenders. The presence and combination of such dynamic risk factors are often evaluated systematically via assessment frameworks such as the Risk of Sexual Violence Protocol, Stable – 2000, or the Structured Assessment of Risk and Need (Thornton, 2002; Webster et al., in press). Such frameworks are popular and are almost certainly improvements upon unstructured clinical judgement. However, research into the reliability and predictive validity of these frameworks is still scarce, and at present there is little basis from which static risk assessments can be reliably adjusted. It follows that there is currently no validated system by which an offender who engages in treatment, such as that described in this chapter, can be said with confidence to have reduced his risk, let alone by what amount. It is our prediction – and our hope – that this question will be a focus for research in the coming decade.

REFERENCES

Abel, G. G. (1976). Assessment of sexual deviation in the male. In A. S. Bellack & M. Hersen (Eds), *Behavioural assessment: A practical handbook* (pp. 437–457). New York: Pergamon Press.

Abel, G. G., Barlow, D. H., Blanchard, E. B. & Guild, D. (1977). The components of rapists' sexual arousal. *Archives of General Psychiatry, 34*, 895–903.

Abel, G. G., Becker, J. V. & Skinner L. (1983). Behavioural approaches to the treatment of the violent person. In L. Roth (Ed.), *Violent behavior: Social learning approaches to prediction, management and treatment* (pp. 116–137). Washington, DC: NIMH Monograph Series.

Abel, G. G., Blanchard, E. B. & Becker, J. V. (1978). An integrated treatment program for rapists. In R. Rada (Ed.), *Clinical aspects of the rapist* (pp. 161–214). New York: Grune and Stratton.

Abel, G. G., Osborn, C. A., Anthony, D. & Gardos, P. (1992). Current treatment of paraphiliacs. *Annual Review of Sex Research, 3*, 255–290.

Abracen, J. & Looman, J. (2004). Issues in the treatment of sexual offenders. *Aggression and Violent Behavior, 9*, 229–246.

Alexander, M. A. (1999). Sexual offender treatment efficacy revisited. *Sexual Abuse: A Journal of Research and Treatment, 11*, 101–116.

Andrews, D. A. & Bonta, J. (2003). *The psychology of criminal conduct (3rd edition)*. Cincinnati, OH: Anderson Publishing.

Andrews, D. A., Zinger, I., Hoge, R. D., Bonta, J., Gendreau, P. & Cullen, F. T. (1990). Does correctional treatment work? A clinically relevant and psychologically informed meta-analysis. *Criminology, 28*, 369–417.

Association for the Treatment of Sexual Abusers (ATSA) (2001). *Ethical standards and principles for the management of sexual abusers*. Beaverton, OR: Author.

Barbaree, H. E. & Cortoni, F. A. (1993). Treatment of the juvenile sex offender within the criminal justice and mental health systems. In H. E. Barbaree, W. L. Marshall & S. M. Hudson (Eds), *The juvenile sex offender* (pp. 243–263). New York: Guilford Press.

Barbaree, H. E., Seto, M. C. & Langton, C. M. (2001). *Psychopathy, treatment behaviour and sex offender recidivism: Extended follow-up*. Paper presented at the annual conference of the Association for the Treatment of Sexual Abusers, San Antonio, TX.

Bartholomew, K. (1993). From childhood to adult relationships: Attachment theory and research. In S. Duck (Ed.), *Learning about relationships* (pp. 30–62). Newbury Park, CA: Sage.

Beech, A. R. (1997). Towards a psychometric typology for assessing pre-treatment levels of problems in child abusers. *Journal of Sexual Aggression, 3,* 87–100.

Beech, A. R. & Fordham, A. S. (1997). Therapeutic climate of sexual offender treatment programs. *Sexual Abuse: A Journal of Research and Treatment, 9,* 219–237.

Beech, A. R., Friendship, C., Erikson, M. & Hanson, R. K. (2002). The relationship between static and dynamic risk factors and reconviction in a sample of UK child abusers. *Sexual Abuse: A Journal of Research and Treatment, 14,* 155–167.

Beech, A. R. & Hamilton-Giachritsis, C. E. (2005). Relationship between therapeutic climate and treatment outcome in group-based sexual offender treatment programs. *Sexual Abuse: A Journal of Research and Treatment, 17,* 127–140.

Blumenthal, S., Gudjonsson, G. & Burns, J. (1999). Cognitive distortions and blame attribution in sex offenders against adults and children. *Child Abuse and Neglect, 23,* 129–143.

Borduin, C. M., Henggeler, S. W., Blaske, D. M. & Stein, R. J. (1990). Multisystemic treatment of adolescent sexual offenders. *International Journal of Offender Therapy and Comparative Criminology, 34,* 105–113.

Bradford, J. M. W. (1985). Organic treatments for the male sexual offender. *Behavioral Sciences and the Law, 3,* 355–375.

Bradford, J. M. W. (1988). Organic treatments for the male sexual offender. *Annals of the New York Academy of Science, 528,* 193–201.

Bradford, J. M. W. (1990). The antiandrogen and hormonal treatment of sex offenders. In W. L. Marshall, D. R. Laws & H. E. Barbaree (Eds), *Handbook of sexual assault: Issues, theories and treatment of the offender* (pp. 297–310). New York: Plenum Press.

Bradford, J. M. W. (1997). Medical interventions in sexual deviance. In D. R. Laws & W. T. O'Donahoe (Eds), *Sexual deviance: Theory, assessment and treatment* (pp. 449–464). New York: Guilford Press.

Bumby, K. (1995). Assessing the cognitive distortions of child molesters and rapists: Development and validation of the RAPE and MOLEST scales. *Sexual Abuse: A Journal of Research and Treatment, 8,* 37–54.

Buschman, J. & van Beek, D. (2003). A clinical model for the treatment of personality disordered sexual offenders: An example of theory knitting. *Sexual Abuse: A Journal of Research and Treatment, 15,* 183–199.

Cortoni, F. A. & Marshall, W. L. (2001). Sex as a coping strategy and its relationship to juvenile sexual history and intimacy in sexual offenders. *Sexual Abuse: A Journal of Research and Treatment, 13,* 27–43.

Craissati, J. & Beech, A. R. (2003). A review of dynamic variables and their relationship to risk prediction in sex offenders. *Journal of Sexual Aggression, 9,* 41–55.

Crawford, D. (1981). Treatment approaches in pedophiles. In M. Cook & K. Howells (Eds), *Adult sexual interest in children* (pp. 181–217). London: Academic Press.

Daniels, M., Mann, R. E. & Marshall, W. L. (2002). The use of role-plays in developing empathy. In Y. Fernandez (Ed.), *In their shoes: Measurement, perspectives and cognitive strategies for developing empathy* (pp. 132–148). Oklahoma City: Wood and Barnes.

Di Fazio, R., Abracen, J. & Looman, J. (2001). Group versus individual treatment of sex offenders: A comparison. *Forum on Corrections Research, 13,* 56–59.

Donato, R. & Shanahan, M. (1999). The economics of implementing intensive in-prison sex-offender treatment programs. *Trends and Issues in Crime and Criminal Justice, No 134.* Canberra: Australian Institute of Criminology.

Drapeau, M. (2005). Research on the processes involved in treating sexual offenders. *Sexual Abuse: A Journal of Research and Treatment, 17,* 117–125.

Falshaw, L., Bates, A., Patel, V., Corbett, C. & Friendship, C. (2003). Assessing reconviction, reoffending and recidivism in a sample of UK sexual offenders. *Legal and Criminological Psychology, 8,* 207–215.

Fedoroff, J. P. & Fedoroff, I. C. (1992). Buspirone and paraphilic sexual behaviour. *Journal of Offender Rehabilitation, 18,* 89–108.

Fernandez, Y. M. (Ed.) (2002*). In their shoes: Measurement, perspectives and cognitive strategies for developing empathy.* Oklahoma City, OK: Wood and Barnes Publishing and Distribution.

Fernandez, Y. M. & Serran, G. (2002). Characteristics of an effective sex offender therapist. In B. Schwartz (Ed.), *The sex offender vol. 4: Current treatment modalities and systems issues* (pp. 9.1–9.12). Kingston, NJ: Civic Research Institute.

Fernandez, Y. M., Shingler, J. & Marshall, W. L. (2006). Putting "behavior" back into the cognitive behavioral treatment of sexual offenders. In W. L. Marshall, Y. M. Fernandez, L. E. Marshall & G. A. Serran (Eds), *Sexual offender treatment: Issues and controversies* (pp. 211–224). Chichester: John Wiley & Sons.

Firestone, P., Bradford, J. M., Greenburg, D. M., Larose, M. R. & Curry, S. (1998). Recidivism factors in convicted rapists. *Journal of the American Academy of Psychiatry and Law, 26*, 185–200.

Fisher, D., Beech, A. R. & Browne, K. D. (1993). Locus of control and its relationship to treatment change and abuse history in child sexual abusers. *Legal and Criminological Psychology, 3*, 1–12.

Friendship, C., Mann, R. E. & Beech, A. R. (2003). Evaluation of a national prison-based treatment programme for sexual offenders in England and Wales. *Journal of Interpersonal Violence, 18*, 744–759.

Friendship, C. & Thornton, D. (2001). Sexual reconviction for sexual offenders discharged from prisons in England and Wales: Implications for evaluating treatment. *British Journal of Criminology, 41*, 285–292.

Gallagher, C. A., Wilson, D. B., Hirschfield, P., Coggeshall, M. B. & MacKenzie, D. L. (1999). A quantitative review of the effects of sex offender treatment on sexual reoffending. *Corrections Management Quarterly, 3*, 19–29.

Garland, R. J. & Dougher, M. (1991). Motivational intervention in the treatment of sex offenders. In W. R. Miller & S. Rollnick (Eds), *Motivational interviewing: Preparing people to change addictive behaviour* (pp. 303–313). New York: Guilford Press.

Garlick, Y., Marshall, W. L. & Thornton, D. (1996). Intimacy deficits and attribution of blame among sexual offenders. *Legal and Criminological Psychology, 1*, 251–258.

Gebhard, G. H., Gagnon, J. H., Pomeroy, W. B. & Christenson, C. V. (1965). *Sex offenders: An analysis of types.* New York: Harper Row.

Groth, A. N. (1979). *Men who rape: The psychology of the offender.* New York: Plenum Press.

Hall, G. C. N. (1995). Sexual offender recidivism revisited: A meta-analysis of recent treatment studies. *Journal of Consulting and Clinical Psychology, 63*, 802–809.

Hanson, R. K. (2000). Treatment outcome and evaluation problems (and solutions). In D. R. Laws, S. M. Hudson & T. Ward (Eds), *Remaking relapse prevention with sexual offenders* (pp. 485–499). Thousand Oaks, CA: Sage Publications.

Hanson, R. K. & Bussière, M. T. (1998). Predicting relapse: A meta-analysis of sexual offender recidivism studies. *Journal of Consulting and Clinical Psychology, 66*, 348–362.

Hanson, R. K. et al. (2002). First report on the collaborative outcome data project on the effectiveness of psychological treatment for sex offenders. *Sexual Abuse: A Journal of Research and Treatment, 14(2)*, 169–197.

Hanson, R. K., Gizzarelli, R. & Scott, H. (1994). The attitudes of incest offenders: Sexual entitlement and acceptance of sex with children. *Criminal Justice and Behavior, 21*, 187–202.

Hanson, R. K. & Harris, A. J. R. (2000). Where should we intervene? Dynamic risk predictors of sexual offence recidivism. *Criminal Justice and Behavior, 27*, 6–35.

Hanson, R. K. & Morton-Bourgon, K. (2004). *Predictors of sexual recidivism: An updated meta-analysis.* Research report 2002–02, Public Safety and Emergency Preparedness Canada.

Hanson, R. K. & Thornton, D. (2000). Improving risk assessments for sexual offenders: A comparison of three actuarial scales. *Law and Human Behavior, 24*, 119–136.

Henggeler, S. W. (1989). *Delinquency in adolescence.* Newbury Park, CA: Sage.

Jennings J. L. & Sawyer, S. (2003). Principles and techniques for maximizing the effectiveness of group therapy with sex offenders. *Sexual Abuse: A Journal of Research and Treatment, 15*, 251–267.

Kear-Colwell, J. & Pollack, P. (1997). Motivation or confrontation: Which approach to the child sex offender? *Criminal Justice and Behavior, 24*, 20–33.

Kenworthy, T., Adams, C. E., Bilby, C., Brooks-Gordon, B. & Fenton, M. (2004). Psychological interventions for those who have sexually offended or are at risk of offending (Cochrane Review). *The Cochrane Library, Issue 3.*

Knight, R. A. & Prentky, R. A. (1990). Classifying sexual offenders: The development and corroboration of taxonomic models. In W. L. Marshall, D. R. Laws & H. E. Barbaree (Eds), *Handbook of sexual abuse: Issues, theories, and treatment of the offender* (pp. 23–52). New York: Plenum Press.

Knopp, F. H. (1984). *Retraining adult sex offenders: Methods and models.* Syracuse, NY: Safer Society Press.

Kravitz, H. M., Haywood, T. W., Kelly, J., Wahlstrom, C., Liles, S. & Cavanaugh, J. L. Jr. (1995). Medroxyprogesterone treatment for paraphiliacs. *Bulletin of the American Academy of Psychiatry and the Law, 23,* 19–33.

Laws, D. R. & Gress, C. L. Z. (2004). Seeing things differently: The viewing time alternative to penile plethysmography. *Legal and Criminological Psychology, 9,* 183–196.

Laws, D. R. & Marshall, W. L. (2003). A brief history of behavioral and cognitive-behavioral approaches to sexual offender treatment: Part 1. Early developments. *Sexual Abuse: A Journal of Research and Treatment, 15,* 75–92.

Lilienfeld, S. O., Lynn, S. J. & Lohr, J. M. (Eds) (2003). *Science and pseudoscience in clinical psychology.* New York: The Guilford Press.

Looman, J., Abracen, J., Serin, R. & Marquis, P. (2005). Psychopathy, treatment change and recidivism in high risk high need sexual offenders. *Journal of Interpersonal Violence, 20,* 549–568.

Malamuth, N. M. & Brown, L. M. (1994). Sexually aggressive men's perceptions of women's communications: Testing three explanations. *Journal of Personality and Social Psychology, 67,* 699–712.

Maletzky, B. M. (1993). Factors associated with success and failure in the behavior and cognitive treatment of sexual offenders. *Annals of Sex Research, 6,* 241–258.

Maletzky, B. M. (1998). The paraphilias: Research and treatment. In P. E. Nathan & J. M. Gorman (Eds), *A guide to treatments that work* (pp. 472–500). New York: Oxford University Press.

Maletzky, B. M. (1999). Groups of one. *Sexual Abuse: A Journal of Research and Treatment, 11,* 179–181.

Mann, R. E. (2005). *An investigation of the role, nature and influence of schemas in sexual offending.* Unpublished doctoral dissertation, University of Leicester.

Mann, R. E. & Beech, A. R. (2003). Cognitive distortions, schemas and implicit theories. In T. Ward, D. R. Laws & S. M. Hudson (Eds), *Sexual deviance: Issues and controversies* (pp. 135–153). Thousand Oaks, CA: Sage Publications.

Mann, R. E. & Shingler, J. (2006). Schema-driven cognition in sexual offenders: Theory, assessment and treatment. In W. L. Marshall, Y. M. Fernandez, L. E. Marshall & G. A. Serran (Eds), *Sexual offender treatment: Issues and controversies* (pp. 173–185). Chichester: John Wiley & Sons.

Mann, R. E. & Thornton, D. (2000). An evidence-based relapse prevention program. In D. R. Laws, S. M. Hudson & T. Ward (Eds), *Remaking relapse prevention with sex offenders* (pp. 341–388). Thousand Oaks, CA: Sage.

Mann, R. E., Webster, S. D., Schofield, C. & Marshall, W. L. (2004). Approach versus avoidance goals in relapse prevention with sexual offenders. *Sexual Abuse: A Journal of Research and Treatment, 16,* 65–75.

Marques, J. K. & Nelson, C. (1992). The relapse prevention model: Can it work with sex offenders? In R. De V. Peters, R. J. McMahon & V, L. Quinsey (Eds), *Aggression and violence throughout the life span* (pp. 222–243). Thousand Oaks, CA: Sage Publications.

Marques, J. K., Nelson, C., Alarcon, J.-M. & Day, D. M. (2000). Preventing relapse in sexual offenders: What we learned from SOTEP's experimental treatment program. In D. R. Laws, S. M. Hudson & T. Ward (Eds), *Remaking relapse prevention with sex offenders* (pp. 39–55). Thousand Oaks, CA: Sage.

Marshall, W. L. (1992). The social value of treatment for sexual offenders. *The Canadian Journal of Human Sexuality, 1,* 109–114.

Marshall, W. L. (1993). A revised approach to the treatment of men who sexually assault adult females. In G. C. Hall, R. Hirschman, J. R., Graham & M. S. Zaragoza (Eds), *Sexual aggression: Issues in etiology, assessment, and treatment* (pp. 143–165). Washington, DC: Taylor & Francis.

Marshall, W. L. (1994). Treatment effects on denial and minimization in incarcerated sex offenders. *Behavior Research and Therapy, 32,* 559–564.

Marshall, W. L., Anderson, D. & Fernandez, Y. (1999). *Cognitive-behavioural treatment of sexual offenders.* Chichester: John Wiley & Sons.

Marshall, W. L. & Barbaree, H. E. (1988). The long-term evaluation of a behavioral treatment program for child molesters. *Behavior Research and Therapy, 26,* 499–511.

Marshall, W. L. & Barbaree, H. E. (1990). An integrated theory of sexual offending. In W. L. Marshall, D. R. Laws & H. E. Barbaree (Eds), *Handbook of sexual assault: Issues, theories, and treatment of the offender* (pp. 257–275). New York: Plenum Press.

Marshall, W. L. & Eccles, A. (1991). Issues in clinical practice with sex offenders. *Journal of Interpersonal Violence, 6,* 68–93.

Marshall, W. L. & Eccles, A. (1993). Pavlovian conditioning processes in adolescent sex offenders. In H. E. Barbaree, W. L. Marshall & S .M. Hudson (Eds), *The juvenile sex offender* (pp. 118–142). New York: Guilford Press.

Marshall, W. L. et al. (2002). Therapist features in sexual offender treatment: Their reliable identification and influence on behaviour change. *Clinical Psychology and Psychotherapy, 9,* 395–405.

Marshall, W. L. et al. (2003). Process variables in the treatment of sexual offenders: A review of the literature. *Aggression and Violent Behavior, 8,* 205–234.

Marshall, W. L. & Hambley, L. S. (1996). Intimacy and loneliness, and their relationship to rape myth acceptance and hostility toward women among rapists. *Journal of Interpersonal Violence, 11,* 586–592.

Marshall, W. L., Jones, R., Ward, T., Johnston, P. & Barbaree, H. E. (1991). Treatment outcome with sex offenders. *Clinical Psychology Review, 11,* 465–485.

Marshall, W. L. & McGuire, J. (2003). Effect sizes in the treatment of sexual offenders. *International Journal of Offender Therapy and Comparative Criminology, 46,* 653–663.

Marshall, W. L. & McKnight, R. D. (1975). An integrated treatment program for sexual offenders. *Canadian Psychiatric Association Journal, 20,* 133–138.

Marshall, W. L. & Williams, S. (1975). A behavioural approach to the modification of rape. *Quarterly Bulletin of the British Association for Behavioural Psychotherapy, 4,* 78.

Marshall, W. L. & Williams, S. (2000). Assessment and treatment of sexual offenders. *Forum on Corrections Research, 12,* 41–44.

McGuire, R. J., Carlisle, J. M. & Young, B. G. (1965). Sexual deviations as conditioned behaviour: A hypothesis. *Behaviour Research and Therapy, 3,* 185–190.

Miller, W. R. & Rollnick, S. (1991). *Motivational interviewing.* New York: Guilford Press.

Perkins, D. (1977). *Development of a psychological treatment programme for sex offenders in a prison setting.* Paper presented at the Annual Conference of the British Psychological Society, Exeter, June.

Piper, W. E., Doan, B. D., Edwards, E. M. & Jones, B. D. (1979). Cotherapy behaviour, group therapy process, and treatment outcome. *Journal of Consulting and Clinical Psychology, 47,* 1081–1089.

Polaschek, D. L. L., Hudson, S. M., Ward, T. & Siegert, R. J. (2001). Rapists' offences processes: A preliminary descriptive model. *Journal of Interpersonal Violence, 16,* 523–544.

Prentky, R. A. & Burgess, A. W. (1990). Rehabilitation of child molesters: A cost-benefit analysis. *American Journal of Orthopsychiatry, 60,* 108–117.

Prentky, R. A. & Knight, R. A. (1986). Impulsivity in the lifestyle and criminal behaviour of sexual offenders. *Criminal Justice and Behavior, 13,* 141–164.

Prentky, R. A., Knight, R. A., Sims-Knight, J. E., Straus, H., Rokous, F. & Cerce, D. (1991). Developmental antecedents of sexual aggression. *Developmental Psychopathology, 1,* 153–169.

Proulx, J., McKibben, A. & Lusignan, R. (1996). Relationships between affective components and sexual behaviour in sexual aggressors. *Sexual Abuse: A Journal of Research and Treatment, 8,* 279–289.

Roger, D. (1995). Emotion control, coping strategies and adaptive behaviour. *Stress and Emotion, 15,* 255–264.

Rutan, J. S. & Stone, W. N. (1993). *Psychodynamic group psychotherapy (2nd edition).* New York: Guilford Press.

Safer Society Press (2000). *North American Survey of sexual abuser treatment and models summary.* Brandon, VT: Safer Society Press.

Scully, D. & Marolla, J. (1984). Convicted rapists' vocabulary of motives, excuses and justifications. *Social Problems, 31,* 530–544.

Seghorn, T. & Cohen, M. (1980). The psychology of the rape assailant. In W. Cerran, A. L. McGarry & C. Petty (Eds), *Modern legal medicine, psychiatry, and forensic science* (pp. 533–551). Philadelphia, PA: F. A. Davis.

Serran, G., Fernandez, Y., Marshall, W. L. & Mann, R. E. (2003). Process issues in treatment: Application to sexual offender programs. *Professional Psychology: Research and Practice, 34,* 368–374.

Seto, M. C. & Barbaree, H. E. (1999). Psychopathy, treatment behaviour and sex offence recidivism. *Journal of Interpersonal Violence, 14,* 1235–1248.

Seto, M. C. & Lalumière, M. L. (2001). A brief screening scale to identify paedophilic interests among child molesters. *Journal of Sexual Abuse and Treatment, 13,* 15–25.

Thornton, D. (2002). Constructing and testing a framework for dynamic risk assessment. *Sexual Abuse: A Journal of Research and Treatment, 14,* 139–153.

Thornton, D. (2005). *Sex offender treatment and sexual recidivism.* Paper in preparation.

Thornton, D., Beech, A. R. & Marshall, W. L. (2004). Pretreatment self-esteem and post-treatment sexual recidivism. *International Journal of Offender Therapy and Comparative Criminology, 48,* 587–599.

Wakeling, H., Webster, S. D. & Mann, R. E. (2005). Sexual offenders' treatment experience: A qualitative and quantitative investigation. *Journal of Sexual Aggression, 11,* 171–186.

Webster, S. D. (2002). Assessing victim empathy in sexual offenders using the victim letter task. *Sexual Abuse: A Journal of Research and Treatment, 14,* 281–300.

Webster, S. D., Bowers, L. E., Mann, R. E. & Marshall, W. L. (2005). Developing empathy in sex offenders: The value of offence re-enactments. *Sexual Abuse: A Journal of Research and Treatment, 17,* 63–77.

Webster, S. D. et al. (in press). Inter-rater reliability of dynamic risk assessment with sexual offenders. *Psychology, Crime, and Law.*

Welsh, B. C. & Farrington, D. P. (2001). A review of research on the monetary value of preventing crime. In B. C. Welsh, D. P. Farrington & L. W. Sherman (Eds), *Costs and benefits of preventing crime* (pp. 87–122). Boulder, CO: Westview Press.

Williams, S. (1995). Sex offender assessment guidelines. In T. A. Leis, L. L. Motiuk & J. R. P. Ogloff (Eds), *Forensic psychology: Policy and practice in corrections* (pp. 122–131). Correctional Services of Canada, Ottawa, Ontario.

Wong, S. (2004). *Treatment of psychopathy: Do we really know where we are going?* Paper presented at the Bergen International Conference on the Treatment of Psychopathy, Norway.

Yalom, I. (1995). *The theory and practice of group psychotherapy (4th edition).* New York: Basic Books.

Chapter 6

DRUG AND ALCOHOL PROGRAMMES: CONCEPT, THEORY, AND PRACTICE

MARY MCMURRAN

University of Nottingham and Llanarth Court Hospital

INTRODUCTION

In England and Wales, accreditation of an offender treatment programme generally requires, amongst other things, evidence that it is targeted at one or more "criminogenic needs" (Correctional Services Accreditation Panel, 2002). This means that the programme designers must say how changing what their programme aims to change will reduce the likelihood of offending among those who participate in it (see Chapter 1). This requirement of proof is waived for programmes targeting substance use, which is taken as self-evidently a criminogenic need. Most people are quite convinced of the connection between substance use and crime, based upon personal experience, media reports, or scientific evidence.

In this chapter, the reasons why substance use is included as a criminogenic need will be described briefly, with reference to the socio-political context in which these behaviours occur. An overview of treatment types will be presented, along with evidence for their effectiveness. Cognitive-behavioural programmes are one type of effective intervention, not only used alone but also often embedded within or used in conjunction with other approaches. The main components of cognitive-behavioural interventions will be described in some detail. The final section of the chapter is devoted to considering how interventions for offenders with problems relating to their substance use may be developed.

RATIONALE FOR DRUG AND ALCOHOL PROGRAMMES

In England and Wales, 63 % of male sentenced prisoners reported hazardous drinking during the year before coming into prison, and 30 % had severe alcohol problems, with the corresponding percentages for convicted women being 39 % and

Offending Behaviour Programmes: Development, Application, and Controversies. Edited by C.R. Hollin and E.J. Palmer.
Copyright © 2006 John Wiley & Sons Ltd.

11 % respectively (Singleton, Farrell & Meltzer, 1999). Of male sentenced prisoners, 43 % reported moderate or severe drug dependence in the year prior to imprisonment, with the percentage for sentenced women prisoners being 42 % (Singleton et al., 1999). These proportions of problematic substance users are far in excess of those observed in the general population, which raises the question of why there is apparently such a strong association between substance use and crime.

One answer is that the relationship is tautological. The possession, sale, and use of certain substances is against the law, hence being caught with an illicit drug is in itself a crime. In this case, stopping people from using prohibited substances, or lessening their use of them, will certainly reduce offending behaviour and possibly also recorded crime. But there is more to drug crimes than the drug-specific crimes of possession and use. In treatment, it is usually *drug-related* crimes that are the targeted criminological outcome of intervention, rather than drug-specific crimes.

The drug-related crimes of principal concern are economically driven offences that are committed in order to support a habit, including shoplifting, burglary, selling drugs, and fraud. In a sample of UK offenders in drug treatment, Turnbull, McSweeney, Webster, Edmunds & Hough (2000) found the average annual expenditure on drugs to be £ 21 000 (about US $40 000) per person. There are, however, a number of other crime connections. Violence is currency in the commercial world of dealing and supplying illicit drugs, but this type of instrumental violence is not the only concern. The use of certain drugs, particularly crack-cocaine, is associated with an increase in the likelihood of violence by the individual who uses (Home Office, 2002a). The illicit drug economy is also tied in with procuration and prostitution, with sex workers (male and female) not only selling sex for drugs but also being vehicles for drug distribution (May, Edmunds & Hough, 1999). There is also concern over the role drug use may play in causing road accidents (National Statistics, 2002). Thus, drug-related crimes are wide in their range and deserve attention in relation both to the reduction of supply and the reduction of demand, the latter being within the treatment domain.

Then there is the interesting anomaly of alcohol. In most countries, alcohol is a legally available substance, albeit with controls placed upon its sale, consumption, and people's behaviour after consumption (for example, drinking and driving or being drunk and disorderly). Major concerns about alcohol and health have led many countries to view excessive alcohol consumption as a major public health issue, and consequently to reduce availability and increase price so as to reduce overall consumption and improve the population's health (Edwards et al., 1994). Such population level controls also reduce alcohol-related violence (Mosher & Jernigan, 2001), a particularly serious problem related to drinking and acknowledged by the World Health Organisation as a public health issue (Krug, Dahlberg, Mercy, Zwi & Lozano, 2002).

Another major alcohol-related problem is drink driving (Ayres & Haward, 2000). In the UK, about 13 % of road deaths occur when someone was driving over the legal limit for alcohol (National Statistics, 2002). Although generally attracting less attention, the cost of supporting a habit of heavy drinking drives some people to commit acquisitive offences (McMurran & Cusens, 2005).

EVIDENCE BASE FOR PROGRAMME TARGETS

Taking one step back at this point, it is important to understand that heavy drinking, drug use, and crime develop over an individual's lifetime, influenced by individual characteristics, family, school and peers, and the social context in which the individual lives. This may be described in a developmental risk factor model, where an accumulation of biological, psychological and social risk factors, along with an absence of protective factors across the lifespan lead eventually to heavy substance use and associated crime (McMurran, 1996; McMurran & Priestley, 2004).

Risk factors for substance use and crime are highly similar along the developmental pathway, meaning that to be at risk of one is to be at risk of the other. These risk factors include early impulsiveness and hyperactivity (Klinteberg, Andersson, Magnusson & Stattin, 1993; White et al., 1994); poor family management practices, such as unclear expectations for behaviour, lax monitoring of behaviour, harsh discipline, and few rewards for positive behaviours (Farrington & Hawkins, 1991; Hawkins, Catalano & Miller, 1992); conduct problems in childhood (Maughan, 1993; Wilens & Biederman, 1993); school failure and truancy (Sher & Trull, 1994), and mixing with delinquent peers in adolescence (Elliott, Huizinga & Ageton, 1985).

Where substances are readily available, experimentation is common in adolescence; indeed, it is more typical to experiment with drugs and alcohol than not. Among antisocial youth it cannot be said that substance use causes crime at this early stage; indeed, antisocial behaviour typically precedes substance use in late childhood/early adolescence. However, once substance use begins, there is potential for the development of subsequent substance-related problems, including crime. For some people, substance use and delinquency interfere with involvement in conventional society leading to the development in adulthood of a lifestyle of substance use and crime (Walters, 1994). Lifestyles of substance use and crime make relationships difficult to sustain, job prospects diminish, and alternative lifestyles seem impossible and the individual eventually becomes trapped in an antisocial way of life.

This pathway describes how early risk factors for both substance use and crime may develop into a generally deviant lifestyle. For most people, the early risk factors are not present or are not permitted to flourish, but experimentation with substance use still occurs in adolescence. Some may experience temporary problems with substance use and crime, from which they soon desist – the so-called "adolescent limited" offenders (Moffitt, 1993). Others may develop primary substance misuse problems that then lead them into crime (Loeber, 1990).

The individual develops within a social and political context, and this is highly important in relation to substance use. Like its fighting partner, the US, the UK has been engaged in the "war on drugs" for many years now. Tracking down traffickers and suppliers and shutting down operations is intended to cut off supply at source and so reduce the drug problem. Few would disagree entirely with this endeavour, although some believe that many drug-related problems are actually created by prohibition.

In the UK, the approach to controlling drinking is considerably less gung-ho. Amongst those countries whose predominant style of drinking has been heavy social drinking at weekends, as opposed to daily drinking mainly at mealtimes, the UK stands out as not only having failed to tighten up on drinking but has actually permitted drinking to become easier; licensing hours are longer, licensed premises are more numerous (on- and off-licenses), and alcohol is cheaper relative to average income than ever before. Indeed, the UK government has, instead, created the conditions where drinks companies can capitalise on the UK population's tendency to binge drink. The creation of super-pubs, extravagant promotions during happy hours, and bullish marketing of high-alcohol designer drinks have all exacerbated the problem of drunkenness, violence, and disorderly conduct, particularly in city centres on weekend nights. It barely needs saying that the war on drugs does not lose the government revenue, whereas a war on alcohol would. Consequently, the UK government bases decisions about alcohol availability not on the advice of researchers or those with an interest in public health but on the advice of the alcohol industry (Drummond, 2004).

In the long term, this is likely to impact on public health but there is no need to wait to discover the impact on antisocial behaviour. Street violence is highly problematic in many UK towns and cities, with young, male binge drinkers being the predominant group of offenders (Richardson & Budd, 2003). Street violence may be the most visible form of alcohol-related violence but alcohol is also very often present in incidents of domestic violence (Gilchrist et al., 2003), increasing the likelihood and degree of violence by some people (Leonard, 2001).

The political and cultural situation has relevance to offender treatments. In the UK, the government at Westminster's drug strategy appeared in 1998 (Home Office, 1998, 2002b) and promised, along with greater efforts in control, prevention, and treatment, a commitment to expand treatment services within the criminal justice system. The revised version in 2002, commits to "using every opportunity from arrest, to court, to sentence, to get drug-misusing offenders into treatment" (Home Office, 2002b, p. 4). The national alcohol strategy for England, which also commits to offender treatment, arrived on the scene much later, in 2004 (Cabinet Office, 2004). Similar strategies have appeared in Scotland (Scottish Office, 1999; Scottish Executive, 2002), Wales (National Assembly for Wales, 2000), and Northern Ireland (Northern Ireland Executive, 1999; DHSSPS, 2000).

The good intentions stated in national strategies seem to translate into practice rather better for drug treatments than for alcohol treatments. Correctional services have had drug strategies in place since the late 1990s, for example, HM Prison Service's (1998) *Tackling Drugs in Prison*, devoted to the control of drugs in prisons and the promotion and coordination of interventions for drug users. Despite the extent of alcohol-related problems among offenders, alcohol strategies have not been put in place, although services are currently working on these. There never has been a coordinator of alcohol interventions in UK Prison and Probation Services, a role that was suggested as far back as 1989 (McMurran, 1989; McMurran & Baldwin, 1989). The result is that treatment programmes in UK criminal justice settings prioritise drugs, and the range of interventions for problem drinkers is limited. Although programmes for substance use in general may include problem drinkers, in reality, services are often not extended to problem drinkers. At present, only one accredited treatment programme specifically for alcohol-related offenders exists, targeting drink driving. If a treatment is not identified as a priority, then resources are not allocated specifically to developing and maintaining that treatment. Clearly, alcohol policies need to be translated into treatments and targets.

There is a strong need for both drug and alcohol treatments in correctional services, and some political and organisational commitment to providing services. What must be examined now is the literature on treatment outcome, so that hard evidence may guide the nature of the services that are developed.

OUTCOME EVIDENCE FOR DRUG AND ALCOHOL PROGRAMMES

Drug and alcohol interventions include medical treatments, educational programmes, therapeutic communities, and psychosocial therapies. These approaches may be used in combination but this is not always the case; therapeutic communities, for example, generally require members to be drug-free, which includes being free of prescribed mood-altering drugs.

Medical treatments include detoxification and pharmacotherapy (Madden, 1991; Raistrick, 2004). Methadone maintenance prescription is commonly used in the treatment of opiate dependence, and in alcohol treatment drugs may be administered to deter drinking (disulfiram), reduce the desire for alcohol (naltrexone), or reduce withdrawal and craving (acamprosate) (Chick, 2004). In most cases, the effectiveness of drug treatments is enhanced by adjunctive psychosocial interventions (Rohsenow, 2004). Combined treatment is possible in prisons, as evidenced by Shewan, Macpherson, Reid & Davies (1996) who evaluated a prison drug treatment programme that combined methadone prescription and counselling with treatment completers, significantly reducing their drug use in prison over those referred but who did not start or did not complete treatment.

The rationale behind drug and alcohol education is to equip people with sufficient knowledge to enable them to make informed choices about substance use. Educational programmes that impart only facts are no longer common, perhaps with the exception of education about safer drug using practices that minimise the likelihood of the spread of infectious diseases. Most educational approaches now also target attitudes to substance use, promote motivation to change, and advise upon strategies for change. As such, the distinction between these and cognitive-behavioural approaches is becoming blurred.

Therapeutic communities (TCs) aim to address dysfunctional living in a democratic setting in which residents confront and correct each other's maladaptive behaviour, offer each other support through the difficult change process, and reward improvement by promoting residents through the community's hierarchy. The term "concept TC" refers to those designed specifically to assist people with substance use problems (Wexler, 1995). The abstinence-oriented, 12-step approach of Narcotics Anonymous (NA) and Alcoholics Anonymous (AA) has been widely adapted by professionals into concept TCs.

Therapeutic communities have been adapted for correctional settings and they have a good track record, particularly in the US (Wexler, 1997). More recently TCs have been introduced in the UK (Malinowski, 2003; Martin & Player, 2000). They have been documented in line with programme accreditation criteria and subsequently accredited (Correctional Services Accreditation Panel, 2004) (see Chapter 1).

Psychological correctional therapies are mainly structured, cognitive-behavioural programmes, in line with the "what works" literature, and a number of such programmes exist. Cognitive-behavioural programmes will be covered in greater detail later in this chapter. First, some evidence of what works in correctional substance abuse treatment will be reviewed.

Pearson & Lipton (1999) reported the first phase of analysis of their Correctional Drug Abuse Treatment Effectiveness (CDATE) project – a meta-analysis of substance use treatment evaluation studies in corrections published between 1968 and 1996. Interventions that were ineffective in terms of reducing reconviction were boot camps (a militaristic experience intended to shock young people into mending their ways) and drug counselling. The therapeutic community (TC) approach was identified as effective and a later report from CDATE indicated that 35 methodologically sound studies of TC or milieu therapy for adults, with almost 11 000 participants, gave a positive mean effect size of 0.14 (Lipton, Pearson, Cleland & Yee, 2002a). Lipton, Pearson, Cleland, and Yee's (2002b) meta-analysis of 68 methodologically acceptable behavioural and cognitive-behavioural programmes with over 10 000 participants gave a positive mean effect size of 0.12. Separate analyses revealed that the 23 evaluations of behavioural programmes (without the cognitive element) produced a mean effect size of 0.07, and that for 44 cognitive-behavioural programmes the mean effect size was 0.14. Effect sizes of 0.12 and 0.14 are quite respectable in comparison with most interventions in offender treatments. Other approaches which showed promise but with too few studies to draw strong conclusions, were methadone maintenance for offenders addicted to heroin, substance abuse education, and 12-step programmes (Pearson & Lipton, 1999).

What works in the US may not work in the UK, and so Perry, McDougall, and Farrington (2005) have reviewed studies of UK criminal justice interventions to reduce crime, including only methodologically acceptable evaluations. McMurran (2005) has reviewed those relating to drug and alcohol interventions.

Only seven eligible studies of drug treatments were identified, and even these had methodological limitations, such as having no control groups or unmatched controls. Five of the studies concerned prescription treatments for heroin users offered in health service clinics. Methadone maintenance was effective in reducing acquisitive crime (Coid et al. 2000, undated; Keen, Rowse, Mathers, Campbell & Seivewright, 2000; Parker & Kirby, 1996), although other studies showed that prescription of pharmaceutical heroin (diamorphine) was superior over methadone at keeping people in treatment and reducing crime (McCusker & Davies, 1996; Metrebian et al., 2001).

Services for drug users in correctional settings targeted drug use more generally. Haynes (1998) compared offending of Probation Service referrals before and after referral to a drug treatment service. Post-treatment, there was a reduction in serious offences of violence and burglary, although there was an increase in less serious property offences. In an evaluation of a 12-step therapeutic community for drug and alcohol misusers in prison, Martin & Player (2000) collected reconviction data from the Home Office's Offender Index at 13 months, showing that significantly fewer graduates than non-graduates had been reconvicted.

Success in treatment for drug users was associated with attending treatment (Haynes, 1998; Martin & Player, 2000), abstaining from the illicit drug of choice (Martin & Player, 2000; Metrebian et al., 2001), finding employment (Parker & Kirby, 1996), and being female (Parker & Kirby, 1996).

With regard to alcohol interventions, only three methodologically acceptable studies were identified (Perry et al., 2005). These were all criminal justice interventions for young offenders, two being brief alcohol education programmes (Baldwin et al., 1991; Singer, 1991), and one being a self-help intervention (McMurran & Boyle, 1990). Baldwin et al. (1991) examined the effectiveness of a 12-hour alcohol education course for male young offenders on average 14 months after release. Compared with an untreated group, the treated group showed significant decreases in drinking and had committed fewer offences against the person. Singer (1991) evaluated a 6-session alcohol education course for young offenders, finding that the actual reconviction rate for high-risk offenders was lower than expected 12 months after completing the course. McMurran & Boyle (1990) investigated the effectiveness of a behavioural self-help manual with male young offenders, finding no significant difference in reconviction at 15 months after release between those offenders who had not participated in the intervention, those given the manual to read alone, and those who had the contents of the manual presented to them.

In summary, pharmacotherapy, education, TCs and cognitive behavioural interventions are the treatments for which there is most positive outcome evidence. As promised earlier, cognitive-behavioural programmes will be covered in greater detail below.

PROGRAMME CONTENT AND APPLICATION ISSUES

To assist in conveying the detail of cognitive-behavioural programmes for substance users in corrections, the focus here will be on examples from Canada and the UK – two jurisdictions with particularly strong connections in programme development and evaluation.

The Correctional Service of Canada has a suite of programmes for offenders with various levels of substance-use problems. The High Intensity Substance Abuse Program (HISAP; Eno, Long, Blanchet, Hansen & Dine, 2001) is a comprehensive treatment programme for imprisoned offenders with severe substance abuse problems, consisting of 100 two-hour sessions delivered at a frequency of 8 sessions per week over 4 to 5 months. The Offender Substance Abuse Pre-Release Program (OSAPP; Lightfoot, 2001) is designed for imprisoned offenders with intermediate to severe alcohol and drug problems and consists of 26 3-hour group sessions plus three individual counselling sessions. *Choices* is a programme consisting of 10 3-hour sessions for offenders with low levels of substance-abuse problems, and who are on conditional release in the community (Lightfoot, 2001). An overview of the content of these programmes is presented in Table 6.1.

An evaluation of OSAPP and *Choices* indicates good completion rates (89% for OSAPP; 91% *Choices*), with readmission to prison for violation of release conditions or a new offence at 1 year after release being significantly less for OSAPP programme completers compared with an untreated matched control

Table 6.1   Canadian Correctional Service substance use programmes

Programme	Content
High Intensity Substance Abuse Program (HISAP)	*Modules:* 1. Programme orientation 2. Motivation 3. Understanding behaviour 4. Behavioural coping 5. Cognitive coping 6. Relapse prevention 7. Life planning 8. Conclusion
Offender Substance Abuse Pre-release Program (OSAPP)	*Units:* 1. Introduction 2. Alcohol and drug education 3. Self-management training 4. Social skills training 5. Job skills refresher 6. Leisure and lifestyle 7. Prerelease planning 8. Relapse prevention and management 9. Conclusion
Choices	*Phases:* 1. Individual assessment 2. Treatment – five sessions on knowledge, motivation, understanding behaviour, problem solving, relapse prevention 3. Maintenance

group (Porporino, Robinson, Millson & Weekes, 2002). Effects were greatest for offenders showing greater levels of substance abuse severity, as measured by psychometric test scores. Interestingly, effects were greater for offenders who had a *less* extensive criminal history. The effects of OSAPP on reducing readmission were significantly greater for offenders who additionally engaged in a community-based programme after release.

Adaptations of the Canadian programmes are used in England and Wales, along with a range of locally developed cognitive-behavioural programmes for substance-misusing offenders (see Chapter 1). There is an intensive programme for offenders in high-security jails (FOCUS), programmes operating in medium-secure settings (STOP, Action on Drugs), and a programme for short duration prisoners (Correctional Services Accreditation Panel, 2004). In addition to these are the earliest developed programmes in the correctional services of England and Wales: Programme for Reducing Individual Substance Misuse (PRISM; Priestley & McMurran, 2001), an individual treatment programme, Addressing Substance-Related Offending (ASRO; McMurran & Priestley, 2001), a group programme designed for offenders in the community, and P-ASRO, an adaptation of ASRO for use in prisons. The ASRO and P-ASRO programmes target medium-risk offenders and consist of 20 2-hour sessions, which are listed in Box 6.1. Hollin et al. (2004) evaluated the outcome of probation treatment programmes in aggregate, finding that, when non-completers were excluded from the analysis, treated offenders

**Box 6.1   Addressing Substance-Related Offending (McMurran &
Priestley, 2001)**

1. Introduction

Section 1 – Enhancing motivation to change
2. The process of change
3. Decision-making
4. Goal-setting

Section 2 – The personal scientist
5. An introduction to enhancing self-control
6. Altering triggers
7. Altering triggers – stress management
8. Altering behaviour
9. Altering consequences
10. Review of methods

Section 3 – Relapse prevention
11. Identifying high-risk situations
12. Coping with cravings
13. Problem solving
14. Managing moods
15. Coping with conflict
16. Review of methods

Section 4 – Lifestyle change
17. Withdrawing from substance users
18. Building new social networks
19. Health and happiness

20. Conclusion

were reconvicted at significantly lower rates than untreated offenders. The ASRO programme was part of this large-scale evaluation, although only a very small number of completers of this programme were included in the analysis.

These sample programmes illustrate the key targets of effective cognitive-behavioural treatments for drug and alcohol use, namely motivation enhancement, behavioural self-control, cognitive coping skills, interpersonal skills, relapse prevention, and lifestyle change, each of which will now be described briefly.

Motivation Enhancement

Motivating substance users to engage in treatment has long been acknowledged as a keystone of treatment effectiveness. In a seminal paper, Miller (1985) addressed the construct of motivation for treatment, with special emphasis on treatment for alcohol problems. In this paper, he summarised the therapist's perception of a client's motivation for treatment as follows:

> A client tends to be judged as motivated if he or she accepts the therapist's view of the problem (including the need for help and the diagnosis), is distressed, and complies with treatment prescriptions. A client showing the opposite behaviours – disagreement, refusal to accept diagnosis, lack of distress, and rejection of treatment prescriptions – is likely to be perceived as unmotivated, denying, and resistant. (Miller, 1985, pp. 87–8)

Miller suggested that judgements of low motivation for treatment based on treatment non-compliance pose the risk of doing clients a disservice by attributing non-compliance to their inherent lack of motivation to change. A more functional approach is to view motivation as a dynamic state that varies with a number of internal and external factors, and the therapy task should be to alter these to increase the probability of a client entering therapy and actively engaging in the treatment process.

Motivational interviewing (MI) developed from this position (Miller & Rollnick, 1991, 2002). MI is a strategic counselling technique that aims to tip ambivalence to change towards taking action, based upon a spirit of collaboration with the client to draw out the client's own capacity and resources for change. Change is encouraged through the expression of empathy, the development of a feeling of a discrepancy between the current situation and a more fulfilling or less problematic one, and supporting the increase of self-efficacy beliefs. Eliciting resistance to change is avoided by using non-directive techniques. The principles of motivational interviewing are seen as important not only to the initial engagement of a client in therapy but also to maintaining the client's engagement throughout, such that training in a motivational style of programme delivery is now considered fundamental to cognitive-behavioural treatment programmes in UK corrections.

Motivational enhancement therapy alone has proven as effective as more intensive interventions for addictions. In Project MATCH, whose aim was to assess the benefits of matching clients with interventions, a four-session motivational enhancement therapy worked as well for most clients in reducing drinking compared with 12 sessions of either cognitive-behaviour therapy or a 12-step programme (Project Match Research Group, 1997). In fact, motivational enhancement therapy was *more* effective than cognitive-behaviour therapy for clients high in anger, as was the 12-step intervention. The possible mechanism for this finding is therapist directiveness, with more directive therapy being less suitable for people high in anger (Karno & Longabaugh, 2004). Anger has relevance to many offenders and so requires consideration in selection for treatment. A project examining the effectiveness of motivational enhancement therapy with UK problem drinkers has yet to report (Copello et al., 2001).

Behavioural Self-Control

The notion of self-control, or lack of it, is fundamental to the understanding of addictive behaviours. Heather (1991) has raised the question of what impaired control means, the gist of which can be extrapolated to drugs as well as alcohol.

When judging impaired control, therapists variously include an inability to stop drinking or drug use, an inability to sustain abstinence for a prolonged period after stopping, trying to cut down but failing, being under the influence at socially inappropriate times or in inappropriate places, solitary drinking or drug use, or simply worrying about one's ability to resist temptation. Impaired control has a range of meanings but it is essentially an inability to adhere to a rule that one has set oneself with regard to changing substance use.

Understanding personal control requires a similar perspective to the understanding of motivation for treatment. Self-control is not a trait: it is the likelihood of drinking or using drugs in response to a range of physical, emotional, and psychological triggers that have a history of substance abuse as a response, with consequent positive outcomes. The task in therapy should be to teach the client to identify the triggers for substance use, resist the urge to respond to those triggers, devise alternative means of coping, recognise and reward personal success in self-control, and view failure as a learning experience on the road to improvement of self-control. In the mid-1970s, Mahoney & Thoresen (1974) encapsulated this approach in the notion of teaching clients to become "personal scientists". Behavioural self-control training has proved effective as a component of intervention (see Miller, 1992) and is now core practice in many cognitive-behavioural interventions.

Cognitive Coping Skills

Cognitive coping includes a range of both specific and general skills. Self-talk derives from the work of Meichenbaum (1977), and includes self-statements and self-instruction. Positive self-statements are taught to assist people cope with cravings ("this feeling won't last; I don't have to use") and avoid the goal-violation effect ("a lapse does not have to become a relapse"). Self-instruction is the construction and use of scripts to use as an internal commentary to support the implementation of new coping skills.

Alcohol and drug outcome expectancies require some attention. An expectancy is a cognitive representation of a person's past learning in the form of an if-then relationship (Goldman, 1994). Expectancies may be positive, for example "if I drink then I will feel more relaxed", or negative, for example, "if I drink then I will say something stupid". Where alcohol is concerned, positive outcome expectancies predict drinking and negative outcome expectancies predict abstinence (Leigh & Stacy, 2004). Holding stronger negative expectancies predicts better treatment outcome (Jones & McMahon, 1996), and changing expectancies in treatment can reduce drinking (Darkes & Goldman, 1993). In relation to crime, specific outcome expectancies require attention, such as the expectancy in rapists whose offences were alcohol-related that they are likely to do something sexually risky after drinking (McMurran & Bellfield, 1993), and the expectancy that alcohol leads to violence (Quigley, Corbett & Tedeschi, 2002; Zhang, Welte & Wieczorek, 2002). Outcome expectancies are less well investigated in and targeted with drug users. Attention has more recently been paid to outcome expectancies for crime in general (Walters, 2003, 2004), and clearly this is an area ripe for further research.

At a broader level, problem-solving skills training, such as that based upon the early work of D'Zurilla & Goldfried (1971) and its more recent developments (Chang, D'Zurilla & Sanna, 2004; D'Zurilla & Nezu, 1999), is usually integrated into cognitive-behavioural treatments. Teaching clients a strategy for solving personal problems increases their independent functioning. Problem-solving therapy has been shown to be effective as part of treatment programmes for anti-social behaviour in general (Friendship, Blud, Erikson, Travers & Thornton, 2003; Lipsey, Chapman & Landenberger, 2001; McGuire & Hatcher, 2001; Robinson, 1995).

Interpersonal Skills

Peer pressure to use drugs is often cited as important in initiation to and maintenance of drug use, particularly in young people. In the 1980s, this led Nancy Reagan, wife of the then US President Ronald Reagan, and Princess Diana, then wife of the UK's Prince Charles, to dissuade youngsters from taking drugs through their "Just Say No" campaigns. While saying no to drugs is essential in preventing or controlling problematic use, resisting peer pressure is rather more complicated than simple assertiveness. Drug use may be a normative behaviour for some sub-groups and the pressure to join one's peers is part of a positive socialisation process, not a skills deficit (May, 1993). Teaching refusal skills is, therefore, only one part of resisting peer pressures, although it is important in helping people resist direct pressure to use drugs. Of course, normative behaviour is in large part defined by the socio-political context, and the issues regarding the availability of drugs and alcohol are pertinent here.

Concerning adults who are changing their behaviour, skills are required to equip the individual to cope with others' disbelief and discouragement. Most people attempt change several times on the route to success, and those close to the person effecting change may well express cynicism and doubt – "I've heard this before". Others who are drinkers or drug users themselves may try to undermine change attempts, because someone stopping makes their continued drinking or drug use more difficult, or makes their inability to change more evident. Interpersonal conflict is a potent risk relapse factor (Marlatt, 1996), and so negotiation and conflict resolution skills are important.

Relapse Prevention

Relapse prevention (RP) is another component of cognitive-behavioural treatment with a long pedigree. In a significant shift of thinking on relapse, Marlatt & Gordon (1985) focused on relapse as part of the change process, not as a separate or distinct event. They identified a number of relapse risk factors that require attention in intervention to increase the likelihood of maintenance of change. A list of relapse risk factors, based on Marlatt's (1996) later work on drinkers, is presented in Box 6.2.

Box 6.2   Relapse risk factors (Marlatt, 1996)

(A) *Intrapersonal (i.e., within the person) determinants*

1. Coping with negative emotional states:
   a. Coping with frustration and/or anger caused by goal frustration, hassles, guilt.
   b. Coping with other negative emotional states, e.g., anxiety, depression, loneliness, worry, stress.
2. Coping with negative physical-physiological states:
   a. Coping with physical states associated with prior substance use, i.e., physical withdrawal.
   b. Coping with other negative physical states not associated with prior substance use, e.g., pain, illness, injury, fatigue, headaches.
3. Enhancement of positive emotional states, e.g., to get high, chill out.
4. Testing personal control, i.e. testing willpower.
5. Giving in to temptations, urges, or cravings:
   a. In the presence of substance-related cues, e.g., passing a bar, seeing tinfoil.
   b. In the absence of substance-related cues, i.e., "out of the blue".

(B) *Interpersonal determinants*

1. Coping with interpersonal conflict:
   a. Coping with frustration or anger, e.g., feel frustrated or angry with someone else and get into arguments or feel jealous.
   b. Coping with other interpersonal conflict, e.g., worry, stress, anxiety, fear.
2. Social pressure:
   a. Direct, e.g., being offered or urged to use substances by someone.
   b. Indirect, i.e., being with people who are using substances and feeling a desire to join in.
3. Enhancement of positive emotional states, e.g., enhance sexual experience, celebrate, party.

Relapse prevention teaches participants first to identify high-risk situations, through examination of past relapses and anticipation of future difficulties. RP then teaches skills for coping with these risks. These skills may be highly specific, such as:

- stimulus control, which is the avoidance of or escape from cues that trigger cravings or urges;
- coping with the problem of immediate gratification (the PIG), which is the strong desire to indulge in substance use;
- managing the goal violation effect, which is where a minor lapse (for example, one drink) turns into a full-blown relapse (for example, the whole bottle); and
- relapse rehearsal, which is where clients are asked to imagine themselves coping effectively in a high risk situation.

Relapse prevention may also tackle broader issues, such as social support for change, stress management, lifestyle balance, and positive substitutes for the addictive behaviour.

In a review of clinical trials, Carroll (1996) found RP to be more effective than no-treatment for substance misuse, but not convincingly superior to other active interventions. There was evidence of a delayed effect, where RP reduced the severity of lapses when they did occur, and that RP was more effective with severely impaired substance users. A meta-analysis of RP with offenders in general (not substance users specifically), showed that offence-related treatment programmes with an RP component were overall effective in reducing recidivism compared with no treatment controls (Dowden, Antonowicz & Andrews, 2003). The most effective RP components were training significant others in the programme model, relapse rehearsal, and understanding the chain of events leading up to relapse.

Lifestyle Change

Developing a non-substance using, non-criminal life often requires general changes in accommodation, work, leisure activities, social networks, and close relationships. In order to achieve these changes, Walters (1998) suggests the following process:

- Identify what needs are being met by the antisocial lifestyle, and in particular, what will the client miss upon stopping drinking, drug use, and crime.
- Identify and support the development of substitute activities that will satisfy these needs.
- Encourage commitment to a new lifestyle and a new personal identity by reviewing the decision to change, developing new social networks, and abandoning the "addict" or "criminal" identity.

So far, we have seen that a number of treatments for offenders with substance use problems show promise, and we have looked more closely at cognitive-behavioural interventions. What becomes important now is to consider how treatments can be made still more effective. This matter needs to be addressed through action at a number of levels, including the socio-political, the design and content of treatment, and the way services are delivered.

FUTURE DIRECTIONS FOR DRUG AND ALCOHOL PROGRAMMES

Diversion of Drug-Using Offenders into Treatment

In developing treatment for offenders with substance use problems, the direction taken has been to support diversion into multi-disciplinary, inter-agency treatments with emphasis on throughcare. Recently, attention has been given to ways of linking offenders into drug and alcohol treatment services. Many of these efforts are linked with drug testing by police, probation and prison personnel. The purposes of testing detainees for drugs are to deter drug use while the person is under the supervision of the criminal justice system, to gather intelligence about the population's drug use, and to encourage people to abstain from drug use, either through self-change or by accessing help. On-charge testing by police opens the opportunity for arrest-referral procedures; pre-sentence testing opens opportunities for probation orders with drug monitoring and treatment provision; and post-sentence testing opens opportunities for drug treatment in prison and follow-through on licence. In conjunction with treatment, drug testing shows promise in reducing drug use and offending (Matrix Research and Consultancy & NACRO, 2004).

Arrest-referral schemes permit the early identification of drug-using offenders by employing drugs workers to approach arrestees in custody and offer advice or channel them into treatment. Evaluations of arrest-referral schemes show positive outcomes in recruiting drug users into treatment and reducing both substance use and crime (Crossen-White & Galvin, 2002; Seeling, King, Metcalfe, Toker & Bates, 2001).

England and Wales' Drug Treatment and Testing Orders (DTTOs) allow offenders to receive treatment as an alternative to custody. Probation services link with other agencies to provide treatment under DTTOs, and offender self-report data indicate substantial reductions in drug use and offending during the DTTO and after its expiry (Turnbull et al., 2000). However, Hough, Clancy, McSweeney & Turnbull (2003) collected recorded crime follow-up data using the Offender Index on 174 DTTO referrals and found a high incidence of reconviction at 2 years (80%), although reconviction was significantly less likely amongst those who completed their order (53%) than those whose order was revoked (91%). The issue of retention and treatment completion is important and will be addressed later (see also Chapter 2).

Recently, in Scotland, special Drug Courts have been set up, with a range of sentencing and treatment options, depending on what services are available locally (Eley, Malloch, McIvor, Yates & Brown, 2002; McIvor, Eley, Malloch & Yates, 2003). Drug courts have been used elsewhere, particularly the US, with some evidence that drug court participants are less likely to recidivate than non-participants on regular probation orders, although failure of individuals to meet the programme's requirements is common (Rodriguez & Webb, 2004).

Diversion from the criminal justice system into treatment requires multidisciplinary and inter-agency working. This has the potential to lead to the best treatment for the client, but it is a weak spot in treatment provision. Turnbull et al. (2000, p. viii) observed that for the English and Welsh Probation Service there was a lack of effective inter-agency working in DTTOs, and suggested that there needs to be investment in "the selection and training of staff, achieving clarity of roles, team building activities and planning better assessment procedures and treatment programmes".

Treatment Setting and Throughcare

A major shortcoming of offender treatment in general, and offender substance misuse treatment in particular, has been its circumscribed nature. That is, treatment happens to an offender in prison or on probation but is not connected to the offender's life outside the criminal justice system. In a study of an arrest-referral scheme, offenders acknowledged the importance of support after treatment to assist them construct new lives without drugs (Crossen-White & Galvin, 2002). Also, as already mentioned in relation to relapse prevention, the community connection is of great importance to effectiveness (Dowden et al., 2003).

In prisons in England and Wales, Counselling, Assessment, Referral, Advice and Throughcare Services (CARATS) provide support and advice for drug misusers during their time in prison and direct prisoners into drug rehabilitation and detoxification programmes. To make throughcare work, inter-agency approaches again need to be effective. One step towards this in England and Wales has been the integration of Prison and Probation Services' work through the creation of a National Offender Management Service (NOMS) (Carter, 2003). Thus, offender management is intended to be a seamless process from sentencing through to post-release.

Drug and alcohol treatments have to be designed differently for application in community and institutional settings. In the community, where drugs and alcohol are available, there exists the opportunity to monitor thoughts, feelings, and behaviour in response to temptation. In institutions, this opportunity is not present in a direct fashion, however, there are advantages in the programme participant being drug- and alcohol-free and in a position to reflect on the past and prepare for the future. Work can be done in secure settings, and Andrews (2001) offers the advice that, although community-based services are to be preferred over institutional treatments, even in custodial settings treatments should be *community-oriented.*

One issue that requires attention in integrating treatments is whether different treatments augment or interfere with each other. Some treatments are conceptually at odds, for example 12-steps abstinence approaches and moderation-oriented behavioural self-control training. Clearly, it would be inadvisable to offer these treatments together to any one person, although one might be offered sequentially if the other failed. Confusion can also arise, however, where programmes based upon the same conceptual foundation use different heuristics and different terminology. In efforts to enhance throughcare, an offender who has graduated from an institutional programme should be offered a community programme upon release. Ideally, the two should connect with each other, continuously building upon prior learning, using the same concepts, skills, and strategies.

Increasing Completion

Retaining offenders in treatment programmes is a topic of current concern in criminal justice settings, given the high non-completion rates (see, for example, Hollin et al., 2002; Hough et al., 2003; Rodriguez & Webb, 2004) and the knowledge that, in some cases, non-completers are more likely to re-offend than untreated offenders (Cann, Falshaw, Nugent & Friendship, 2003). In Hough et al.'s (2003) study, not only was reconviction at 2 years significantly less likely amongst those who completed their order compared with those whose order was revoked, but completers showed an upward trend of offending, peaking the year before the DTTO and dropping thereafter. With 67 % of the sample (N = 108) having their orders revoked, the authors commented that "the key to success in DTTOs lies in retaining people on their orders" (Hough et al., 2003, p. 5). Attention to methods of retaining offenders in treatment is clearly required. However, programme non-completers may be higher risk offenders than completers and the same factors may predict non-completion, therefore it is not logical to assume that retention in treatment will necessarily lead to success with this group. Attention to methods of selection is also required to minimise the dropout problem.

Protecting Treatment Integrity

Meta-analyses have shown that outcome effectiveness is greatest for small-scale programmes where the evaluator is involved in the design and implementation (Dowden et al., 2003). Despite this, large-scale programme rollout has been driven in the UK, as elsewhere, by the political agenda. In 1999, a target was set for the English and Welsh Probation Service to have 60 000 offenders on programmes by 2003/4, with an expected 5 % reduction in crime (Crime Reduction Website). Targets of such celestial proportions pose serious challenges to treatment integrity. To achieve the targeted number of offenders graduating from treatment programmes (and hence secure financial resources for the service), there is the risk of lowering standards in a number of areas: selecting less well-suited staff to facilitate; cutting their hours of training; paring programme preparation and debriefing time; and selecting less motivated offenders for programmes. As the quality of programmes diminishes, so does the confidence of correctional services' staff and offenders, and eventually outcome suffers (see Chapter 7).

In England and Wales, the general cognitive skills programmes, Reasoning and Rehabilitation (R & R) and Enhanced Thinking Skills (ETS), gave good results in prisons in the early years (Friendship et al., 2003), but later results were disappointing (Cann et al., 2003) (see Chapters 1 and 3 for fuller discussion of these studies). In the later study, reduced recidivism was observed only when non-completers were excluded; analysis with all programme starters showed no reduction in recidivism compared with untreated matched controls. In response to these findings, it would have been logical to pay attention to why people do not complete R & R and ETS and to make adjustments to reduce non-completion. Are selection criteria being adhered to? Is the programme being implemented in a motivational style? Are operational decisions interfering with offenders' completion of programmes? Questions such as these could be asked and answered to good effect but the response was rather different and relevant to the topic of this chapter.

The politically driven organisational response to disappointing outcomes for R & R and ETS was to divert resources with great speed into drug treatment programmes. This rapid response required intensive staff training, with experienced trainers asked to train others to train facilitators and so speed up the capacity to deliver. The risk that has been created is, of course, that the integrity of drug interventions may be compromised and this could reflect in future outcomes.

Clarifying Treatment Goals

Accreditation criteria for programmes in the Correctional Services for England and Wales state that the risk factor is "dependency on alcohol and drugs" (Correctional Services Accreditation Panel, 2002, p. 4). That is, it is not problematic use but rather *dependency* that is the explicit risk factor, and this is applied to illicit drugs and alcohol alike. Following implicitly from this, the rationale behind drug treatment is that dependency can be cured, or at least arrested, only by stopping drug use. This, of course, will theoretically eradicate drug-specific and drug-related crimes. Consequently, treatment is targeted primarily at those who are dependent on drugs, rather than those who are "recreational" drug users or are merely experiencing problems as a result of their drug use.

The problems created by the dependency/abstinence approach are most clearly evident in relation to alcohol. One example is binge drinking and violence. Although young women binge drink (Williamson, Sham & Ball, 2003), the main culprits in terms of violence are young men, for whom heavy weekend drinking is a cultural norm, at least in the UK. These young men are unlikely to be dependent on alcohol; most are unlikely to wish to abstain from drinking. To select these young men for treatment on the basis of dependence on alcohol is likely to exclude many with serious problems of alcohol-related violence, and to promote abstinence as the treatment goal is likely to disaffect many of those offered treatment.

One controversy is what to do with people who do not wish to abstain from taking drugs. Would a crime harm reduction approach be acceptable, where the reduction of drug-related crime was the main treatment goal and the actual use of substances was of lesser priority? In health settings, harm reduction is a well accepted approach to treating and caring for drug users. The desire to control the spread of infectious diseases led to the prioritisation of the health of self and others over the cessation of drug use. In criminal justice settings, to accept harm minimisation as a valid treatment goal, without necessarily requiring abstinence, may be seen as failing to address drug use or even condoning a criminal behaviour. In most criminal justice services, this issue appears to be fudged. That is, practitioners promote abstinence from illicit drug use, but they may be willing to accept that individuals may be unwilling or unable to abstain completely and under these circumstances harm minimisation is desirable. It would be helpful to practitioners and clients if harm reduction goals were explicitly endorsed.

Specific Programmes

Generic programmes that aim to reduce or stop substance use can be effective. There are, however, many different substances with varied effects on people's behaviour, which raises the issue of whether programmes aimed at specific drug- and alcohol-related offences may be more useful in some cases.

Programmes for drink-impaired drivers are one example. In a meta-analytic study of the effectiveness of treatment programmes for drink-drivers, 215 evaluation studies were identified (Wells-Parker, Bangert-Drowns, McMillen & Williams, 1995). The treatments included education and psychological therapies, and the aims were to separate drinking from driving and to avoid future drink-driving offences.

Overall, the mean effect size was 0.19, representing an 8% to 9% reduction in recidivism for treated over untreated participants. The most effective interventions combined education, psychological therapy, and supervision.

As mentioned earlier, intoxicated aggression is a problem that requires specific attention. Graham et al. (1998, p. 670) highlighted the need for interventions that "not only employ standard treatment techniques (for example, anger management), but also use knowledge of the effects of alcohol and the process of aggression in treating violent individuals." The Control of Violence for Angry Impulsive Drinkers (COVAID) programme integrates anger management with an approach to tackling drinking (McMurran & Cusens, 2003).

The basic framework of COVAID is the systems approach to angry aggression described by Robins & Novaco (1999), where anger provocations are appraised in light of hostile beliefs, which leads to physiological arousal that is readily labelled anger, and hence to aggression or violence, which are overlearned behaviours. In COVAID, consideration is then given to the effect of drinking on this system, for example increasing the likelihood of meeting with provocations to anger; changing perceptions and cognitions; removing violence inhibitions, and reducing the accessibility of alternatives to aggression. The intervention teaches participants to address all parts of the system, plus moderating their drinking and especially their *drunkenness*, to reduce the likelihood of aggression and violence. A pilot study has shown that COVAID has promise in that programme participants were less likely than those who were referred but untreated to have been reconvicted of a violent offence in the short-term, and self-reported aggression and violence was low in COVAID participants (McMurran & Cusens, 2003). Psychometric data support the notion that the mediators of anger and impulsivity were successfully addressed.

Intensity

The question of how intensive a substance-use treatment programme needs to be requires further examination. In meta-analyses of offender treatment studies, Lipsey (1992, 1995) identified higher "dosage" treatments as most effective in reducing recidivism. These intensive treatments were at least 26 weeks duration, with two or more contacts per week, and amounting to more than 100 hours of treatment.

However, the offender treatment literature and the clinical treatment literature, particularly that concerning alcohol treatment, are somewhat at odds with regard to treatment intensity. In alcohol treatments, brief interventions, including advice, self-help manuals, and brief motivational enhancement therapy, have a good record of effectiveness, particularly with people with less severe drinking problems who request help (see review by Heather, 2004). The drive towards accreditation of intensive programmes for high-risk offenders means that there is little interest in supporting the design and evaluation of briefer programmes. This is different from the approach in clinical settings, where cognisance of limited resources and the need for cost-effectiveness has led to a stepped care model of treatment, where a minimal intervention is given first, and, if that does not work, successively more intensive interventions are given until the client shows signs of benefit. Economising in this way means that scarce resources can be shared among more people.

Undoubtedly, high-risk offenders and serious, long-term drug users are unlikely to benefit from minimal interventions, yet there are offenders passing through the criminal justice system for whom early stage interventions may have a beneficial effect. It seems likely that stepped care with substance users in the community, which is effective and efficient, could translate in some way to criminal justice settings.

Responsivity

One issue of concern in correctional treatment is the mismatch between programme materials and the literacy levels and cognitive abilities of offenders (Davies, Lewis, Byatt, Purvis & Cole, 2004). General responsivity demands that programmes be accessible to and engaging for the offenders for whom the programme is designed. This encompasses a long list of requirements, such as that materials should be relevant, readable, and eye-catching; that teaching methods should be varied, active, and participative; and that complex ideas should be conveyed simply, graphically, and memorably. Most programmes could improve in these areas. There is considerably creativity evident in the delivery of programmes, and good ideas need to be captured and shared.

Finally, one aspect that is under-investigated is what works for specific groups, for example women offenders, Black and minority ethnic groups, young offenders, and offenders with mental health problems. There may be different antecedents to and criminal consequences of women's substance use, with abuse and sex work figuring more prominently, yet services specific to their needs remain underdeveloped. Cultural and religious backgrounds may be of particular relevance to the understanding of substance-use problems, particularly where the use of alcohol or drugs is proscribed by religious rules. Programmes for young offenders need to take into account developmental issues, for instance the relative lack of impact of health and mortality messages and the greater importance of social image. Mental illness has special importance in the treatment of substance use in that sufferers may be cognitively less able to assimilate programme information and they may also have to cope with being super-sensitive to alcohol and drugs, either because of the mental condition or because of interactions with their prescribed medication (Mueser, Drake & Wallach, 1998). Personality disorder also needs to be considered because this moderates the effectiveness of treatment (Brooner, Kidorf, King & Stoller, 1998; Cecero, Ball, Tennen, Kranzler & Rounsaville, 1999). For people with concurrent mental health problems, integrated treatment for the mental disorder and substance use is the preferred approach.

Manuals

Not only do programme content and materials for offenders require some attention to improve their appeal and appropriateness, but consideration also needs to be given to the treatment manuals (for a detailed consideration of this area, see Chapter 2). In particular, there is room for improvement in the quality, style, and ease of use of the facilitators' manuals – those manuals that guide the professional

through the treatment sessions. Surprisingly, despite the proliferation of manualised treatments for offenders, relatively little attention has been paid to what
makes a good treatment manual.

Treatment manuals offer several advantages, notably that they enhance treatment integrity, facilitate staff training and supervision and permit treatments to
be replicated (McMurran & Duggan, 2005). There are, however, different types of
manual explaining different types of therapy for different types of problem to be
used by practitioners from a range of professional backgrounds. It is likely that
there is a client × therapist × therapy × manual interaction in achieving successful
therapeutic outcome.

Looking at the therapist, treatment manuals have a particularly important role in
providing support and structure to less experienced practitioners. Crits-Cristoph
et al. (1991), in a meta-analysis of psychotherapy outcome, found that the use
of treatment manuals reduced variability in treatment outcome across therapists.
This means that manuals may reduce the effectiveness of the best therapists, but
adherence to manuals offers a minimum quality assurance.

Experience of training professionals in the use of our manualised treatments
showed us that, as academics, we had concentrated on substance over form. Although the manual's instructions were clear to us, and the procedures easy to
follow, others did not share our views. Consequently, we have turned our attention to issues of layout and style – larger font, graphics to highlight the purpose of
each section at-a-glance, reproducible materials on CD. Rather than guess the best
way to design a treatment manual to be of most use to practitioners, we surveyed
views on what makes a good treatment manual. Using the Delphi method, Mc-
Murran & McCulloch (in press) surveyed experienced trainers – those who train
programme facilitators. Trainers are an interesting group because they have usually
been programme facilitators and many are familiar with a number of programmes
and so they can compare different manuals. Some preliminary information about
identifiers of a good facilitator's manual is presented in Box 6.3. This research will

Box 6.3 Identifiers of a good facilitator's manual

- There is a clear theory manual
- Theory and practice are linked
- Learning points are listed throughout
- There is a clear framework for sessions
- Layout is clear (big font, well spaced)
- Different types of activity are visibly distinguished (e.g., by icons, different
  font, section demarcation)
- Plain English is used
- The sessions are not too prescriptive
- Creativity is permitted within boundaries of integrity
- There is information on style of delivery
- Assessment materials are integral
- Materials are available on CD

help us answer the question, "What kind of manuals used by which workers, with what type of clients, and in which settings work best to reduce reoffending?"

Cultural and Regional Variations

Drinking and drug use varies across cultures. Much of the research comes from the US, and its application to other cultures cannot be assumed. US research is conducted within a culture where, often for funding reasons, the disease model of addiction prevails. Consequently, medical diagnoses and the exhortation to abstain are commonplace, and little tolerance for controlled consumption among former "addicts" exists. This holds true for drinking alcohol, where the differences between the US and the UK are greatest. Controlled drinking as a viable treatment goal for problem drinkers is more readily accepted in the UK (Cox, Rosenberg, Hodgins, Macartney & Maurer, 2004).

Hough et al.'s (2003) DTTO study identified regional variations in treatment outcome even within the UK. This may be explained by regional variations in drug use (Turnbull et al., 2000), and also regional variations in services. This suggests that there is value in regional research, comparing client groups, service provision, and ways of working to identify what works with whom and where.

Research Methodology

In researching the effectiveness of criminal justice drug and alcohol interventions, key methodological points should be taken into consideration (see Chapter 2 for a full discussion of these issues). It is only through collecting high-quality information that we can genuinely know what does work and what does not, and consequently develop valid evidence-based practice.

First, if offending is to be used as an outcome measure, then offenders selected for treatment should be those who commit drug- or alcohol-related offences. Second, and related to the first point, is that crime outcome measures should be rationally selected to reflect the types of crime one might logically expect to reduce after treatment. For example, if there is an underpinning rationale that heroin use is costly and so users are driven by economic necessity to commit acquisitive crimes, then, logically, one can expect that reducing heroin use will lead to a reduction in acquisitive offending. Other types of offending may not be affected. If these logical connections between the behaviour targeted in treatment and the crime outcome by which success is judged are missing, then the likelihood is that crime reduction will not be seen to occur. Evaluations that show treatments to be ineffective may risk contributing to a revival of the "nothing works" pessimism. It is the duty of researchers to ensure that they do not contribute to this potential revival through false conclusions based on inadequate research methods.

Third, if tackling drug or alcohol consumption is intended to reduce offending, then it is useful to measure the impact of treatment on substance use. Measuring change in substance use is common in health-service research, where this is a targeted outcome. It is less common in criminal justice setting research, where the targeted outcome is crime and substance use is a mediating variable. In understanding crime outcomes, whether successful or unsuccessful, it is important to know if drug and alcohol interventions are having the desired effect on substance use.

Fourth, control or comparison groups are essential to understanding treatment effectiveness, and these should be comparable to the treatment group on a number of relevant measures. Two obviously important variables in drug and alcohol research are substance use and crime risk. Differences on these variables mean that any observed treatment effects are confounded by the different initial status of the control or comparison groups.

Fifth, where there is attrition in samples, data on treatment completers do not necessarily represent data on the sample as a whole, and assuming so can inflate the observed treatment effects. Treatment non-completers have been shown to be high-risk for re-offending as measured by statistical risk calculation scales (Wormith & Olver, 2002). Care must be taken, therefore, to minimise missing cases and, where data are missing, this should be handled in a statistically appropriate manner (Hollis & Campbell, 1999).

Finally, correctional services are quite rightly concerned not just with the effectiveness of interventions to reduce re-offending but also with their cost relative to other strategies, and this is an important area for research. One important saving to take into account is that the effects of substance use treatment programmes in prisons may also include the reduction of violence related to supply and dealing inside, and improvements in the manageability of prisons (Lipton, 1998).

CONCLUSIONS

The development of effective interventions requires attention to the complex question: "what works best with whom for which problem and delivered under what conditions?" The range of factors within each of these sections can be unpacked. "What works?" includes what types of programmes, components of programmes, and combinations of programmes. "For whom?" includes a range of different offender characteristics, including age, culture, cognitive abilities, and dependence level. "Which problem?" addresses the substance type, the offence type, and the relationship between the two. "What conditions?" relates obviously to location – institution or community – but also to treatment directions or orders, multi-agency working, and throughcare. When we consider the number of factors and the number of combinations of them possible within the clinical question posed above, the magnitude of the undertaking that is required becomes clear.

Developing effective interventions will always be a work in progress, with new ideas and new methods demanded in response to changing circumstances. Some may ask whether the outcomes are worth the effort. Reducing crime is of considerable importance, not only in reducing the number of victims of crime, but also in reducing our fears of the possibility of becoming a victim, making work safer for criminal justice personnel, and reducing the financial costs to society of dealing with crime. Interventions to help people change will also help reduce the experiences of exclusion and alienation of our most risky fellow citizens, and instead promote inclusion and acceptance. This is not only the most humane position, but also the safest one.

REFERENCES

Andrews, D. A. (2001). Principles of effective correctional programs. In L. L. Motiuk & R. C. Serin (Eds), *Compendium 2000 on effective correctional programming* (pp. 9–17). Ottawa: Correctional Service Canada.

Ayres, M. & Hayward, P. (2000). *Motoring offences and breath test statistics.* Home Office Statistical Bulletin No. 24/01. London: Home Office.

Baldwin, S. et al. (1991). Effectiveness of pre-release alcohol education courses for young offenders in a penal institution. *Behavioural Psychotherapy, 19*, 321–331.

Brooner, R. K., Kidorf, M., King, V. L. & Stoller, K., (1998). Preliminary evidence of good treatment response in antisocial drug abusers. *Drug and Alcohol Dependence, 49*, 249–260.

Cabinet Office (2004). *Alcohol harm reduction strategy for England.* London: Cabinet Office Strategy Unit.

Cann, J., Falshaw, L., Nugent, F. & Friendship, C. (2003). Understanding What Works: Accredited cognitive skills programmes for adult men and young offenders. Home Office Research Findings No. 226. London: Home Office.

Carroll, K. M. (1996). Relapse prevention as a psychosocial treatment: A review of controlled clinical trials. *Experimental and Clinical Psychology, 4*, 46–54.

Carter, P. (2003). *Managing offenders, reducing crime: A new approach.* London: Cabinet Office Strategy Unit.

Cecero, J. J., Ball. S. A., Tennen, H., Kranzler, H. R. & Rounsaville, B. J. (1999). Concurrent and predictive validity of antisocial personality disorder subtyping among substance users. *Journal of Nervous and Mental Diseases, 187*, 478–486.

Chang, E. C., D'Zurilla, T. J. & Sanna, L. J. (Eds) (2004). *Social problem solving: Theory, research and training.* Washington, DC: American Psychological Association.

Chick, J. (2004). Pharmacological treatments. In N. Heather & T. Stockwell (Eds), The *essential handbook of treatment and prevention of alcohol problems* (pp. 53–68). Chichester: John Wiley & Sons.

Coid, J., Carvell, A., Kittler, Z., Healey, A. & Henderson, J. (2000). *The impact of methadone treatment on drug misuse and crime.* Home Office Research Findings No. 120. London: Home Office.

Coid, J., Carvell, A., Kittler, Z., Healey, A. & Henderson, J. (undated). Opiates, criminal behaviour and methadone treatment. Accessed 21 September 2004. http://www.homeoffice.gov.uk/rds/pdfs/crimbehav.pdf

Copello, A. et al. (2001). United Kingdom Alcohol Treatment Trial (UKATT): Hypotheses, design, and methods. *Alcohol and Alcoholism, 36*, 11–21.

Correctional Services Accreditation Panel (2002). *Programme accreditation criteria.* London: Home Office.

Correctional Services Accreditation Panel (2004). *The Correctional Services Accreditation Panel Report, 2003–2004.* London: Home Office.

Cox, W. M., Rosenberg, H., Hodgins, C. H. A., Macartney, J. I. & Maurer, K. A. (2004). United Kingdom and United States healthcare providers' recommendations of abstinence versus controlled drinking. *Alcohol and Alcoholism, 39*, 130–134.

Crime Reduction (undated). Crime reduction programme. <http://www.crimereduction.gov.uk/crpinit3.htm>. Accessed 16th November 2004.

Crits-Cristoph, P. et al. (1991). Meta-analysis of therapist effects in psychotherapy outcome studies. *Psychotherapy Research, 1*, 81–91.

Crossen-White, H. & Galvin, K. (2002). A follow-up study of drug misusers who received an intervention from a local arrest-referral scheme. *Health Policy, 61*, 153–171.

Darkes, J. & Goldman, M. S. (1993). Expectancy challenge and drinking reduction. *Journal of Consulting and Clinical Psychology, 61*, 344–353.

Davies, K., Lewis, J., Byatt, J., Purvis, E. & Cole, B. (2004). *An evaluation of the literacy demands of general offending behaviour programmes.* Home Office Research Findings No. 223. London: Home Office.

DHSSPS (2000). *Strategy for reducing alcohol related harm.* Belfast: Northern Ireland Executive, Department of Health, Social Services, and Public Safety.

Dowden, C., Antonowicz, D. & Andrews, D. A. (2003). The effectiveness of relapse prevention with offenders: A meta-analysis. *International Journal of Offender Therapy and Comparative Criminology, 47*, 516–528.

Drummond, C. (2004). An alcohol strategy for England: The good, the bad and the ugly. *Alcohol and Alcoholism, 39*, 377–379.

D'Zurilla, T. J. & Goldfried, M. R. (1971). Problem solving and behavior modification. *Journal of Abnormal Psychology, 78*, 107–126.

D'Zurilla, T. J. & Nezu, A. M. (1999). *Problem solving therapy: A social competence approach to clinical intervention (2nd edition).* New York: Springer Publishing Company.

Edwards, G. et al. (1994). *Alcohol policy and the public good.* Oxford: Oxford University Press.

Eley, S., Malloch, M., McIvor, G., Yates, R. & Brown, A. (2002). *The Glasgow drug court in action: The first six months.* Edinburgh: Scottish Executive Social Research.

Elliott, D. S., Huizinga, D. & Ageton, S. S. (1985). *Explaining delinquency and drug use.* Newbury Park, CA: Sage.

Eno, J., Long, C., Blanchet, S., Hansen, E. & Dine, S. (2001). High intensity substance abuse programming for offenders. *Forum on Corrections Research, 13*, 45–47.

Farrington, D. P. & Hawkins, J. D. (1991). Predicting participation, early onset, and later persistence in officially recorded offending. *Criminal Behaviour and Mental Health, 1*, 1–33.

Friendship, C., Blud, L., Erikson, M., Travers, R. & Thornton, D. M. (2003). Cognitive-behavioural treatment for imprisoned offenders: An evaluation of HM Prison Service's cognitive skills programmes. *Legal and Criminological Psychology, 8*, 103–114.

Gilchrist, E., Johnson, R., Takriti, R., Weston, S., Beech, A. R. & Kebbell, M. (2003). *Domestic violence offenders: Characteristics and offending related needs.* Home Office Research Findings No. 217. London: Home Office.

Goldman, M. S. (1994). The alcohol expectancy concept: Applications to assessment, prevention and treatment of alcohol abuse. *Applied and Preventive Psychology, 3*, 131–144.

Graham, K. et al. (1998). Current directions in research on understanding and preventing intoxicated aggression. *Addiction, 93*, 659–676.

Hawkins, J. D., Catalano, R. F. & Miller, J. Y. (1992). Risk and protective factors for alcohol and other drug problems in adolescence and early adulthood: Implications for substance abuse prevention. *Psychological Bulletin, 112*, 64–105.

Haynes, P. (1998). Drug using offenders in south London: Trends and outcomes. *Journal of Substance Abuse Treatment, 15*, 449–456.

Heather, N. (1991). Impaired control over alcohol consumption. In N. Heather, W. R. Miller & J. Greeley (Eds), Self-*control and the addictive behaviours* (pp. 153–179). Botany, Australia: Maxwell Macmillan.

Heather, N. (2004). Brief interventions. In N. Heather & T. Stockwell (Eds), *The essential handbook of treatment and prevention of alcohol problems* (pp. 117–138). Chichester: John Wiley & Sons.

HM Prison Service. (1998). *Tackling drugs in prisons.* London: HM Prison Service.

Hollin, C. R. et al. (2004). *Pathfinder programmes in the Probation Service: A retrospective analysis.* Home Office Online Report No. 66/04. London: Home Office. http://www.homeoffice.gov.uk/rds/pdfs04/rdsolr6604.pdf. Accessed 12 January 2005.

Hollin, C. R., McGuire, J., Palmer, E. J., Bilby, C., Hatcher, R. & Holmes, A. (2002). *Introducing Pathfinder programmes into the Probation Service: An interim report.* Home Office Research Study No. 247. London: Home Office.

Hollis, S. & Campbell, F. (1999). What is meant by intention to treat analysis? Survey of published randomised controlled trials. *British Medical Journal, 319*, 670–674.

Home Office (1998). *Tackling drugs to build a better Britain.* London: Home Office.

Home Office (2002a). *Tackling crack: A national plan.* London: Home Office.

Home Office (2002b). *Tackling drugs to build a better Britain.* London: Home Office.

Hough, M., Clancy, A., McSweeney, T. & Turnbull, P. J. (2003). *The impact of Drug Treatment and Testing Orders on offending: Two-year reconviction results.* Home Office Research Findings No. 184. London: Home Office.

Jones, B. T. & McMahon, J. (1996). A comparison of positive and negative alcohol expectancy and value and their multiplicative composite as predictors of post-treatment abstinence survivorship. *Addiction, 91,* 89–99.

Karno, M. P. & Longabaugh, R. (2004). What do we know? Process analysis and the search for a better understanding of Project MATCH's anger-by-treatment matching effect. *Journal of Studies on Alcohol, 65,* 501–512.

Keen, J., Rowse, G., Mathers, N., Campbell, M. & Seivewright, N. (2000). Can methadone maintenance for heroin-dependent patients retained in general practice reduce criminal conviction rates and time spent in prison? *British Journal of General Practice, 50,* 48–49.

Klinteberg, B. A., Andersson, T., Magnusson, D. & Stattin, H. (1993). Hyperactive behavior in childhood as related to subsequent alcohol problems and violent offending: A longitudinal study of male subjects. *Personality and Individual Differences, 15,* 381–388.

Krug, E. G., Dahlberg, L. L., Mercy, J. A., Zwi, A. B. & Lozano, R. (Eds) (2002). *World report on violence and health.* Geneva: World Health Organization.

Leigh, B. C. & Stacy, A. W. (2004). Alcohol expectancies and drinking in different age groups. *Addiction, 99,* 215–227.

Leonard, K. E. (2001). Domestic violence and alcohol: What is known and what do we need to know to encourage environmental interventions? *Journal of Substance Use, 6,* 235–247.

Lightfoot, L. O. (2001). Programming for offenders with substance abuse and dependence problems. In L. L. Motiuk & R. Serin (Eds), *Compendium on effective correctional programming 2000* (pp. 98–112). Ottawa: Correctional Service Canada.

Lipsey, M. W. (1992). Juvenile delinquency treatment: A meta-analytic inquiry into the variability of effects. In T. D. Cook, H. Cooper, D. S. Cordray, H. Hartman, L. V. Hedges, R. J. Light, T. A. Louis & F. Mosteller (Eds), *Meta-analysis for explanation: A casebook* (pp. 83–127). NY: Russell Sage Foundation.

Lipsey, M. W. (1995). What do we learn from 400 research studies on the effectiveness of treatments with juvenile delinquents? In. J. McGuire (Ed.), *What works: Reducing reoffending* (pp. 63–78). Chichester: John Wiley & Sons.

Lipsey, M. W., Chapman, G. L. & Landenberger, N .A. (2001). Cognitive-behavioral programs for offenders. *The Annals of the American Academy of Political and Social Science, 578,* 144–157.

Lipton, D. S. (1998). Treatment for drug abusing offenders during correctional supervision: A nationwide overview. *Journal of Offender Rehabilitation, 26,* 1–45.

Lipton, D. S., Pearson, F. S., Cleland, C. M. & Yee, D. (2002a). The effects of therapeutic communities and milieu therapy on recidivism. In J. McGuire (Ed.), *Offender rehabilitation and treatment: Effective programmes and policies to reduce re-offending* (pp. 39–77). Chichester: John Wiley & Sons.

Lipton, D. S., Pearson, F. S., Cleland, C. M. & Yee, D. (2002b). The effectiveness of cognitive-behavioural treatment methods on offender recidivism. In J. McGuire (Ed.), *Offender rehabilitation and treatment: Effective programmes and policies to reduce re-offending* (pp. 79–112). Chichester: John Wiley & Sons.

Loeber, R. (1990). Development and risk factors of juvenile antisocial behavior and delinquency. *Clinical Psychology Review, 10,* 1–41.

Madden, J. S. (1991). Detoxification, pharmacotherapy, and maintenance: drugs. In I. B. Glass (Ed.), *The international handbook of addiction behaviour* (pp. 216–224). London: Routledge.

Mahoney, M. J. & Thoresen, C. E. (1974). *Self-control: Power to the person.* Monterey, CA: Brookes/Cole.

Malinowski, A. (2003). "What works" with substance users in prison? *Journal of Substance Use, 8,* 223–233.

Marlatt, G. A. (1996). Taxonomy of high-risk situations for alcohol relapse: Evolution and development of a cognitive behavioural model. *Addiction, 91 (Supplement),* S37–S49.

Marlatt, G. A. & Gordon, J. R. (Eds) (1985). *Relapse prevention.* New York: Guilford.

Martin, C. & Player, E. (2000). *Drug treatment in prison: An evaluation of the RAPt treatment programme.* Winchester: Waterside Press.

Matrix Research and Consultancy and NACRO (2004). *Evaluation of drug testing in the criminal justice system.* Home Office Research Study No. 286. London: Home Office.

Maughan, B. (1993). Childhood precursors of aggressive offending in personality disordered adults. In S. Hodgins (Ed.), *Mental disorder and crime* (pp. 119–139). Newbury Park, CA: Sage.

May, C. (1993). Resistance to peer group pressure: An inadequate base for alcohol education. *Health Education Research: Theory & Practice, 8,* 159–165.

May, Y., Edmunds, M. & Hough, M. (1999). *Street business: The links between sex and drug markets.* Police Research Series, Paper 118. London: Home Office.

McCusker, C. & Davies, M. (1996). Prescribing drug of choice to illicit heroin users: The experience of a UK community drug team. *Journal of Substance Abuse Treatment, 13,* 521–531.

McGuire, J. & Hatcher, R. (2001). Offense-focused problem solving: Preliminary evaluation of a cognitive skills program. *Criminal Justice and Behavior, 28,* 564–587.

McIvor, G., Eley, S., Malloch, M. & Yates, R. (2003). *Establishing Drug Courts in Scotland: Early experiences of the pilot Drug Courts in Glasgow and Fife.* Crime and Criminal Justice Research Programme, Research Findings No. 71. Edinburgh: Scottish Executive.

McMurran, M. (1989). Services for prisoners who drink. *Prison Service Journal, 75,* 5–6.

McMurran, M. (1996). Substance use and delinquency. In C. R. Hollin & K. Howells (Eds), *Clinical approaches to working with young offenders* (pp. 209–235). Chichester: John Wiley & Sons.

McMurran, M. (2005). Alcohol and drug treatments. In A. Perry, C. McDougall & D. Farrington (Eds), *Reducing crime: The effectiveness of criminal justice interventions* (pp. 33–52). Chichester: John Wiley & Sons.

McMurran, M. & Baldwin, S. (1989). Services for prisoners with alcohol-related problems: A survey of UK prisons. *Addiction, 84,* 1053–1058.

McMurran, M. & Bellfield, H. (1993). Sex-related alcohol expectancies in rapists. *Criminal Behaviour and Mental Health, 3,* 76–84.

McMurran, M. & Boyle, M. (1990). Evaluation of a self-help manual for young offenders who drink. *British Journal of Clinical Psychology, 29,* 117–119.

McMurran, M. & Cusens, B. (2003). Controlling alcohol-related violence: A treatment programme. *Criminal Behaviour and Mental Health, 13,* 59–76.

McMurran, M. & Cusens, B. (2005). Alcohol and violent and non-violent acquisitive offending. *Addiction Research and Theory, 13,* 439–443.

McMurran, M. & Duggan, C. (2005). The manualisation of offender treatment. *Criminal Behaviour and Mental Health, 15,* 17–27.

McMurran, M. & McCulloch, A. (in press). The features of a good offender treatment programme manual: A Delphi survey of experts. *Psychology, Crime and Law.*

McMurran, M. & Priestley, P. (2001). *Addressing Substance-Related Offending (ASRO).* London: National Probation Directorate.

McMurran, M. & Priestley, P. (2004). Addressing Substance-Related Offending (ASRO): A structured cognitive-behavioural programme for drug users in probation and prison services. In B. Reading & M. Weegman (Eds), *Group psychotherapy and addiction* (pp. 194–210). London: Whurr.

Meichenbaum, D. (1977). *Cognitive-behavior modification.* New York: Plenum.

Metrebian, N. et al. (2001). Prescribing drug of choice to opiate dependent drug users: A comparison of clients receiving heroin with those receiving injectable methadone at a West London drug clinic. *Drug and Alcohol Review, 20,* 267–276.

Miller, W. R. (1985). Motivation for treatment: A review with special emphasis on alcoholism. *Psychological Bulletin, 98,* 84–107.

Miller, W. R. (1992). The effectiveness of treatment for substance abuse. *Journal of Substance Abuse Treatment, 9,* 93–102.

Miller, W. R. & Rollnick, S. (1991). *Motivational interviewing: Preparing people to change addictive behavior.* New York: Guilford.

Miller, W. R. & Rollnick, S. (2002). *Motivational interviewing: Preparing people for change (2nd edition)*. New York: Guilford.

Moffitt, T. E. (1993). Adolescent-limited and life-course-persistent antisocial behavior: A developmental taxonomy. *Psychological Review, 100*, 674–701.

Mosher, J. & Jernigan, D. (2001). Making the link: A public health approach to preventing alcohol-related violence and crime. *Journal of Substance Use, 6*, 273–289.

Mueser, K. T., Drake, R. E. & Wallach, M. A. (1998). Dual diagnosis: A review of etoiological theories. *Addictive Behaviors, 23*, 717–734.

National Assembly for Wales (2000). *Tackling substance misuse in Wales*. Cardiff: National Assembly for Wales.

National Statistics (2002). Casualties from road accidents involving illegal alcohol levels, 1986–2000. *Social Trends* 32. <http://www.statistics.gov.uk/STATBASE/ssdataset.asp?vlnk=5179>. Accessed 16 December 2004.

Northern Ireland Executive (1999). *Drug Strategy for Northern Ireland*. Belfast: Northern Ireland Executive.

Parker, H. & Kirby, P. (1996). *Methadone maintenance and crime reduction on Merseyside*. Police Research Group, Crime Detection and Prevention Series, Paper 72. London: Home Office.

Pearson, F. S. & Lipton, D. S. (1999). A meta-analytic review of the effectiveness of corrections-based treatments for drug abuse. *The Prison Journal, 79*, 384–410.

Perry, A., McDougall, C. & Farrington, D. P. (Eds) (2005). *Reducing crime: The effectiveness of criminal justice interventions*. Chichester: Wiley.

Porporino, F. J., Robinson, D., Millson, B. & Weekes, J. R. (2002). An outcome evaluation of prison-based treatment programming for substance users. *Substance Use and Misuse, 37*, 1047–1077.

Priestley, P. & McMurran, M. (2001). *Programme for Reducing Individual Substance Misuse*. London: National Probation Directorate.

Project Match Research Group (1997). Project MATCH secondary a priori hypotheses. *Addiction, 92*, 1671–1698.

Quigley, B. M, Corbett, A. B. & Tedeschi, J. T. (2002). Desired image of power, alcohol expectancies, and alcohol-related aggression. *Psychology of Addictive Behaviors, 16*, 318–324.

Raistrick, D. (2004). Alcohol withdrawal and detoxification. In N. Heather & T. Stockwell (Eds), *The essential handbook of treatment and prevention of alcohol problems* (pp. 35–51). Chichester: John Wiley & Sons.

Richardson, A. & Budd, T. (2003). Young adults, alcohol, crime, and disorder. *Criminal Behaviour and Mental Health, 13*, 5–17.

Robins, S. & Novaco, R. W. (1999). Systems conceptualization and treatment of anger. *Journal of Clinical Psychology, 55*, 325–337.

Robinson, D. (1995). *The impact of cognitive skills training on post-release recidivism among Canadian federal offenders*. Ottawa: Correctional Services of Canada.

Rodriguez, N. & Webb, V. J. (2004). Multiple measures of juvenile drug court effectiveness: Results of a quasi-experimental design. *Crime and Delinquency, 50*, 292–314.

Rohsenow, D. J. (2004). What place does naltrexone have in the treatment of alcoholism? *CNS Drugs, 18*, 547–560.

Scottish Executive (2002). *Plan for action on alcohol problems*. Edinburgh: Scottish Executive.

Scottish Office (1999). *Tackling drugs in Scotland: Action in partnership*. Edinburgh: The Scottish Office.

Seeling, C., King, C., Metcalfe, E., Tober, G. & Bates, S. (2001). Arrest referral – A proactive multi-agency approach. *Drugs: Education, Prevention, and Policy, 8*, 327–333.

Sher, K. J. & Trull, T. J. (1994). Personality and disinhibitory psychopathology: Alcoholism and antisocial personality disorder. *Journal of Abnormal Psychology, 103*, 92–102.

Shewan, D., Macpherson, A., Reid, M. M. & Davies, J. B. (1996). The impact of the Edinburgh prison (Scotland) drug reduction programme. *Legal and Criminological Psychology, 1*, 83–94.

Singer, L R. (1991). A non-punitive paradigm of probation practice: Some sobering thoughts. *British Journal of Social Work, 21*, 611–626.

Singleton, N., Farrell, M. & Meltzer, H. (1999). *Substance misuse among prisoners in England and Wales*. London: Office for National Statistics.

Turnbull, P. J., McSweeney, T., Webster, R., Edmunds, M. & Hough, M., (2000). *Drug Treatment and Testing Orders: Final evaluation report*. Home Office Research Study No. 212. London: Home Office.

Walters, G .D. (1994). *Drugs and crime in lifestyle perspective*. Thousand Oaks, CA: Sage Publications.

Walters, G. D. (1998). *Changing lives of crime and drugs*. Chichester: John Wiley & Sons.

Walters, G. D. (2003). Changes in outcome expectancies and criminal thinking following a brief course of psychoeducation. *Personality and Individual Differences, 35*, 691–701.

Walters, G. D. (2004). Changes in positive and negative crime expectancies in inmates exposed to a brief psychoeducational intervention: Further data. *Personality and Individual Differences, 37*, 505–512.

Wells-Parker, E., Bangert-Drowns, R., McMillen, R. & Williams, M. (1995). Final results from a meta-analysis of remedial interventions with drink/drive offenders. *Addiction, 90*, 907–926.

Wexler, H. (1995). The success of therapeutic communities for substance abusers in American prisons. *Journal of Psychoactive Drugs, 27*, 57–66.

Wexler, H. (1997). Therapeutic communities in American prisons. In E. Cullen, L. Jones & R. Woodward (Eds), *Therapeutic communities for offenders* (pp. 161–179). Chichester: John Wiley & Sons.

White, J. L., Moffitt, T. E., Caspi, A., Bartusch, D. J., Needles, D. J. & Stouthamer-Loeber, M. (1994). Measuring impulsivity and examining its relationship to delinquency. *Journal of Abnormal Psychology, 103*, 192–205.

Wilens, T. E. & Biederman, J. (1993). Psychopathology in preadolescent children at high risk for substance abuse. A review of the literature. *Harvard Review of Psychiatry, 1*, 207–218.

Williamson, R. J., Sham, P. & Ball, D. (2003). Binge drinking trends in a UK community-based sample. *Journal of Substance Use, 8*, 234–237.

Wilson, G. T. (1996). Manual-based treatments: The clinical application of research findings. *Behaviour Research and Therapy, 34*, 295–314.

Wormith, J. S. & Olver, M. E. (2002). Offender treatment attrition and its relationship with risk, responsivity, and recidivism. *Criminal Justice and Behavior, 29*, 447–471.

Zhang, L., Welte, J. W. & Wieczorek, W. W. (2002). The role of aggression-related alcohol expectancies in explaining the link between alcohol and violent behavior. *Substance Use and Misuse, 37*, 457–471.

Chapter 7

THE IMPLEMENTATION AND MAINTENANCE OF QUALITY SERVICES IN OFFENDER REHABILITATION PROGRAMMES

CLAIRE GOGGIN* AND PAUL GENDREAU[†]
*St Thomas University, Fredericton, New Brunswick, Canada
†University of New Brunswick, Saint John, New Brunswick, Canada

INTRODUCTION

Robert Martinson's (1974) landmark publication[1] declaring offender treatment to be relatively ineffective (see also Lipton, Martinson & Wilks, 1975) was the spark that renewed interest amongst corrections researchers, particularly North American supporters of offender rehabilitation (Cullen, 2004; Ellis & Winstone, 2002; McGuire, 2004), to generate the data necessary to refute the "nothing works" doctrine. During the 15 years that followed Martinson's (1974) proclamation, researchers began systematically to examine treatment programme outcomes (see, for example, Lipsey's 1989 summary of 400 studies) with the result that, to date, at least 42 meta-analyses of the effectiveness of correctional treatments have been conducted (McGuire, 2004). On the basis of the collected results from these studies and summaries thereof (Andrews, 1995; Andrews & Bonta, 2003; Andrews, Zinger, Hoge, Bonta, Gendreau & Cullen 1990b; Davidson, Gottschalk, Gensheimer & Mayer, 1984; Dowden & Andrews, 1999a, 1999b; Garrett, 1985; Gendreau, 1996a; 1996b; Gendreau, Goggin, French & Smith, 2006; Hollin, 1999; Lipsey, 1992, 1995; Lipsey & Wilson, 1998; Lösel, 1995; McGuire, 2002, 2004; McGuire & Priestley, 1995; Palmer, 1992, 1994, 1995; Whitehead & Lab, 1989; Wilson, Lipsey & Soydan, 2003) one can now state unequivocally that, not only do correctional treatment

---

[1] For a comment on the substance of the studies Martinson (1974) relied upon to support his claims, see Cullen & Gendreau (2000).

Offending Behaviour Programmes: Development, Application, and Controversies. Edited by C.R. Hollin and E.J. Palmer.
Copyright © 2006 John Wiley & Sons Ltd.

programmes "work", but many of the requisite conditions for their optimal effect are known.

Despite such advances in our knowledge of "what works", and a broad consensus supporting the benefits of empirically validated programme standards, the majority of "real world" offender treatment programmes continue to be relatively unsuccessful in reducing recidivism. Indeed, the percentage of treatment studies founded upon principles of offender programming known to generate positive outcomes has actually declined over the past 15 years from 20 % in 1990 (Andrews et al., 1990b) to the current rate of 13 % (Andrews, Dowden & Gendreau, 2004).

This rather woeful state of affairs has far-reaching consequences. It opens the door to revanchist academics trapped in the "nothing works" time warp (cf. Cullen & Gendreau, 2001; Latessa & Holsinger, 1998; Raynor, 2004), to advocates who espouse retributive correctional philosophies, typified by "get tough" and "doing better justice" policies (Cullen & Gendreau, 1989, 2000), and to "common-sense" entrepreneurs promoting alternative, if not eccentric, correctional interventions (Gendreau, Goggin, Cullen & Paparozzi, 2002; Latessa, Cullen & Gendreau, 2002).[2] It encourages the media to skew debate by relentlessly trumpeting "cure-all" programmes of little substance (for example, Cullen, Blevins, Trager & Gendreau, in press), some no better than correctional quackery (Latessa et al., 2002). One can only imagine how the public feels – confused and cynical perhaps – as they read in the press of spectacular, seemingly contradictory, findings. Taken together, the effect of failed programmes ultimately hinders the progress of the rehabilitation agenda (Latessa & Holsinger, 1998). As such, it behoves corrections professionals (policy-makers, researchers, programme developers) to examine why such failures occur and work towards solutions for their remediation.

The purpose of this chapter, therefore, is to provide a comprehensive update regarding developments in the area of offender programming practices. The framework for our presentation is as follows. Firstly, we briefly review the research that has contributed to our understanding of what makes correctional programmes effective in reducing offender recidivism. We hasten to emphasise that, without such basic knowledge, the application of even the most sophisticated programme implementation and maintenance strategies will be in vain. Secondly, we discuss the utility of one specific measure, the Correctional Programme Assessment Inventory – 2000 (CPAI – 2000) (Gendreau & Andrews, 2001) as a reliable means of evaluating correctional programme validity. Finally, we document efforts under way in several jurisdictions to establish programme accreditation systems and close with a review of preliminary data on the outcome of accredited programmes in England and Wales.

ESTABLISHING "WHAT WORKS"

During the period of "therapeutic nihilism" (Cooke & Philip, 2001, p. 17) that followed in the wake of Martinson's (1974) publication, correctional treatment

---

[2] Hunt's (1999) treatise on the rise of the "know-nothings" is delightful reading as applied to social policies in general. In our view, his insights apply equally to the field of corrections (see Gendreau, Goggin, Cullen, et al., 2002).

researchers redoubled their efforts to produce the data necessary to respond to his claim. At the time, proponents of offender rehabilitation, such as Rezmovic (1979) and Palmer (1975), were optimistic that meaningful gains in treatment success would ensue once researchers learned more about programme/offender interactions, or in Palmer's (1975, p. 150) words, "which methods work best for which type of offenders and under which conditions". Of note, developments in the corrections field paralleled a general interest among the broader health and human service communities in strengthening the link between research results and professional practice by more systematically integrating the two (McGuire, 2001). As McGuire (2001) commented, such initiatives were fuelled both by a public policy agenda whose objective was "value for money" (p. 26) as well as practitioners' concerns regarding the consequences of their treatments.

The impetus to revivify correctional rehabilitation came primarily from within the discipline of psychology, in particular from the so-called "Canadian school" (Cullen, 2002, 2004) of scientist-practitioners.[3] In their roles as clinical and community psychologists, this group was involved in implementing, administering, and evaluating offender assessment and treatment programmes within correctional and governmental jurisdictions that, fortunately, were generally supportive of rehabilitation policies. Professionally, they were *au courant* with learning theory (Gendreau & Smith, in press) as well as related behavioural treatments, and championed the perspective that criminal behaviour, like most social behaviours, is largely learned and can, therefore, be modified through the use of ethical and appropriate behaviour reinforcement contingencies (rewards and punishers).[4] Of equal importance, the Canadian school contested the notion implied by the "nothing works" doctrine that offenders are somehow "different" and, *ergo*, incapable of learning new behavioural repertoires (Gendreau & Ross, 1979).

As a first step, these researchers undertook a number of demonstration projects and literature reviews (for example, Andrews, 1979, 1980; Andrews & Kiessling, 1980; Andrews, Kiessling, Robinson & Mickus, 1986; Gendreau & Andrews, 1979; Gendreau & Ross, 1979, 1981a, 1981b, 1983–84, 1987; Ross & Fabiano, 1985; Ross & Gendreau, 1980; Ross & McKay, 1978) whose results, it was hoped, would validate the utility of the rehabilitative ideal. The central purpose of the research was an attempt to examine treatment's "black box". As Gendreau (1996a) later stated:

> Unlike Martinson and his followers, we believe it is not sufficient just to sum across studies or file them into general categories. The salient question is what are the principles that distinguish between effective and ineffective programs? – what exactly was accomplished under the name of "employment"? As a result

---

[3] For a less complimentary view of this "school", consult Logan et al. (1991). We would also be remiss in not acknowledging the enormous contributions of *non*-Canadian researchers in the early days – people like Vicki Agee, Michael Milan, Ted Palmer, William Davidson II, Marguerite Warren, and Frank Cullen, amongst others.

[4] For a detailed discussion regarding changing behaviour, readers may wish to consult psychology source material on behavioural programmes in general (Fishbein, 1995; Masters, Burish, Hollon & Rimm, 1987; Spiegler & Guevremont, 1998) and offender programming in particular (Andrews & Bonta, 2003; Gendreau, 1996a, pp. 120–122; Lester & Van Voorhis, 1997).

of endorsing the perspective of opening the "black box", we have been able to generate a number of principles of effective and ineffective intervention. (Gendreau, 1996a, p. 118)

Gendreau & Ross (1979) also provided what they termed "bibliotherapy for cynics" by uncovering scores of treatment studies that reported reductions in offender recidivism, some in the range of 20 % to 50 %. Reviews of this type provided the foundation for the development of some elementary principles of effective intervention (see also Andrews, 1979). For example, it was noted early on that a majority of the most effective programmes were behavioural in nature (Gendreau & Ross, 1979).

Secondly, as psychologists, the members of this group were sensitive to the notion of individual differences, a concept to which many criminologists were inimical (Andrews & Wormith, 1989). In fact, by the late 1970s and early 1980s, a large body of research had confirmed the importance of individual differences in treatment response (which offenders respond best to what types of treatments and therapies) (Andrews, Bonta & Hoge, 1990a; Gendreau & Ross, 1987). Offender risk was identified as a potentially useful moderator; that is, offenders rated as higher risk (for example, those with more extensive anti-social attitudes, substance abuse problems, criminal histories) appeared to benefit more from intensive behavioural treatments than did their lower risk counterparts (for example, Andrews, Kiessling, Mickus & Robinson, 1986). In addition, the data suggested that, with lower risk offenders, even behavioural type treatment programmes had little effect on rates of criminal activity (recidivism). Modalities such as Rogerian non-directive and psychodynamic type treatments were also notably ineffective in terms of reducing recidivism (Andrews, 1979; Gendreau & Ross, 1983–4).

A singular development in literature review methodologies in the early 1980s proved timely for attempts to demonstrate the capacity of treatment programmes to reduce offender recidivism. Meta-analysis supplanted the narrative as the review standard in medicine and psychology (Glass, McGaw & Smith, 1981; Hollin, 1999; Hunt, 1997; Rosenthal, 1991), affording researchers the opportunity to more precisely establish "what works" with offenders by quantifying the results of correctional treatment studies. While the narrative format might produce some general truths ("treatment works"), such broad conclusions obviously lacked precision (Gendreau, 1996a). Nor could the technique account for the effects of potentially important moderators (Gendreau & Andrews, 1990).

What, then, did meta-analysis reveal about the effectiveness of offender rehabilitation? The earliest reviews dating from the mid-1980s (Davidson et al., 1984, also reported in more detail in Apter & Goldstein, 1986; Garrett, 1985; for a review see Gendreau & Ross, 1987, pp. 391–394; Ross & Fabiano, 1985) furnished the first quantitative confirmation of the results from earlier narrative reviews that, in fact, correctional treatment did work. For example, Garrett (1985) reported an average effect size (ES) of $r = 0.12$ among well-designed studies of juvenile offenders ($k_{ES} = 433$). She also noted that cognitive behavioural therapies produced the greatest mean effect ($r = 0.22$) among more rigorous designs and studies with more than 10 ES. The Ross and Fabiano (1985) study, akin to a box-score analysis, also agreed that the greatest effects could be anticipated from cognitive-behavioural interventions. In addition, the results of Davidson et al.'s (1984) analysis of the potential influence of moderators indicated that professional training (for example, psychology, education), and degree of evaluator involvement in the design, implementation, and control of an intervention were positively correlated with successful programmes.

A later summary of a vast database of juvenile treatments ($k_{ES} = 443$) by Lipsey (1995) indicated that for a majority (64 %) of interventions the outcome was positive (reduced recidivism), a noticeable improvement over the 50 % baseline reported by Martinson (1974) and Palmer (1975) almost 20 years previously. Subsequently, Lösel (1995) conducted a comprehensive assessment of 13 meta-analyses of treatment studies published between 1985 and 1995. He reported that mean ES ranged from 0.05 to 0.18, with an approximate mean of $r = 0.10$ among samples of adult and juvenile and adult offenders.[5] The results of later meta-analyses (Andrews et al., 2004; Redondo, Sanchez-Meca & Garrido, 1999) concurred with Lösel's findings. Of note, mean effects were not attenuated by methodological factors such as sample attrition, quality of research design, follow-up period, or publication status (Lipsey, 1992).

Given the variability among study samples, coding schemes, and researchers, such robust replications of the positive effects of offender treatment were impressive. Even criminologists, generally less supportive of rehabilitation (Cullen & Gendreau, 2001), produced positive results using meta-analysis (Whitehead & Lab, 1989). Additionally, Lösel (1995) and Lipsey (1992) suggested that the overall treatment ES was likely underestimated as the studies they reviewed did not routinely include well-matched experimental and comparison groups and tended to include dichotomous criterion measures that were insensitive to differences in outcome (recidivism). Nevertheless, the general trend among these results indicated that behaviourally oriented programmes, at least those with considerable structure (for example, some academic, vocational, family therapy programmes) typically produced the greatest reductions in recidivism and their mean effects were larger than those of non-behavioural or relatively unfocused interventions (such as "group therapy", psychodynamic or *milieu* type therapies), with the latter occasionally producing slight increases in recidivism.

Two meta-analyses (Andrews et al., 1990b; Andrews et al., 2004) from this period provided the first empirical test of the principles of effective correctional intervention. The development of these principles – offender risk, need, and responsivity – has been extensively documented elsewhere (see Andrews, 1995; Andrews & Bonta, 2003; Gendreau, 1996a, 1996b; Gendreau, Cullen & Bonta, 1994; Gendreau, French & Gionet, 2004); a brief summary of their key points is provided in Box 7.1, highlighting their value to the design, implementation, and maintenance of effective offender treatment programmes.

---

[5] An $r = 0.10$ can be interpreted as a mean difference of 10 % in the recidivism rates of the two groups. Rosenthal's (1991) BESD statistic is another means of conveying the practical meaning of r. Firstly, one computes the recidivism rate for the treatment and comparison groups from a base rate of 50 %. With an $r = 0.10$ between programme and outcome – with positive values indicating a reduction in recidivism – one can conclude that the recidivism rate for the treatment group is 45 % (50 % minus 5 %) as compared to 55 % for the comparison group (50 % plus 5 %). Under most circumstances – where recidivism rates are not extreme and the ratio of the treatment and comparison group sample sizes are within 3:1 – the r value can be taken at face value, even when the criterion base rate is not precisely 50 % (Cullen & Gendreau, 2000).

Box 7.1 Principles of effective correctional programming

---

1. Risk
- Higher risk offenders are characterised by greater criminogenic need.
- Use a valid/reliable measure to assess offender risk.
- Target higher risk offenders for treatment.

2. Need
- Target offender characteristics most predictive of recidivism.
- Predictors are classed as static (i.e., criminal history) or dynamic (i.e., anti-social attitudes).
- Dynamic factors, or *criminogenic needs*, are appropriate treatment targets.
- Criminogenic needs that are *robust* predictors of recidivism: anti-social attitudes/values, pro-criminal associates, impulsiveness/poor self-control.
- Criminogenic needs that are *poor* predictors of recidivism: self-esteem, depression, anxiety.
- Target more criminogenic than non-criminogenic needs (3:1 ratio).

3. Responsivity
- Use potent behaviour change strategies (i.e., cognitive/behavioural) incorporating operant conditioning principles to modify behaviour.
- Replace anti-social cognitions with more adaptive cognitive/social skills.
- Consider "specific responsivity", match service delivery style with offender abilities/learning style (i.e., take into account lack of motivation, intellectual deficits, feelings of depression/anxiety).

4. Other considerations
- Treatment context: deliver in the community when possible.
- Employ interpersonally sensitive, clinically well trained and supervised staff.
- Offer structured relapse prevention (i.e., "throughcare").
- Include offenders' significant others when feasible.

Source: From Andrews & Bonta (2003).

In their initial meta-analysis, Andrews et al. (1990b) coded the treatment literature ($k_{ES} = 154$) along a variety of dimensions including "treatment quality", which they defined as either:

- appropriate – consistent with the principles outlined in Box 7.1;
- inappropriate – not consistent with said principles; or
- unspecified – undetermined treatment quality due to a lack of information.

They found that treatment quality was an important factor in determining programme outcome, with "appropriate" treatments producing a 30% reduction in recidivism. In contrast, the mean ES among programmes delivering "inappropriate" treatments showed a slight increase in recidivism ($r = -0.06$). Moreover, when the effect of programme setting were examined, appropriate treatments delivered in the community produced better outcomes than those delivered in institutional settings ($r = 0.35$ versus $r = 0.17$, respectively).

Later updates of the Andrews et al. (1990b) meta-analysis increased the number of ES to 374 (see Andrews & Bonta, 2003; Andrews et al., 2004) and the initial results were replicated. That is, the mean ES for programmes which adhered to all of the principles from Box 7.1 (risk/need/responsivity) was $r = 0.28$ as compared with $r = 0.05$ for those that did not. Programmes that targeted criminogenic needs and used behavioural treatment strategies produced robust effects ($r = 0.20$ and $r = 0.19$, respectively), as did programmes located in the community ($r = 0.29$). Furthermore, these findings apply to a variety of discrete offender groups including males, females, adults, youth, various minorities, as well as the mentally disordered (Andrews, Dowden & Rettinger, 2001; Dowden & Andrews, 2000). Unexpectedly, Andrews et al. (2004) found only marginal support for the risk principle ($r = 0.07$), although this might be attributed to how offender risk is variously operationalised when cumulating across a sample of studies (variable cut-off scores, different risk criteria, and so forth) (see Smith, Goggin & Gendreau, 2002).

In closing this section, we highlight some preliminary results of the application of Andrews & Bonta's (2003) treatment principles to prison-based programming. To wit, Bourgon & Armstrong (2005) report on the effectiveness of a programme whose treatment protocol was based explicitly on the principles laid out in Box 7.1. Conducted during the late 1990s at Rideau Correctional and Treatment Centre (RCTC), a medium security provincial facility in Canada, the programme employed a broad spectrum of risk/need measures (Level of Service Inventory – Revised (LSI-R)) (Andrews & Bonta, 1995), Criminal Sentiments Scale, Beck Depression Inventory, and so forth). Psychometric assessments were supplemented by a comprehensive questionnaire detailing aspects of social and criminal behaviour (interpersonal relations, literacy, substance abuse, and so forth). Assignment to one of three structured cognitive-behavioural treatment programmes (5 weeks, 10 weeks, or 15 weeks in duration) was made on the basis of assessed risk/need. At one year post-release, the authors report a mean ES of $r = 0.10^6$, with a statistically lower recidivism rate among those who received treatment ($n = 482$, 31%) versus those who did not ($n = 138$, 41%) (Bourgon & Armstrong, 2005).

Most recently, French & Gendreau (in press) have compiled a sizeable database ($k_{ES} = 105$, $n = 23\,000$) by updating two earlier reviews (Gendreau & Keyes, 2001; Morgan & Flora, 2002) of the effects of prison-based treatment programmes on rates of institutional misconducts. Their results ($r = 0.14$) paralleled those reported for community-based programmes, with behavioural treatments producing the best outcomes ($r = 0.26$). Similarly, programmes that targeted three to eight criminogenic needs were more successful ($r = 0.29$) than those which targeted none

---

[6] Those who would dismiss a 10% reduction in recidivism as having little applied value are misinformed (see Lipsey & Wilson, 1998). As noted by Lipsey and Wilson (1998) and Rosnow and Rosenthal (1999), many medical treatments have proven to be cost-effective when the incidence of serious illness is reduced by only a few percentage points through effective treatment. With respect to offender programming, Cohen (2001) has calculated the cost-effectiveness of "saving" high-risk juvenile offenders. Admittedly, crime cost-benefit analyses are imprecise as they are based on estimates of the rate of criminal participation and include categories such as "prison" and "suffering" along with "property loss" and "lost wages". Notwithstanding these caveats, Cohen (2001) found that the criminal career of the average high-risk youth incurs costs of between US\$1.7 million and US\$2.3 million (approximately £ 903 000 million to £ 1.2 million). Depending on the "career" point at which the intervention occurs and its attendant costs, treatment programmes can be demonstrably cost-effective when even "small" reductions in recidivism result (see also Aos, Lieb, Mayfield, Miller & Pennucci, 2004; Aos, Phipps, Barnoski & Lieb, 1999; Farrington, Petrosino & Welsh, 2001; Lösel, 2001).

($r = 0.06$). Further, programmes high in therapeutic integrity, as measured by the CPAI-2000 (discussed below), produced an ES of $r = 0.38$ as compared with those scoring low on that construct ($r = 0.13$). The authors argue that such findings among prison-based samples are important for two reasons. Firstly, it suggests the potential to realise significant cost-savings given the economic implications of high rates of institutional misconducts (see Lovell & Jemelka, 1996). Secondly, graduates of programmes which were most effective in reducing prison misconducts were also amongst those with lower post-release recidivism rates ($r = 0.13$), implying that one may regard institutional misconduct as a criterion equivalent to community-based recidivism (Gendreau, Goggin & Law, 1997; Hill, 1985).

In toto, the collected findings from the available meta-analyses of correctional programme outcomes stand as substantive empirical refutation of the "nothing works" apophthegm in confirming that appropriate correctional treatments can be effective in reducing offender recidivism, particularly among programmes that follow the principles deduced by the Canadian school ($r_{range} = 0.25$ to 0.35).

TRANSFERRING "WHAT WORKS" FROM THE "RESEARCH LAB" TO THE "REAL WORLD"

Given the evidence generated since the mid-1970s in support of the rehabilitative ideal, one might optimistically expect its pre-eminence on the correctional landscape to have been re-established with ease. The question being, have the obvious changes in the "general vocabulary" (Ellis & Winstone, 2002, p. 334) of twenty-first century corrections ("what works") been embodied in measurable improvements in programme effectiveness? Regrettably, it appears that such a transfer has been less than complete and, in truth, remains an ongoing challenge (Leschied, 2001).[7] The principal reasons for this are fourfold.

Since the 1980s, the dominant political ideology among most Western governments has increasingly favoured the Right wing (Gendreau, Goggin, Cullen, et al., 2002). In the criminal justice area, this has been exemplified by "get tough" policies (Gendreau, Goggin & Cullen, 1999; Harris & Smith, 1996), which, consequently, have resulted in reduced support for programmes that emphasise treatment over sanctions (Hamm & Schrink, 1989). A growing trend towards the hiring of content-free managers in government, some appointed simply through nepotism, has resulted in a relative policy vacuum (loss of "institutional" memory) among senior government mandarins (Gendreau, Goggin & Fulton, 2001a; Gendreau, Goggin & Smith, 2000). Given their consequent sensitivity to political machinations, such managers in the correctional treatment arena have been readily seduced by "buzzwords" (Cochran, 1992, p. 309) and "quick-fix" solutions (boot camps), in the absence of any empirical evidence to support their effectiveness (Harris & Smith, 1996).

---

[7] Such concerns are not entirely new. Jerome Miller (1986) also noted the criminal justice system's penchant for semantic versus substantive reform citing, by way of illustration, the putative "renaissance" (Miller, 1986, p. 261) in American corrections in the 1960s, which he suggests was more myth than reality. Nor is a preoccupation with effective technology transfer exclusive to corrections. Related social services domains (medicine, substance abuse treatment, psychiatry, community mental health, social work, and so forth) have also documented systemic failures to inform clinical practice through research (Cabana et al., 1999; Corrigan, Steiner, McCracken, Blaser & Barr, 2001; Herie & Martin, 2002; Simpson, 2002; Slavin, 2002; Torrey et al., 2001).

A second barrier to effective knowledge transfer is found within academic and applied settings where, as noted previously, disciplines such as criminology, have been, at best, ambivalent towards a correctional rehabilitation agenda (Cullen & Gendreau, 2001). We are aware of only one academic criminology programme in North America, that at the University of Cincinnati, which, in our opinion, places appropriate emphasis on offender rehabilitation as part of its criminal justice curriculum. Based on our reading of the literature, there also continue to be too few university-based graduate training programmes in clinical psychology which focus on salient aspects of correctional psychology (offender assessment and treatment) (Ax & Morgan, 2002; Gendreau, 1996b). Our supposition, and one that we hope will be challenged in the near future, is that relatively few contemporary graduates are aware of the principles of effective correctional programming (cf. Andrews & Bonta, 2003).

As a case in point, an integral prerequisite to the provision of effective treatment is an offender risk measure with robust predictive validities (for recidivism) that can also measure changes in the level of offenders' criminogenic needs over time. One such measure is the LSI-R (Andrews & Bonta, 1995; see Gendreau, Goggin & Smith, 2002), yet very few psychologists have ever heard of the instrument (Boothby & Clements, 2000). We fear that such a critical deficiency of well-trained corrections professionals may bear problematic fruit as successive cohorts of university graduates rise to positions of responsibility within the criminal justice system and academia. Undoubtedly, they will serve as poor advocates of rehabilitative policies and, in all likelihood, be less committed to an ongoing programme of offender treatment research (Brodsky, 2000; Gendreau et al., 2006; Knott, 1995).

A third delimiting condition in successful technology transfer is the failure to inform practitioners about the requisites of effective correctional programming. By way of example, Backer & David (1995) have reported that, among substance abuse treatment programmes, neither management policies nor clinical decisions are necessarily derived from a reading of professional journals. Instead, treatment-relevant information is usually provided to clinicians through workshops, and, even then, is only of benefit to a relatively small percentage of participants. Simpson (2002) illustrates the limited impact of differing staff training modalities on skills transfer. He reports that, among drug treatment programmes offering employment services for offenders, only 28 % of those whose staff received personalised, on-site training were successful in fully implementing the treatment protocol. Among programmes whose staff received workshop-based training, that rate fell to 19 %. For programmes that used manuals only as training media, the rate of full implementation stood at 1 % (Simpson, 2002). We hazard that such problems are not unique to the realm of substance abuse programming.

The final impediment to transferring what is known about effective programming occurs at the field level where the nexus of the aforementioned political and academic influences shape critical aspects of programme implementation. This, in turn, has a direct impact on the potential effectiveness of programmes. As noted previously, extensive surveys of the quality of treatment services delivered in "real world" settings have revealed that less than 15 % of programmes follow the guidelines ensuing from the known principles of effective treatment (Andrews et al., 2004; Gendreau & Goggin, 1996). Among the most common shortcomings is the failure to assess offenders comprehensively using valid risk measures, the targeting of proportionally more non-criminogenic than criminogenic needs for treatment, the use of treatments that lack empirical validity, and the employment of staff who are poorly trained and do not hold the necessary credentials (Gendreau, Goggin & Smith, 2001b; see also Porporino, 1997).

In brief, there has been a dearth of therapeutic integrity[8] in many field-based correctional programmes (Andrews & Bonta, 2003; Cooke & Philip, 2001; Gendreau, Goggin & Smith, 1999; Hollin, 1995; Lösel, 2001; Salend, 1984). This deficiency muddies the debate regarding the "why" of programme failures: is it a function of the treatment protocol or its implementation or some interplay between the two (Debidin & Lovbakke, 2004; Hamm & Schrink, 1989; Harris & Smith, 1996; Petersilia, 1990; Raynor, 2004; Sechrest, White & Brown, 1979; Van Voorhis, Cullen & Applegate, 1995)? Certainly, any conclusions regarding correctional treatment effectiveness that are made in the absence of adequate therapeutic integrity are clearly an unfair test of the treatment (Rezmovic, 1979). According to Harris and Smith (1996), the inability to distinguish treatment failure from implementation failure may stand, collectively, as correction's "greatest irony" (p. 186).

Several researchers have suggested that a common feature of ineffective or failed correctional programmes is, in fact, a lack of sufficient attention to aspects of programme implementation and process (Bonta, Bogue, Crowley & Motiuk, 2001; Gendreau & Andrews, 1979; Gendreau et al., 1999; Gendreau et al., 2001b; Hamm & Schrink, 1989; Harris & Smith, 1996; Petersilia, 1990). The gravity and diuturnal nature of this problem is revealed in Walter Williams' (1976, p. 267) observation that a "Lack of concern for implementation is currently *the* crucial impediment to improving complex operating systems, policy analysis, and experimentation in social policy areas." In point of fact, as early as 1979 Gendreau and Ross had observed that a key indicator of the success or failure of offender treatments was the extent to which correctional programmes maintained therapeutic integrity in delivering service. As they queried:

> To what extent do treatment personnel actually adhere to the principles and employ the techniques of the therapy they purport to provide? To what extent are the treatment staff competent? How hard do they work? How much is treatment diluted in the correctional environment so that it becomes treatment in name only? (Gendreau & Ross, 1979, p. 467)[9]

Harris & Smith (1996) (see also Ellickson & Petersilia, 1983; Petersilia, 1990) have reviewed the development of community-based offender treatment programmes (intensive supervision programmes, juvenile diversion, and so forth)

---

[8] The term "therapeutic integrity" refers to the correspondence between treatment as conceptualised and treatment as delivered (Andrews & Dowden, 2006; Harris & Smith, 1996; Salend, 1984; Yeaton & Sechrest, 1981).

[9] Gendreau and Ross (1979) found answers to their questions in studies such as Quay's (1977) re-assessment of Kassebaum, Ward, and Wilner's (1971) famous prison counselling programme, which was trumpeted at the time as an example of a methodologically rigorous evaluation that demonstrated the ineffectiveness of offender treatment. Upon further inspection, however, Quay (1977) (see also Sechrest et al., 1979) concluded that Kassebaum et al.'s (1971) programme lacked therapeutic integrity, as defined by a weak conceptual base, the use of unstable counselling groups, and the employment of poorly trained, unqualified counsellors who expressed little faith in the programme's potential utility. In a related example, Emery and Marholin (1977) examined 27 empirical investigations of applied behavioural programmes for delinquency prevention and reported that in only 9 % of cases were the behaviours targeted for change identified per individual. Further, in 70 % of studies the behaviours for which youth were referred were not reflected in the behaviours targeted for treatment (referred for stealing cars but treated for tardiness).

and enumerated several implementation conditions characteristic of successful and failed programmes. Common to the latter was a tendency to exclude front-line staff from the planning and development stages, to "dictate" new operational standards (such as caseload modifications) without sufficient pre-programme consultation or resource allocation (Byrne & Kelly, 1989), to identify multiple programme goals and over-state them, to provide complex and vaguely defined treatment interventions (Salend, 1984), to operate extant from mainstream criminal justice components (judges, prosecutors) upon whom they were dependent for referrals, and, ultimately, to fail to adapt to local environments (Harris & Smith, 1996). Noteworthy among successful implementations were theoretically grounded programmes (Borum, 2003) whose goals were discrete, clearly articulated, and well understood by both staff and relevant third parties, whose treatment procedures were thoroughly delineated and easily integrated into existing operational components, whose jurisdictions (agency administration, senior managers) were supportive, whose resource requirements (staff, space) were secure, and whose procedures were sufficiently flexible to accommodate local contingencies, such as a need for ongoing feedback to stakeholders (Harris & Smith, 1996).

The importance of attending to what is known about therapeutic integrity in implementing effective programmes is also supported by outcome data from a variety of sources. For example, Andrews & Bonta (2003) report that treatment programmes which employed therapists who have adequate relationship skills produced lower recidivism rates ($r = 0.34$) than programmes that did not ($r = 0.07$). Programmes with which evaluators were directly involved and who, consequently, had greater control over therapeutic and evaluative components, also showed meaningful reductions in recidivism ($r = 0.19$).[10] In addition, Dowden, Antonowicz & Andrews (2003) reported a mean ES of $r = 0.15$ ($k = 40$) among programmes that provided booster/aftercare and relapse prevention training (for example, working with offenders and their significant others to help them better identify the precursors of anti-social behaviour).

Consider also the results of a recent study examining the predictive validity of the LSI-R (Andrews & Bonta, 1995) in which the effect of the quality of the risk assessment procedure on recidivism was evaluated (Lowenkamp, 2003). Specifically, the author rated nine community-based correctional agencies according to the type of LSI-R training received by staff (staff trained by LSI-R qualified trainer versus "train-the-trainer" graduates) and the extent to which the agency was committed to using the measure (less than 3 years versus more than 3 years). In analysing the relationship between LSI-R total score and recidivism (technical violation, re-arrest, re-incarceration) among a sample of 2 030 adult offenders, Lowenkamp (2003) reported larger ES among agencies which had been using the LSI-R for 3 years or

---

[10] Prendergast, Podus & Chang (2000) reported similar results in a meta-analysis of the effects of drug treatment programmes with non-offenders in which self-reported criminal activity ($k = 59$) was one of the criteria. Among programmes that included a treatment-comparison group design ($k = 17$), the authors reported an ES of $r = 0.42$ for those in which the researcher was "highly involved" and an ES of $r = 0.13$ for more "mature" programmes (in operation for more than 2 years) (Prendergast et al., 2000). The effect of "therapeutic alliance" is also a subject of interest to researchers in the mental health domain where a weighted mean ES of $r = 0.23$ has been reported in a recent meta-analysis ($k = 261$) of its relationship with clinical outcomes (such as decreased symptoms of depression) (Martin, Garske & Davis, 2000).

more ($r_{yes} = 0.22, k = 2; r_{no} = 0.13, k = 7$) and whose staff were formally trained in its use ($r_{yes} = 0.23, k = 3; r_{no} = 0.10, k = 6$).

A recent meta-analysis by Andrews & Dowden (2006) provides the first systematic review of the effects of correctional programme integrity on offender recidivism. The authors identified 10 indicators of programme integrity, among them, the programme's basis in theory, the particulars of staff selection, training, and supervision, the quality of the programme's manuals and process monitoring, the specifics of sample size and treatment dosage, as well as the degree of involvement of the programme's evaluator. Programmes were also rated according to appropriateness of treatment per Andrews et al.'s (1990b) guidelines. The inclusion criteria limited the sample to studies comparing the post-programme recidivism of treatment and comparison groups ($k = 273$), the majority of which (58% of studies) were randomly constituted.

The frequency with which studies reported sufficient integrity descriptors for coding did vary considerably (from 5% for "details of staff selection" to 59% for "programme has specific theoretical model"), but Andrews & Dowden (2006) report that when the effects of such indicators were measured by treatment quality, none were found to be significantly correlated with ES under inappropriate treatment conditions ($r_{range} = -0.03$ to 0.08). They also found no evidence of greater reductions in recidivism among inappropriate treatments even when rated higher on integrity. In contrast, under appropriate treatment conditions, correlations between programme integrity indicators and outcome ranged from $r = 0.20$ to $r = 0.34$. Moreover, the impact of programme integrity on treatment effectiveness was equally relevant among diverse populations (males: $r = 0.35, k = 238$; females: $r = 0.35, k = 35$; adults: $r = 0.38, k = 127$; youth: $r = 0.39, k = 146$; minorities: $r = 0.31, k = 92$) and within different settings (community: $r = 0.44, k = 175$; institution: $r = 0.31, k = 98$) (Andrews & Dowden, 2006).

Finally, Melnick, Hawke & Wexler (2004) have examined the potential impact of therapeutic integrity on treatment outcome from a slightly different perspective, that of programme participants. In a study designed to evaluate the quality of prison-based substance abuse treatment programmes in the US, the authors surveyed 1 059 adult offenders involved in 13 programmes across four states using the Multimodality Quality Assurance (MDA) scale (Melnick & Pearson, 2000). The MDA taps four strategic domains, among them organisational and offender characteristics, treatment elements, and programme climate. Offenders were grouped according to mean scores on the scale's four domains, with higher scores indicating greater endorsement of the program: "elevated" ($n = 459$) – scores above the mean; "moderate" ($n = 413$) – scores just below the mean; and "low" ($n = 187$) – scores well below the mean. Melnick et al. (2004) reported that respondents in the "elevated" group had significantly higher ratings on the programme outcomes (self-reported treatment participation, rapport with counselling process, programme satisfaction) than either those in the "moderate" or "low" groups. Albeit preliminary, such findings suggest that offender perspective is an important dimension to sample when assessing the therapeutic integrity of correctional programming.

EVALUATING CORRECTIONAL PROGRAMME QUALITY: THE CPAI-2000

In a comparative review of the effects of so-called "real world" ($k = 196$) and "demonstration" programmes ($k = 205$), Lipsey (1999) noted a disturbing trend in the pattern of results. That is, the former were, on average, only half as effective as the latter in reducing recidivism, with "demonstration" projects typically being the recipients of generous external support (for example, informed evaluators, academic links).[11] Even under conditions of optimal programme quality, this "demonstration" effect persists. In a meta-analysis of the outcome of cognitive-behavioural treatments in which inclusion was limited to high quality studies (random assignment, non-random but no selection bias), Lipsey, Chapman & Landenberger (2001) observed that, although the overall results supported the effectiveness of cognitive-behavioural strategies in reducing offender recidivism, the magnitude of that effect varied by study design. The most effective programmes were community based (probation/parole) demonstration projects (smaller ns, less than 6 months follow-up) whose design and implementation were systematically controlled by the researchers directly involved in programme development (treatment manuals), the selection, training, and monitoring of staff, as well as aspects of programme delivery (Lipsey et al., 2001). Short-term (less than 6 months) recidivism rates among such programmes ($k = 4$; $n < 75$) were dramatically reduced in the treatment (15 %) versus comparison groups (52 %). In contrast, existing programmes ($k = 6$), those delivered and evaluated by one person, most often treating larger institution-based samples, were associated with the weakest mean effects. Although differences in long-term (≥ 6 months) recidivism rates among this sample of programmes also favoured the treatment group, they did so by a much narrower margin (T $= 26$ % versus C $= 31$ %).

Farabee et al. (1999) heralded similar foreboding regarding the recent expansion of substance abuse treatment programmes in US prisons. They too highlighted concerns that transfer of "model" programmes, those typically nurtured in environments characterised by stable funding and supportive infrastructures, to the "real world", where they are commonly subjected to the mundane demands of social service settings (budget, staffing, and resource constraints – see Bauman, Stein & Ireys, 1991), often fall victim to hyperbole surrounding expectations of the magnitude of their effectiveness (Farabee et al., 1999).

In light of the potential threats to validity posed by inadequately conceptualised and poorly implemented correctional programs, a number of researchers (Latessa & Holsinger, 1998; Leschied, 2001; Lipton, Thornton, McGuire, Porporino & Hollin, 2000) have called for a reliable means of measuring the degree to which treatment programmes are consistent with the empirically validated principles of effective correctional treatments (Andrews & Bonta, 2003). Cooke & Philip (2001, p. 30), for example, have emphasised that sponsoring agencies and programme designers

---

[11] Andrews and Dowden (2006) speculate that those responsible for "demonstration"-type programmes are more aware of the principles of effective correctional treatment and, therefore, better able to design evaluations that will enhance programme effects.

must not regard the capacity to monitor and evaluate programme implementation and process as an "optional extra".

The CPAI-2000 (Gendreau & Andrews, 2001) is one measure that has been designed expressly to evaluate empirically correctional programme quality according to the principles developed by Andrews and Bonta (2003) (see Box 7.1).[12] The CPAI-2000's 131 items assess aspects of therapeutic integrity across eight domains: organisational culture, programme implementation/maintenance, management/staff characteristics, client risk-need assessment practices, programme characteristics, several dimensions of core correctional practice, inter-agency communication, and evaluation.

To date, the CPAI-2000 has been used to evaluate almost 400 "real world" programmes (cf. Gendreau et al., 2001c; Lowenkamp, 2004; Matthews, Hubbard & Latessa, 2001), the majority (approximately 70%) of which, regrettably, have not received a passing grade.[13] While predictive validities for the CPAI-2000 have only recently been reported in the literature, they confirm a positive relationship between ratings of higher programme integrity and better offender outcome (greater reductions in recidivism). For example, using an earlier version of the CPAI-2000 (70 items, six domains), Nesovic (2003) examined the effects of programme integrity on offender recidivism across 173 treatment studies. In her meta-analysis ($k = 266$), she reported a mean ES of $r = 0.12$ with recidivism. Using programme descriptions as detailed in the studies, Nesovic (2003) assessed their quality with the CPAI and then correlated CPAI scores with ES for each programme (some studies described more than one programme and, therefore, produced more than one ES). Overall, CPAI scores correlated well with reductions in recidivism ($r = 0.46$), although the "programme implementation" domain reported the weakest validity ($r = 0.10$). In contrast, the "client assessment" and "programme characteristics" domains were among the most robust ($r = 0.41$ and $r = 0.43$, respectively).

Nesovic (2003) also examined correlations between individual scale items and ES and identified the following as being positively correlated with outcome ($r \geq 0.25$): offenders are appropriate for the programme, their dynamic risk factors are assessed, the programme has a written manual, relapse prevention is practised, staff are trained and hired based on their knowledge of effective relationship and therapeutic skills, and evaluators are involved in the programme. Finally, she categorised treatment programmes in terms of quality (high, medium, or low) based on CPAI score and reported mean effects with outcome of $r = 0.20$, $r = 0.11$, and $r = 0.01$, respectively.

One notable problem, however, when using study documentation to assess programme specifics, is the routine scarcity of descriptive information in primary studies (Andrews & Dowden, 2006). Lowenkamp (2004) overcame this confound by using the CPAI to conduct 38 *in situ* reviews of Ohio-based offender treatment programmes whose designs included matched treatment and comparison groups

---

[12] Domain-specific measures of correctional programme quality are also available. For example, readers may wish to consult the work of Dr Dwayne Simpson and colleagues at Texas Christian University's Institute for Behavioral Research (http://www.ibr.tcu.edu) for details of scales developed to evaluate substance abuse programmes for offenders.

[13] Of note, the RCTC programmes (Bourgon & Armstrong, 2005) are the highest scoring amongst those evaluated using the CPAI-2000 (Gendreau, Smith & Goggin, 2001c).

(gender, race, actuarial risk measure score) and used reincarceration as the criterion. Even though the results for many programmes were poor – it was common to find lower recidivism rates among the comparison groups – the predictive validity of total CPAI score was supported. Across all programme participants, the correlation with outcome was $r = 0.41$; amongst programme completers only, it was $r = 0.32$. In contrast to Nesovic's (2003) results, Lowenkamp (2004) found the "programme implementation" domain to be a powerful predictor of recidivism (rs of 0.54 and 0.46 for each of his samples) while the "staff characteristics" domain was not. In keeping with Nesovic's (2003) findings, Lowenkamp (2004) also reported robust correlations for the "client assessment" and "programme characteristics" domains (rs from 0.30 to 0.52 for each study). When CPAI items which correlated well with treatment outcome were isolated, the mean ES between total scale score and outcome was $r = 0.60$ for all offenders and $r = 0.47$ among programme completers only (Lowenkamp, 2004).

PROGRAMME ACCREDITATION: THE NEXT WAVE IN ADVANCING THE REHABILITATION AGENDA

Notwithstanding the valuable contributions of many localised agencies (Rideau Correctional Treatment Centre) and teams of researchers through their commitment to the rehabilitative ideal, the availability of effective treatment programmes in the "real world" has, thus far, been as much a function of serendipity as design. Until recently, the collective research enterprise had yet to produce a wholesale shift in the correctional treatment *zeitgeist*. That is, it had not spawned a broad-based and coordinated approach to the standardised design, implementation, and evaluation of correctional treatment programmes. Since the mid-1990s, however, governments in some jurisdictions,[14] notably those in England and Wales (Lipton et al., 2000), Scotland (Wozniak, 2001), and Canada (Concilio, 2003; Porporino, 1997), have undertaken just such an initiative by introducing comprehensive correctional programme accreditation systems (see Chapter 1). Based upon the principles of effective correctional programming cumulated from the extensive post-Martinson research literature (Andrews & Bonta, 2003), these accreditation initiatives include the establishment of standards for the design, delivery, and evaluation of treatment programmes as well as the auditing of the institutional and community settings in which they are located. Preliminary outcome data on the impact of the accreditation process in England and Wales and the comparative effectiveness of its accredited programmes are now available and will occupy the remainder of this section.

---

[14] Broad-based accreditation initiatives in the US have not developed apace (Rex, Lieb, Bottoms & Wilson, 2003), in part, because of the lack of a "federal" criminal justice infrastructure (Cadigan & Pelissier, 2003). American accreditation programmes typically focus more on aspects of facility standards (Rowland, 2000; Youngken, 2000) than programme content, although there are notable exceptions, including the *Blueprints for Violence Prevention* initiative at the University of Colorado (Mihalic, Irwin, Elliott, Fagan & Hansen, 2001; Mihalic, Irwin, Fagan, Ballard & Elliott, 2004), the empirically based treatment projects pilot in Illinois and Maine, co-sponsored by the National Institute of Corrections and Crime and Justice Institute (National Institute of Corrections, 2004), and the introduction of the CPAI-2000 by Indiana's Department of Corrections as a means of assessing treatment programme quality (contact Klisby@coa.doc.state.in.us).

Table 7.1 Chronology of England and Wales' correctional programmes accreditation initiative

1991	"What Works" conference
1992	HM Prison Service introduces cognitive skills programming (i.e. R & R, TF)
1993	HM Prison Service develops and implements ETS
1995	McGuire publishes "What Works" conference proceedings
1996	HM Prison Service introduces accreditation process
1998	Underdown Report: 4/267 community-based programmes deemed "effective"
1999	Home Office launches Pathfinder initiative to develop "model" programmes for HM Probation Service
	JAP established
2000	HM Probation Service introduces Pathfinder programmes, adopts accreditation system
2001	Creation of NPS
	NAPO rejects aspects of "What Works" at national conference
2002	JAP becomes CSAP
2003	Carter Report: revamping of service delivery within corrections
2004/5	Prison and Probation Services merge to become NOMS

Note R & R = Reasoning and Rehabilitation, TF = Think First, JAP = Joint Prison/Probation Accreditation Panel, NPS = National Probation Service, NAPO = National Association of Probation Officers, CSAP = Correctional Services Accreditation Panel, NOMS = National Offender Management Services.
Source Correctional Services Accreditation Panel (2004); Debidin and Lovbakke (2004); Ellis & Winstone (2002), Friendship, Blud, Erikson, Travers & Thornton (2003a); Hollin et al. (2004); Homel, Nutley, Webb & Tilley (2004); Raynor (2003; 2004), and Stewart-Ong, Harsent, Roberts, Burnett & Al-Attar (2004).

Firstly, we provide a brief history of the English and Welsh accreditation initiative (see Table 7.1).[15] A fuller description of these events is provided in Chapter 1. In contrast to the North American response to Martinson's (1974) "nothing works" publication (Palmer, 1975; Ross & Gendreau, 1980), little or no government-sponsored research examining the relative effectiveness of correctional programming was undertaken in Britain until the early 1990s (Ellis & Winstone, 2002; Raynor, 2004). In 1991, international data from several studies examining outcomes of offender treatment were presented at a "What Works" conference, the proceedings of which were later published by McGuire (1995). In large part, circulation of this new information acted as a catalyst in spurring a rapid succession of policy developments during the following decade.

Between 1992 and 1993, HM Prison Service introduced three cognitive skills treatment programmes, Think First (TF), a programme developed in-house by Professor James McGuire (Joint Prison/Probation Accreditation Panel, 2001), Reasoning and Rehabilitation (R & R), a programme originating in Canada (Ross, Fabiano & Ewles, 1988) and later revised for use in England and Wales (Porporino & Fabiano, 2000), and Enhanced Thinking Skills (ETS) (Clark, 2000), an updated version of TF (Friendship et al., 2003a). In 1996, the Prison Service added treatment

---

[15] This initiative was but one component of a sweeping Crime Reduction Programme (CRP) adopted in 1999 by Her Majesty's government whose aim was to reduce the incidence of anti-social behaviour and broaden the knowledge base regarding the effectiveness and cost-benefits of correctional programming in the UK by proactively incorporating empirical evidence into criminal justice policy (Homel et al., 2004; Maguire, 2004). For a more detailed discussion of the programme accreditation initiative in particular, see Correctional Services Accreditation Panel (2004), Joint Prison/Probation Accreditation Panel (2001; 2002), Lipton et al. (2000), Raynor (2003, 2004), Rex et al. (2003), and Thornton (1998/9).

and site accreditation systems as a means of ensuring consistent standards for both programme content and delivery across its facilities.

Shortly thereafter, standards were also developed for programmes offered by HM Probation Service. Their necessity was reinforced by the results of a 1996 survey of 55 Probation Service managers regarding the effectiveness of existing community programmes (Underdown, 1998), which indicated that only four of the 267 identified programmes were sufficiently rigorous in the quality of their design and implementation to detect evidence of a treatment effect (Raynor & Vanstone, 2001). Such findings fuelled the political agenda (Ellis & Winstone, 2002) and, within a year of the Underdown (1998) report had resulted in a plan by the Home Office to develop a series of "template" or Pathfinder programmes for application in Probation Service settings. As had been the case with the Prison Service initiative, the purpose of standardising the Probation Service's programme content and delivery was to reduce re-offending by improving the correspondence between what research said about effective correctional programming and the quality of the programmes provided by the Service.

The coordinating body designated to oversee this standardisation was the Joint Prison/Probation Service Accreditation Panel (JAP) (since renamed the Correctional Services Accreditation Panel (CSAP)), a non-governmental advisory committee comprised of independent experts and representatives from the Home Office Research Development and Statistics Directorate, and the prison and probation services (Joint Prison/Probation Accreditation Panel, 2001; Rex et al., 2003). Established in 1999, CSAP's mandate included the following among its principal responsibilities:

1. To develop and review annually programme accreditation standards against which existing and future correctional programmes provided by both HM Prison and Probation Services can be evaluated as to their potential to effectively reduce recidivism.
2. To review and accredit applicant programmes for both Services *per* the aforementioned standards.
3. To develop agency auditing standards for use by both the Prison and Probation Services and to authorise annual audits in order to evaluate the fidelity with which accredited treatment programmes are delivered as planned.
4. To review the results of the agency audits, and provide on-going feedback and consultation as required.
5. To act as an *ad hoc* resource for HM Prison and Probation Services, as well as the Home Office, on general issues of correctional treatment programme design, delivery, and evaluation.

As of December 2004, 27 different programmes had been accredited by CSAP for use in HM Prison and Probation Services, including three cognitive skills programmes, eight drug treatment programmes, and seven sex offender programmes (Correctional Services Accreditation Panel, 2004) (see Chapter 1). Since 1999, several thousand offenders have participated in accredited treatment programmes delivered by scores of trained staff in a host of prison and probation sites (Blud, Travers, Nugent & Thornton, 2003; Debidin & Lovbakke, 2004; Falshaw, Friendship,

Travers & Nugent, 2004; Hollin et al., 2004). Results from the first set of follow-up studies are now available and a summary of their findings regarding programme effectiveness is timely as it provides a first-hand opportunity to examine the impact in "real world" settings of what the research literature says works in correctional treatment (see also Chapters 1 and 3).[16]

Outcome of Accredited Programmes

On balance, the effectiveness of the Prison Service's accredited programmes in reducing offender recidivism has not been in the range mandated by government policy (5 % between 1997 and 2004)[17] (Merrington & Stanley, 2004; Prime, 2002) nor that anticipated by programme designers and facilitators (Correctional Services Accreditation Panel, 2004; HM Prison Service, 2004; Raynor, 2004), particularly when compared with results reported elsewhere (Porporino & Robinson, 1995; Van Voorhis, Spruance, Ritchey, Listwan & Seabrook, 2004).

In the first post-accreditation follow-up study, two year reconviction rates for R & R and ETS participants ($n = 649$) were virtually identical to those of the comparison group ($n = 1\,947$) (39.4 % versus 39.2 %, respectively) (Falshaw et al., 2004). Such findings also did not differ from those of Friendship et al. (2003a) who reported a slightly higher recidivism rate ($r = -0.03$) for pre-accredited versions of R & R and ETS programmes among treatment participants (treatment: $n = 667$, 44 %; comparison: $n = 1\,801$, 40 %). The Falshaw et al. (2004) study also reported no differences in the recidivism rates of the treatment and comparison groups after removing from analysis programme non-completers or those who attended programmes that had failed to meet accreditation standards. (The issue of programme completion is considered in more detail in Chapter 2.) Moreover, neither "time since programme inception" nor "type of programme" (R & R versus ETS) were associated with differences in outcome.

A second post-accreditation follow-up examined the effectiveness of R & R and ETS in reducing recidivism among juveniles as well as adults (Cann, Falshaw, Nugent & Friendship, 2003) and reported results in keeping with those of the two previous samples. That is, among both adults and juveniles, treatment and comparison group recidivism rates were approximately equal at 1 and 2 years post-programme. The R & R programme was notably ineffective for both groups at either follow-up, while the effects of ETS among moderate/high risk complements showed some promise at 1 year (adults: $r = 0.05$; juveniles: $r = 0.03$) but not 2 years (no significant difference between treatment and comparison groups).

Among accredited prison-based programmes, there has been some indication of positive effects, at least over the short term (Blud et al., 2003). The authors examined the impact of R & R and ETS relative to aspects of programme delivery and found that, across more than 4 000 offenders ($n_{range} = 4\,042$ to $4\,814$) in 103 prisons, higher

---

[16] By virtue of distance we may be at once more objective in our review of the English and Welsh accreditation initiative and less sensitive to the subtle nuances attendant in such a large-scale implementation. We trust that neither condition has adulterated the quality of our observations.

[17] A reduction of 5 % in the "rate of re-conviction of all offenders punished by imprisonment or by community supervision" (Prime, 2002) should not necessarily be interpreted as a programme effect of 5 % given that the entire offender cohort includes both treatment participants and non-participants.

programme quality (more experienced tutors, more institutional support, more throughcare) was associated with lower treatment dropout rates.

Regarding the effectiveness of programmes delivered by HM Probation Service, early results from a study of TF were consistent with what the literature suggests for community-based cognitive skills treatments (Andrews & Bonta, 2003). That is, at 6 months post-programme reconviction rates were notably reduced ($r = 0.14$) for the treatment ($n = 116$) versus comparison group ($n = 174$) (26.7 % versus 40.2 %, respectively) (Stewart-Ong et al., 2004). This trend persisted at both 9 months ($r = 0.21$) and 12 months ($r = 0.29$) (recidivism rates: 35.4 % versus 56.9 % and 44.4 % versus 73.7 %, respectively), but generalisability of these findings is severely hampered by the limited number of probation areas involved ($n = 3$) and the low completion rate (28 %) among treatment recipients (Stewart-Ong et al., 2004) (cf. Chapter 2).

In evaluating the effectiveness of accredited community-based treatment programmes, it is prudent, therefore, to give more weight to results from nationally representative samples, such as HM Probation Service's Pathfinders initiative. Implemented by the Home Office in 2000, the Pathfinders project involved the development of model treatment programmes designed to address offenders' empirically confirmed criminogenic needs (cognitions, basic skills, resettlement, and so forth). In all, seven programmes were piloted in 16 Probation Areas and their outcomes have been independently evaluated (Raynor, 2004).

Hollin et al.'s (2004) report on the effects of Pathfinder programmes, the largest study to date of the outcome of accredited probation programmes, includes data on 4 875 offenders (treatment: $n = 2 230$; comparison: $n = 2 645$), with the majority (96 %) of the treatment group having attended one of three accredited cognitive skills programmes (TF: $n = 1 262$; R & R: $n = 250$; ETS: $n = 629$).

Based on recidivism rates during follow-up, the effects of the Pathfinder programmes have been, on the whole, negligible ($r = 0.03$) (Correctional Services Accreditation Panel, 2004; Hollin et al., 2004). For example, 54.5 % of programme completers ($n = 748$) recidivated during the nearly 2 year follow-up as compared with 57.9 % of the comparison group ($n = 2 645$). Among male completers, the ES was $r = 0.05$ (treatment: $n = 680$, 54.4 %; comparison: $n = 2 156$, 59.8 %), while for female completers ($n = 68$), recidivism rates were actually higher ($r = -0.04$) than for the comparison group ($n = 489$) (56 % versus 50 %, respectively). In examining the progress of all offenders by risk level, Hollin et al. (2004) noted a slight but detectable treatment effect, and in the direction predicted by the risk principle (Andrews & Bonta, 2003). That is, the ES among low risk offenders was $r = -0.001$ whereas that among the moderate- and high-risk samples was $r = 0.10$ and 0.09, respectively.

Although these studies represent only the first stage of the research effort to track the effects of accredited programmes delivered by the prison and probation services, the relatively weak ESs have been a cause for concern, especially given the scope of the British government's commitment (Blunkett, 2004; Homel et al., 2004) and the potential threat they pose to the future of the initiative. It is important, therefore, to determine what might be behind such findings. Do they simply represent the random variation one might expect in a distribution of programme outcomes (Andrews & Bonta, 2003) or, as some have speculated, are they indicative of more systemic problems with programme delivery and evaluation design (Homel et al., 2004; Wrench, 2004) (cf. Chapter 2)?

One of the confounds faced by Hollin et al. (2004) in attempting to evaluate the relative effectiveness of the Pathfinder programmes was the study's excessive number of treatment non-completers (see Chapter 2 for a full discussion of this issue). Only 33.5 % of those who began a treatment programme actually completed it. Further, recidivism rates among non-completers surpassed those of the comparison group by a wide margin (77.6 % versus 57.9 %, respectively). When considered as a group, the recidivism rate of completers plus non-completers exceeded that of the comparison group by 12 percentage points (69.9 % versus 57.9 %). Hollin et al. (2004, p. 13) questioned whether the apparent lack of effectiveness of the Pathfinder programmes might have more to do with "A failure of implementation rather than programme failure" and advised that completion rates and treatment "dosage" be given due consideration in the design of future programme evaluations (cf. Chapter 2). Non-completion rates have also been noted among the prison-based studies of accredited programmes (Cann et al., 2003; Falshaw et al., 2004), but given their relative values (11.1 % and 10.0 %, respectively), they are within an acceptable range (see Lösel, 2001).

Programme Audit Results

The principal mechanism designed to monitor the strengths and weaknesses of the accreditation initiative is the programme audit. It is intended to provide both the necessary guidelines for effective programme implementation and delivery, as well as a means by which to measure the fidelity of that process vis-à-vis outcome (Correctional Services Accreditation Panel, 2004; see Scheirer & Rezmovic, 1983). As such, audit results may shed light on the causes for events such as the high non-completion rates, especially among probation samples.

The audit protocols for each Service are similar in content but differ procedurally (see Chapter 3). For instance, audits were initially conducted for each of the services by separate agencies, HM Inspectorate of Probation for community-based programmes and HM Prison Service's Offending Behaviour Prevention Unit (OBPU) for institutional programmes.[18] The existing audit protocols for both Services measure largely similar constructs. They include three common performance standards governing aspects of "institutional/management support" (programme adequately resourced and scheduled, tutors sufficiently prepared, etc.), "treatment/programme management" (selection, training, and supervision of skilled tutors, delivery monitored by video-tape, participants selected on risk/need/responsivity basis, etc.), and "quality of programme delivery" (intervention follows prescribed treatment, high completion rates, and so forth) (HM Inspectorate of Probation, 2002; Prison Service Order 4360, 2004). A fourth performance standard reflects treatment functions that are unique

---

[18] The lack of independence in having the OBPU carry out programme audits within the Prison Service has been a concern to CSAP (Correctional Services Accreditation Panel, 2004; see Rex et al., 2003). A streamlining of audit standards and procedures was first advocated for both Services by CSAP in 2001, although progress to date has been less than anticipated (Correctional Services Accreditation Panel, 2004). Probation Service audits have most recently become the responsibility of the National Probation Service, although since early 2004 their regular completion has been hampered by funding problems (Correctional Services Accreditation Panel, 2004). At the time of this writing, both services have committed to collaborate in the development of a conjoint audit process.

to each Service: "continuity and resettlement" (progress reviews, appropriate throughcare, and so forth) in the case of the Prison Service and "case management" (enforcement of attendance, and so forth) for the Probation Service. Among prison programmes, the percentage value assigned to each audit standard is generally 25 % (Prison Service Order 4360, 2004). Equivalent values for probation standards are set at 20 %, 30 %, 30 %, and 20 %, respectively (Joint Prison/Probation Accreditation Panel, 2002).

For both services, audit data is gathered from file reviews, individual and group interviews with staff and offenders, site visits, and evaluation of treatment delivery quality through reviews of session videotapes (HM Inspectorate of Probation, 2002; Prison Service Order 4360, 2004). Programme progress is evaluated against each of the standards, "scored" according to the above-noted schedule, and summed to yield an implementation quality rating (IQR). The IQR benchmark in the Prison Service is set at 60 % (Prison Service Order 4360, 2004) while that of the Probation Service is 70 % (HM Inspectorate of Probation, 2002). Programmes that receive IQRs below 40 % are considered as "failures" in both services and are subject to follow-up review.

In their 2003/4 annual report, CSAP noted that attrition posed a serious problem to measurement of programme effectiveness, especially among probation programmes (Correctional Services Accreditation Panel, 2004). A summary of initial Probation Service IQR data ($n = 14$) suggests that, with mean scores of 66.4 % on "leadership commitment", 57.7 % on "programme management", 52.8 % on "quality of programme delivery", and 46.8 % on "case management" (HM Inspectorate of Probation, 2002), few programmes were meeting the criterion IQR for effective implementation and delivery.[19] Specific deficiencies were noted in the following areas: offender targeting and risk assessment, use of video monitoring, and sufficient training for case managers.

Successive annual reports from the Probation Inspectorate have documented little change over time in mean initial IQR ratings ($\overline{X} \leq 62$ %) and continue to emphasise the need for the probation service to bolster specific components of programme delivery, notably the targeting of offenders for treatment and case management practices (HM Inspectorate of Probation, 2003, 2004; see also National Probation Service for England and Wales, 2004; Rex et al., 2003). The question remains: what effect are programmes with mean IQR scores in the "unsatisfactory" range having on completion rates and would an increase in average ratings translate into better retention rates and, consequently, decreased recidivism among treatment recipients (HM Inspectorate of Probation, 2002)? Thus far, the necessary data are not available to answer such questions.

Some (Clarke, Simmonds & Wydall, 2004; Debidin & Lovbakke, 2004; Rex et al., 2003) have speculated that offender motivation could be an important predictor of programme completion, although the results of a study by Stewart & Millson (1995) suggest that it may not play as important a role as criminogenic need (cf. Chapter 2). The latter followed a cohort of 2 400 Canadian federal parolees for 2 years and

---

[19] The first author used Prison Service IQR data presented by Wrench (2004) for the fiscal year 2002/3 to calculate a mean score of 93.9 % for all programmes, with 93.8 % having an IQR $\geq$ 90 %. Among cognitive programmes (ETS and R & R), the mean IQR was 96.4 % with 97.4 % achieving IQRs $\geq$ 90 %.

assessed the effect of motivation for treatment[20] on suspension within 6 months of conditional release from prison. Stewart & Millson (1995) reported that, although those who were rated as "high motivation" (self-motivated, addressing problem areas) generally fared better in treatment than those rated as "low motivation", motivation in itself was not a mediating factor when its influence was examined in the context of criminogenic need (employment, attitudes, substance abuse, and so forth). That is, within the "high-need" group, recidivism rates were approximately equivalent regardless of level of motivation ("high motivation" = 36.2% versus "low motivation" = 35.4%) (Stewart & Millson, 1995).

Such findings reinforce the importance of using a valid and reliable means of assessing criminogenic need in determining offenders' risk of re-offending and, therefore, appropriateness for treatment. Debidin & Lovbakke (2004), for example, note that over the course of successive prison studies of accredited programme effectiveness, the proportion of high-risk offenders in the samples actually declined relative to that of moderate and lower risk offenders (see Wrench, 2004). This contrasts with what the empirical literature has confirmed regarding the effectiveness of treatment with lower risk offenders (Andrews & Bonta, 2003), particularly probationers (Walker, Farrington & Tucker, 1981). As Raynor (2004) notes, lower risk offenders were also more likely to complete probation's Pathfinder programmes, but, given floor effects, this could not be expected to have any discernible impact on their already low recidivism rates.

A second advantage of an appropriate risk/needs assessment instrument, one that samples dynamic as well as static offender attributes, is its use in enhancing the "match" between treatment and comparison group cohorts. In the first wave of post-accreditation studies, CSAP (2004, p. 14) identified a "lack of adequacy" in treatment/comparison group matching as a problem that may have forestalled any definitive conclusions regarding programme effectiveness. For instance, in the Falshaw et al. (2004) study, offenders in the treatment and comparison groups were matched according to ethnicity, sentence length, offence type, and Offender Group Reconviction Score – 2 (OGRS2) (Taylor, 1999), a risk assessment tool comprising static offender characteristics (such as age and number of previous convictions). Data from North American samples have suggested that similar static offender variables such as race ($r = 0.13$) (Gendreau, Little & Goggin, 1996) or situational factors such as sentence length ($r_{range} = 0.03$ to 0.07) (Smith et al., 2002) are not as robust predictors of recidivism as are dynamic offender characteristics (anti-social companions: $r = 0.18$; criminogenic needs: $r = 0.18$) (Gendreau et al., 1996).

Comprehensive pre-programme assessments of offenders (Bourgon & Armstrong, 2005) can also detect mismatches between the literacy demands of cognitive skills programmes and the literacy skills of referrals. Davies, Lewis, Byatt, Purvis & Cole (2004) rated the reading ability of a sample of offenders ($n = 473$) from six probation areas and found that 57% of those enrolled in ETS were assessed at less than level 1 (able to identify main points and specific details

---

[20] Approximately equal proportions of the sample were rated as "high motivation" or "high need" but cell frequencies were notable skewed: high motivation/high need ($n = 287$, 36.2% recidivism), high motivation/low need ($n = 913$, 8.5% recidivism), low motivation/high need ($n = 854$, 35.4% recidivism), low motivation/low need ($n = 346$, recidivism percentage not cited) (Stewart & Millson, 1995).

in text) according to the UK's National Standards of Adult Literacy, while 100% of the programme's 20 sessions required that same rating. At least a third of ETS's 20 sessions required level 2 skills (accurately read and understand text of varying complexity). Similar discrepancies were noted between the literacy requirements of both the TF and R & R programmes and the average literacy skills of offenders. Overall, only 9.5% of offenders were rated at level 2 while level 2 requirements for the three programmes' sessions varied from 35% to 68%. The observation by one programme participant "I didn't understand what they were going on about" (Davies et al., 2004, p. 13) may shed some light on the treatment retention problem. Of note, the Home Office has recently moved to address this disparity through a literacy initiative (cf. Davis et al., 1997).

Programme completion rates have been just one of several significant challenges experienced in the course of the accreditation roll-out. To its credit, the project stands as an "unprecedented" (Ellis & Winstone, 2002, p. 334) government commitment to implement a system-wide regime of clinically relevant and empirically informed correctional treatments (see Homel et al., 2004). Given the dynamic political context in which the implementation has taken place, it is perhaps not surprising that the initiative has experienced a number of problems that collectively may have contributed to the attenuated effects reported thus far (see Box 7.2).

Box 7.2   Limitations in the design and implementation of England and Wales's correctional programmes accreditation initiative

---

1. Research design
- quasi-experimental rather than random assignment
- high treatment non-completion rates (i.e., $\geq 65\%$)
- outcome data collected before programme "bugs" fully worked out
- reliability of recidivism data in national databases (i.e., Offenders Index, National Identification System)

2. Programme
- adequacy of matching between treatment and comparison cohorts
- appropriateness of programme referrals (i.e., more low than high risk)
- literacy demands of cognitive programmes exceed offenders' abilities
- physical resources (i.e., programme facilities) not secured
- programme process not being systematically evaluated (i.e., treatment video tapes not being monitored)

3. Personnel
- professional resistance to "new" methods, adherence to "nostalgia" mythology (i.e., "why change what we're doing, when we know it works")
- limited "buy in": staff express lack of involvement, poor communication, inadequate preparation/training to deliver programmes
- lack of national training standards for programme facilitators
- inadequate staff resources to meet increased demands (i.e., trained qualified facilitators, support staff)   (*Cont.*)

Box 7.2   Continued

- increases in probation caseloads parallel increased demands to meet programme targets
- sufficient and adequate case management services not being delivered in timely manner
- tension between programme staff and non-programme staff regarding programme versus agency (i.e., probation, prison services) service delivery priorities
- non-programme staff feel "marginalised", "not appreciated"

4. Organisation
- scope of undertaking leads to unrealistic expectations regarding potential impact of programmes (i.e., meaningful reductions in recidivism within 3 years)
- programme referral targets tied to operational budgets
- computerised risk assessment not systematically available in timely fashion (i.e., software support for Offender Assessment System: anticipated delivery in 2000, still not fully operational in 2004)
- concurrent agency restructuring and reorganisation of previously semi-autonomous probation offices into the National Probation Service (i.e., new legislation, changes in funding, boundary re-definitions)
- semantic modifications to standard probation orders (i.e., Community Service Order becomes Community Punishment Order) in April 2001 adds confusion

Note. From Clarke et al. (2004); Debidin & Lovbakke (2004); Ellis & Winstone (2002); Friendship, Thornton, Erikson & Beech (2001); Friendship, Falshaw & Beech (2003b); HM Inspectorate of Probation (2002; 2004); Hollin et al. (2002; 2004); Homel et al. (2004); Merrington & Stanley (2004); Raynor (2003; 2004); Raynor & Vanstone (2001); Rex, Gelsthorpe, Roberts & Jordan (2004); Wozniak (2001).

Several researchers have emphasised that more sophisticated research designs are essential to improving detection of treatment effects (Correctional Services Accreditation Panel, 2004) (cf. Chapter 2). In particular, Merrington & Stanley (2004) have noted that not all of the post-accreditation evaluations (Wilson, Attrill & Nugent, 2003) have included comparison groups. Even among studies with matched treatment/comparison cohorts, most studies do so using the OGRS2, which, as noted previously, captures only static offender characteristics (Cann et al., 2003). As well, Rex et al. (2003) have suggested that failure more assertively to interest offenders in treatment may have left programmes, especially those offered in community settings, vulnerable to poor completion rates. Cann et al. (2003) note that it is equally important to clarify the nature of the service received by the comparison group as they commonly receive some form of treatment ("service as usual") and this undoubtedly reduces comparative differences in outcome between the two groups (Lösel, 2001).

In addition, Webster, Hedderman, Turnbull & May (2001) have highlighted problematic aspects of programme monitoring in a review of prison-based employment programs in England and Wales. The authors surveyed 103 facilities as to the number and nature of the offenders attending their programmes and found that less than one-third systematically collect any information on programme participants. Most programmes could provide only estimates of the numbers of offenders who had participated in programmes for which eligibility was more often determined by budgetary concerns (unused programme "seats" threatened by budget cuts) than by risk/needs assessment. A lack of aftercare coordination with community probation staff was also an issue raised by both prison workers and offenders (probation officers too busy, too disinterested, and so forth). These are consistent with many of the deficiencies detailed by Homel et al. (2004) in their review of the CRP undertaking as a whole for example, difficulties recruiting and retaining qualified programme and evaluation staff.

Raynor (2004, p. 312) has also noted the potential impact that political decisions (programme targets tied to "treasury targets") (see Homel et al., 2004) and delays in software implementation (OASys risk assessment support delivery anticipated in 2000, still not fully operational by 2004) may have had on decisions regarding which offenders and how many are identified for treatment. As mentioned, the most widely used assessment tool at present, the OGRS2, includes exclusively static variables (Taylor, 1999) and may, therefore, fail to detect meaningful differences among offenders on treatment-responsive criminogenic factors (Andrews & Bonta, 2003). As Falshaw et al. (2004) suggest, offenders whose risk level is derived only from ratings of static factors may well differ on critical dynamic attributes (cognitive skills, drug use, and so forth) and which could account, at least in part, for the lack of treatment effect reported in their study.

Given its importance for both methodological and clinical reasons (Ellis & Winstone, 2002; Lösel, 2001), addressing programme retention rates must be made a priority in future evaluations (Hollin et al., 2004). Results from the English and Welsh initiative (Cann et al., 2003; Debidin & Lovbakke, 2004; Hollin et al., 2004) and elsewhere (Lösel, 2001; Van Voorhis et al., 2004) repeatedly confirm that treatment non-completers have higher recidivism rates than either treatment completers or comparison cohorts. By including non-completers in the treatment group when assessing programme outcome, measures of effectiveness will necessarily be dampened, thereby doing a disservice to the programme (Lösel, 2001) (cf. Chapter 2). For instance, in analysing differences between treatment completers and non-completers in their Georgia sample, Van Voorhis et al. (2004) found the latter to be younger, less educated, and more likely to have a history of violent conviction.

Germane to the English and Welsh accreditation context, Friendship et al. (2003b) note that the specific characteristics of comparison group members are rarely known as they are neither as routinely nor as thoroughly screened as treatment referrals, pre-empting analysis of possible associations between salient offender attributes and outcome. In fact, the Probation Inspectorate indicated in 2002 that, although the research design identified "offender interviews" as one of the data sources for programme audits, only a limited number had thus far been conducted and then only with treatment completers (HM Inspectorate of Probation, 2002). More detailed knowledge of the characteristics of non-completers would undoubtedly provide information that could help in better targeting their treatment needs and keep non-completion rates to a minimum (approximately 10 %) in future studies.

Improving offender participation rates, however, also depends upon improving staff "buy-in". In a comprehensive review of CSAP's role in the accreditation implementation process, Rex et al. (2003) reported an overall rate of return of 28.9 % in a questionnaire survey of 1 384 stakeholders. Responses were received from 65.7 % ($n = 254$) of programme staff in six prisons and five probation areas, 20.2 % ($n = 247$) of non-programme prison personnel, 1.4 % ($n = 500$) of non-programme probation personnel, and 46.2 % ($n = 383$) of sentencers (judges, magistrates). In addition, key informant interviews were conducted with all of the CSAP members ($n = 25$) and smaller samples of implementation managers and programme developers from both services ($n = 18$) as well as programme staff ($n = 46$) and judges ($n = 8$) drawn from the original sample of questionnaire respondents.

Some programme facilitators, particularly within the Probation Service, were reportedly piqued by the "psychological language and structured style" (Rex et al., 2003, p. 45) in some programmes (ETS, TF), describing them as "deskilling" (p. 45). Probation officers also expressed a sense that, in the move to implement standardised programme delivery nationwide, their traditional skills were being devalued (Rex et al., 2003). These views contrast somewhat with impressions gained from site visits by HM Inspectorate of Probation during which programme staff were generally enthusiastic about their participation in the project. The statements were, however, consistent with reports from non-programme staff who indicated they felt harried by time constraints resulting from increased caseloads, and who felt that their work had been "marginalised" and was "little appreciated" (HM Inspectorate of Probation, 2004, p. 9).[21] Responses by Prison Service programme staff documented their concerns regarding a lack of supportiveness *vis-à-vis* programme delivery within the prison environment (see Clarke et al., 2004).

It is notable that the nature of the relationship between CSAP and programme staff differed somewhat by service (prison versus probation) (Rex et al., 2003). Respondents in prison-based sites were almost twice as likely as probation staff to rate CSAP's decisions as "good" or "very good" (62 % versus 36 %), although both groups were only moderately supportive regarding the "fairness" of CSAP's advice (≈ 50 % agreement). Rex et al.'s (2003) findings suggest that there have been significant difficulties in effectively communicating to front-line staff not only the objectives of the accreditation initiative but also the rudiments of its successful implementation (Homel et al. 2004). An improved sense of programme "ownership" by facilitators, especially among those in the Probation Service, might translate into better treatment retention rates among offenders.

Certainly, the empirical literature is unambiguous as regards the importance of safeguarding all aspects of therapeutic integrity if programme implementation is to be successful and the test of programme effectiveness fair. In their 5-year review of the panel's activities, CSAP (2004) detailed a number of key deficiencies in programme delivery, which they recommended be addressed by the Home Office if the quality of programme implementation and effectiveness are to improve. These include more comprehensive assessment and targeting of treatment participants, improvements in the quality of programme delivery (data collection,

---

[21] The depth of probation officer discontent was confirmed in a formal rejection of aspects of the "what works" initiative at the National Association of Probation Officers annual conference in 2001 (Raynor, 2004).

video monitoring reviews, and so forth) and the supportiveness of the respective prison and community treatment environments (dedicated treatment facilities and resources), better programme attendance and completion rates, and greater emphasis on evaluating post-programme offender performance (recidivism as well as changes in life circumstances/opportunities). The CSAP's Chair relayed the Panel's conclusions to the government in early 2004, writing:

> At present the research available on the use of accredited programmes in England and Wales is still unable to answer some of the key questions about their use, value and relative effectiveness, particularly in relation to which types of offenders, in which circumstances and contexts, are most likely to benefit from the existing range of programmes. We also still have very little evidence of the likely duration of any positive effects on the longer-term criminal careers of offenders. (Correctional Services Accreditation Panel, 2004, p. 14)

The problems summarised by the CSAP (2004) number among those that have been well documented by others involved in implementing empirically-based treatment regimes, albeit, on a smaller scale (Byrne & Kelly, 1989; Ellickson & Petersilia, 1983). For instance, Borum (2003) has documented the results of efforts to implement empirically validated treatment programmes for juveniles in four pilot sites in the US and confirmed that locales that maintained better levels of therapeutic integrity were associated with decreased recidivism rates. The English and Welsh accreditation experience points up the very real difficulties inherent in transferring a research-based treatment paradigm to the "real world", particularly one on such a large scale, even under circumstances where what is known to be effective has been widely confirmed (Andrews & Bonta, 2003; McGuire, 1995) and is broadly accepted (Homel et al., 2004; Rex et al., 2002). As Borum (2003, p. 129), however, notes: "Good intentions and good ideas are not sufficient to produce a successful intervention."

For some (Ellis & Winstone, 2002; Raynor, 2004), the accreditation initiative's lacklustre results have echoed like a radar "ping" heralding the potential resurgence of the *ennui* regarding offender rehabilitation that characterised the post-Martinson period in Britain. Given the initiative's attendant costs (approximately £400 million) (Homel et al., 2004), it will not be surprising to find critics of the project snapping at its heels should succeeding treatment evaluations continue to report only minimal reductions in recidivism. A more parsimonious response to these findings (Raynor, 2004) suggests that the initial results from the accreditation initiative be regarded as "pilot" data, especially given the absence of treatment effectiveness research in Britain before 1990. At the very least, the lessons learned from reviews of this first phase of the accreditation implementation can provide useful directions to improve not only the implementation process but also the quality of programme delivery and the evaluations designed to measure their effects.

In the end, however, it may be as Raynor (2004) suggests, that expectations in Britain of dramatic programme effects (significant reductions in recidivism) were running considerably higher than they should have been given the very daunting risks attendant such a grand scale roll-out. As well as newly minted programmes, both services, but more so Probation, have been challenged to implement the initiative in a political context which has concurrently ordained a significant re-organisation of duties, responsibilities, and changes in funding structure, not all of which were related to the accreditation project (Carter, 2003; HM Inspectorate of Probation, 2004; Raynor, 2003, 2004). For example, since 2001, the Probation Service has experienced organisational restructuring and new legislation, and is currently facing an impending merger with the much larger Prison Service (to be known henceforth as the National Offender Management Service (NOMS)), *per* the government's commitment to streamline offender service delivery over the entire sentence period, regardless of where served (Carter, 2003) – a move that the Probation Inspectorate warns may lead to "organisation exhaustion" on the part of service staff (HM Inspector of Probation, 2003, p. 5).

While Lipsey et al. (2001) have advised that the mean effect of "real-world" programmes can and must be improved by transferring the conditions for effective programming beyond the experimental or "demonstration" context, Lösel (2001) has warned of the consequences of such evident disparity between the mean effects of "research" versus "routine" programmes. Persistent attenuation of treatment effects, like those reported thus far for outcome evaluations of the British "real world" programmes, can lead to antipathy among agencies, staff, and offenders (see Hamm & Schrink, 1989), and, ultimately, have the potential to derail the rehabilitative ideal in the process (Lösel, 2001).

In the years that have passed since Martinson's (1974) seminal publication, an impressive volume of research has documented that correctional treatments that are founded upon sound behavioural principles can indeed be demonstrably effective in reducing anti-social behaviour. With remarkable consistency, the effectiveness of correctional treatments has been empirically demonstrated across a variety of offender populations and settings. The prerequisites for and circumstances under which programming is optimally effective have been disseminated widely, culminating in large scale treatment programme applications in at least three national jurisdictions during the last decade. Despite what we know about effective treatments and the colossal commitment by a vast coterie of corrections professionals,[22] researchers, and programme facilitators, criminal justice systems continue to be dogged by evidence from "real-world" programmes that outcomes are less substantive than the research literature suggests they can be. One constructive consequence of this conundrum has been a greater focus on critical aspects of treatment delivery, notably the quality of programme implementation and the degree to which therapeutic integrity is maintained throughout the process. A second, more disturbing, consequence has been a growing disillusionment with the "what works" agenda (Ellis & Winstone, 2002; Lösel, 2001; Gendreau & Smith, 2005; Raynor, 2003, 2004; Wozniak, 2001). In order to ensure that the progress made since the mid-1970s is not invalidated by a generalised disaffection with the rehabilitative ideal, we must be vigilant in ensuring the delivery of appropriate and effective correctional programming, thereby safeguarding the mutual interests of both the public and offenders. To do less would be irremissible.

---

[22] We trust that the efforts of professionals such as White (2004) and Ferguson (2002) are representative of programme administrators and facilitators whose commitment to implementing effective correctional programming is not diminished by the practical hurdles experienced in doing so.

REFERENCES

Andrews, D. A. (1979). *The dimensions of correctional counseling and supervision process in probation and parole.* Toronto, Ontario: Ontario Ministry of Correctional Services.

Andrews, D. A. (1980). Some experimental investigations of the principles of differential association through deliberate manipulations of the structure of service systems. *American Sociological Review, 45,* 448–462.

Andrews, D. A. (1995). The psychology of criminal conduct and effective treatment. In J. McGuire (Ed.), *What works: Reducing reoffending – Guidelines from research and practice* (pp. 35–62). Chichester: John Wiley & Sons.

Andrews, D. A. & Bonta, J. (1995). *The Level of Service Inventory – Revised.* Toronto, Ontario: Multi-Health Systems.

Andrews, D. A. & Bonta, J. (2003). *The psychology of criminal conduct (3rd edition).* Cincinnati, OH: Anderson Publishing Co.

Andrews, D. A., Bonta, J. & Hoge, R. D. (1990a). Classification for effective rehabilitation: Rediscovering psychology. *Criminal Justice and Behavior, 17,* 19–52.

Andrews, D. A. & Dowden, C. (2005). Managing correctional treatment for reduced recidivism: A meta-analytic review of programme integrity. *Legal and Criminological Psychology, 10,* 173–187.

Andrews, D. A. & Dowden, C. (2006) Risk principle of case classification in correctional treatment: A meta-analytic investigation. *International Journal of Offender Therapy and Comparative Criminology, 50,* 88–100.

Andrews, D. A., Dowden, C. & Gendreau, P. (2004). *Clinically relevant and psychologically informed approaches to reduce re-offending: A meta-analytic study of human service, risk, need, responsivity, and other concerns in justice contexts.* Unpublished manuscript.

Andrews, D. A., Dowden, C. & Rettinger, L. J. (2001). Special populations within corrections. In J. A. Winterdyk (Ed.), *Corrections in Canada* (pp. 170–212). Toronto, Ontario: Prentice Hall.

Andrews, D. A. & Kiessling, J. J. (1980). Program structure and effective correctional practices: A summary of the CaVIC research. In R. R. Ross & P. Gendreau (Eds), *Effective correctional treatment* (pp. 441–463). Toronto, Ontario: Butterworths.

Andrews, D. A., Kiessling, J. J., Mickus, S. & Robinson, D. (1986). The construct validity of interview-based risk assessment in corrections. *Canadian Journal of Behavioral Science, 18,* 460–471.

Andrews, D. A., Kiessling, J. J., Robinson, D. & Mickus, S. (1986). The risk principle of case classification: An outcome evaluation with young adult probationers. *Canadian Journal of Criminology, 28,* 377–383.

Andrews, D. A. & Wormith, J. S. (1989). Personality and crime: Knowledge destruction and construction in criminology. *Justice Quarterly, 6,* 289–309.

Andrews, D. A., Zinger, I., Hoge, R. D., Bonta, J., Gendreau, P. & Cullen, F. T. (1990b). Does correctional treatment work? A clinically relevant and psychologically-informed meta-analysis. *Criminology, 28,* 369–404.

Aos, S., Lieb, R., Mayfield, J., Miller, M. & Pennucci, A. (2004). *Benefits and costs of prevention and early intervention programs for youth.* Olympia, WA: Washington State Institute for Public Policy.

Aos, S., Phipps, P., Barnoski, R. & Lieb, R. (1999). *The comparative costs and benefits of programs to reduce crime: A review of national research findings with implications for Washington state.* Olympia, WA: Washington State Institute for Public Policy.

Apter, S. J. & Goldstein, A. P. (1986). *Youth violence: Program and prospects.* New York: Pergamon Press.

Ax, R. K. & Morgan, R. D. (2002). Internship training opportunities in correctional psychology: A comparison of settings. *Criminal Justice and Behavior, 29,* 332–347.

Backer, T. E. & David, S. L. (1995). Synthesis of behavioral science learning about technology transfer. In T. E. Backer, S. L. David & G. Saucy (Eds), *Reviewing the behavioral science knowledge base on technology transfer NIDA Monograph 155* (pp. 262–279). Washington, DC: U.S. Department of Health and Human Services.

Bauman, L. J., Stein, R. E. K. & Ireys, H. T. (1991). Reinventing fidelity: The transfer of social technology among settings. *American Journal of Community Psychology, 19,* 619–639.

Blud, L., Travers, R., Nugent, F. & Thornton, D. (2003). Accreditation of offending behaviour programmes in HM prison service: "What works" in practice. *Legal and Criminological Psychology, 8,* 69–81.

Blunkett, D. (2004, January). *Reducing crime, changing lives: The government's plans for transforming the management of offenders.* London: Home Office.

Bonta, J., Bogue, B., Crowley, M. & Motiuk, L. (2001). Implementing offender classification systems: Lessons learned. In G. A. Bernfeld, D. P. Farrington & A. W. Leschied (Eds), *Offender rehabilitation in practice: Implementing and evaluating effective programs* (pp. 226–245). Chichester: John Wiley & Sons.

Boothby, J. L. & Clements, C. B. (2000). A national survey of correctional psychologists. *Criminal Justice and Behavior, 27,* 715–731.

Borum, R. (2003). Managing at-risk juvenile offenders in the community: Putting evidence-based principles into practice. *Journal of Contemporary Criminal Justice, 19,* 114–137.

Bourgon, G. & Armstrong, B. (2005). Transferring the principles of effective treatment into a "real world" prison setting. *Criminal Justice and Behavior, 32,* 3–25.

Brodsky, S. (2000). Guest editorial: Judging the progress of psychology in corrections – The verdict is not good. *International Journal of Offender Therapy and Comparative Criminology, 44,* 141–145.

Byrne, J. M. & Kelly, L. M. (1989). *Restructuring probation as an intermediate sanction: An evaluation of the implementation and impact of the Massachusetts Intensive Probation Supervision Program.* Final report to the National Institute of Justice (85-IJ-CX-0036). Washington, DC.

Cabana, M. D., Rand, C. S., Powe, N. R., Wu, A. W., Wilson, M. H., Abboud, P. A. C., et al. (1999). Why don't physicians follow clinical practice guidelines? *Journal of the American Medical Association, 282,* 1458–1465.

Cadigan, T. P. & Pelissier, B. (2003). Moving towards a federal criminal justice "system". *Federal Probation, 67,* 61–63.

Cann, J., Falshaw, L., Nugent, F. & Friendship, C. (2003). *Understanding what works: Accredited cognitive skills programmes for adult men and young offenders.* Home Office Research Findings No. 226. London: Home Office.

Carter, P. (2003, December). *Managing offenders, reducing crime: A new approach.* London, UK: Cabinet Office.

Clark, D. (2000). *Theory manual for Enhanced Thinking Skills.* Prepared for Joint Accreditation Panel, UK.

Clarke, A., Simmonds, R. & Wydall, S. (2004). *Delivering cognitive skills programmes in prison: A qualitative study.* Home Office Research Findings No. 242. London: Home Office.

Cochran, D. (1992). The long road from policy development to real change in sanctioning practice. In J. M. Byrne, A. J. Lurigio & J. Petersilia (Eds), *Smart sentencing: The emergence of intermediate sanctions* (pp. 307–318). Newbury Park, CA: Sage Publications.

Cohen, M. A. (2001). To treat or not to treat? A financial perspective. In C. Hollin (Ed.), *Handbook of offender assessment and treatment* (pp. 35–49). Chichester: John Wiley & Sons.

Concilio, A. (2003). Correctional program and site accreditation in Canada. *Forum on Correctional Research, 15,* 32–35.

Cooke, D. J. & Philip, L. (2001). To treat or not to treat? An empirical perspective. In C. Hollin (Ed.), *Handbook of offender assessment and treatment* (pp. 17–34). Chichester: John Wiley & Sons.

Correctional Services Accreditation Panel. (2004, April). *The Correctional Services Accreditation Panel report: 2003–2004.* London: Prison and Probation Services.

Corrigan, P. W., Steiner, L., McCracken, S. G., Blaser, B. & Barr, M. (2001). Strategies for disseminating evidence-based practices to staff who treat people with serious mental illness. *Psychiatric Services, 52,* 1598–1606.

Cullen, F. T. (2002). Rehabilitation and treatment programs. In J. Q. Wilson & J. Petersilia (Eds), *Crime: Public policies for crime control,* (pp. 253–289). Oakland, CA: ICS Press.

Cullen, F. T. (2004, November). *The twelve people who saved rehabilitation: How the science of criminology made a difference*. 2004 Presidential Address, American Society of Criminology.

Cullen, F. T., Blevins, K. R., Trager, J. S. & Gendreau, P. (2005). The rise and fall of boot camps: A case study in common-sense corrections. *Journal of Offender Rehabilitation, 40,* 53–70.

Cullen, F. T. & Gendreau, P. (1989). The effectiveness of correctional treatment: Reconsidering the "nothing works" debate. In L. Goodstein & D. L. MacKenzie (Eds), *The American prison: Issues in research and policy* (pp. 23–44). New York: Plenum.

Cullen, F. T. & Gendreau, P. (2000). Assessing correctional rehabilitation: Policy, practice, and prospects. In J. Horney (Ed.), *National Institute of Justice criminal justice 2000: Changes in decision making and discretion in the criminal justice system* (pp. 109–175). Washington, DC: Department of Justice, National Institute of Justice.

Cullen, F. T. & Gendreau, P. (2001). From nothing works to what works: Changing professional ideology in the 21st century. *The Prison Journal, 81,* 313–338.

Davidson, W., Gottschalk, R., Gensheimer, L. & Mayer, J. (1984). *Interventions with juvenile delinquents: A meta-analysis of treatment efficacy.* Washington, DC: National Institute of Juvenile Justice and Delinquency Prevention.

Davies, K., Lewis, J., Byatt, J., Purvis, E. & Cole, B. (2004). *An evaluation of the literacy demands of general offending behaviour programmes and their compatibility with the literacy skills of offenders.* Home Office Research Findings No. 233. London: Home Office.

Davis, G. et al. (1997). *Addressing the literacy needs of offenders under probation supervision.* Home Office Research Study No. 169. London: Home Office.

Debidin, M. & Lovbakke, J. (2004). Offending behaviour programmes in prison and probation. In G. Harper & C. Chitty (Eds), *The impact of corrections on re-offending: A review of "what works"* (pp. 31–54). Home Office Research Study No. 291. London: Home Office.

Dowden, C. & Andrews, D. A. (1999a). What works for female offenders: A meta-analytic review. *Crime and Delinquency, 45,* 438–452.

Dowden, C. & Andrews, D. A. (1999b). What works in young offender treatment: A meta-analysis. *Forum on Corrections Research, 11,* 21–24.

Dowden, C. & Andrews, D. A. (2000). Effective correctional treatment and violent reoffending: A meta-analysis. *Canadian Journal of Criminology, 42,* 449–467.

Dowden, C., Antonowicz, D. & Andrews, D. A. (2003). The effectiveness of relapse prevention with offenders: A meta-analysis. *International Journal of Offender Therapy and Comparative Criminology, 47,* 516–528.

Ellickson, P. & Petersilia, J. (1983). *Implementing new ideas in criminal justice* (R-2929-NIJ). Santa Monica, CA: RAND Corporation.

Ellis, T. & Winstone, J. (2002). The policy impact of a survey of programme evaluations in England and Wales. In J. McGuire (Ed.), *Offender rehabilitation and treatment: Effective programmes and policies to reduce re-offending* (pp. 333–357). Chichester: John Wiley & Sons.

Emery, R. E. & Marholin, D. (1977). An applied behavior analysis of delinquency: The irrelevancy of relevant behavior. *American Psychologist, 32,* 860–873.

Falshaw, L., Friendship, C., Travers, R. & Nugent, F. (2004). Searching for "What Works": HM Prison Service accredited cognitive skills programmes. *The British Journal of Forensic Practice, 6,* 3–13.

Farabee, D., Prendergast, M., Cartier, J., Wexler, H., Knight, K. & Anglin, M. D. (1999). Barriers to implementing effective correctional drug treatment programs. *The Prison Journal, 79,* 150–162.

Farrington, D. P., Petrosino, A. & Welsh, B. C. (2001). Systematic reviews and cost-benefit analyses of correctional interventions. *Prison Journal, 81,* 339–359.

Ferguson, J. L. (2002). Putting the "What Works" research into practice: An organizational perspective. *Criminal Justice and Behavior, 29,* 472–492.

Fishbein, M. (1995). Developing effective behavior change interventions: Some lessons learned from behavioral research. In T. E. Backer, S. L. David & G. Saucy (Eds), *Reviewing the behavioral science knowledge base on technology transfer NIDA Monograph 155* (pp. 246–261). Washington, DC: US Department of Health and Human Services.

French. S. A. & Gendreau, P. (2006). Reducing prison misconducts: What works! *Criminal Justice and Behavior, 33*, 185–218.

Friendship, C., Blud, L., Erikson, M., Travers, R. & Thornton, D. (2003a). Cognitive-behavioural treatment for imprisoned offenders: An evaluation of HM Prison Service's cognitive skills programmes. *Legal and Criminological Psychology, 8*, 103–114.

Friendship, C., Falshaw, L. & Beech, A. R. (2003b). Measuring the real impact of accredited offending behaviour programmes. *Legal and Criminological Psychology, 8*, 115–127.

Friendship, C., Thornton, D., Erikson, M. & Beech, A. (2001). Reconviction: A critique and comparison of two main data sources in England and Wales. *Legal and Criminological Psychology, 6*, 121–129.

Garrett, C. J. (1985). Effects of residential treatment on adjudicated delinquents: A meta-analysis. *Journal of Research in Crime and Delinquency, 22*, 287–308.

Gendreau, P. (1996a). The principles of effective intervention with offenders. In A. Harland (Ed.), *Choosing correctional options that work* (pp. 117–130). Thousand Oaks, CA: Sage Publications.

Gendreau, P. (1996b). Offender rehabilitation: What we know and what needs to be done. *Criminal Justice and Behavior, 23*, 144–161.

Gendreau, P. & Andrews, D. A. (1979). Psychological consultation in correctional agencies: Case studies and general issues. In J. J. Platt & R. J. Wicks (Eds), *The psychological consultant* (pp. 177–212). New York: Grune and Stratton.

Gendreau, P. & Andrews, D. A. (1990). Tertiary prevention: What the meta-analyses of the offender treatment literature tells us about "what works". *Canadian Journal of Criminology, 32*, 173–184.

Gendreau, P. & Andrews, D. A. (2001). *Correctional Program Assessment Inventory – 2000 (CPAI-2000)*. Saint John, New Brunswick, Canada: University of New Brunswick.

Gendreau, P., Cullen, F.T. & Bonta, J. (1994). Intensive rehabilitation supervision: The next generation in community corrections? *Federal Probation, 58*, 72–78.

Gendreau, P., French, S. A. & Gionet, A. (2004). What works (what doesn't work): The principles of effective correctional treatment. *Journal of Community Corrections, 13*, 4–6, 27–30.

Gendreau, P. & Goggin, C. (1996). Principles of effective correctional programming. *Forum on Corrections Research, 8*, 38–41.

Gendreau, P., Goggin, C. & Cullen, F. T. (1999). *The effects of prison sentences on recidivism* (Research Report No. J42-87/1999E). Ottawa, Ontario: Corrections Research and Development and Aboriginal Policy Branch, Solicitor General of Canada.

Gendreau, P., Goggin, C., Cullen, F. & Paparozzi, M. (2002). The common sense revolution and correctional policy. In J. McGuire (Ed.), *Offender rehabilitation and treatment: Effective programmes and policies to reduce reoffending* (pp. 359–386). Chichester: John Wiley & Sons.

Gendreau, P., Goggin, C., French, S. & Smith, P. (2006). Practicing psychology in correctional settings. In A. K. Hess & I. B. Weiner, (Eds), *The handbook of forensic psychology (3rd edition)* (pp. 722–750). Chichester: John Wiley & Sons.

Gendreau, P., Goggin, C. & Fulton, B. (2001a). Intensive supervision in probation and parole settings. In C. R. Hollin (Ed.), *Handbook of offender assessment and treatment* (pp. 195–204). Chichester: John Wiley & Sons.

Gendreau, P., Goggin, C. & Law, M. A. (1997). Predicting prison misconducts. *Criminal Justice and Behavior, 24*, 414–431.

Gendreau, P., Goggin, C. & Smith, P. (1999). The forgotten issue in effective correctional treatment: Program implementation. *International Journal of Offender Therapy and Comparative Criminology, 43*, 180–187.

Gendreau, P., Goggin, C. & Smith, P. (2000). Generating rational correctional policies: An introduction to advances in cumulating knowledge. *Corrections Management Quarterly, 4*, 52–60.

Gendreau, P., Goggin, C. & Smith, P. (2001b). Implementation guidelines for correctional programs in the "real world." In G. A. Bernfeld, D. P. Farrington & A. W. Leschied (Eds), *Offender rehabilitation in practice* (pp. 247–268). Chichester: John Wiley & Sons.

Gendreau, P., Goggin, C. & Smith, P. (2002). Is the PCL-R really the "unparalleled" measure of offender risk? *Criminal Justice and Behavior, 29*, 397–426.

Gendreau, P. & Keyes, D. (2001). Making prisons safer and more humane environments. *Canadian Journal of Criminology, 43*, 123–130.

Gendreau, P., Little, T. & Goggin, C. (1996). A meta-analysis of the predictors of adult offender recidivism: What works! *Criminology, 34*, 575–607.

Gendreau, P. & Ross, R. R. (1979). Effective correctional treatment: Bibliotherapy for cynics. *Crime and Delinquency, 25*, 463–489.

Gendreau, P. & Ross, R. R. (1981a). Correctional potency: Treatment and deterrence on trial. In R. Roesch & R. Corrado (Eds), *Evaluation and criminal justice policy* (pp. 29–57). Beverly Hills, CA: Sage.

Gendreau, P. & Ross, R. R. (1981b). Offender rehabilitation: The appeal of success. *Federal Probation, 45*, 45–48.

Gendreau, P. & Ross, R. R. (1983–84). Correctional treatment: Some recommendations for successful intervention. *Juvenile and Family Court, 34*, 31–40.

Gendreau, P. & Ross, R. R. (1987). Revivification of rehabilitation: Evidence from the 1980s. *Justice Quarterly, 4*, 349–408.

Gendreau, P. & Smith, P. (2005). Effective correctional treatment: Contributions from theory, common sense and meta-analysis. In F. T. Cullen, J. P. Wright & K. R. Blevins (Eds), *Taking stock: The status of criminological theory* (pp. 419–446). Piscataway, NJ: Transaction Press.

Gendreau, P., Smith, P. & Goggin, C. (2001c). Treatment programs in corrections. In J. Winterdyk (Ed.), *Corrections in Canada: Social reaction to crime* (pp. 238–263). Scarborough, Ontario: Prentice-Hall.

Glass, G., McGaw, B. & Smith, M. L. (1981). *Meta-analysis in social research*. Beverly Hills, CA: Sage.

Hamm, M. S. & Schrink, J. L. (1989). The conditions of effective implementation: A guide to accomplishing rehabilitative objectives in corrections. *Criminal Justice and Behavior, 16*, 166–182.

Harris, P. & Smith, S. (1996). Developing community corrections: An implementation perspective. In A. T. Harland (Ed.), *Choosing correctional options that work* (pp. 183–222). Thousand Oaks, CA: Sage Publications.

Herie, M. & Martin, G. W. (2002). Knowledge diffusion in social work: A new approach to bridging the gap. *Social Work, 47*, 85–95.

Hill, G. (1985). Predicting recidivism using institutional measures. In D. P. Farrington & R. Tarling (Eds), *Prediction in criminology* (pp. 96–118). Albany, NY: State University of New York Press.

HM Inspectorate of Probation (2002). *Annual report 2001/2002*. London: Home Office.

HM Inspectorate of Probation (2003). *Annual report 2002/2003*. London: Home Office.

HM Inspectorate of Probation (2004). *Annual report 2003/2004*. London: Home Office.

HM Prison Service (2004). *HM Prison Service (public sector prisons): Annual report and accounts 2003/2004*. London: HM Prison Service.

Hollin, C. R. (1995). The meaning and implications of "programme integrity". In J. McGuire (Ed.), *What works in reducing reoffending: Guidelines from research and practice* (pp. 195–208). Chichester: John Wiley & Sons.

Hollin, C. R. (1999). Treatment programs for offenders: Meta-analysis, "What Works", and beyond. *International Journal of Law and Psychiatry, 22*, 361–372.

Hollin, C. R. et al. (2004). *Pathfinder programmes in the Probation Service: A retrospective analysis*. Home Office Online Report 66/04. London: Home Office.

Hollin, C. R., McGuire, J., Palmer, E. J., Bilby, C., Hatcher, R. & Holmes, A. (2002). *Introducing Pathfinder programmes into the Probation Service: An interim report*. Home Office Research Study No. 247. London: Home Office.

Homel, P., Nutley, S., Webb, B. & Tilley, N. (2004). *Investing to deliver: Reviewing the implementation of the UK Crime Reduction Programme*. Home Office Research Study No. 281. London: Home Office.

Hunt, M. (1997). *How science takes stock: The story of meta-analysis*. New York: Russell Sage Foundation.

Hunt, M. (1999). *The new know-nothings: The political foes of the scientific study of human nature.* London: Transaction Publishers.

Joint Prison/Probation Accreditation Panel (2001, April). *What works 2000–2001.* London: Prison and Probation Services.

Joint Prison/Probation Accreditation Panel (2002, April). *What works 2001–2002.* London: Prison and Probation Services.

Kassebaum, G., Ward, D. A. & Wilner, D. M. (1971). *Prison treatment and parole survival: An empirical assessment.* New York: John Wiley.

Knott, C. (1995). The STOP programme: Reasoning and rehabilitation in a British setting. In J. McGuire (Ed.), *What Works: Reducing Reoffending – Guidelines from Research and Practice* (pp. 115–126). Chichester: John Wiley & Sons.

Latessa, E. J., Cullen, F. T. & Gendreau, P. (2002). Beyond correctional quackery – Professionalism and the possibility of effective treatment. *Federal Probation, 66,* 43–49.

Latessa, E. & Holsinger, A. (1998). Importance of evaluating correctional programs: Assessing outcome and quality. *Corrections Management Quarterly, 2,* 22–29.

Leschied, A. W. (2001). Implementation of effective correctional programs. In L. L. Motiuk & R. C. Serin (Eds), *Compendium 2000 on effective correctional programming* (pp. 41–46). Ottawa, Ontario: Correctional Service of Canada.

Lester, D. & Van Voorhis, P. (1997). Cognitive therapies. In P. Van Voorhis, M. Braswell & D. Lester (Eds), *Correctional counseling and rehabilitation (3rd edition)* (pp. 109–125). Cincinnati, OH: Anderson Publishing.

Lipsey, M. (1989). *The efficacy of intervention for juvenile delinquency.* Paper presented at the American Society of Criminology annual meeting, Reno, NV.

Lipsey, M. W. (1992). Juvenile delinquency treatment: A meta-analytic inquiry into the variability of effects. In T. D. Cook, H. Cooper, D. S. Cordray, H. Hartmann, L. V. Hedges, R. J. Light, et al. (Eds), *Meta-analysis for explanation: A casebook* (pp. 83–127). New York: Russell Sage.

Lipsey, M. W. (1995). What do we learn from 400 research studies on the effectiveness of treatment with juvenile delinquents? In J. McGuire (Ed.), *What works: Reducing reoffending – Guidelines from research and practice* (pp. 63–78). Chichester: John Wiley & Sons.

Lipsey, M. W. (1999). Can rehabilitative programs reduce the recidivism of juvenile offenders? An inquiry into the effectiveness of practical programs. *Virginia Journal of Social Policy and Law, 6,* 611–641.

Lipsey, M. W., Chapman, G. L. & Landenberger, N. A. (2001). Cognitive-behavioral programs for offenders. *The Annals of the American Academy of Political and Social Science, 578,* 144–157.

Lipsey, M. W. & Wilson, D. B. (1998). Effective intervention for serious juvenile offenders. In R. Loeber & D. P. Farrington (Eds), *Serious and violent juvenile offenders: Risk factors and successful interventions* (pp. 313–345). Thousand Oaks: Sage Publications Inc.

Lipton, D., Martinson, R. & Wilks, J. (1975). *The effectiveness of correctional treatment: A survey of treatment evaluation studies.* New York: Praeger.

Lipton, D. S., Thornton, D., McGuire, J., Porporino, F. J. & Hollin, C. R. (2000). Program accreditation and correctional treatment. *Substance Use and Misuse, 35,* 1705–1734.

Logan, C. H., Gaes, G. G., Harer, M., Innes, C. A., Karacki, L. & Saylor, W. G. (1991). *Can meta-analysis save correctional rehabilitation?* Washington, DC: Department of Justice, Federal Bureau of Prisons.

Lösel, F. (1995). The efficacy of correctional treatment: A review and synthesis of meta-evaluations. In J. McGuire (Ed.), *What works: Reducing reoffending – Guidelines from research and practice* (pp. 79–111). Chichester: John Wiley & Sons.

Lösel, F. (2001). Evaluating the effectiveness of correctional programs: Bridging the gap between research and practice. In G. A. Bernfeld, D. P. Farrington & A. W. Leschied (Eds), *Offender rehabilitation in practice* (pp. 67–92). Chichester: John Wiley & Sons.

Lovell, D. & Jemelka, R. (1996). When inmates misbehave: The costs of discipline. *Prison Journal, 76,* 165–179.

Lowenkamp, C. (2003). *Predicting outcome with the Level of Service Inventory – Revised: The importance of quality assurance.* Unpublished manuscript.

Lowenkamp, C. (2004). *A program level analysis of the relationship between correctional program integrity and treatment effectiveness.* Unpublished doctoral dissertation, University of Cincinnati, Ohio.

Maguire, M. (2004). The Crime Reduction Programme in England and Wales. *Criminal Justice, 4,* 213–237.

Martin, D. J., Garske, J. P. & Davis, M. K. (2000). Relation of the therapeutic alliance with outcome and other variables: A meta-analytic review. *Journal of Consulting and Clinical Psychology, 68,* 438–450.

Martinson, R. (1974). What works? Questions and answers about prison reform. *The Public Interest, 35,* 22–54.

Masters, J. C., Burish, T. G., Hollon, S. D. & Rimm, D. C. (1987). *Behavior therapy: Techniques and empirical findings.* San Diego, CA: Harcourt Brace Jovanovich, Inc.

Matthews, B., Hubbard, D. J. & Latessa, E. (2001). Making the next step: Using evaluability assessment to improve correctional programming. *The Prison Journal, 81,* 454–472.

McGuire, J. (Ed.) (1995). *What works in reducing reoffending: Guidelines from research and practice.* Chichester: John Wiley and Sons.

McGuire, J. (2001). What works in correctional intervention? Evidence and practical implications. In G. A. Bernfeld, D. P. Farrington & A. W. Leschied (Eds), *Offender rehabilitation in practice: Implementing and evaluating effective programs* (pp. 25–43). Chichester: John Wiley & Sons.

McGuire, J. (2002). *Evidence-based programming today.* Draft paper for the International Community Corrections Association (ICCA) Annual Conference 2002, Boston, MA.

McGuire, J. (2004). *Understanding psychology and crime: Perspectives on theory and action.* Berkshire: Open University Press.

McGuire, J. & Priestley, P. (1995). Reviewing what works: Past, present and future. In J. McGuire (Ed.), *What works: Reducing reoffending – Guidelines from research and practice* (pp. 3–34). Chichester: John Wiley & Sons.

Melnick, G., Hawke, J. & Wexler, H. K. (2004). Client perceptions of prison-based therapeutic community drug treatment programs. *The Prison Journal, 84,* 121–138.

Melnick, G. & Pearson, F. (2000). *A Multimodality Quality Assurance instrument.* New York: National Development and Research Institutes, Inc.

Merrington, S. & Stanley, S. (2004). "What Works?": Revisiting the evidence in England and Wales. *Probation Journal: The Journal of Community and Criminal Justice, 51,* 7–20.

Mihalic, S., Irwin, K., Elliott, D., Fagan, A. & Hansen, D. (2001, July). *Blueprints for Violence Prevention.* Washington, DC: US Department of Justice, Office of Justice Programs.

Mihalic, S., Irwin, K., Fagan, A., Ballard, D. & Elliott, D. (2004, July). *Successful program implementation: Lessons from Blueprints.* Washington, DC: US Department of Justice, Office of Justice Programs.

Miller, J. (1986). Sentencing: What lies between sentiment and ignorance. *Justice Quarterly, 3,* 231–239.

Morgan, R. D. & Flora, D. B. (2002). Group psychotherapy with incarcerated offenders: A research synthesis. *Group Dynamics, 6,* 203–218.

National Institute of Corrections (2004). *Implementing effective correctional management of offenders in the community: An integrated model.* Washington, DC: National Institute of Corrections.

National Probation Service for England and Wales (2004). *Annual report 2003/2004.* London: National Probation Directorate.

Nesovic, A. (2003). Psychometric evaluation of the Correctional Program Assessment Inventory. *Dissertation Abstracts International, 64* (09), 4674B. (UMI No. AAT NQ83525).

Palmer, T. (1975). Martinson revisited. *Journal of Research in Crime and Delinquency, 12,* 133–152.

Palmer, T. (1992). *The re-emergence of correctional interventions.* Newbury Park, CA: Sage.

Palmer, T. (1994). *Profile of correctional effectiveness and new directions for research.* Albany, NY: State University of New York Press.

Palmer, T. (1995). Programmatic and non-programmatic aspects of successful intervention: New directions for research. *Crime and Delinquency, 41*, 100–131.

Petersilia, J. (1990). Conditions that permit intensive supervision programs to survive. *Crime and Delinquency, 36*, 126–145.

Porporino, F. J. (1997). *Developing program accreditation criteria for the Correctional Service of Canada: Issues and a suggested approach.* Toronto, Ontario: T3 Associates.

Porporino, F. J. & Fabiano, E. A. (2000). *Theory manual for Reasoning and Rehabilitation* (Rev.). Ottawa, Ontario: T3 Associates.

Porporino, F. J. & Robinson, D. (1995). An evaluation of the reasoning and rehabilitation program with Canadian federal offenders. In R. R. Ross & R. D. Ross (Eds), *Thinking Straight: The Reasoning and Rehabilitation program for delinquency prevention and offender rehabilitation* (pp. 155–191). Ottawa, Ontario: Air Training & Publications.

Prendergast, M. L., Podus, D. & Chang, E. (2000). Program factors and treatment outcomes in drug dependence treatment: An examination using meta-analysis. *Substance Use and Misuse, 35*, 1931–1965.

Prime, J. (2002, October). *Progress made against Home Office Public Service Agreement target 10.* Home Office Online Report 16/02. London: Home Office.

Prison Service Order 4360 (2004, June 25). London: HM Prison Service (http://www. hmprisonservice.gov.uk/resourcecentre/psispsos/listpsos/).

Quay, H. C. (1977). The three faces of evaluation: What can be expected to work. *Criminal Justice and Behaviour, 4*, 21–25.

Raynor, P. (2003). Evidence-based probation and its critics. *Probation Journal: The Journal of Community and Criminal Justice, 50*, 334–345.

Raynor, P. (2004). The Probation Service "Pathfinders": Finding the path and losing the way? *Criminal Justice, 4*, 309–325.

Raynor, P. & Vanstone, M. (2001). "Straight Thinking on Probation": Evidence-based practice and the culture of curiosity. In G. A. Bernfeld, D. P. Farrington & A. W. Leschied (Eds), *Offender rehabilitation in practice: Implementing and evaluating effective programs* (pp. 189–203). Chichester: John Wiley & Sons.

Redondo, S., Sanchez-Meca, J. & Garrido, V. (1999). The influence of treatment programmes on the recidivism of juvenile and adult offenders: A European meta-analytic review. *Psychology, Crime and Law, 5*, 251–278.

Rex, S. et al. (2002). *Crime reduction programme: An evaluation of community service Pathfinder projects – Final report.* RDS Occasional Paper No. 87. Cambridge: The Institute of Criminology, University of Cambridge.

Rex, S., Gelsthorpe, L., Roberts, C. & Jordan, P. (2004). *What's promising in community service: Implementation of seven Pathfinder projects.* Home Office Research Findings No. 231. London: Home Office.

Rex, S., Lieb, R., Bottoms, A. & Wilson, L. (2003). *Accrediting offender programmes: A process-based evaluation of the Joint Prison/Probation Services Accreditation Panel.* Home Office Research Study No. 273. London: Home Office.

Rezmovic, E. L. (1979). Methodological considerations in evaluating correctional effectiveness: Issues and chronic problems. In L. Sechrest, S. O. White & E. D. Brown (Eds), *The rehabilitation of criminal offenders: Problems and prospects* (pp. 163–209). Washington, DC: National Academy of Science, Panel on Research on Rehabilitative Techniques.

Rosenthal, R. (1991). *Meta-analytic procedures for social research.* Beverly Hills, CA: Sage.

Rosnow, R. L. & Rosenthal, R. (1999). *Beginning behavioral research: A conceptual primer (3rd edition).* Upper Saddle River, NJ: Prentice Hall.

Ross, R. R. & Fabiano, E. A. (1985). *Time to think: A cognitive model of delinquency prevention and offender rehabilitation.* Johnson City, TN: Institute of Social Science and Arts.

Ross, R. R., Fabiano, E. A. & Ewles, C. D. (1988). Reasoning and rehabilitation. *International Journal of Offender Therapy and Comparative Criminology, 32*, 29–35.

Ross, R. R. & Gendreau, P. (1980). *Effective correctional treatment.* Toronto, Ontario: Butterworths.

Ross, R. R. & McKay, B. (1978). Treatment in corrections: Requiem for a panacea. *Canadian Journal of Criminology, 20,* 279–295.

Rowland, C. (2000). Discovering the new world of accreditation standards. *Corrections Today, 62,* 76–80.

Salend, S. J. (1984). Therapy outcome research: Threats to treatment integrity. *Behavior Modification, 8,* 211–222.

Scheirer, M. A. & Rezmovic, E. L. (1983). Measuring the degree of program implementation: A methodological review. *Evaluation Review, 7,* 599–633.

Sechrest, L., White, S. O. & Brown, E. D. (1979). *The rehabilitation of criminal offenders: Problems and prospects.* Washington, DC: National Academy of Science, Panel on Research on Rehabilitative Techniques.

Simpson, D. D. (2002). A conceptual framework for transferring research into practice. *Journal of Substance Abuse Treatment, 22,* 171–182.

Slavin, R. E. (2002). Evidence-based education policies: Transforming educational practice and research. *Educational Researcher, 37,* 15–21.

Smith, P., Goggin, C. & Gendreau, P. (2002). The effects of prison sentences and intermediate sanctions on recidivism: General effects and individual differences. *A Report to the Corrections Research Branch.* Ottawa, Ontario: Solicitor General of Canada.

Spiegler, M. D. & Guevremont, D. C. (1998). *Contemporary behavior therapy (3rd edition).* Pacific Grove, CA: Brooks/Cole.

Stewart, L. & Millson, W. A. (1995). Offender motivation for treatment as a responsivity factor. *Forum on Corrections Research, 7,* 5–7.

Stewart-Ong, G., Harsent, L., Roberts, C., Burnett, R. & Al-Attar, Z. (2004, June). *Think First prospective research study: Effectiveness and reducing attrition.* London: National Probation Service.

Taylor, R. (1999). *Predicting reconvictions for sexual and violent offences using the revised Offender Group Reconviction Scale.* Home Office Research Findings No. 104. London: Home Office.

Thornton, D. (1998/9). *Criteria for accrediting programmes.* London: HM Prison Service, Offending Behaviour Programmes Unit.

Torrey, W. C. et al. (2001). Implementing evidence-based practices for persons with severe mental illnesses. *Psychiatric Services, 52,* 45–50.

Underdown, A. (1998). *Strategies for effective offender supervision: Report of the HMIP What Works project.* London: HM Inspectorate of Probation.

Van Voorhis, P., Cullen, F. T. & Applegate, B. (1995). Evaluating interventions with violent offenders: A guide for practitioners and policymakers. *Federal Probation, 59,* 17–28.

Van Voorhis, P., Spruance, L. M., Ritchey, P. N., Listwan, S. J. & Seabrook, R. (2004). The Georgia cognitive skills program: A replication of reasoning and rehabilitation. *Criminal Justice and Behavior, 31,* 282–305.

Walker, N., Farrington, D. P. & Tucker, G. (1981). Reconviction rates of adult males after different sentences. *British Journal of Criminology, 21,* 357–360.

Webster, R., Hedderman, C., Turnbull, P. J. & May, T. (2001, September). *Building bridges to employment for prisoners.* Home Office Research Study No. 226. London: Home Office.

White, T. F. (2004, February). *A framework for implementing evidence-based practice in probation and parole.* Hartford, CT: Court Support Services Division, Judicial Branch, State of Connecticut.

Whitehead, J. T. & Lab, S. P. (1989). A meta-analysis of juvenile correctional treatment. *Journal of Research in Crime and Delinquency, 26,* 276–295.

Williams, W. (1976). Implementation analysis and assessment. In W. Williams & R. Elmore (Eds), *Social program implementation* (pp. 267–292). New York: Academic Press.

Wilson, S., Attrill, G. & Nugent, F. (2003). Effective interventions for acquisitive offenders: An investigation of cognitive skills programmes. *Legal and Criminological Psychology, 8,* 83–101.

Wilson, S. J., Lipsey, M. W. & Soydan, H. (2003). Are mainstream programs for juvenile delinquency less effective with minority youth than majority youth? A meta-analysis of outcomes research. *Research on Social Work Practice, 13,* 3–26.

Wozniak, E. (2001). Programme accreditation: Perceptions and realities. *International Community Corrections Journal, July*, 7–11.

Wrench, P. (2004, May 5). Justice 1 Committee: HM Prison Service memorandum to the Home Affairs Committee Inquiry into the rehabilitation of prisoners. http://www.scottish.parliament.uk/business/committees/justice1/currentInquiries.htm. (October 29, 2004).

Yeaton, W. H. & Sechrest, L. (1981). Critical dimensions in the choice and maintenance of successful treatments: Strength, integrity, and effectiveness. *Journal of Consulting and Clinical Psychology, 49*, 156–167.

Youngken, M. (2000). The Commission on Accreditation for Corrections: Raising the bar of excellence. *Corrections Today, 62*, 98–101.

Chapter 8

OFFENDING BEHAVIOUR PROGRAMMES: CONTROVERSIES AND RESOLUTIONS

CLIVE R. HOLLIN AND EMMA J. PALMER

University of Leicester

This closing chapter seeks to draw together the key points that we perceive to have emerged in the preceding chapters. The points that we have gathered are presented under three main headings – "programme delivery", "programme evaluation", and "is there a future for offending behaviour programmes?" – within which cluster various areas of debate. These areas of debate arise because of the difficulties and controversies they pose, at several levels, for all those concerned with the delivery, evaluation, and development of offending behaviour programmes.

PROGRAMME DELIVERY

Are Groups the Optimum Means of Programme Delivery?

Controversies

The first issue here relates to the relative advantages and disadvantages of delivering programmes either in groups or on an individual basis. As outlined in Chapter 2, there are a number of advantages to treating offenders in groups with respect to efficiency. Delivering interventions via groupwork is likely to be more financially cost-effective in terms of use of staff, resources, and time. Use of manualised groupwork programmes can also allow for a wide variety of staff to be trained to deliver interventions, including prison and probation officers as well as psychologists. Along with the economic advantages to group delivery of programmes, there are a number of clinical advantages to group delivery. As was noted in Chapter 5, the dynamics of groupwork can lead offenders to challenge distorted beliefs of other group members, as well as providing support to each other (Jennings & Sawyer, 2003; Rutan & Stone, 1993; Yalom, 1995). Group delivery can also help to ensure uniformity of treatment across offenders, something that is also useful when evaluating the effectiveness of an intervention. Furthermore, uniformity of delivery may contribute to the maintenance of therapeutic integrity.

There are advantages to the groupwork mode of delivery but this approach does have some disadvantages. As discussed in Chapter 2, manualised group programmes are often criticised on the grounds that, for example, they compromise clinical artistry, and they are not tailored to offender's individual needs. This assessment issue relates not only to criminogenic needs but also to responsivity issues, as discussed in more detail later in this chapter. Therefore, even if a programme's content is appropriate for all of the group members, differences in learning styles or literacy levels may compromise its effect. Finally, problems can occur in groups that relate to the offenders' own behaviours. Within group sessions there is potential for offenders to collude with each other to maintain problematic thinking and beliefs, some offenders may be disruptive, and others not suitable for groupwork for reasons such as chronic mental health problems.

The delivery of programmes in groups can also prove problematic due to organisational difficulties. The need to have an adequate number of offenders in a group can lead to time lags between referral and commencement of treatment, which may be damaging to an offender's willingness to participate. Managing groups of offenders can also present difficulties and requires staff delivering programmes to have groupwork skills to ensure the smooth running of sessions. Finally, groupwork can sometimes raise problems of confidentiality as offenders may feel unable openly to discuss issues in the presence of other offenders for fear of ridicule or recrimination (Abracen & Looman, 2004).

A further issue that has arisen with groupwork programmes is that levels of completion of programmes are not always high, with particularly poor performance among sexual offenders (see, for example, Abel, Mittelman, Becker, Rathner & Rouleau, 1988; Browne, Foreman & Middleton, 1998; Marques, Day, Nelson & West, 1994), violent offenders (see, for example, Dalton, Major & Sharkey, 1998; Hird, Williams & Markham, 1997), and domestic violence offenders (Gondolf & Foster, 1991).

The large-scale implementation of offending behaviour programmes in the English and Welsh Probation Service provides a further example of this phenomenon, with non-start rates of almost 50 % of all offenders allocated to programmes (Hollin et al., 2005). Further, Hollin et al. reported that, of those offenders who did start a programme, 44.0 % dropped out without completing. Similar problems have been experienced by other initiatives within the Probation Service, with the basic skills Pathfinders having high levels of attrition at all stages of screening, assessment, referral, and treatment (McMahon, Hall, Hayward, Hudson & Roberts, 2004). As discussed in Chapter 2, it is becoming clear that for an offender to start a programme but to fail to complete may be disadvantageous with respect to recidivism (Cann, Falshaw, Nugent & Friendship, 2003; Hanson et al., 2002; Hollin et al., 2004, 2005; Robinson, 1995).

The scale of non-completion is increasingly being recognised but less is known about which offenders are more likely to not complete treatment, and reasons why this occurs. Studies that have examined the offender characteristics of non-completers have found a number of variables that are also associated with an increased risk of recidivism (for example, Van Voorhis, Spruance, Ritchey, Listwan & Seabrook, 2004).

Wormith & Olver (2002) also considered the role of treatment process variables in attrition from programmes. They distinguished those offenders who elected to withdraw from treatment from those expelled from treatment, reporting few differences in terms of offender characteristics. McMurran & McCulloch (in press) conducted interviews with prisoners who did not complete a programme (ETS) and, like Wormith and Olver, found a number of reasons for non-completion: some prisoners were expelled from the group; some left due to health problems; some chose to leave. Other non-completers stated that they did not like the group format and would prefer one-to-one work. In a qualitative study examining the delivery of cognitive skills programmes in prisons, Clarke, Simmonds & Wydall (2004) commented that organisational factors, such as a long delay before starting the programme and the link between programme completion and parole, could impact on a prisoner's willingness to enter and complete a programme. In a probation-based study Briggs & Turner (2003) looked at why offenders with an order to attend an accredited programme failed to start their programme. Briggs and Turner reported three reasons why those offenders who were referred to a programme failed to start: first, no group was available; second, the offender was breached; and third, a cluster of "indeterminate" reasons such as travel problems, health, missed communications, and so on.

Thus, there are many reasons for programme non-completion, relating to offender characteristics and treatment process variables. Offenders may choose to dropout of a programme, or they may be removed from programmes for reasons such as being disruptive in group sessions. Alternatively, offenders can leave programmes due to administrative reasons that are unrelated to treatment participation, as with transfer to another institution.

Towards a Resolution

As discussed above, the format of programme delivery presents a dilemma: should the apparently cost-effective approach of groupwork be used or should an individualised approach that allows for a fine-grained analysis of offenders' behaviour and greater focus on their specific needs be favoured. It is not necessarily the case that group and one-to-one work are mutually exclusive and some programmes have attempted to combine the two approaches.

Jones & Hollin (2004) describe a pilot study of a 36-session anger management programme for personality disordered forensic patients in a high security setting, which involves both individual and group-based sessions. The programme delivers skills training in group sessions using a manualised format. There are also individual sessions with a mentor to allow for practice of skills and to help patients generalise these skills to everyday situations. Patients have the same mentor throughout the programme, with this person also taking responsibility for support and liaison with the clinical team outside of the sessions. Jones and Hollin reported full completion of the programme with the number of sessions attended ranging from 30 to 36, with an average of 33 sessions. Further, pre-post psychometric and behavioural ratings showed reductions in anger over the course of the programme.

On a larger scale, as discussed in Chapter 1, recent developments have seen the establishment of intervention programmes that engage a wider system, with a number of different agencies working together to contribute to the rehabilitation of offenders. Some of these programmes involve multi-agency work within one setting, such as the community, while others have been designed to be delivered "through the prison door" as with, for example, resettlement programmes for prisoners (see Lewis et al., 2003). An example of this approach is the STOP START programme developed by County Durham Probation Service for delivery to women prisoners serving short-term sentences (Hollin, 2002). This programme takes a systems approach, with an emphasis on case management, rather than following the format of a traditional programme. Thus, STOP START was designed in a modular format to be delivered across the prison walls into the community by prison and probation staff using community resources (for example, health and education services). In order to address the high level of multiple needs exhibited by women prisoners after release from custody (Maguire, Raynor, Vanstone & Kynch, 2000), each woman's progress through the modularised programme was determined by her assessed individual profile of needs.

This multi-agency approach to working is also seen in the citizenship education projects set up by the Department for Education and Skills (DfES) in schools and colleges. Originally incorporated into the school national curriculum, since 2001, citizenship education is also being implemented for young people age 16–19 years, with a number of projects being run by groups of education/training providers working in partnership with voluntary and community groups (DfES, 2000).

Turning to the problem of treatment completion, there are a number of strategies that can be employed to enhance the retention of offenders within programmes. A key issue is whether individual offenders wish to reduce or desist from their offending – whether they are ready to enter a programme and change their behaviour (Ward, Day, Howells & Birgden, 2004). Motivation to change is often highlighted as critical, and is commonly one of the criteria for selection into an intervention (McMurran, 2002). However, motivation is a complex concept and has traditionally been defined by therapists rather than from an offender's perspective (Miller, 1985). Thus, it is expected motivation to change is evinced by admitting the offence, showing regret, expressing a wish to stop offending, and asking for help. Although these sentiments might indicate a motivation to participate in a programme, there are questions as to whether they also represent motivation actually to engage in the programme and a real desire to change behaviour. These issues are important as participation in programmes is often linked to tangible benefits for the offender, for example, granting of parole, getting privileges in an institution, or being a condition of a community sentence order.

More recently, attention has turned to other factors that are involved in engagement in treatment, leading to the notion of "readiness to change" (Serin, 1998; Serin & Kennedy, 1997). The concept of readiness to change includes motivation to change *plus* the individual and situational factors (including therapeutic situation) that can impact on treatment engagement (Howells & Day, 2002). As Ward et al. (2004, p. 6) note, it means the person is motivated (i.e., wants to, has the will to), is able to respond to appropriately (i.e., perceives he or she can), finds it relevant and meaningful (i.e., can engage), and has the capacities (i.e., is able to) to successfully enter the treatment programme.

Ward et al. outline a number of personal characteristics that can impact on an offender's readiness to change, which they refer to as "internal readiness conditions". These internal conditions include cognitive, affective, volitional, behavioural, and identity variables.

Cognitive variables include attitudes to treatment and practitioners, and the offender's expectations of success. Affective/emotional variables include both the high level of generalised psychological distress that many offenders experience at the point of entry to the criminal justice system (especially for custodial sentences), and offence-related emotions (such as shame, guilt, remorse) that may impact on treatment readiness. The volitional factors are similar to the traditional concept of motivation to change, and include the offender's goals and wishes and their desire to change and engage in treatment. Participation in programmes requires behavioural skills and competencies, including interpersonal skills (for example, communication and conversation skills) and literacy and numeracy skills. Finally, personal and social identity variables relating to an individual's values, as well as contextual factors relating to their age, gender, ethnicity, and social class, can also impact on readiness to change.

There is, therefore, a need to ensure that assessments of readiness to change are incorporated into the selection of offenders into programmes. These assessments should include an appraisal of offenders' individual characteristics and their environmental situation. Furthermore, these factors should also be taken into consideration when designing the content of programmes.

Various strategies have been used to increase participation and engagement in treatment in clinical and offender treatment. Walitzer, Dermen & Connors (1999) present a review of preparatory techniques, used mostly in psychotherapy, including role induction interview, vicarious therapy pre-training, and cognitive-experiential preparatory exercises. These techniques aim to reduce attrition from treatment and increase the benefit of interventions by familiarising clients with the rationale for and the processes of treatment. The evidence shows these techniques to have some success, especially with respect to treatment attendance, and there is some evidence of positive impact on treatment process and outcome. It is thought that the techniques work through education of the client, with provision of information to increase positive outcome expectancy, and encourage realistic expectations of outcome.

A second set of techniques used to enhance retention and treatment engagement are motivational enhancement techniques, initially developed in psychotherapy to address problems of attrition and non-compliance (Garfield, 1994; Miller, 1985). The most well known of these techniques is motivational interviewing (MI), which is a "directive, client-centred counselling style for eliciting behavior change by helping clients to explore and resolve ambivalence" (Rollnick & Miller, 1995, p. 326). Rather than being a list of techniques, motivational interviewing is a set of principles for therapists to work within including expression of empathy throughout treatment; development of a discrepancy between the client's values and beliefs and the behaviour to be changed (for example, offending behaviour); avoiding arguments during therapy; using client resistance in a constructive way rather than confronting it head on; trying to get the client to make self-motivational statements; and emphasising choice (Miller & Rollnick (1991).

Although motivational interviewing was initially developed for interventions with problem drinking, it has been incorporated into offender treatment programmes, particularly with sexual offenders and domestic violence offenders (see, for example, Kear-Colwell & Pollack, 1997; Mann, Ginsburg & Weekes, 2002; Murphy & Baxter, 1997). It has been suggested that motivational interviewing may be useful at pre-treatment to enhance readiness to change and participation in treatment, and during programmes to maintain motivation and engagement (Mann et al., 2002). To date, there is little empirical evidence as to the utility of motivational interviewing with offender populations. Ginsburg (2000) reported one study that has examined this issue in an offender treatment programme addressing alcohol dependency. Offenders who had a motivational interview before treatment improved their problem recognition and contemplation skills as compared to a control group. However, this study did not explore the key issue of whether motivational interviewing helped to increase the offenders' motivation to change their offending behaviour.

Going to Scale

Controversies

A number of implementation issues have arisen in the drive to deliver offending behaviour programmes on a large scale, with a poor transferral of the "what works" research findings from the "research laboratory" to the "real world" of practice. These problems have led some commentators to ask whether it is possible to replicate the findings from small-scale evaluations on a larger scale. Lipsey (1999) makes the distinction between *demonstration* projects and *practical* interventions. Demonstration projects are small-scale pilots, which are often used as the source for research to be included in meta-analyses and systematic reviews. Practical interventions, in contrast, refer to the routine implementation of programmes.

Research comparing the results of these two types of interventions consistently shows that demonstration projects produce better results. Studies of offending behaviour programmes in the English and Welsh Prison Service have mirrored this pattern, with evaluations carried out pre-accreditation yielding more positive results than those conducted post-accreditation. These results have led Friendship, Blud, Erikson, Travers & Thornton (2003) to suggest that the scale of implementation might be one factor for the differences in these results. Friendship et al. propose that the small scale nature of early implementation in which participants and tutors were volunteers could have meant levels of motivation and enthusiasm were higher. They go on to suggest that the large-scale implementation of programmes post-accreditation could have led to the dilution of the positive effects found in the initial evaluations.

Within the Probation Service, the pace of implementation and the timetables for evaluation also often meant that data were collected prior to the projects running in their fully developed format. This situation was accompanied by problems with obtaining data, with the data-reporting tool not being ready when initially antic-ipated, data not being available at all or not being in the appropriate format, and a lack of cooperation by probation staff with researchers' requests (Hollin et al., 2005).

The decision to expand the use of programmes on a national scale in England and Wales, first within the Prison Service, then later in the Probation Service, raised several issues. As noted by Goggin and Gendreau in Chapter 7, it appears that the transfer of knowledge from the "what works" literature to the real world has been problematic (Leschied, 2001). The difficulties have been exacerbated by over-optimistic expectations given the limited time scale of the implementation process, increasing pressure on staff and leading to short cuts being taken. For example, the setting of unrealistic targets for the Probation Service relating to reduction of national reconviction rates at an early stage led to a rush for the national roll-out of programmes instead of a number of considered, small scale pilot projects. Meeting these targets has been hampered by what some commentators view as the impos-ition of tough enforcement policies, which have increased attrition problems. The fact that these policies have undoubtedly contributed to non-completion of pro-grammes raises questions about the utility and effectiveness of current approaches to enforcement (Ellis, 2000; Hedderman & Hearndon, 2001).

These issues have been especially problematic in the English and Welsh Proba-tion Service, where the large-scale organisational changes that the Probation Service has undergone in the past few years have clearly contributed to implementation problems (cf. Raynor, 2004). Among these problems is the creation of the National Probation Service, which has led to new arrangements for governance and man-agement, alongside an amalgamation of geographical areas. The accompanying complexities of these changes have led to a disruption in the implementation of the "what works" agenda. Furthermore, more reorganisation is now expected with the recent amalgamation of the Prison and Probation Services (Carter, 2003; Home Office, 2004) and the establishment of the National Offender Management System (NOMS). None of this enhances the likelihood that programmes will be resourced and managed effectively.

Some of the issues that have arisen in the implementation of the "what works" agenda can be attributed to the scale and pace of the implementation but other problems have been generated by organisational non-compliance. This organisa-tional resistance has been a particular issue within the Probation Service (cf. Raynor, 2004) where there has been resistance to programme implementation on a number of levels (Blumson, 2004; NAPO, 2001). Indeed, the pace and scale of the introduc-tion of programmes has led many practitioners to claim to feel deskilled (Rex, Lieb, Bottoms & Wilson, 2003) and alienated from the "what works" agenda. Further-more, a lack of resources on the ground has led to increases in workloads, result-ing in widespread dissatisfaction that included industrial action. As discussed in Chapter 7, these problems highlight the importance for effective implementation of educating staff about the latest developments in the field of corrections and their implications for effective practice.

Towards a Resolution

These implementation issues are reflected in a classic paper by Laws (1974), which documents the organisational barriers encountered in establishing an intervention for offenders within a residential setting. Laws describes clashes between administrators and clinicians over the ownership of the programme and resources for it, clashes with other professionals who did not agree with the programme and undermined its integrity, and disagreements over who was responsible for staff training. Thus, although the organisation had approved the introduction of the programme, there had not been sufficient preparation in setting up local systems to introduce and support the programme. This meant that the organisation was not robust enough to cope with the threats to the programme's integrity, leading ultimately to its collapse.

These issues highlight the importance of "organisational readiness" for programmes so that programmes are implemented correctly, to a high quality, and can provide more adequate examination of utility of intervention. The concept of readiness is complex and concerns abstract ideas such as "support" and "open decision-making". However, there has been an increasing awareness of the importance of management in the implementation of treatment (see, Hollin, Epps & Kendrick, 1995), with Bernfeld (2001) noting that "Administration [is] *integral* to effective treatment services." From this perspective, "there is no such thing as an administrative decision – every decision is a clinical decision" (Bernfeld, 2001, p. 183). These comments are supported by research that has examined the role of organisational factors in the delivery of services. The developers of multisystemic therapy (MST) have consistently included treatment integrity in their evaluations (Brown et al., 1997; Henggeler, Melton, Brondino, Scherer & Hanley, 1997; Henggeler, Pickrel & Brondino, 1999). This body of research has shown that the active support by administrators of MST therapists' work is crucial in terms of organisational policies, commitment of resources, and competitive salaries (Edwards, Schoenwald, Henggeler & Strother, 2001). It has also been noted by both Bouffard, Taxman & Silverman (2003) and Edwards et al. (2001) that therapists should not be overburdened with documentation and data collection.

With reference to the Aggression Replacement Training programme for violent young offenders (cf. Chapter 4), Goldstein & Glick (2001) outlined several broad management principles for its implementation. First, they emphasise the importance of managers respecting their own work and that of the people who deliver the programme. Second, there is the need for open and honest communication among the programme team, which includes the offenders participating in the programme. Third, there is the need to define clearly the roles and responsibilities to allow for accountability. Finally, Goldstein and Glick propose that joint ownership of the programme by all staff should be promoted through involving everyone in the planning of implementation and delivery. Bernfeld (2001) has highlighted similar issues as important in the delivery of the teaching-family model interventions for young offenders (Phillips, Phillips, Fixen & Wolf, 1974), in which treatment is delivered in a large number of small-group settings (for example, families).

Box 8.1   Organisational factors characteristic of successful programme implementation (after Gendreau, Goggin & Smith, 1999)

1. The organisation has a history of adopting new initiatives.
2. The organisation puts new initiatives into place efficiently.
3. The bureaucratic structure of the organisation is moderately decentralised, allowing for flexible responses to problems.
4. Problems are resolved in a timely manner.
5. Problems are resolved in a non-confrontational style.
6. There is little task/emotional-personal conflict within the organisation at the interdepartmental, staff, management, and/or management-staff levels.
7. There has been a staff turnover of less than 25% at all levels during the previous 2 years.
8. The organisation has formal training in the assessment and treatment of offenders on a biannual basis.
9. The organisation has formal links with educational institutions and/or consultants for the purpose of seeking guidance and training on service and clinical matters.

In light of these and other examples in the literature, along with their own practical experience of offender programmes, Gendreau, Goggin & Smith (1999) have identified nine organisational factors characteristic of successful implementation (see Box 8.1).

To summarise, the concept of "organisational readiness for programmes" is complex. As Reppucci proposed in the 1970s (Reppucci 1973; Reppucci & Saunders, 1974), it requires organisations to have a clear philosophy underpinning treatment that is understood and adhered to by all staff; an organisational structure that facilitates accountability and communication; staff involvement in decision making; and realistic objectives as to what can be achieved in set time periods. There should, therefore, be minimum requirements for organisations wishing to implement programmes. These requirements should then be evaluated with respect to their utility in practice and their impact on outcomes. It is difficult to see how, on the basis of experience, this demanding agenda can be achieved at a national level.

Responsivity

Controversies

As outlined in Chapter 1, one of the key findings from the meta-analytic reviews of offending behaviour programmes was the importance of the responsivity principle. This principle emphasises the need for offending behaviour programmes that are accessible and engaging for offenders, and also take into account individual learning styles (Andrews & Bonta, 2003; Andrews et al., 1990). The responsivity principle states that the mode and style of treatment should be matched to the characteristics of the offender population it is delivered to in order for offenders to achieve maximum benefit from it in terms of behaviour change. Andrews (2001) distinguishes between *internal* and *external* responsivity. Internal responsivity refers to those offender characteristics that can impede understanding of and ability to benefit from programmes, including factors such as age, gender, ethnicity, personality characteristics, intellectual deficits, and motivation (Kennedy, 2000, 2001). Such issues, therefore, require programme designers and practitioners to match the content and pace of treatment to specific offender characteristics. In contrast, external responsivity refers to staff and programme setting and delivery characteristics (Kennedy, 2000, 2001). Staff factors include individuals' preferences for certain modes of treatment delivery, settings, and client groups. As Kennedy argues, matching staff with offenders, delivery style, and setting will lead to a maximisation of the therapeutic alliance and, hopefully, treatment effectiveness.

The importance of the responsivity principle has been shown in a number of meta-analyses (for example, Andrews et al., 1990; Garrett, 1985; Lipsey, Chapman & Landenberger, 2001; Redondo, Sánchez-Meca & Garrido, 2002). More recently these results have been replicated with specific offender populations, including women offenders (Andrews & Dowden, 1999; Dowden & Andrews, 1999a), violent offenders (Dowden & Andrews, 2000), young offenders (Dowden & Andrews, 1999b) and sexual offenders (Gallagher, Wilson, Hirschfield, Coggleshall & MacKenzie, 1999; Polizzi, MacKenzie & Hickman, 1999).

The impact of responsivity issues on engagement in and completion of treatment has been shown in a number of studies. Davies, Lewis, Byatt, Purvis & Cole (2004) examined the literacy demands of three general offending behaviour programmes (R & R, ETS, Think First) in six probation areas in England. The skills levels required for the programmes were assessed and then compared to the literacy skills of offenders required to attend the programmes. As outlined in Chapter 7, Davies et al. reported that the literacy demands of the programmes were high, although there were some variations between the three programmes with regard to levels of reading and writing. The speaking and listening demands were found to be very high for all three programmes. It was also suggested that the effects of these demands may be cumulative, with very high demands placed by most sessions. In contrast, Davies et al. reported that offenders typically have poor literacy skills that were often below the requirements of the programmes. Thus, there was a mismatch between the literacy demands of the programmes and the literacy skills of the offenders participating in them. Furthermore, although tutors had some discretion in the delivery of the programmes, interviews with tutors and offenders showed that tutors' attempts to address literacy problems were not always successful. Tutors were often not aware of the literacy levels of offenders to whom they were delivering programmes, and had not always received training in literacy issues. Given these results there is a clear need to provide tutors with training in the area of literacy, to ensure there is appropriate assessment of offenders, to adapt programme materials and manuals, and to provide literacy support to offenders.

In interviews with non-completers of ETS in prison, McMurran & McCulloch (in press) reported that the non-completers said that initially they were motivated to stop offending and engage in treatment but had subsequently felt that the programme was not relevant to their needs (as may be true if, say, substance use is a primary problem). With respect to the programme material, some non-completers said that ETS was too slow and patronising, whereas others felt that it was too demanding. In a study of ETS in a probation setting, Briggs, Gray & Stephens (2003) reported that offenders with literacy problems were more likely to drop out of the programme than offenders without such problems. Referring back to the high non-completion rates reported by Hollin et al. (2004, 2005) for three programmes in the Probation Service, it is clear that responsivity issues have implications for offenders' engagement in and completion of programmes. Thus, there is an onus on programme designers to make offending behaviour programmes accessible and engaging for offenders, and to ensure that they are relevant to their needs.

The role of practitioners should also not be underestimated in terms of the therapeutic skills they bring to their work. It has been shown that effective practitioners need to have the skills, ability, and knowledge to deliver a programme. In a recent meta-analysis Dowden & Andrews (2004) found effective treatment to be associated with practitioners who used a "firm-but-fair" approach in which official rules were clearly explained and upheld; who modelled and reinforced prosocial attitudes and behaviours; who taught problem-solving skills that were relevant to the offenders' lives; who used community resources when necessary; and who built a high quality therapeutic relationship with offenders. Tutors' attitudes to treatment in general and specific programme approaches are also important (Lösel, 1996), while Preston & Murphy (1997) emphasise the personal attributes necessary for working with offenders as being enthusiastic, flexible, tolerant, trustworthy, and having good communication skills.

Towards a Resolution

Given the level of literacy problems among offender populations, together with the findings of Davies et al. (2004) relating to the discrepancy between programme demands and the literacy skills of offenders, it is clear that treatment provision needs to take literacy into account. As recommended by Davies et al., tutors and other correctional staff need to receive training in literacy issues that allows them better to interpret and understand assessments, and more appropriately to adapt their delivery to take account of the needs of offenders with poor literacy. At the same time, attention should be paid to ensuring that all offenders are screened for literacy problems prior to being allocated to a programme.

Programme designers should also be aware of the problems facing offenders and tutors in the area of literacy, and ensure that programmes are developed which are appropriate for offenders who experience difficulties in their reading and writing. This attention to literacy should result in added guidance for tutors on ways to maintain the engagement of offenders experiencing problems, while ensuring integrity of delivery is not compromised. Literacy support for offenders, both within and outside of the sessions, could also play a role.

Practitioner skills are important factors in treatment outcomes, but as Andrews et al. (1990) note these can be divided into *general* skills for working with offenders and skills that are *specific* to certain client groups. Following the responsivity principle there is, therefore, a need to match practitioners and client groups. The therapeutic relationship between practitioners and offenders is increasingly being seen as playing an important role in treatment outcome (Andrews et al., 1990; Averbeck & Lösel, 1994; Cooke, 1997), with recent work on sexual offender treatment showing the importance of having an effective therapeutic alliance (for example, Marshall et al., 2002). The importance of the therapeutic alliance in clinical treatment was highlighted in a meta-analysis of 79 studies (Martin, Garske & Davis, 2000), and an association has also been reported between poor therapeutic alliance and non-completion of treatment (for example, Piper et al., 1999; Samstag, Batchelder, Muran, Safran & Winston, 1998).

Marshall et al. (2003) examined the therapist features that were associated with treatment outcome in the general psychotherapy and clinical literature, with a view to applying this knowledge to sexual offender programmes. Positive outcomes were associated with a range of therapist behaviours, including empathy, emotional responsiveness, warm interpersonal style, acceptance and support, genuineness, respect, use of open-ended questions, directiveness, encouragement of the client to participate in therapy, self-confidence, moderate levels of self-disclosure, flexibility, use of humour, and a non-confrontational style.

A similar review by Keijsers, Schaap & Hoogduin (2000) found two clusters of therapist interpersonal behaviour associated with positive outcome in cognitive behavioural treatment. The first cluster related to the use of Rogerian values (empathy, non-possessive warmth, positive regard for clients, and genuineness), and the second cluster to the establishment of a good therapeutic alliance with the client. Three clusters of client behaviour were also associated with positive outcome: clients' perceptions of the therapist as self-confident, skilful and active; a willingness to discuss problems; and a willingness at pre-treatment to change and accept treatment to achieve that change. The similarities in the findings of the Marshall et al. (2003) and Keijsers et al. (2000) reviews suggest some common ground in identifying strong therapist skills.

Marshall et al. (2002) showed positive outcomes of sexual offender treatment to be predicted by high levels of practitioner empathy and warmth, and by the use of directive and rewarding behaviours during treatment. Beech & Fordham (1997) examined the relationship between group cohesiveness and treatment outcome in sexual offenders. The most substantial therapeutic changes were found in those groups with the highest level of cohesiveness, in turn associated with participants rating the group leaders as supportive but challenging. In contrast, the group with the lowest cohesiveness score had a therapist with an aggressive, confrontational style of delivery. Thus, the emerging research supports the important role of therapist skills in treatment effectiveness and outcome.

While there is a need for further research in this area, there are clear implications of this work for practitioner recruitment, selection, and training. As knowledge increases so it needs to be incorporated into recruitment and selection procedures, whilst taking into account the skills that can be taught during training. Once recruited, staff should receive high quality training that enables them to gain the varied, active, and participatory teaching methods that will allow them to convey complex ideas in a simple, graphic, and memorable style.

Controversies

A further issue to consider is whether all programmes are suitable for specific groups of offenders such as women, black and ethnic minorities, young offenders, offenders with mental health problems, and very high risk and psychopathic offenders. The meta-analyses suggests that, as a population, offenders respond better to programmes based on behavioural, cognitive-behavioural, and social learning theories than those underpinned by psychodynamic principles (for a review, see McGuire, 2002). However, offenders are not a homogenous population and various offender characteristics can impact on responsiveness to interventions, perhaps through their interaction with therapist characteristics or service delivery mode. Ogloff (2002) points out that offender treatment programmes are typically designed for white, male, adult offenders, with minor adaptations for other groups of offenders. He argues that this position needs to be expanded so as to include women offenders, young offenders, and offenders from different ethnic and cultural groups, who may all be likely to have different personal, social, and cultural treatment needs. Therefore, interventions need to be sensitive to these specific needs with programme design being guided by empirical research into the treatment needs of these groups.

A good example of specific treatment needs within an offender population can be found in the provision of treatment for women offenders. Given Ogloff's (2002) point, there is a service delivery issue as to whether offending behaviour programmes designed for men take into account the specific criminogenic needs of women offenders, as well as their specific treatment delivery needs. This issue can be explored by examining the extant literature, as in the following section, in order to illustrate the point.

An examination of the literature on female criminogenic needs shows that the criminogenic needs that have emerged from research from male offenders have traditionally been applied to women offenders. However, it has been argued that the concepts of risk and need are "gendered", and that it is likely that there will be some differences between male and female offenders (Blanchette, 2002). This view is supported by recent reviews of the literature that have highlighted particular criminogenic needs relevant to women offenders (Blanchette, 2002; Hollin & Palmer, in press; Howden-Windell & Clark, 1999; Sorbello, Eccleston, Ward & Jones, 2002).

Briefly, offending has been shown to be associated with education and employment among female offenders, although the level of need appears to be lower among female than male offenders (Blanchette, 2002; Home Office, 2002). Problems with finances have also been shown to be a criminogenic need among women, with many women prisoners being financially dependent on their families after release (Sorbello et al., 2002). Accommodation problems have been reported to be prevalent among female offenders, particularly in terms of finding suitable housing after release from prison (Home Office, 2002). These problems may be compounded by the association between homelessness, substance use, and family conflict and abuse among young people (Wincup, Buckland & Bayliss, 2003).

The research findings demonstrate a need to design interventions for women offenders that include practical input on these issues. This input may include training in basic skills and employment skills for those who are able to work, and information on financial and accommodation issues, including eligibility for benefits and budgeting skills. Putting women in contact with relevant community agencies is also important, and is a feature of many of the new resettlement projects (Lewis et al., 2003).

Family and marital relationships have been highlighted as a key issue in female offending. For example the association of early and current abusive family relationships with offending is well established among both male and female offenders (Hawkins et al., 1998). While these relationship issues may not in themselves predict later offending (see, for example, Lowenkamp, Holsinger & Latessa, 2001), it has been suggested that abuse in personal relationships may interact with other factors to impact on later behaviour (Hollin & Palmer, in press). To address these issues, programmes are required that can deal with both previous and current abuse. In particular, attention should be paid to problems that have arisen as a result of these experiences, for example drug abuse, which are clearly identifiable as criminogenic.

Emotional and mental health problems, including self-harm and suicide, have been shown to be particularly high among women offenders (Gorsuch, 1998; O'Brien, Mortimer, Singleton & Meltzer, 1997; Parsons, Walker & Grubin, 2001). However, the research suggests that mental health problems are not a criminogenic need *per se*, but play a key role in offending in terms of their interaction with other variables. Therefore, as well as providing interventions that address women offenders' immediate mental health problems, attention also needs to be paid to the causes of these problems.

The research evidence suggests a strong association between substance use and an elevated risk of offending among women offenders (Byrne & Howells, 2002; Gorsuch, 1998; Henderson, 1998). There appear, however, to be differences between men and women in their reasons and motivations for drug use (Langan & Pelissier, 2001), leading to suggestions that there may be qualitative differences between the two genders in the role of drugs in offending (Hollin & Palmer, 2004). These findings have direct implications for the design of treatment programmes for women offenders with substance use problems. While services clearly need to have an explicit focus on substance use, it appears that without attending to issues of abuse, mental health and so on, there is likely to be a limited treatment effect on both substance use and offending. There are good grounds for suggesting that treatment should focus on the complex patterns of need found in many women substance-using offenders.

In summary, there are obvious areas of overlap in the criminogenic needs of male and female offenders, but also some areas of difference. This view leads to the suggestion that there may be different pathways to offending among male and female offenders, meaning that it is crucial that these differences are taken into account when designing treatment programmes for women offenders.

Responsivity challenges are also posed by women offenders in terms of both treatment setting and staff issues (Sorbello et al., 2002). Educational research has revealed differences in the learning styles of men and women, with women responding better to empathy, collaboration, and listening (Belenky, Clinchy, Goldberger & Tarule, 1986). There is, therefore, a need to ensure that staff working with women offenders are trained and skilled in these techniques.

Overall, it is clear that the issue of responsivity in determining treatment process and outcomes is of paramount importance. This position has led commentators to argue that offender classification systems should include assessment of offender characteristics that are likely to impact on their responsiveness to treatment (Kennedy, 2000; Van Voorhis, 1997).

PROGRAMME EVALUATION

Controversies

The issues in programme evaluation that give rise to controversy lie in the deceptively simple question, "What works best, for whom, for which problem, in what conditions?" The meta-analyses that principally informed "what works" and the development of offending behaviour programmes set up a testable hypothesis that may provide an answer to this question: if services can be configured in accordance with the principles of effective practice, as indicated by the meta-analyses, then there is a likelihood of lowering rates of recidivism. There is therefore a bottom line, as Friendship, Falshaw & Beech (2003, p. 115) state: "The aim of accredited offending behaviour programmes is to reduce re-offending post-treatment." It can be argued that offending behaviour programmes perform other functions, but there is an agreed bottom line: if offending behaviour programmes do not reduce re-offending then the "what works" hypothesis does not stand.

At face value the task of evaluation appears to be straightforward: do offending behaviour programmes delivered to offenders reduce their rates of re-offending? However, in order to reach the bottom line of changes in rates of re-offending there are many paths to tread. Working from the starting point of an *accredited* programme, evaluation rests on several initial assumptions: first, that a given programme is nested in appropriate theory; second, it uses methods appropriate for given offender characteristics, such as age, gender, and intellectual ability; third, that it is designed appropriately for purpose with regard to behaviour change, as with problem substance use, sexual offending, domestic violence, and so on; fourth, that it is being delivered, either in institutions or the community, to appropriate standards of integrity by trained staff (Andrews & Dowden, 2005). Of course, some of these assumptions will be testable in an evaluation, but the starting point for researchers will be that the programme is fit for purpose.

Friendship et al. (2003) present an integrated model to evaluate the effectiveness of accredited offending behaviour programmes. They suggest that there are four elements to an evaluation. First, the organisational climate in which the delivery of the programme takes place; second, the level of programme integrity; third, the cost-effectiveness of the programme; fourth, the short-term and long-term outcomes of the programme. Friendship et al. also advocate a within-subject design in which the long-term effects of the programme are considered in relation to the short-term effects. Thus, an offender's reconviction might be looked at in relationship to their change on a measure, say change in anger management, or their responsiveness to the programme. As Friendship et al. note, this approach has the advantage of using each offender as their own control, eliminating all the arguments about matching experimental and control groups as discussed in Chapter 2.

The model presented by Friendship et al. is helpful in bringing attention to a wide range of factors that are important in evaluating programmes. However, the Friendship et al. model can be refined, in moving towards a plan for comprehensive evaluation of programmes, by reframing the components of the model around important research questions. The first research question, central to a sound structural framework for evaluating complex interventions (Everitt & Wessely, 2004; Medical Research Council, 2000), concerns *modelling*. The process of modelling relies on gathering data that will illuminate understanding of the way in which the components of the intervention influence the outcome. In an ideal world, the intervention would be based on *theory* but as Everitt and Wessely note, "The idea that one should develop the theoretical basis of the intervention as a first step is rarely, if ever, observed in practice" (p. 65). Nonetheless, research intended to inform modelling should help enlighten theoretical understanding of the effects of the intervention.

Following modelling, the second research question addresses what happens when the intervention is applied in practice. This question is addressed within the context of an *exploratory trial* in which the intervention is put into practice and preliminary evidence is gathered on its delivery, functioning of the outcome measures, and so on. The exploratory trial is then followed by the full-scale testing of the fully-defined intervention. In traditional clinical trials this full-scale testing would be a *definitive randomised control trial (RCT)*, although as discussed in Chapter 2 it is debatable whether the arguments for an RCT are as strong with offending behaviour programmes as they are with some drug-based and medical treatments. Indeed, Everitt and Wessely (2004) make this very point in noting that RCTs may not be justifiable with some complex interventions, particularly the psychotherapies, as there may be important variables that cannot be randomised: "Even when the intervention has been manualised, there can still be substantial differences between treatments given to patients under the same label (the issue of 'treatment fidelity'), and also, to put it simply, not all the therapists are equally good" (Everitt & Wessely, 2004, p. 66). Thus, there is a strong case for considering a range of designs as either alternatives to RCTs, or as complementary to RCTs.

Towards a Resolution

Modelling

Intuitively, there are two principal areas to consider in setting up research to understand the processes that influence the outcome of an offending behaviour programme. The first area is the environment in which the programme is to be delivered; the second is the processes that occur during the actual delivery of the programme.

As illustrated in Figure 8.1, the environment in which programmes are delivered can be conceived as beginning with social, political, and professional factors. These broad factors include the formulation of policy financially to support programmes

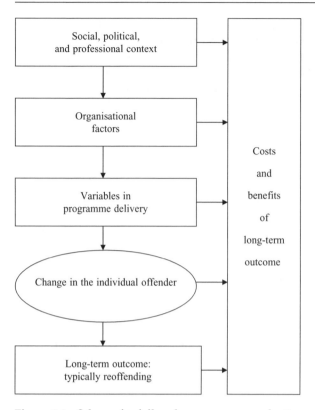

Figure 8.1 Scheme for full-scale programme evaluation

and the vested professional interests in adopting offending behaviour programmes. For example, Mair (2004) describes the (alleged) professional and political manoeuvrings that led to the implementation of offending behaviour programmes within the English and Welsh Probation Service.

More immediate environmental influences with respect to programme delivery lie in the organisational factors that are important with regard to programme implementation. These factors may be thought of in terms of organisational "readiness for change", as discussed above and in Chapters 1 and 7. Of course, the nature of the relationship between the wider social, political, and professional factors and the narrower organisational factors is one that continually shifts and changes. A sophisticated analysis of this relationship would primarily be the province of researchers, such as sociologists, expert in the analysis of social trends and forces.

The analysis of the processes involved in the delivery of offending behaviour programmes flows from organisational readiness for change. Thus, there are issues that are directly dependent upon organisational readiness, such as the resources given to the programme as seen, for example, in terms of the physical location for programmes, the level and effectiveness of staff training, and commitment to staff support. Moving yet closer to the delivery of the intervention, as defined by the group interaction during programme sessions, is the programme being delivered with integrity? Closer still, now at the micro level, concern may be with the characteristics of skilled and effective programme deliverers, the importance of the therapeutic alliance, group dynamics and the therapeutic climate, and offenders' perceptions and responses to the programme (see above and Chapter 5). Researchers concerned with the finer points of programme organisation and delivery can draw, for example, on a long tradition of research in social psychology, organisational psychology, group work, counselling, and clinical, criminological, and experimental psychology.

Thus, modelling of the effective delivery of offending behaviour programmes may move through the stages outlined in Figure 8.1. It is evident that understanding the journey from broad social and political factors, through organisational influences, to the dynamics of group interactions is a complex task. A planned programme of research that sought to integrate these various levels of activity, understanding how each stage interacts with and impacts upon the next, would prove valuable in the extreme and would necessitate the application of a range of research methods. However, it is also the case that all this complex activity is (overtly at least) directed at one specific objective, bringing about some level of change in the individual offender's functioning. The exact nature of that change will, of course, vary from programme to programme, but the fact is that the stated aim of programmes is to bring about that individual level of change. This point raises three issues. First, how do researchers measure change at the level of the individual offender? Second, how are levels of change related to the social, organisational, and programme variables discussed above? Third, what is the relationship between level of offender change and eventual long-term outcome, principally with respect to re-offending? Finally, once outcome is known, questions may be asked about whether the costs and benefits associated with the programme delivers value for money. While financial cost is not everything, clearly the costs and benefits of programmes that spend public money must be considered.

Measuring Change

If programmes are designed to bring about change in some level of the individual offender's functioning – in terms of his or her functioning at a cognitive, emotional, or skills level – then clearly the measurement of that individual change is central to evaluative research. Programme evaluation, along with the measures to carry out the evaluation, is built into the accreditation criteria for programme development. Typically, the evaluation hinges on the use of various psychometric scales, appropriately linked to the programme's targets for change, themselves based on established criminogenic needs. As well as psychometric tests, there may also be other measures of the effect of the programme, as might be gathered using interviews, screening for substance use, and institutional behaviour. In addition, information may be gathered on treatment integrity, typically using video-recording of programme sessions and post-session and post-programme reports from staff and offenders. Rarely, there may also be systematic collection of financial data for the purposes of cost-effectiveness and cost-benefit analyses.

In most evaluations the process is twofold: first, has the programme been delivered with integrity? Second, if integrity can be assured, has the programme achieved its aim of bringing about change? In order to answer the latter point, the typical research strategy, say with psychometric data, is to compare statistically pre-programme scores with post-programme scores. If there has been statistically significant change then it would be said that the programme has been successful. However, it would be wrong just to rely on significance testing: as Borenstein (1997) explains

> In the vast majority of clinical trials, the goal of significance testing is inappropriate because it addresses the wrong question. Usually, when we test a new treatment, we are not interested in whether the treatment has *any* effect. Rather, we are interested in estimating the size of the effect. The significance test addresses the first question only. (Borenstein, 1997, p. 8)

Yet further, as Friendship et al. (2003) note, there is a contrast to be made between *statistical* significance and *clinical* significance. Jacobson, Roberts, Berns & McGlinchey (1999) make the point that in the context of treatment the degree of change can be statistically significant (there is, probably, an effect of treatment), and it is possible to estimate the effect size (the amount of change attributable to treatment). However, statistically reliable change does not mean that the individual is at an acceptable level of functioning: as Jacobson et al. state, the question is whether after the intervention individuals have changed in a way that "renders them indistinguishable from well-functioning people" (Jacobson et al., 1999, p. 301).

The concept of clinical significance is critically important in working with offenders. For example, if offenders' risk of violent conduct is heightened when they are angry, then an anger management programme may be seen as appropriate. Following the programme, offenders may show statistically significant change on measures of anger and the magnitude of that change may be substantial. However, if the improvement is considered in relation to population norms with respect to anger, the offender may have moved from an anger problem of chronic proportions to an anger problem that would be of serious concern. Another offender completing the same programme may have made statistically similar, or even less, change, but have moved from an anger problem of serious proportions to a position where the problem is not considered critical. Thus, the statistical change may be similar in the two cases but the clinical significance of the change is very different. It might be said, with justification, that the former offender posed a greater risk of violent conduct than the latter, even though they had both responded similarly to the programme. As Jacobson et al. (1984) have demonstrated, using the example of behavioural marital therapy, there are marked differences in "success" depending on whether statistical or clinical criteria are used. Further, as Follette & Callaghan (2001) explain, meta-analyses deal in effect sizes that do not easily translate into estimates of clinical importance.

Connecting Change

A comprehensive research programme with a focus on change in the individual offender, could move either up or down the stages in Figure 8.1. Moving up the stages, from individual change to broad context, would produce a complex model of the various interactions between the different stages. The environment immediately surrounding the actual delivery of the programme, from group dynamics and staff characteristics to levels of training and programme management, is likely to have the most demonstrable relationship with the effectiveness of the programme. Certainly, in terms of modelling the effects of the programme with respect to offender change, and thereby gaining greater understanding about how the programme works, analysis of the associations between these immediate relationships is likely to be highly informative. However, moving further up the chain to the interaction between organisational and wider social and professional issues is also likely to be instructive.

Finally, moving down a stage, the association between the effects of the programme at the level of individual change and later criminal behaviour, typically measured through reconviction, should be gauged in order to complete the chain and hence the modelling. It is often the case in the literature that this absolutely fundamental and critical issue – the relationship between offender change (statistical and clinical) – is omitted in outcome studies. It is evident, however, that without addressing this basic question then a complete model of how a programme works is impossible to formulate. More studies of the type reported by Beech, Fisher & Beckett (1999), which employ clinical significance, are necessary in order to determine convincingly that programme effects translate into meaningful long-term change.

With a working model of the programme in place, based on theory and preliminary research, it is then possible to move to an exploratory trial.

Exploratory Trial

Following modelling, at this stage attention is turned to the collection of preliminary evidence in advance of a definitive trial of the intervention. In effect, the model is put to the test based on what has been learned during the modelling phase. This testing may mean that variations of a treatment programme, say by dose, are compared, appropriate control groups are gathered, targeting matrices are applied to real populations in order to determine the numbers they produce, and different research designs tested. As suggested by the Medical Research Council framework (MRC, 2000, p. 4), "A key and distinctive possibility of studies at this point could therefore be the adaptive nature of interventions, study design, analyses (being modified over time in the course of the study phase)." In effect, the exploratory trial is a comprehensive pilot, or "test drive" as the MRC framework prefers, of the treatment, paying careful and measured attention to both content and delivery. In particular, monitoring at this stage should take note of rates of compliance and drop out from the treatment. Indeed, as the MRC framework suggests with regard to drop out, "This may be particularly problematic with behavioural interventions" (MRC, 2000, p. 12). The attendant problems for evaluation caused by high rates of drop out were discussed in Chapter 2.

The UK Government's Cabinet Office report, *The Role of "Pilots" in Policy-making*, published in 2003, emphasises the role and nature of pilots:

> A policy pilot should be seen above all as a "test run" the results of which will help to influence the shape and delivery of the final policy. It follows that a policy pilot must be allowed to run its course and produce its findings before the policy is rolled out. (p. 8).

Definitive Trial

Having moved through the modelling and exploratory phases, the next step is a full-scale evaluation of the treatment programme. Traditionally this would involve a randomised control trial (RCT), appropriately designed for the context of the study, incorporating treatment, cost, and other measures as necessary. However, in the specific case of programmes aimed at behaviour change there is some debate about the use of RCTs (see Chapter 2). Thus, while the choice of design may be open to debate, a definitive trial should be the end product of a great deal of meticulous planning and gathering of preliminary evidence.

Nevertheless, a definitive trial is still a trial, an investigation of the effects of an intervention. The final phase in the MRC framework, following the findings from the definitive trial, is therefore to look at the real-life *long-term implementation* of the intervention. At this stage concern may be with effectiveness when the intervention is delivered in uncontrolled settings, or with any longer-term effects not seen in the previous trials.

Research Design

Overlaying the whole process, from modelling to long-term implementation, is the issue of research design and its potential impact upon research outcome. It is clear that when viewed as a process, beginning with theory and modelling and ending with long-term implementation, the evaluation of the effectiveness of offending behaviour programmes is a highly complex task. A full research programme will therefore use a variety of research methods, quantitative and qualitative, to answer different questions. Along the way, researchers will have to weigh their choice of research design against ethical and methodological issues particular to the criminal justice system. Interestingly, the Cabinet Office (2003, p. 20) report took the view that "Insufficient use is made of combined methodologies in pilot evaluations, which can provide insights that are inaccessible to any single method."

Informing Policy

Research in criminal justice settings will, almost inevitably, be affected by the political context in which it is commissioned (Blumson, 2004; Hedderman, 2004). Further, there are likely to be demands for quick outputs: Pawson (2002, p. 157) comments that "Evaluation research is tortured by time constraints. The policy cycle revolves quicker than the research cycle, with the results that 'real time' evaluations often have little influence on policy making." There is an evident tension with the view, expressed above, that pilots must be allowed to run their course and produce findings before policy is eventually rolled out. Further, a long trial may even outlast a government's term of office so producing pressure for "good news" quickly, even blurring the distinction between "evidence-led policy" and "policy-led evidence". These pressures may give rise to difficult waters for independent researchers to navigate (Hope, 2004; Raynor, 2004).

Dissemination

Finally, there is the important issue of how the research findings are placed in the public domain. Naturally, researchers will want to communicate their findings to other researchers via the traditional academic outlet of journal publication. Publication in a high-quality journal, in which research findings are subjected to rigorous peer review, is crucial as a means of establishing the quality of the research and demonstrating its standing to the research community. However, there are other forms of publication to consider in order that the research findings reach a wide readership. Publication of the messages from the research for policy and practice in professional journals, rather than the finer academic points of research design and tables of data and accompanying statistical analysis, may serve the purpose of communicating findings to those more concerned with implementation of policy and delivery of services. Further, the popular media, highbrow and lowbrow, are always alive to a story. Uninformed or misinformed newspaper articles have, for example, presented offending behaviour programmes as naïve, too expensive, and not working. The popular media give the legions of critics their day in the sun, variously blaming everything on the government, the prison service, research findings, and even psychologists! Smart researchers need to consider how best to manage the dissemination of their findings across all these different outlets, each with its own rules, demands, and consequences.

IS THERE A FUTURE FOR OFFENDING BEHAVIOUR PROGRAMMES?

Controversies

As with any treatment innovation, particularly when evidence based for some reason, there are bound to be critics. Listening to informed criticism is an important part of the process of implementation and evaluation of any new departure. The right criticism might be helpful in improving treatment, or in informing decisions about whether a treatment can continue. The criticism may be based in empiricism, asking what do the relevant data say and how robust is the research? Alternatively, there may be critical debate, within and across professions, based on working principles and practice. However, less helpfully, criticism may be couched in political and professional game-playing, overt hostility, academic slight of hand and, regrettably, name calling and personal innuendo. In part, the future development of offending behaviour programmes rests on criticism and so it is worth considering some of the main critical points.

Evidence-Based Criticism

Two types of evidence-based criticism can be distinguished. The first type of criticism concerns the evidence base, drawn from the meta-analyses, which provided the impetus for the wider development of programmes. The second criticism is of the type of evidence that is gathered in an attempt to evaluate offending behaviour programmes.

As with any research method, in this case a statistical method, there are criticisms to be levelled at meta-analysis. Sharpe (1997) notes three points that may threaten the validity of meta-analytic findings: first, the "apples and oranges" effect of mixing dissimilar studies in the analysis, so producing meaningless findings; second, the "file drawer" issue of only selecting published studies for inclusion in the analysis; third, the matter of "garbage in garbage out", leading to the undue influence within the analysis of poorly designed and conducted original studies. Further critical points range from the rationale for the technique itself, to selection of the studies to enter into a meta-analysis, and the subjective nature of the coding of the studies to be entered into the meta-analysis. While these points have their own specific implications for the reading of the meta-analyses (Hollin, 1999), the over-arching point is that the meta-analytic procedures are both clear and replicable. Thus, coding schemes can be criticised and refined, more studies can be added, and weight can be given in the meta-analysis to the strength of the research design. As is clear from the reviews, a reasonably consistent picture emerges from the various meta-analyses (Cooke & Philip, 2001; McGuire, 2002). This consistency should be seen in light of differences across the various meta-analyses in terms of number of studies sampled, coding schemes, and so on. While critics such as Mair (2004) suggest that the meta-analyses have little to say about the organisation and context of treatment (which is itself a debatable statement), if the primary studies are not available that is hardly a fault of the technique of meta-analysis. Indeed, to follow the point, as indicated in Chapter 7 considerable thought and attention has been given to the optimum context for the delivery of effective treatment.

In summary, meta-analysis is a statistical technique that allows transparent aggregation of data from many separate studies to determine the size of any consistent effects within that data set. Taken alone a single meta-analysis may be a strong indication of a given effect, depending on the parameters of the analysis; replication of the same effect across several meta-analyses lends weight to the likelihood of a real effect. However, it is only by the actual testing of the hypotheses derived from the meta-analyses that the likelihood of an effect can be tested.

Once formulated and part of practice, evidence regarding the effectiveness of offending behaviour programmes is the next step. In England and Wales a range of offending behaviour programmes have gradually been introduced by various agencies, but mainly by the Prison and Probation Services, since 2000. An overview of these programmes (Merrington & Stanley, 2004) reaches the inevitable conclusion that given the time-scales involved it is too early to comment on outcomes. However, reviews of recent evidence from a wider geographical base than just England and Wales give support to the effectiveness of offending behaviour programmes in reducing offending (Tong & Farrington, 2006; Wilson, Bouffard & Mackenzie, 2005). Similarly, outcome studies published since 2000 have continued to add to the evidence base (Bourgon & Armstrong, 2005; Van Voorhis et al., 2004). It is of note that the analysis and depth of questioning in both the Bourgon & Armstrong (2005) and Van Voorhis et al. (2004) studies rises to a new level of sophistication. These studies are not just outcome studies but are attempting, using complex research designs and methods of data analysis, to relate organisational and treatment factors to outcome. It can be anticipated that this emerging trend towards more intricate outcome studies will be one that continues into the future.

Professional Debate

It would be a strange world if a new development did not attract professional debate as to its merits and shortcomings. Thus, the introduction of offending behaviour programmes has led to questioning about the real purpose of probation within the criminal justice system (Robinson & McNeill, 2004), questions about management and its role in the implementation of change (Blumson, 2004), the involvement of unions (see Raynor, 2004), and associated questions about the meaning of treatment and its evaluation (Seligman & Levant, 1998). All this debate can be seen as healthy if it espouses a spirit of curiosity: Raynor & Vanstone (2001, p. 201) make the observation that "Curiosity drives the spirit of experimentation which allows organizations to learn." Organisations and the individuals within them can take a great deal from adopting a positive spirit of curiosity, or even what might be called a "scientist-practitioner" approach (Long & Hollin, 1997), in reflecting on their practice and use of evidence in learning, developing and improving.

In contrast to a positive, constructive stance, it often seems that a great deal of professional debate adopts a highly critical, negative stance. Ironically, the criticisms are often at their most trenchant between professional groups who are, at face value at least, working towards the same goal. There is something terribly paradoxical when professional groups with the same aim harshly criticise and fight with each other. It is not difficult to find examples, both in the popular press and in academic publications, along the lines of "my theory is better than yours", "my practice is better than yours", and "your understanding is wrong and mine is right". This destructive in-fighting acts as a diversion when there are real arguments to be had: for example, Raynor (2004, p. 321) comments that

> Already some right-wing commentators on criminal justice (Green et al., 2004) are citing the probation pathfinder research in support of their contention that rehabilitation does not work, and prison does. So could we be in for another 20 years of "nothing works"?

The report that Raynor refers to by Green, Grove, and Martin (2004), published by Civitas: The Institute for the Study of Civil Society, is a curious mix of selections from the research literature and half-hidden slurs: "Clive Hollin . . . revealed the semi-religious nature of belief in rehabilitation when he remarked how a small group of academics 'kept faith with the rehabilitation ideal'" (Green, Grove & Martin, p. 40). (Actually I wrote "kept faith with the *rehabilitative* ideal" (Hollin & McMurran, 1995): always best to get it right, sloppy quotes, sloppy scholarship.) Of course, the word "faith" has meaning outside its theological use but how clever to write off as quasi-religious zealots those academics that read the published evidence as supportive of rehabilitation and maintain that view despite an adverse prevailing academic and political climate.

In the context of offending behaviour programmes, for example, as various critics have noted, there is certainly more to be learned with regard to gender and diversity, bedding programmes in organisational structures, and connecting programmes to the local context in working towards building local communities. However, these points do not negate what is already known, rather they direct attention to what needs to be added to current knowledge and understanding. This point extends to the place of offending behaviour programmes within an organisation's practice. With reference to the Probation Service, for example, Farrall (2004, p. 202) rightly states, "Cognitive behavioural work should thus complement the social and economic interventions undertaken to assist probationers." Did anyone say otherwise?

Given mutual respect, academics from different disciplines can work together constructively to develop and enhance understanding through theory building, through joint research, and informed debate. Destructive criticism, in the guise of academic debate, is less than helpful and works against collaboration across disciplines. Such destructive criticism is sometimes based on presenting the "other side" in a one-dimensional way: for example, advocates of offending behaviour programmes are said universally to embrace a pathological model of offenders as people with deficits and dysfunctions (see Chapter 3). It is self-evident that this position is based either on a limited portrayal of theory or a limited theoretical understanding. At other times, the evidence is attacked not on technical grounds but with accusations of "positivism". The charge that research, and hence those who report it, is positivistic is one that is seldom thoroughly substantiated or precise in clarifying what is meant by positivism. Halfpenny (1982/1992) identifies the three broad churches of positivism – sociological positivism, positivism associated with statistical influences, and logical positivism – with several variations inside all three. As Halfpenny comments

> Controversy over positivism begins immediately "positivism" is used, for there are so many different understandings about how the term can or should be used. There are differences that depend upon whether the term is used to label oneself or one's enemies, for the positivism of positivists differs from the positivism of anti-positivists. (Halfpenny, 1982/1992, p. 11)

Finally, the debate descends to one-sided, selective attacks on disciplines and on particular, named individuals (Kendall, 2004). What is particularly unfortunate about this "them and us" approach is that it polarises disciplines and the strong messages in any analysis are regrettably lost in the almost inevitable low quality exchanges that follow.

Towards a Resolution

It is clear that offending behaviour programmes touch upon many different chords, not all harmonious, in the lives of policy-makers, managers, academics, professionals, and practitioners. There is much to learn from all this discussion, debate, and research evidence, which, hopefully, will serve to strengthen understanding and practice in delivering effective services within the criminal justice and allied systems. Doubtless there are areas of controversy where a resolution is unlikely to be forthcoming, but it is worth maintaining a high level of professional and academic standards in the conduct of the debate. If the impetus to effective and constructive work with offenders is lost, a very different agenda emerges and it may well be a long way back.

REFERENCES

Abel, G. G., Mittelman, M. S., Becker, J. V., Rathner, J. & Rouleau, J. L. (1988). Predicting child molesters' response to treatment. In R. A. Prentky & V. L. Quinsey (Eds), *Human sexual aggression: Current perspectives* (pp. 223–234). New York: Annals of the New York Academy of Sciences.

Abracen, J. & Looman, J. (2004). Issues in the treatment of sexual offenders. *Aggression and Violent Behavior, 9,* 229–246.

Andrews, D. A. (2001). Principles of effective correctional programs. In L. L. Motiuk & R. C. Serin (Eds), *Compendium 2000 on effective correctional programming, Volume 1* (pp. 9–17). Ottawa, Correctional Services Canada.

Andrews, D. A. & Bonta, J. (2003). *The psychology of criminal conduct (3rd edition).* Cincinnati, OH: Anderson.

Andrews, D. A. & Dowden, C. (1999). A meta-analytic investigation into effective correctional intervention for female offenders. *Forum on Corrections Research, 11,* 18–21.

Andrews, D. A. & Dowden, C. (2005). Managing correctional treatment for reduced recidivism: A meta-analytic review of programme integrity. *Legal and Criminological Psychology, 10,* 173–187.

Andrews, D. A., Zinger, I., Hoge, R. D., Bonta, J., Gendreau, P. & Cullen, F. T. (1990). Does correctional treatment work? A psychologically informed meta-analysis. *Criminology, 28,* 369–404.

Averbeck, M. & Lösel, F. (1994). Subjective theories on juvenile delinquency. In M. Stellar, K. P. Dahle & M. Basque (Eds), *Straftaterbehandlung Argumente für Eine Revitalisierung in Forschung und Praxis* (pp. 213–226). Pfaffenweiler: Centaurus.

Beech, A., Fisher, D. & Beckett, R. (1999). *Step 3: An evaluation of the prison sex offender treatment programme.* London: Home Office.

Beech, A. & Fordham, A. S. (1997). Therapeutic climate of sexual offender treatment programs. *Sexual Abuse: A Journal of Research and Treatment, 9,* 219–237.

Belenky, M. F., Clinchy, B. M, Goldberger, N. R. & Tarule, J. M. (1986). *Women's ways of knowing: The development of self, voice and mind.* New York: Basic Books.

Bernfeld, G. A. (2001). The struggle for treatment integrity in a "dis-integrated" service delivery system. In G. A. Bernfeld, D. P. Farrington & A. W. Leschied (Eds), *Offender rehabilitation in practice: Effective programs and policies to reduce re-offending* (pp. 168–188). Chichester: John Wiley & Sons.

Blanchette, K. (2002). Classifying female offenders for effective intervention: Application of the case-based principles of risk and need. *Forum on Corrections Research, 14,* 31–35.

Blumson, M. (2004). First steps and beyond: The pathway to our knowledge of delivering programmes. *Vista, 8,* 171–176.

Borenstein, M. (1997). Hypothesis testing and effect size estimation in clinical trials. *Annals of Allergy, Asthma, and Immunology, 78,* 5–11.

Bouffard, J. A., Taxman, F. S. & Silverman, R. (2003). Improving process evaluations of correctional programs by using a comprehensive evaluation methodology. *Evaluation and Program Planning, 26,* 149–161.

Bourgon, G. & Armstrong, B. (2005). Transferring the principles of effective practice into a "real world" prison setting. *Criminal Justice and Behavior, 32,* 3–25.

Briggs, S., Gray, B. & Stephens, K. (2003). *Offender literacy and attrition from the Enhanced Thinking Skills programme.* National Probation Service, West Yorkshire.

Briggs, S. & Turner, R. (2003). *Barriers to starting programmes: Second phase report.* National Probation Service, West Yorkshire.

Brown, T. L., Swenson, C. C., Cunningham, P. B., Henggeler, S. W., Schoenwald, S. K. & Rowland, M. D. (1997). Multisystemic treatment of violent and chronic juvenile offenders: Bridging the gap between research and practice. *Administration and Policy in Mental Health, 25,* 221–238.

Browne, K. D., Foreman, L. & Middleton, D. (1998). Predicting treatment drop-out in sex offenders. *Child Abuse Review, 7,* 402–419.

Byrne, M. K. & Howells, K. (2002). The psychological needs of women prisoners: Implications for rehabilitation and management. *Psychiatry, Psychology and Law, 9*, 34–43.

Cabinet Office. (2003). *The role of "pilots" in policy-making*. London: Government Chief Social Researcher's Office.

Cann, J., Falshaw, L., Nugent, F. & Friendship, C. (2003). *Understanding what works: Accredited cognitive skills programmes for adult men and young offenders*. Home Office Research Findings No. 226. London: Home Office.

Carter, P. (2003). *Managing offenders, reducing crime*. London: Strategy Unit.

Clarke, A., Simmonds, R. & Wydall, S. (2004). *Delivering cognitive skills programmes in prison: A qualitative study*. Home Office Online Report 27/04. London: Home Office.

Cooke, D. J. (1997). The Barlinnie Special Unit: The rise and fall of a therapeutic experiment. In E. Cullen, L. Jones & R. Woodward (Eds), *Therapeutic communities in prison* (pp. 101–120). Chichester: John Wiley & Sons.

Cooke, D. J. & Philip, L. (2001). To treat or not to treat? An empirical perspective. In C. R. Hollin (Ed.), *Handbook of offender assessment and treatment* (pp. 17–34). Chichester: John Wiley & Sons.

Dalton, R., Major, S. & Sharkey, M. (1998). Nonattenders and attrition from a forensic psychology outpatient service. *International Journal of Offender Therapy and Comparative Criminology, 42*, 174–180.

Davies, K., Lewis, J., Byatt, J., Purvis, E. & Cole, B. (2004). *An evaluation of the literacy demands of general offending behaviour programmes*. Home Office Research Findings No. 233. London: Home Office.

DfES (2000). *Citizenship for 16–19 year olds in education and training*. Report of the Advisory Group to the Secretary of State for Education and Employment. Coventry: The Further Education Funding Council.

Dowden, C. & Andrews, D. A. (1999a). What works for female offenders: A meta-analytic review. *Crime and Delinquency, 45*, 438–452.

Dowden, C. & Andrews, D. A. (1999b). What works in young offender treatment: A meta-analytic review. *Forum on Corrections Research, 11*, 21–24.

Dowden, C. & Andrews, D. A. (2000). Effective correctional treatment and violent reoffending: A meta-analysis. *Canadian Journal of Criminology, 42*, 449–467.

Dowden, C. & Andrews, D. A. (2004). The importance of staff practice in delivering effective correctional treatment: A meta-analytic review of Core Correctional Practice. *International Journal of Offender Therapy and Comparative Criminology, 48*, 203–214.

Edwards, D. L., Schoenwald, S. K., Henggeler, S. W. & Strother, K. B. (2001). A multilevel perspective on the implementation of Multisystemic Therapy (MST): Attempting dissemination with fidelity. In G. A. Bernfeld, D. P. Farrington & A. W. Leschied (Eds), *Offender rehabilitation in practice: Effective programs and policies to reduce re-offending* (pp. 97–120). Chichester: John Wiley & Sons.

Ellis, T. (2000). Enforcement policy and practice: Evidence-based or rhetoric-based? *Criminal Justice Matters, 39*, 6–8.

Everitt, B. S. & Wessely, S. (2004). *Clinical trials in psychiatry*. Oxford: Oxford University Press.

Farrall, S. (2004). Supervision, motivation and social context: What matters most when probationers desist? In G. Mair (Ed.), *What matters in probation* (pp. 187–209). Cullompton: Willan Publishing.

Follette, W. C. & Callaghan, G. M. (2001). The evolution of clinical significance. *Clinical Psychology: Science and Practice, 8*, 431–435.

Friendship, C., Blud, L., Erikson, M., Travers, R. & Thornton, D. (2003). Cognitive-behavioural treatment for imprisoned offenders: An evaluation of HM Prison Service's cognitive skills programmes. *Legal and Criminological Psychology, 8*, 103–114.

Friendship, C., Falshaw, L. & Beech, A. R. (2003). Measuring the real impact of accredited offending behaviour programmes. *Legal and Criminological Psychology, 8*, 115–127.

Gallagher, C. A., Wilson, D. B., Hirschfield, P., Coggleshall, M. B. & MacKenzie, D. L. (1999). A quantitative review of the effects of sexual offender treatment on sexual re-offending. *Corrections Management Quarterly, 3*, 19–29.

Garfield, S. L. (1994). Research on client variables in psychotherapy. In A. E. Bergin & S. L. Garfield (Eds), *Handbook of psychotherapy and behavior change (4th edition)* (pp. 190–228). New York: John Wiley & Sons.

Garrett, C. J. (1985). Effects of residential treatment on adjudicated delinquents: A meta-analysis. *Journal of Research in Crime and Delinquency, 22,* 287–308.

Gendreau, P., Goggin, C. & Smith, P. (1999). The forgotten issue in effective correctional treatment: Program implementation. *International Journal of Offender therapy and Comparative Criminology, 43,* 180–187.

Ginsburg, J. I. D. (2000). *Using motivational interviewing to enhance treatment readiness in offenders with symptoms of alcohol dependence.* PhD thesis, Carleton University, Ottawa, Ontario, Canada.

Goldstein, A. P. & Glick, B. (2001). Aggression Replacement Training: Application and evaluation management. In G. A. Bernfeld, D. P. Farrington & A. W. Leschied (Eds), *Offender rehabilitation in practice: Implementing and evaluating effective programs* (pp. 122–148). Chichester: John Wiley & Sons.

Gondolf, E. W. & Foster, R. A. (1991). Pre-program attrition in batterer programs. *Journal of Family Violence, 6,* 337–349.

Gorsuch, N. (1998). Unmet need among disturbed female offenders. *Journal of Forensic Psychiatry, 9,* 556–570.

Green, D. G., Grove, E. & Martin, N. A. (2004). *How can the criminal justice system reduce the criminal activities of known offenders?* Civitas Final Report for the Rethinking Crime and Punishment Project. Available at www.civitas.org.uk/pdf/CivitasRCP_Report. pdf.

Halfpenny, P. (1982/1992). *Positivism and sociology: Explaining social life.* London: Allen & Unwin/Aldershot, Hants: Gregg Revivals.

Hanson, R. K. et al. (2002). First report on the collaborative outcome data project on the effectiveness of psychological treatment for sex offenders. *Sexual Abuse: A Journal of Research and Treatment, 14(2),* 169–197.

Hawkins, J. D., Herrenkohl, T., Farrington, D. P., Brewer, D., Catalano, R. F. & Harachi, T. W. (1998). A review of predictors of youth violence. In R. Loeber & D. P. Farrington (Eds), *Serious and violent juvenile offenders: Risk factors and successful interventions* (pp. 106–146). Thousand Oaks, CA: Sage.

Hedderman, C. (2004). Testing times: How the policy and practice environment shaped the creation of "what works" evidence-base. *Vista, 8,* 182–188.

Hedderman, C. & Hearndon, I. (2001). To discipline or to punish? Enforcement under National Standards. *VISTA, 6,* 215–224.

Henderson, D. J. (1998). Drug use and incarcerated women: A research review. *Journal of Substance Abuse Treatment, 15,* 579–587.

Henggeler, S. W., Melton, G. B., Brondino, M. J., Scherer, D. G. & Hanley, J. H. (1997). Multisystemic Therapy with violent and chronic juvenile offenders and their families: The role of treatment fidelity in successful dissemination. *Journal of Consulting and Clinical Psychology, 65,* 821–833.

Henggeler, S. W., Pickrel, S. G. & Brondino, M. J. (1999). Multisystemic treatment of substance-abusing and – dependent delinquents: Outcomes, treatment fidelity, and transportability. *Mental Health Services Review, 1,* 171–184.

Hird, J., Williams, P. & Markham, D. (1997). Survey of attendance at a community-based anger control treatment programme with reference to source of referral, age of client, and external motivating factors. *Journal of Mental Health, 6,* 47–54.

Hollin, C. R. (1999). Treatment programmes for offenders: Meta-analysis, "what works", and beyond. *International Journal of Law and Psychiatry, 22,* 361–372.

Hollin, C. R. (2002). An overview of offender rehabilitation: Something old, something borrowed, something new. *Australian Psychologist, 37,* 159–164.

Hollin, C. R., Epps, K. J. & Kendrick, D. J. (1995). *Managing behavioural treatment: Policy and practice with delinquent adolescents.* London: Routledge.

Hollin, C. R. et al. (2004). *Pathfinder Programmes in the Probation Service: A retrospective analysis.* Online Report 66/04. London: Home Office.

Hollin, C. R. & McMurran, M. (1995). Series preface. In J. McGuire (Ed.), *What works: Reducing reoffending* (pp. ix–x). Chichester: John Wiley & Sons.

Hollin, C. R. & Palmer, E. J. (2004). *The special needs of women substance-using offenders*. Commissioned Report for the Women's Prison Estate, Home Office.

Hollin, C. R. & Palmer, E. J. (in press). Criminogenic need and women offenders: A critique of the literature. *Legal and Criminological Psychology*.

Hollin, C. R., Palmer, E. J., McGuire, J., Hounsome, J., Hatcher, R. & Bilby, C. (2005). *An evaluation of Pathfinder Programmes in the Probation Service*. Unpublished research report to the Home Office Research, Development and Statistics Directorate.

Home Office (2002). *Statistics on women and the criminal justice system*. London: Home Office.

Home Office (2004). *Reducing crime, changing lives*. London: Home Office.

Hope, T. (2004). Pretend it works: Evidence and governance in the evaluation of the Reducing Burglary Initiative. *Criminal Justice, 4*, 287–308.

Howden-Windell, J. & Clark, D. (1999). *Criminogenic needs of female offenders: A literature review*. London: HM Prison Service.

Howells, K. & Day, A. (2002). Readiness for anger management: Clinical and theoretical issues. *Clinical Psychology Review, 23*, 319–337.

Jacobson, N. S., Follette, W. C., Revenstorf, D., Baucom, D. H., Hahlweg, K. & Margolin, G. (1984). Variability in outcome and clinical significance of behavioral marital therapy: A reanalysis of outcome data. *Journal of Consulting and Clinical Psychology, 52*, 497–504.

Jacobson, N. S., Roberts, L. J., Berns, S. B. & McGlinchey, J. B. (1999). Methods for defining and determining the clinical significance of treatment effects: Description, application, and alternatives. *Journal of Consulting and Clinical Psychology, 67*, 300–307.

Jennings J. L. & Sawyer, S. (2003). Principles and techniques for maximizing the effectiveness of group therapy with sex offenders. *Sexual Abuse: A Journal of Research and Treatment, 15*, 251–267.

Jones, D. & Hollin, C. R. (2004). Managing problematic anger: The development of a treatment programme for personality disordered patients in high security. *International Journal of Forensic Mental Health, 3*, 197–210.

Kear-Colwell, J. & Pollack, P. (1997). Motivation or confrontation: Which approach to the child sex offender? *Criminal Justice and Behavior, 24*, 20–33.

Keijsers, G. P. J., Schaap, C. P. D. R. & Hoogduin, C. A. L. (2000). The impact of interpersonal patient and therapist behavior on outcome in cognitive-behavior therapy: A review of empirical studies. *Behavior Modification, 24*, 264–297.

Kendall, K. (2004). Dangerous thinking: A critical history of correctional cognitive behaviouralism. In G. Mair (Ed.), *What matters in probation* (pp. 53–89). Cullompton: Willan Publishing.

Kennedy, S. M. (2000). Treatment responsivity: Reducing recidivism by enhancing treatment effectiveness. *Forum on Corrections Research, 12*, 19–23.

Kennedy, S. M. (2001). Treatment responsivity: Reducing recidivism by enhancing treatment effectiveness. In L. L. Motiuk & R. C. Serin (Eds), *Compendium 2000 on effective correctional programming, Volume 1*. Ottawa, Correctional Services Canada.

Langan, N. P. & Pelissier, B. M. M. (2001). Gender differences among prisoners in drug treatment. *Journal of Substance Abuse, 13*, 291–301.

Laws, D. R. (1974). The failure of a token economy. *Federal Probation, 38*, 33–38.

Leschied, A. W. (2001). Implementation of effective correctional programs. In L. L. Motiuk & R. C. Serin (Eds), *Compendium 2000 on effective correctional programming* (pp. 41–46). Ottawa, Ontario: Correctional Service of Canada.

Lewis, S. et al. (2003). *The resettlement of short-term prisoners: An evaluation of seven Pathfinders*. RDS Occasional Paper 83. London: Home Office.

Lipsey, M. W. (1999). Can rehabilitative programs reduce the recidivism of juvenile offenders? An inquiry into the effectiveness of practical programs. *Virginia Journal of Social Policy and Law, 6*, 611–641.

Lipsey, M. W., Chapman, G. L. & Landenberger, N. A. (2001). Cognitive-behavioral programs for offenders. *Annals of the American Academy of Political and Social Science, 578*, 144–157.

Long, C. G. & Hollin, C. R. (1997). The scientist-practitioner model in clinical psychology: A critique. *Clinical Psychology and Psychotherapy, 4,* 75–83.

Lösel, F. (1996). Effective correctional programming: What empirical research tells us and what it doesn't. *Forum on Corrections Research, 6,* 33–37.

Lowenkamp, C. T., Holsinger, A. M. & Latessa, E. J. (2001). Risk/need assessment, offender classification, and the role of childhood abuse. *Criminal Justice and Behavior, 28,* 543–563.

Maguire, M., Raynor, P., Vanstone, M. & Kynch, J. (2000). Voluntary after-care and the Probation Service: A case of diminishing responsibility. *The Howard Journal of Criminal Justice, 39,* 234–248.

Mair, G. (2004). The origins of What Works in England and Wales: A house built on sand? In G. Mair (Ed.) *What matters in probation* (pp. 12–33). Cullompton: Willan Publishing.

Mann, R. E., Ginsburg, J. I. D. & Weekes, J. R. (2002). Motivational interviewing with offenders. In M. McMurran (Ed.), *Motivating offenders to change: A guide to enhancing engagement in therapy* (pp. 87–102). Chichester: John Wiley & Sons.

Marques, J. K., Day, D. M., Nelson, C. & West, M. A. (1994). Effects of cognitive-behavioral treatment on sex offender recidivism. *Criminal Justice and Behavior, 21,* 28–54.

Marshall, W. L. et al. (2002). Therapist features in sexual offender treatment: Their reliable identification and influence on behaviour change. *Clinical Psychology and Psychotherapy, 9,* 395–405.

Marshall, W. L. et al. (2003). Process variables in the treatment of sexual offenders: A review of the literature. *Aggression and Violent Behavior, 8,* 205–234.

Martin, D. J., Garske, J. P. & Davis, M. K. (2000). Relation of the therapeutic alliance with outcome and other variables: A meta-analytic review. *Journal of Consulting and Clinical Psychology, 68,* 438–450.

McGuire, J. (2002). Integrating findings from research reviews. In J. McGuire (Ed.), *Offender rehabilitation and treatment: Effective programmes and policies to reduce re-offending* (pp. 3–38). Chichester: John Wiley & Sons.

McMahon, G., Hall, A., Hayward, G., Hudson, C. & Roberts, C. (2004). *Basic skills programmes in the Probation Service: An evaluation of the basic skills Pathfinder.* Home Office Research Findings No. 203. London: Home Office.

McMurran, M. (2002). Preface. In M. McMurran (Ed.), *Motivating offenders to change: A guide to enhancing engagement in therapy* (pp. xii–xiii). Chichester: John Wiley & Sons.

McMurran, M. & McCulloch, A. (in press). *Why don't offenders complete treatment? Prisoners' reasons for non-completion of a cognitive skills programme. Psychology, Crime, & Law.*

Medical Research Council. (2000). *A framework for development and evaluation of RCTs for complex interventions to improve health.* London: Medical Research Council.

Merrington, S. & Stanley, S. (2004). "What works?": Revisiting the evidence in England and Wales. *Probation Journal, 51,* 7–20.

Miller, W. M. (1985). Motivation for treatment: A review with special emphasis on alcoholism. *Psychological Bulletin, 98,* 84–107.

Miller, W. M. & Rollnick, S. (Eds). (1991). *Motivational interviewing: Preparing people to change addictive behavior.* New York: Guilford.

Murphy, C. M. & Baxter, V. A. (1997). Motivating batterers to change in the treatment context. *Journal of Interpersonal Violence, 12,* 607–619.

NAPO (2001). AGM resolutions 2001. *NAPO News, 134,* 10–15.

O'Brien, M., Mortimer, L., Singleton, N. & Meltzer, H. (1997). *Psychiatric morbidity among women prisoners in England and Wales.* London: Office of National Statistics.

Ogloff, J. R. P. (2002). Offender rehabilitation: From "nothing works" to what next? *Australian Psychologist, 37,* 245–252.

Parsons, S., Walker, L. & Grubin, D. (2001). Prevalence of mental disorder in female remand prisoners. *Journal of Forensic Psychiatry, 12,* 194–202.

Pawson, R. (2002). Evidence-based policy: In search of a method. *Evaluation, 8,* 157–181.

Phillips, E. L., Phillips, E. A., Fixen, D. L. & Wolf, M. M. (1974). *The Teaching-Family handbook (2nd edition).* Lawrence, KS: University of Kansas Press.

Piper, W. E. et al. (1999). Prediction of dropping out in time-limited interpretive individual psychotherapy. *Psychotherapy: Theory, Research and Practice, 36,* 114–122.

Polizzi, D. M., MacKenzie, D. L. & Hickman, L. J. (1999). What works in adult sex offenders treatment? A review of prison- and non-prison based treatment programs. *International Journal of Offender Therapy and Comparative Criminology, 43*, 357–374.

Preston, D. L. & Murphy, S. (1997). Motivating treatment resistant clients in therapy. *Forum on Corrections Research, 9*, 39–43.

Raynor, P. (2004). The Probation Service "Pathfinders": Finding the path and losing the way? *Criminal Justice, 4*, 309–325.

Raynor, P. & Vanstone, M. (2001). "Straight Thinking on Probation": Evidence-based practice and the culture of curiosity. In G. A. Bernfeld, D. P. Farrington & A. W. Leschied (Eds), *Offender rehabilitation in practice: Implementing and evaluating effective programmes* (pp. 189–203). Chichester: John Wiley & Sons.

Redondo, S., Sánchez-Meca, J. & Garrido, V. (2002). Crime treatment in Europe: A review of outcome studies. In J. McGuire (Ed.), *Offender rehabilitation and treatment: Effective programmes and policies to reduce re-offending* (pp. 113–141). Chichester: John Wiley & Sons.

Reppucci, N. D. (1973). Social psychology of institutional change: General principles for intervention. *American Journal of Community Psychology, 1*, 330–341.

Reppucci, N. D. & Saunders, J. T. (1974). Social psychology of behavior modification: Problems of implementation in natural settings. *American Psychologist, 29*, 649–660.

Rex, S., Lieb, R., Bottoms, A. & Wilson, L. (2003). *Accrediting offender programmes: A process-based evaluation of the Joint Prison/Probation Services Accreditation Panel.* Home Office Research Study No. 273. London: Home Office.

Robinson, D. (1995). *The impact of cognitive skills training on post-release recidivism among Canadian federal offenders.* (Research Report No. R-41). Ottawa, Correctional Service of Canada.

Robinson, G. & McNeill, F. (2004). Purposes matter: Examining the "ends" of probation. In G. Mair (Ed.), *What matters in probation* (pp. 277–304). Cullomptom: Willan Publishing.

Rollnick, S. & Miller, W. M. (1995). What is motivational interviewing? *Behavioral and Cognitive Psychotherapy, 12*, 325–334.

Rutan, J. S. & Stone, W .N. (1993). *Psychodynamic group psychotherapy (2nd edition).* New York: Guilford Press.

Samstag, L. W., Batchelder, S. T., Muran, J. C., Safran, J. D. & Winston, A. (1998). Early identification of treatment failures in short-term psychotherapy: An assessment of therapeutic alliance and interpersonal behavior. *Journal of Psychotherapy Practice and Research, 7*, 126–143.

Seligman, M. E. P. & Levant, R. F. (1998). Managed care policies rely on inadequate science. *Professional Psychology: Research and Practice, 29*, 211–212.

Serin, R. C. (1998). Treatment responsivity, intervention and reintegration: A conceptual model. *Forum on Corrections Research, 10*, 29–32.

Serin, R. C. & Kennedy, S. M. (1997). *Treatment readiness and responsivity: Contributing to effective correctional programming.* Research Report, Correctional Service of Canada.

Sharpe, D. (1997). Of apples and oranges, file drawers and garbage: Why validity issues in meta-analysis will not go away. *Clinical Psychology Review, 17*, 881–901.

Sorbello, L., Eccleston, L., Ward, T. & Jones, R. (2002). Treatment needs of female offenders: A review. *Australian Psychologist, 37*, 198–205.

Tong, L. S. J. & Farrington, D. P. (2006). How effective is the "Reasoning and Rehabilitation" programme in reducing re-offending? A meta-analysis of evaluations in four countries. *Psychology, Crime, and Law, 12*, 3–24.

Van Voorhis, P. (1997). Correctional classification and the "responsivity principle". *Forum on Corrections Research, 9*, 46–50.

Van Voorhis, P., Spruance, L. M., Ritchey, P. N., Listwan, S. J. & Seabrook, R. (2004). The Georgia Cognitive Skills experiment: A replication of Reasoning and Rehabilitation. *Criminal Justice and Behavior, 31*, 282–305.

Walitzer, K. S., Dermen, K. H. & Connors, G. J. (1999). Strategies for preparing clients for treatment: A review. *Behavior Modification, 23*, 129–151.

Ward, T., Day, A., Howells, K. & Birgden, A. (2004). The multifactor offender readiness model. *Aggression and Violent Behavior, 9*, 645–673.

Wilson, D. B., Bouffard, L. A. & Mackenzie, D. L. (2005). A quantitative review of structured, group-orientated, cognitive-behavioural programs for offenders. *Criminal Justice and Behavior, 32*, 172–204.

Wincup, E., Buckland, G. & Bayliss, R. (2003). *Youth homelessness and substance abuse: Report to the drugs and alcohol research unit.* Home Office Research Findings No. 191. London: Home Office.

Wormith, J. S. & Olver, M. E. (2002). Offender treatment attrition and its relationship with risk, responsivity, and recidivism. *Criminal Justice and Behavior, 29*, 447–471.

Yalom, I. (1995). *The theory and practice of group psychotherapy (4th edition).* New York: Basic Books.